RFAR

The Billboard Book of

Gold & Platinum Records

ADAM WHITE

BILLBOARD BOOKS
An imprint of Watson-Guptill Publications/New York

The publisher wishes to acknowledge the cooperation of the Recording
Industry Association of America (RIAA) in the preparation of this book.

Chart typesetting by TGA Communications, Inc.
Senior Editor: Tad Lathrop
Jacket illustration by David Myers

First published 1990 by Billboard Publications, Inc.
1515 Broadway, New York, NY 10036.

Library of Congress Cataloging-in-Publication Data

White, Adam.
    The Billboard book of gold and platinum records / Adam White.
        p.   cm.
    ISBN 0-8230-7547-8 :
    1. Music—Discography.   I. Title.
ML156.2.W48   1990
016.78′026′6—dc20   89-18566
                                                                 CIP
                                                                 MN

Manufactured in the United States of America
First Printing, 1990

1 2 3 4 5 6 7 8 9 / 91 90

CONTENTS

INTRODUCTION

From Gene Autry to Zapp, Rick Astley to Zager & Evans, Anthrax to the Zombies.

These are the inhabitants of this volume: the 1,000-plus recording artists whose music has been certified gold, platinum, and multi-platinum by the Recording Industry Association of America (RIAA) between March 1958 and August 1989.

They reflect the transcendent, the bizarre, and the mundane in popular music—and probably do so as well as any other list of names you could assemble.

This book identifies everyone who belongs to that gold and platinum club. If you're interested in music and musicmakers, I hope you won't leave home without it.

The RIAA, formed in 1952, is the trade association of America's record companies. It introduced its gold record awards in 1958, although the idea of precious metal as a measure of recording success was established at least 50 years earlier.

Female violinist Marie Hall was possibly the first to receive such an honor, when Britain's Gramophone Company gave her a bracelet in 1905 to mark the popularity of her music. According to author Joseph Murrells, the bracelet was made of gold and pearls and featured a tiny violin, a tapered gramophone arm, and seven tiny gold discs—to represent her seven most successful recordings.

Another significant gold record award of the past, also noted by Murrells, was presented to bandleader Glenn Miller by RCA-Victor for more than a million copies sold of "Chattanooga Choo Choo." That was in 1942.

By the late '50s, an increasingly prosperous music industry was dispensing gold to artists left, right, and center, using various criteria, some questionable.

According to the RIAA, the situation at that time was "chaotic." There was a proliferation of awards "with no basis in fact, no method for verification or authentication." Even worse, commented the association, "the veracity of all award claims was held in disrepute in and outside the industry."

While it's doubtful that record buyers were preoccupied with the problem, the RIAA decided to take action. In 1958, the certified gold record award was created.

With record company claims to be audited by independent accountants, the gold standards were set. For albums, the benchmark was $1 million in sales at manufacturer wholesale prices, based on one-third of the list price for each record. For singles, gold meant one million copies sold.

The program began modestly. In 1958, four singles (the first was Perry Como's "Catch A Falling Star") and one album (the *Oklahoma!* soundtrack) went gold. The next year, one single and four albums were certified.

By 1964, the awards were gathering momentum. Thirty-five albums and singles were certified gold that year; the Beatles grabbed nine of them.

As the industry grew exponentially through the '60s and '70s, so did the stature of the RIAA honors. In 1970, the number of gold albums topped 100 for the first time—and sales of prerecorded tape were counted into the qualifying equation.

In 1975, the awards criteria were amended for gold albums, to require a minimum sale of 500,000 copies as well as the $1 million in wholesale value. The following year, the RIAA officially launched the platinum era: awards based on authenticated sales of one million albums (and $2 million in wholesale value) or two million singles.

The first release thus certified was a compilation featuring the Eagles, *Their Greatest Hits 1971-1975*, on Asylum Records. It went platinum on February 24, 1976. The same day, Johnnie Taylor's "Disco Lady" on Columbia Records became the first official platinum single. By the end of that year, a total of 37 albums were certified for one million sales, and 4 singles verified at two million apiece.

Unfortunately, the recording industry's vigorous growth during the '70s encouraged more hype than ever. Gold and platinum awards were used increasingly as marketing tools—or the means to persuade (or placate) artists that their record company was on the case—rather than as mementos of genuine success.

Labels sought instant certification: trade-press advertisements proclaimed albums as "shipping gold" or "shipping platinum," in part to encourage retailers and wholesalers not to miss the boat on a particular release.

But generous sale-or-return policies meant that retailers could ship poor-selling albums right back to the record companies. And they did. The standard industry joke at the time was that this or that release may have shipped gold, but it returned platinum—meaning hundreds of thousands of unsold copies.

This hardly enhanced the credibility of the RIAA honors. So, in 1979, the association introduced a post-release certification delay: a minimum of 120 days after a record first went on sale. No more instant gold or platinum.

Most record-industry professionals said they had never done that—or they put a safe distance between themselves and the practice. "I suspect that dumping product in front to obtain immediate certification was done far more frequently three or four years ago," one senior label executive told *Billboard* magazine, in a 1979 article about the new RIAA rules. "With the cost of manufacturing, shipping and returns, it's absolutely insane to consider this today."

With shipment abuses discouraged by those rules and tough economic realities, the RIAA cut the four-month certification delay. From 1980 onwards—to this day—a record can be certified gold or platinum 60 days after release, or any time thereafter.

The years 1979 through 1983 were tough for the industry. Record sales slumped significantly, as reflected by the number of RIAA awards. Gold albums tumbled from 193 in 1978 to 111 in 1983; platinum albums fell from 102 to 49 during the same period.

That was the low point. Subsequently, sales improved, spurred by the growing popularity of prerecorded cassettes and the debut of the compact disk. In December 1984, the RIAA introduced the multi-platinum award. This enabled the industry to not only trumpet its turnaround—Michael Jackson's *Thriller* was among the first with multi-platinum honors, certified for sales of 20 million—but also bask in the glory of past megahits, such as Fleetwood Mac's *Rumours* and the *Saturday Night Fever* soundtrack.

Yet as the music business returned to health, it was apparent that vinyl was dying as a music medium. For RIAA-certified albums, this wasn't a problem: sales on cassette and compact disk—the formats replacing the vinyl LP in popularity—were easily counted into gold and platinum qualification totals.

The single was different. The music on a seven-inch 45 or twelve-inch single wasn't available in any other comparable format, and sales were falling: from 164 million units in 1980 to 94 million in 1986. The decline was reflected in the number of gold-single certifications: from 42 to 7 between 1980 and 1986.

Record companies responded in 1987 by introducing the cassette single, which began to replace vinyl as music buyers' preferred medium. Then the RIAA reduced the qualifying sales criteria, to help bring back some of the excitement and kudos of a gold or platinum single.

From January 1989, a single required 500,000 unit sales to go gold, and one million to reach platinum. The result was an immediate surge in certifications: 72 gold singles for the first six months of 1989—including roughly 30 older titles which couldn't attain gold under the previous criteria —*versus* half-a-dozen for all of 1988.

It's likely there will be other changes in the way the Recording Industry Association of America measures and honors the gold, platinum, and multi-platinum hits of the day. Technology influences the way music is delivered to people. People influence the way music companies sign, develop, and market artists.

The future may contain gold DATs or platinum microchips, or an album may be declared multi-platinum on the basis of the number of homes to which it's beamed directly by satellite at 3:00 AM. Chances are, though, that the precious metal metaphor will still be used.

I t's important to know that every single and album which qualified for an RIAA gold or platinum award these past 31 years did *not* automatically receive one.

From the very beginning of the awards, it's been up to the individual record company to decide which of its hits should be certified, then apply to the RIAA for that certification.

Each record is audited by the independent accounting firm to corroborate the required sales levels. Then the gold, platinum, or multi-platinum certification is issued, and the label buys official award plaques through the RIAA from a licensed plaque manufacturer.

A record company doesn't have to belong to the association to have any of its releases certified, but—member or not—nothing goes gold or platinum without an application. The application fee is currently $275 per title for RIAA members, $425 for non-members.

Most of the biggest hit albums of the past three to four decades *have* been certified gold. That's certainly the case with popular music's superstars, such as Frank Sinatra, Elvis Presley, the Beatles, and the Rolling Stones. Likewise, the platinum award has been widely used since it was introduced in 1976, and, rather more selectively, the multi-platinum award, created in 1984.

But not every megahit is platinum. Carole King's *Tapestry* is widely acknowledged as one of the biggest-selling releases of the '70s, with U.S. sales well over five million. So is Pink Floyd's *Dark Side Of The Moon*, a chart fixture for years since its 1973 release.

As of this writing, neither *Tapestry* nor *Dark Side* have been certified beyond gold. No one doubts that both have sold multi-platinum, but the awards haven't been applied for. In King's case, the rights to market *Tapestry* have been given to two record companies on separate occasions. Perhaps only the singer, her accountant, and the album's producer know the full picture.

Hit singles are yet another matter. You can be sure that every single certified between 1958 and 1988 sold at least one million copies. But the earliest hits of rock & roll weren't submitted for certification—and not all of them necessarily sold a million, anyway.

Record companies often inflated sales figures for publicity's sake. That's part of the hyperbole of the business. But the truth, not to mention what the artist's royalty statements showed, was often quite different. And a lot of the smaller, independent record labels of rock's first ten to fifteen years weren't willing to let outside accountants go through their books.

The most significant company not to use the RIAA awards was Motown Records. Label founder Berry Gordy, Jr. said he never wanted to pay membership dues to the association—although that wouldn't have prevented him from applying for gold—and so the celebrated Motown sound of the '60s is disappointingly absent from this book.

Motown's more recent music *was* submitted for certification, however. This was partly due to the outlook of Jay Lasker, the company's president for most of the '80s, who wanted to show that, for example, Lionel Richie's *Can't Slow Down* was one of the biggest-selling albums in music history.

Aside from Motown, all the major record companies have used the RIAA awards to authenticate their hits. They include such famous names (past and present) as A&M, Atlantic/Atco, Apple, Arista, Capitol, Casablanca, Columbia, Decca, EMI, Elektra/Asylum, Epic, Island, Kapp, Liberty, MCA, Mercury, Polydor, RCA, United Artists, Virgin, and Warner Bros.

And from the maverick ranks—embodying the spirit of rock 'n' soul—you'll find certifications for labels like Alston, Capricorn, Curtom, Enigma, Gamble, Hot Wax, IRS, Profile, Rounder, Scepter, Sleeping Bag, T-Neck, Tommy Boy, and Stax.

This book owes its existence to the encouragement, help, and involvement of many people. I am grateful to the Recording Industry Association of America for their approval and (of course) truckloads of information.

Particular thanks to RIAA president Jay Berman, executive director Jim Fishel, vice president/public relations Trish Heimers, gold/platinum administrator Angie Corio, and public relations assistant Tanya Blackwood.

At record companies, rights organizations, and the like, the following were tremendously helpful: Greg Brodsky at Atlantic, Sue Satriano at EMI Music, (the inimitable!) Andy McKaie at MCA, Julie Friedenthal at RCA, Angela Aguillar at CBS, Bill Word at Walt Disney, Vivian Reid at Benson, Mary Mossberg at Sparrow, Tom Ramsey at Word, Joe Quirk at PolyGram, and Mark Marone of *Billboard*'s charts department.

Also, in London: Phil Graham and Nicky Campbell at BMI, James Fisher and Michael Donovan at ASCAP, John Tracey at Decca International, and Luke Crampton at MRIB.

These colleagues and friends helped (and endured) my quest: John Thorogood, Alan Warner, Bob Fisher, Chris Poole, and Harry Weinger. The aforementioned Jim Fishel and Trish Heimers should be included in this category, too.

Friend and author (*The Billboard Book Of Number One Hits*) Fred Bronson deserves special mention, not least for advice and encouragement in navigating contracts, charts, and deadlines. *Billboard* colleague Paul Grein, the Chartbeat master, is also due thanks.

Acknowledgments to the following as reference points and sources: *Billboard*, *Cash Box*, the Joel Whitburn chronicles (including *Top Pop Albums* and *Top Pop Singles*), *The Rolling Stone Encyclopedia Of Rock & Roll*, *Million-Selling Records* by Joseph Murrells, and the *Guinness Book Of Rock Stars*.

Thanks are hardly enough for Tad Lathrop at Billboard Books, a patient, painstaking, and truly professional editor who probably hopes he won't have to edit another book of mine. I hope he will. Also appreciated: the contributions of associate editor Fred Weiler and (from an earlier era) Marisa Bulzone.

And I *know* thanks are insufficient for my wife, Anne, who might have preferred to learn less about gold and platinum records these past 18 months—but who is #1 and multi-platinum, regardless.

ADAM WHITE
November 11, 1989

GOLD & PLATINUM RECORDS

RIAA AWARDS CRITERIA

Gold Singles

From 1958 through 1988, a single had to sell a minimum of one million copies to qualify for gold certification. Most singles were seven-inch, 45 r.p.m. records.

When the twelve-inch single was introduced commercially in the '70s, each copy sold counted as two units for certification purposes.

Sales of the twelve-inch could be combined with sales of the seven-inch, provided the former had one selection (song) per side, and the music on both sides was identical to the seven-inch in terms of artist and title.

Later, the RIAA amended the criteria so that twelve-inch singles with one song per side counted as one unit towards certification. It also decreed that only the A side of a single had to be the same (in terms of title and artist) on different configurations; the B side could vary.

From January 1, 1989, the gold-single certification requirement was cut from a minimum sale of one million to a minimum sale of 500,000 copies—the criterion in effect today.

Extended-play versions of a single (vinyl EP, cassette maxi-single, three-inch CD maxi) count as two units for certification. The A side or its equivalent must be the same on all configurations to combine sales.

Platinum Singles

This certification level was introduced from January 1, 1976, and required a minimum sale of two million copies. All other criteria were the same as for gold singles.

From January 1, 1989, the platinum-single requirement was reduced to a minimum sale of one million copies, with all other criteria—such as extended-play versions—the same as for gold singles.

Gold Albums

From 1958 through 1974, the minimum requirement for a gold album was $1 million in sales at manufacturer wholesale prices, based on 33⅓ percent of the list price for each album. From January 1, 1975, an additional requirement was that an album sold a minimum of 500,000 copies.

These standards—in unit sales and manufacturer dollar volume—continue to apply today.

Platinum Albums

This award requires that an album has a minimum sale of one million copies, with at least $2 million in manufacturer wholesale value, based on 33⅓ percent of the list price of each album. This criteria has remained constant since platinum was introduced by the RIAA on January 1, 1976.

Multi-Platinum Awards

Effective from January 1, 1985, the multi-platinum award enables a platinum album to be certified each time it reaches an additional million-unit sales level: two million, three million, and so on.

Also required: manufacturer sales value of at least $4 million for two million units, $6 million for three million, and so on. These dollar volumes are based on 33⅓ percent of the suggested list price of each album sold.

Singles can also qualify for multi-platinum at successive million-unit sales levels, although it happens rarely.

Multi-Album Sets

A gold certification for a three-record (or more) set—or its tape/CD equivalent—requires that at least 250,000 sets be shipped. They must have a wholesale value of at least $2 million, based on 33⅓ percent of the suggested list price.

For a platinum award, at least 500,000 sets ($4 million in wholesale value) must be shipped. For certification, sets cannot be combined with sales of individual LP/tape/CD equivalents within those sets.

These criteria were introduced from January 1, 1983, and continue to apply today.

General Criteria

When applying for an RIAA certification, record companies cannot include promotional copies (for broadcast and/or review purposes) of a single or album in the sales figures. They can include recordings given free with quantities bought: by retailers, for example.

Sales through record/tape/compact disk clubs count towards certification, but club bonus recordings or membership-enrollment inducement packages do not.

At least 50 percent of sales must go through normal retail outlets, and only recordings sold in the U.S. count for certification. Export sales and sales to military post exchanges overseas are excluded, as are special packages sold only through clubs or mail.

A post-release qualification delay of 60 days applies to all certifications, which means that two months must pass from the date a recording is released commercially before it can be certified. This rule was made effective for all recordings released on or after January 4, 1980.

For the preceding six months of 1979, the post-certification delay had been 120 days. Before that, an album or single could be certified on the day of release, or any time afterwards—and some albums (on the basis of advance orders) were certified before they were shipped!

Video

In 1981, the RIAA extended its awards program to home video and began certifying major movies released in this format, as well as commercially-available music video. Six years later, it left the movie business (so to speak) and narrowed its focus to non-theatrical music video titles.

This book does not include the association's venture into the broad range of home video, or its music video awards. The latter may be included in a future volume.

HOW TO USE THIS SECTION

With a pinch of salt, naturally. To minimize hunting high and low, here's what you need to know.

This book lists all the recordings certified by the RIAA from March 14, 1958 through August 31, 1989. They appear under the names of the recording artists, which are listed alphabetically. Singles and albums are shown by title under each artist entry, with:

- month and year of release;
- gold, platinum, and/or multi-platinum certification level;
- RIAA certification date(s);
- *Billboard* chart peak;
- record label and catalog number.

It's easy to differentiate singles from albums—*all* singles show writer and producer credits. *All* albums show just the title.

The alphabetical listing of artist names conforms to the usual A-Z rules, with a couple of exceptions. Rappers are difficult to classify—musically as well as alphabetically—so you'll locate the likes of M.C. Hammer and D.J. Jazzy Jeff under the first letter of their names (M and D respectively), rather than under H and J. The same applies to Big Daddy Kane, who's under B, not K or D. Use your imagination in tracking them down.

Orchestras such as the New York Philharmonic and the Royal Philharmonic are entered by the conductor's name, e.g. Leonard Bernstein and Louis Clark. Unfortunately, there aren't that many—or fortunately, if you're trying to find them.

The month/year of a recording's release is self-explanatory. Most dates come from the record companies themselves, or from trade-magazine editorial and/or advertisements.

This is surprisingly difficult information to obtain. Many labels no longer have dependable release data about old recordings they originated or acquired. Some (the largest record company in the world, for instance) have submitted incorrect details to the RIAA. Others have long disappeared into the mists of obscurity and bankruptcy.

So it's probably fair to state that 80 percent of release dates in this book are correct; 10 percent are informed estimates; and the balance are guesses. I've limited this data to month and year of release, because locating the day would be impossible for almost everything prior to the '70s, especially singles. Anyone want to pinpoint, say, the date that "Love (Can Make You Happy)" by Mercy on Sundi Records first hit the streets?

The specific gold, platinum, and multi-platinum certification levels appear in the second column of the listings, as G, P, or 2P (for double platinum), 3P (triple platinum), and so on.

An album doesn't reach platinum without first going gold, but record companies don't have to seek certification for each subsequent million-unit sales level. Most do, a few don't. One example: Columbia had Barbra Streisand's album *Guilty*, certified at four million and five million, but not at two and three million. So on those occasions when the logical G/P/2P/3P sequence does not appear, it's because of the record company's preference, not the author's.

When an asterisk appears by the gold, platinum or multi-platinum designation, it means that the release has been certified at a higher sales level after the cutoff date for this book's main text: August 31, 1989.

The third column identifies the month/day/year when a single or album was certified gold, platinum, and/or multi-platinum. Up to July 1, 1979, this could have been in the same month (or even on the same day) as a recording's release. From January 4, 1980, it couldn't have been less than 60 days after release.

Nothing prevents a label from certifying a record years after it's sold a million or more—and they sometimes do that for promotional reasons.

For example: on September 2, 1987, seven Barry Manilow albums were certified at various platinum and multi-platinum levels. They all didn't reach the required sales mark at the same time, but Arista did want to mark Manilow's re-signing with the label by celebrating his past achievements. You get the picture.

Also note that all singles certified after January 1, 1989 (whatever their original release date) are subject to the lower gold/platinum sales criteria. So, for instance, Michael Jackson's 1980 single, "Off The Wall," was certified gold in 1989—but sold half as many copies as his 1987 release, "I Just Can't Stop Loving You," certified gold in '87.

Column four indicates the peak position a single reached on *Billboard*'s Hot 100 (in the case of singles) or Top Pop Albums chart. A boldface entry indicates that a recording reached #1 on its particular chart.

A small number of certified releases didn't chart at all. In the case of singles, this was mostly where a release sold a million in a specialist market—country music, for instance, or rhythm & blues—without crossing over to the pop Hot 100.

In the case of albums, this was most often where a release didn't cross from its specialist market, or where the certification level was attained by sales over a long period (as with classical releases) rather than in a compressed, chart-targeted duration.

In addition, a number of Christmas albums were ranked by *Billboard* between 1963 and 1973 on a separate seasonal chart, not on the main album listing. In such cases, this book shows no chart peak.

The title of the certified recording appears in column five. With singles, the names of the songwriter(s) and producer(s) are also included, immediately under the title.

In the handful of cases where a single's producer is unknown or unverifiable, no name appears. Where a song was written by the group which recorded it, the composite name—rather than that of the individual members—is listed.

If an album is a movie soundtrack, the symbol [S] appears after its title. Such recordings are also listed separately in the Original Soundtracks section, which begins on page 258.

The final column lists each recording's original record label and catalog number. Some abbreviations, for reasons of space, have been used.

And in a couple of instances, one label name appears even though the company modfied that name over the years. In the '50s and '60s, RCA was known as RCA-Victor; later it became just RCA. In this book, it's listed only as RCA. The same applies to Warner Bros., which began with that name, later became Warner-7 Arts, and eventually changed back to Warner Bros.

The album catalog numbers are the stereo numbers in cases where a recording originally came out in mono and stereo—a data preference in which I've been influenced by ace chartologist Joel Whitburn. In the mid-'60s, of course, mono releases disappeared, and record companies subsequently used only one catalog number.

A few more explanatory comments are necessary. There is a cross-reference notation in the main listing for artists involved in duets or multi-artist recordings.

There is a complete song title index, beginning on page 271. It applies only to certified singles.

As noted earlier, soundtrack albums appear under an artist's entry where they carry a specific artist credit, and also in a separate Original Soundtracks section, beginning on page 258.

Children's recordings appear in a separate category, on pages 265-267. As with soundtracks, where a children's release carries a specific artist credit—for example, the Muppets or the Chipmunks—those artists have their own distinct entry in the book's main listing.

Original cast recordings are shown in a separate category, on page 264. Just one of these albums also appears in the book's main section under the artist's name (Barbra Streisand).

On those rare occasions when a certified recording is a reissue (for example, Perry Como's *Merry Christmas Music*), the reissue catalog number and chart position (none in Como's case) is shown.

One gold single, Barbra Streisand and Donna Summer's "No More Tears," was released on different labels: Columbia (the seven-inch version) and Casablanca (the twelve-inch). Their sales were combined for certification purposes.

Separate seven-inch and twelve-inch versions of another single, Frankie Smith's "Double Dutch Bus," sold well enough to gain separate gold certifications.

Miscellaneous albums (mostly those by various performers) which are not easily categorized under an artist's name appear on page 267.

Two spoken-word tuition recordings certified by the RIAA in 1966, *Young People's Living Language/French* and *Young People's Living Language/Spanish*, are not listed because of difficulties in securing release date and catalog number information.

Release Date	Certification	Date of Certification	Chart Peak	ARTIST/Title Songwriter ● Producer (singles only)	Label & Number
				A	
				ABBA	
11/76	G	3/29/77	1	**Dancing Queen** Benny Andersson/Bjorn Ulvaeus/Stig Anderson • Andersson/Ulvaeus	Atlantic 3372
4/78	G	8/8/78	3	Take A Chance On Me Andersson/Ulvaeus • Andersson/Ulvaeus	Atlantic 3457
9/76	G P	12/30/76 7/20/78	48	Greatest Hits	Atlantic 18189
1/77	G	4/4/77	20	Arrival	Atlantic 18207
2/78	G P	3/10/78 8/8/78	14	The Album	Atlantic 19164
6/79	G	11/14/79	19	Voulez-Vous	Atlantic 16000
12/79	G	4/23/80	46	Greatest Hits, Vol.2	Atlantic 16009
12/80	G	2/6/81	17	Super Trouper	Atlantic 16023
				GREGORY ABBOTT	
8/86	G	2/2/87	22	Shake You Down	Columbia 40437
				PAULA ABDUL	
11/88	G P	2/8/89 3/29/89	1	**Straight Up** Elliot Wolff • Wolff/Keith Cohen	Virgin 99256
2/89	G	5/24/89	1	**Forever Your Girl** Oliver Leiber • Leiber	Virgin 99230
6/89	G	8/30/89	1	**Cold Hearted** Wolff • Wolff/Cohen	Virgin 99196
6/88	G P 2P*	2/14/89 3/9/89 7/19/89	1	Forever Your Girl	Virgin 90943
				AC/DC	
10/76	G	3/2/81	146	High Voltage	Atco 142
6/77	G	10/14/80	154	Let There Be Rock	Atco 151
5/78	G	7/2/81	133	Powerage	Atlantic 19180
12/78	G	10/14/80	113	If You Want Blood You've Got It	Atlantic 19212
8/79	G	12/6/79	17	Highway To Hell	Atlantic 19244

Release Date	Certification	Date of Certification	Chart Peak	ARTIST/Title Songwriter ● Producer (singles only)	Label & Number
	P 2P	3/18/80 10/30/84			
8/80	G P 5P	10/13/80 10/13/80 10/30/84	4	Back In Black	Atlantic 16018
4/81	G P 2P	6/3/81 6/3/81 10/30/84	3	Dirty Deeds Done Dirt Cheap	Atlantic 16033
11/81	G P 2P	1/20/82 1/20/82 10/30/84	1	**For Those About To Rock We Salute You**	Atlantic 11111
8/83	G	1/25/84	15	Flick Of The Switch	Atlantic 80100
7/85	G	8/29/85	32	Fly On The Wall	Atlantic 81263
5/86	G P	8/19/86 3/24/87	33	Who Made Who [S]	Atlantic 81650
2/88	G P	4/6/88 4/29/88	12	Blow Up Your Video	Atlantic 81828
				BRYAN ADAMS	
1/83	G P	5/31/83 8/17/83	8	Cuts Like A Knife	A&M 4919
10/84	G P 4P	2/5/85 2/5/85 1/30/86	1	**Reckless**	A&M 5013
3/87	G P	6/8/87 6/8/87	7	Into The Fire	A&M 3907
				AEROSMITH	
1/73	G P 2P	9/11/75 11/21/86 11/21/86	21	Aerosmith	Columbia 32005
3/74	G P 2P	4/18/75 11/21/86 11/21/86	74	Get Your Wings	Columbia 32847
4/75	G P 4P 5P	8/11/75 11/21/86 11/21/86 12/21/88	11	Toys In The Attic	Columbia 33479
5/76	G P 2P 3P	5/21/76 7/9/76 10/19/84 12/21/88	3	Rocks	Columbia 34165
12/77	G P	12/9/77 12/13/77	11	Draw The Line	Columbia 34856

11

Release Date	Certification	Date of Certification	Chart Peak	ARTIST/Title Songwriter ● Producer (singles only)	Label & Number
10/78	G P	10/31/78 12/26/78	13	Live! Bootleg	Columbia 35564
11/79	G	3/13/80	14	Night In The Ruts	Columbia 36050
10/80	G P 2P 4P	3/3/81 1/27/86 11/24/86 11/21/88	53	Aerosmith's Greatest Hits	Columbia 36865
8/87	G P 2P	11/10/87 12/8/87 5/24/88	11	Permanent Vacation	Geffen 24162
				A-HA	
6/85	G P	10/22/85 3/17/86	15	Hunting High And Low	Warner 25300
				AIR SUPPLY	
5/80	G	10/10/80	2	All Out Of Love Graham Russell/Clive Davis • Robie Porter	Arista 0520
5/81	G	8/12/81	1	**The One That You Love** Russell • Harry Maslin	Arista 0604
7/83	G	12/16/83	2	Making Love Out Of Nothing At All Jim Steinman • Steinman	Arista 9056
5/80	G P	10/1/80 1/12/81	22	Lost In Love	Arista 4268
5/81	G P	7/20/81 10/7/81	10	The One That You Love	Arista 9551
6/82	G P	7/27/82 2/1/83	25	Now And Forever	Arista 9587
8/83	G P 3P 4P	10/12/83 10/12/83 7/31/85 8/28/89	7	Greatest Hits	Arista 8024
6/85	G	7/29/85	26	Air Supply	Arista 8283
				ALABAMA	
5/80	G P 2P	7/14/81 6/30/82 8/20/86	71	My Home's In Alabama	RCA 3644
3/81	G P 3P 4P	5/27/81 9/15/81 10/25/84 7/30/85	16	Feels So Right	RCA 3930

Release Date	Certification	Date of Certification	Chart Peak	ARTIST/Title Songwriter ● Producer (singles only)	Label & Number
2/82	G P 3P 4P	4/29/82 4/29/82 10/25/84 7/30/85	14	Mountain Music	RCA 4229
3/83	G P 2P 3P	5/3/83 5/3/83 10/25/84 7/30/85	10	The Closer You Get…	RCA 4663
2/84	G P 2P*	4/2/84 4/2/84 10/25/84	21	Roll On	RCA 4939
2/85	G P*	4/1/85 4/1/85	28	40 Hour Week	RCA 5339
10/85	G P	11/15/85 11/15/85	75	Alabama Christmas	RCA 7014
1/86	G P*	3/31/86 3/31/86	24	Greatest Hits	RCA 7170
9/86	G P	1/6/87 1/6/87	42	The Touch	RCA 5649
9/87	G	9/9/88	55	Just Us	RCA 6495
5/88	G	8/11/88	76	Alabama Live	RCA 6825
1/89	G	4/4/89	62	Southern Star	RCA 8587
				MORRIS ALBERT	
4/75	G	11/13/75	6	Feelings Morris Albert • Albert	RCA 10279
				THE ALLMAN BROTHERS BAND	
7/71	G	10/25/71	13	At Fillmore East	Capricorn 802
2/72	G	4/13/72	4	Eat A Peach	Capricorn 0102
2/73	G	9/25/73	25	Beginnings	Atco 805
8/73	G	8/21/73	1	**Brothers And Sisters**	Capricorn 0111
8/75	G	10/6/75	5	Win, Lose Or Draw	Capricorn 0156
3/79	G	3/5/79	9	Enlightened Rogues	Capricorn 0218
				DUANE ALLMAN	
11/72	G	12/21/72	28	An Anthology	Capricorn 0108

Release Date	Certification	Date of Certification	Chart Peak	ARTIST/Title Songwriter ● Producer (singles only)	Label & Number
				GREGG ALLMAN	
10/73	G	3/5/74	13	Laid Back	Capricorn 0116
				HERB ALPERT	
5/68	G	7/19/68	1	**This Guy's In Love With You** Burt Bacharach/Hal David • Herb Alpert/ Jerry Moss	A&M 929
6/79	G	9/25/79	1	**Rise** Randy Badazz/Andy Armer • Alpert/Badazz	A&M 2151
10/79	G P	2/5/80 2/5/80	6	Rise	A&M 4790
2/87	G	6/17/87	18	Keep Your Eye On Me	A&M 5125
				HERB ALPERT & THE TIJUANA BRASS	
12/62	G	5/9/66	24	The Lonely Bull	A&M 101
5/63	G	5/9/66	17	Herb Alpert's Tijuana Brass, Volume 2	A&M 103
10/64	G	5/9/66	6	South Of The Border	A&M 108
4/65	G	12/15/65	1	**Whipped Cream & Other Delights**	A&M 110
10/65	G	12/15/65	1	**Going Places**	A&M 112
5/66	G	5/9/66	1	**What Now My Love**	A&M 4114
11/66	G	1/19/67	2	S.R.O.	A&M 4119
5/67	G	8/25/67	1	**Sounds Like**	A&M 4124
12/67	G	12/8/67	4	Herb Alpert's Ninth	A&M 4134
4/68	G	7/19/68	1	**The Beat Of The Brass**	A&M 4146
11/68	G	12/16/68	—	Christmas Album	A&M 4166
6/69	G	3/26/70	28	Warm	A&M 4190
3/70	G	4/12/71	43	Greatest Hits	A&M 4245
				AMERICA	
1/72	G	3/24/72	1	**A Horse With No Name** Dewey Bunnell • Ian Samwell	Warner 7555
1/72	G P	3/10/72 10/13/86	1	**America**	Warner 2576
11/72	G	12/18/72	9	Homecoming	Warner 2655
6/74	G	10/30/74	3	Holiday	Warner 2808
3/75	G	6/12/75	4	Hearts	Warner 2852
10/75	G	12/1/75	3	History/America's Greatest Hits	Warner 2894

Release Date	Certification	Date of Certification	Chart Peak	ARTIST/Title Songwriter ● Producer (singles only)	Label & Number
	P 4P	10/13/86 10/13/86			
4/76	G	5/19/76	11	Hideaway	Warner 2932
				THE AMERICAN BREED	
10/67	G	1/31/68	5	Bend Me, Shape Me Scott English/Laurence Weiss • Bill Traut	Acta 811
				ED AMES	
2/67	G	5/19/67	4	My Cup Runneth Over	RCA 3774
2/68	G	2/17/69	13	Who Will Answer? And Other Songs Of Our Time	RCA 3961
				ANDERSON/BRUFORD/WAKEMAN/HOWE **[see also Rick Wakeman]**	
6/89	G	8/30/89	30	Anderson/Bruford/Wakeman/Howe	Arista 8590
				JOHN ANDERSON	
1/83	G	6/14/83	43	Swingin' John Anderson/Lionel Delmore • Anderson/Frank Jones	Warner 29788
10/82	G	5/15/84	58	Wild & Blue	Warner 23721
				LYNN ANDERSON	
10/70	G	2/3/71	3	Rose Garden Joe South • Glenn Sutton	Columbia 45252
12/70	G P	3/25/71 11/21/86	19	Rose Garden	Columbia 30411
				MAURICE ANDRE/PAILLARD CHAMBER ORCHESTRA	
1/77	G	12/11/85	—	The Pachelbel Canon	RCA 5468
				THE ANIMALS	
1/66	G	7/28/66	6	The Best Of The Animals	MGM 4324

Release Date	Certification	Date of Certification	Chart Peak	ARTIST/Title Songwriter ● Producer (singles only)	Label & Number
				PAUL ANKA	
6/74	G	8/14/74	1	**(You're) Having My Baby** Paul Anka • Rick Hall	United Art. 454
8/74	G	11/20/74	9	Anka	United Art. 314
11/75	G	11/15/76	22	Times Of Your Life	United Art. 569
				ADAM ANT	
10/82	G	3/14/83	16	Friend Or Foe	Epic 38370
				ANTHRAX	
11/87	G	8/19/88	53	I'm The Man	Megaforce 90685
9/88	G	2/8/89	30	State Of Euphoria	Megaforce 91004
				APRIL WINE	
10/79	G	10/22/81	64	Harder…Faster	Capitol 12013
1/81	G P	4/2/81 9/21/81	26	The Nature Of The Beast	Capitol 12125
				ARCADIA	
11/85	G P	1/22/86 1/22/86	23	So Red The Rose	Capitol 12428
				THE ARCHIES	
5/69	G	8/30/69	1	**Sugar, Sugar** Jeff Barry/Andy Kim • Barry	Calendar 1008
11/69	G	1/29/70	10	Jingle Jangle Barry/Kim • Barry	Kirshner 5002
				LOUIS ARMSTRONG	
5/64	G	8/10/64	1	**Hello, Dolly!**	Kapp 3364
				EDDY ARNOLD	
9/65	G	5/12/66	7	My World	RCA 3466
4/67	G	3/28/68	34	The Best Of Eddy Arnold	RCA 3565

Release Date	Certification	Date of Certification	Chart Peak	ARTIST/Title Songwriter ● Producer (singles only)	Label & Number
				ASHFORD & SIMPSON	
9/77	G	6/21/78	52	Send It	Warner 3088
8/78	G	10/10/78	20	Is It Still Good To Ya	Warner 3219
8/79	G	12/11/79	23	Stay Free	Warner 3357
10/84	G	3/7/85	29	Solid	Capitol 12366
				ASIA	
3/82	G P 3P	6/2/82 6/2/82 10/22/84	1	**Asia**	Geffen 2008
8/83	G P	10/11/83 10/11/83	6	Alpha	Geffen 4008
				THE ASSOCIATION	
8/66	G	10/18/66	1	**Cherish** Terry Kirkman • Curt Boettcher	Valiant 747
5/67	G	7/14/67	1	**Windy** Ruthann Friedman • Bones Howe	Warner 7041
8/67	G	11/27/67	2	Never My Love Don & Dick Addrisi • Howe	Warner 7074
8/66	G	11/27/66	5	And Then…Along Comes The Association	Valiant 5002
7/67	G	12/28/67	8	Insight Out	Warner 1696
10/68	G P 2P	3/3/69 10/13/86 6/1/89	4	Greatest Hits	Warner 1767
				RICK ASTLEY	
10/87	G	2/24/89	1	**Never Gonna Give You Up** Mike Stock/Matt Aitken/Pete Waterman • Stock/Aitken/Waterman	RCA 5347
12/87	G P	2/26/88 5/20/88	10	Whenever You Need Somebody	RCA 6822
				ATLANTA RHYTHM SECTION	
12/76	G	4/12/77	11	A Rock And Roll Alternative	Polydor 6080
3/78	G P	4/11/78 9/26/78	7	Champagne Jam	Polydor 6134
6/79	G	6/12/79	26	Underdog	Polydor 6200

Release Date	Certification	Date of Certification	Chart Peak	ARTIST/Title Songwriter ● Producer (singles only)	Label & Number
				ATLANTIC STARR	
4/85	G	2/12/86	17	As The Band Turns	A&M 5019
3/87	G	6/2/87	18	All In The Name Of Love	Warner 25560
				PATTI AUSTIN with JAMES INGRAM	
2/82	G	3/1/83	1	**Baby, Come To Me** Rod Temperton • Quincy Jones	Qwest 50036
				AUTOGRAPH	
11/84	G	4/1/85	29	Sign In Please	RCA 8040
				GENE AUTRY	
11/49	G	11/10/69	1	**Rudolph The Red-Nosed Reindeer** Johnny Marks	Columbia 38610
				AVERAGE WHITE BAND	
10/74	G	3/6/75	1	**Pick Up The Pieces** Roger Ball/Hamish Stuart • Arif Mardin	Atlantic 3229
8/74	G	1/14/75	1	**AWB**	Atlantic 7308
6/75	G	7/24/75	4	Cut The Cake	Atlantic 18140
7/76	G P	8/12/76 12/30/76	9	Soul Searching	Atlantic 18179
1/77	G	5/20/77	28	Person To Person	Atlantic 1002
3/78	G	5/16/78	28	Warmer Communications	Atlantic 19162
				B	
				BURT BACHARACH **[Chorus and Orchestra]**	
9/67	G	11/13/70	96	Reach Out	A&M 4131
6/69	G	11/13/70	51	Make It Easy On Yourself	A&M 4188
10/69	G	5/22/70	16	Butch Cassidy & The Sundance Kid [S]	A&M 4227
6/71	G	7/21/71	18	Burt Bacharach	A&M 3501

Release Date	Certification	Date of Certification	Chart Peak	ARTIST/Title Songwriter ● Producer (singles only)	Label & Number
				BACHMAN-TURNER OVERDRIVE	
9/74	G	12/13/74	1	**You Ain't Seen Nothing Yet** Randy Bachman • Bachman	Mercury 73622
5/73	G	10/11/74	70	Bachman-Turner Overdrive	Mercury 673
12/73	G	5/9/74	4	Bachman-Turner Overdrive II	Mercury 696
8/74	G	8/23/74	1	**Not Fragile**	Mercury 1004
5/75	G	5/27/75	5	Four Wheel Drive	Mercury 1027
12/75	G	12/23/75	23	Head On	Mercury 1067
8/76	G	9/21/76	19	Best Of BTO (So Far)	Mercury 1101
				BAD COMPANY	
6/74	G	9/19/74	1	**Bad Company**	Swan Song 8410
4/75	G	5/8/75	3	Straight Shooter	Swan Song 8413
2/76	G P	2/10/76 12/1/76	5	Run With The Pack	Swan Song 8415
3/77	G	3/15/77	15	Burnin' Sky	Swan Song 8500
3/79	G P	3/20/79 4/26/79	3	Desolation Angels	Swan Song 8506
12/85	G P	9/21/87 2/14/89	137	10 From 6	Atlantic 81625
8/88	G	6/21/89	58	Dangerous Age	Atlantic 81884
				BADFINGER	
11/71	G	3/4/72	4	Day After Day Peter Ham • George Harrison	Apple 1841
				JOAN BAEZ	
7/71	G	10/22/71	3	The Night They Drove Old Dixie Down Robbie Robertson • Norbert Putnam/Jack Lothrop	Vanguard 35138
10/60	G	1/29/66	15	Joan Baez	Vanguard 2077
9/61	G	1/29/66	13	Joan Baez, Vol.2	Vanguard 2097
9/62	G	1/29/66	10	Joan Baez In Concert	Vanguard 2122
1/69	G	1/31/72	30	Any Day Now	Vanguard 79306
9/71	G	1/31/72	11	Blessed Are…	Vanguard 6570
5/75	G	11/11/75	11	Diamonds And Rust	A&M 4527

Release Date	Certification	Date of Certification	Chart Peak	ARTIST/Title Songwriter ● Producer (singles only)	Label & Number
				PHILIP BAILEY	
11/84	G	3/11/85	2	Easy Lover [with PHIL COLLINS] Philip Bailey/Phil Collins/Nathan East • Collins	Columbia 04679
10/84	G	3/11/85	.22	Chinese Wall	Columbia 39542
				ANITA BAKER	
3/86	G P 2P 3P 4P	8/4/86 10/24/86 3/3/87 10/21/87 9/27/88	11	Rapture	Elektra 60444
10/88	G P 2P 3P	12/12/88 12/12/88 12/12/88 3/9/89	1	**Giving You The Best That I Got**	Elektra 60827
				AFRICA BAMBAATAA & SOULSONIC FORCE	
4/82	G	9/16/82	48	Planet Rock [12-inch single] Arthur Baker/John Robie/Soulsonic Force • Baker	Tommy Boy 823
				BANANARAMA	
7/86	G	10/1/86	15	True Confessions	London 828013
				THE BAND	
9/69	G	11/26/69	9	The Band	Capitol 132
8/70	G	10/19/70	5	Stage Fright	Capitol 425
8/72	G	11/2/72	6	Rock Of Ages	Capitol 11045
				BAND AID	
12/84	G	12/19/84	13	Do They Know It's Christmas? Midge Ure/Bob Geldof • Ure	Columbia 04749
				BANGLES	
7/86	G	4/17/89	1	**Walk Like An Egyptian** Liam Sternberg • David Kahne	Columbia 06257
1/89	G	4/17/89	1	**Eternal Flame** Billy Steinberg/Tom Kelly/Susanna Hoffs • Davitt Sigerson	Columbia 68533

Release Date	Certification	Date of Certification	Chart Peak	ARTIST/Title Songwriter ● Producer (singles only)	Label & Number
1/86	G P 2P	4/28/86 12/16/86 2/2/87	2	Different Light	Columbia 40039
10/88	G P	12/21/88 4/17/89	15	Everything	Columbia 44056
				BAR-KAYS	
11/77	G	5/10/78	47	Flying High On Your Love	Mercury 1181
10/79	G	2/15/80	35	Injoy	Mercury 3781
11/81	G	3/3/82	55	Nightcruising	Mercury 4028
				ROB BASE & DJ E-Z ROCK	
2/88	G	2/17/89	36	It Takes Two Robert Ginyard • Base/William Hamilton	Profile 5186
9/88	G P	11/29/88 6/12/89	31	It Takes Two	Profile 1267
				BASIA	
8/87	G*	11/10/88	36	Time And Tide	Epic 40767
				TONI BASIL	

8/82	G
	P
		12/21/82
		3/7/83
			1	**Mickey**
				    Nicky Chinn/Mike Chapman • Greg Mathieson/
				    Trevor Veitch
					Chrysalis 2638

10/82	G	3/7/83	22	Word Of Mouth	Chrysalis 1410
				BAY CITY ROLLERS	
9/75	G	12/16/75	1	**Saturday Night** Bill Martin/Phil Coulter • Martin/Coulter	Arista 0149
9/75	G	12/31/75	20	Bay City Rollers	Arista 4049
3/76	G	10/26/77	31	Rock 'n' Roll Love Letter	Arista 4071
9/76	G	11/23/77	26	Dedication	Arista 4093
7/77	G	8/17/77	23	It's A Game	Arista 7004
11/77	G	12/7/77	77	Greatest Hits	Arista 4158

1. No bull: the most successful instrumental group of the past 30 years is Herb Alpert & The Tijuana Brass, with 13 gold albums. No other act on A&M Records — the A is for Alpert — tops that total, either.

2. Fronting Aerosmith's formidable collection of nine platinum albums — six of 'em consecutive — is *Toys In The Attic* at 5 million. Cumulatively, the band has walked their way to sales of more than 20 million.

3. At a certified 4 million, Bryan Adams' *Reckless* is A&M Records' biggest-selling album by a male soloist since *Frampton Comes Alive!*

1

2

3

4

4. The most popular album by an Australian band? AC/DC claims that title with *Back In Black,* which contributed a high-voltage 5 million to their cumulative 16 million sales.

5. John Anderson's country music smash ''Swingin' '' couldn't crack the Top 40, but sold a million all the same — and secured him a gold album, too.

5

6

7　　　　　　　　　　　　　　　　　　　　8

9

10

6. Alabama has nine consecutive platinum albums to their credit, more than any other group except Chicago. Must be something in those geographical names.

7. With five consecutive gold albums between 1974 and '79, Bad Company was good company for Swan Song Records, the label formed by Led Zeppelin.

8. The oldest gold single is yodeling cowboy Gene Autry's "Rudolph The Red Nosed Reindeer," released in 1949 and certified as a million-seller 20 years later.

9. The South rose again with the Allman Brothers Band, one of the few groups whose first gold album was a live recording.

10. Lynn Anderson's "Rose Garden" won a Grammy (for best country female vocal performance) as well as a gold award. It was one of two million-selling singles written by Joe South.

Release Date	Certification	Date of Certification	Chart Peak	ARTIST/Title Songwriter ● Producer (singles only)	Label & Number
				THE BEACH BOYS	
5/64	G	2/22/82	1	**I Get Around** Brian Wilson • Wilson	Capitol 5174
10/66	G	12/21/66	1	**Good Vibrations** Mike Love/Wilson • Wilson	Capitol 5676
6/88	G P	1/10/89 1/10/89	1	**Kokomo** Love/Terry Melcher/John Phillips/Scott McKenzie • Melcher	Elektra 69385
4/63	G	11/15/65	2	Surfin' U.S.A.	Capitol 1890
7/63	G	11/15/65	7	Surfer Girl	Capitol 1981
10/63	G	12/21/66	4	Little Deuce Coupe	Capitol 1998
3/64	G	12/21/66	13	Shut Down, Volume 2	Capitol 2027
7/64	G	2/18/65	4	All Summer Long	Capitol 2110
10/64	G	2/18/65	1	**Beach Boys Concert**	Capitol 2198
10/64	G	4/6/82	—	The Beach Boys' Christmas Album	Capitol 2164
3/65	G	10/1/65	4	The Beach Boys Today!	Capitol 2269
7/65	G	2/7/66	2	Summer Days (And Summer Nights!!)	Capitol 2354
7/66	G	4/12/67	8	Best Of The Beach Boys	Capitol 2545
7/67	G	12/10/76	50	Best Of The Beach Boys, Vol.2	Capitol 2706
11/73	G	10/4/74	25	The Beach Boys In Concert	Brother 6484
7/74	G	8/14/74	1	**Endless Summer**	Capitol 11307
4/75	G	4/30/75	8	Spirit Of America	Capitol 11384
7/76	G	9/1/76	8	15 Big Ones	Brother 2251
6/86	G	5/26/88	96	Made In The USA	Capitol 12396
				BEASTIE BOYS	
10/86	G P 3P 4P	2/2/87 2/2/87 4/6/87 10/20/87	1	**Licensed To Ill**	Def Jam 40238
				THE BEATLES	
12/63	G	2/3/64	1	**I Want To Hold Your Hand** John Lennon/Paul McCartney • George Martin	Capitol 5112
3/64	G	3/31/64	1	**Can't Buy Me Love** Lennon/McCartney • Martin	Capitol 5150
7/64	G	8/25/64	1	**A Hard Day's Night** Lennon/McCartney • Martin	Capitol 5222

Release Date	Certification	Date of Certification	Chart Peak	ARTIST/Title Songwriter ● Producer (singles only)	Label & Number
11/64	G	12/31/64	1	**I Feel Fine** Lennon/McCartney • Martin	Capitol 5327
2/65	G	9/16/65	1	**Eight Days A Week** Lennon/McCartney • Martin	Capitol 5371
7/65	G	9/2/65	1	**Help!** Lennon/McCartney • Martin	Capitol 5476
9/65	G	10/20/65	1	**Yesterday** Lennon/McCartney • Martin	Capitol 5498
12/65	G	1/6/66	1	**We Can Work It Out** Lennon/McCartney • Martin	Capitol 5555
2/66	G	4/1/66	3	Nowhere Man Lennon/McCartney • Martin	Capitol 5587
5/66	G	7/14/66	1	**Paperback Writer** Lennon/McCartney • Martin	Capitol 5651
8/66	G	9/12/66	2	Yellow Submarine Lennon/McCartney • Martin	Capitol 5715
2/67	G	3/20/67	1	**Penny Lane** Lennon/McCartney • Martin	Capitol 5810
7/67	G	9/11/67	1	**All You Need Is Love** Lennon/McCartney • Martin	Capitol 5964
11/67	G	12/15/67	1	**Hello Goodbye** Lennon/McCartney • Martin	Capitol 2056
3/68	G	4/8/68	4	Lady Madonna Lennon/McCartney • Martin	Capitol 2138
8/68	G	9/13/68	1	**Hey Jude** Lennon/McCartney • Martin	Capitol 2276
5/69	G	5/19/69	1	**Get Back** [with BILLY PRESTON] Lennon/McCartney • Martin	Apple 2490
6/69	G	6/16/69	8	The Ballad Of John And Yoko Lennon/McCartney • Martin	Apple 2531
10/69	G	10/27/69	1	**Something** George Harrison • Martin	Apple 2654
3/70	G	3/17/70	1	**Let It Be** Lennon/McCartney • Martin	Apple 2764
1/64	G	2/3/64	1	**Meet The Beatles!**	Capitol 2047
4/64	G	4/13/64	1	**The Beatles' Second Album**	Capitol 2080
7/64	G	8/24/64	2	Something New	Capitol 2108
12/64	G	12/31/64	7	The Beatles' Story	Capitol 2222
12/64	G	12/31/64	1	**Beatles '65**	Capitol 2228
3/65	G	1/8/74	43	The Early Beatles	Capitol 2309
6/65	G	7/1/65	1	**Beatles VI**	Capitol 2358

Release Date	Certification	Date of Certification	Chart Peak	ARTIST/Title Songwriter ● Producer (singles only)	Label & Number
8/65	G	8/23/65	1	**Help!** [S]	Capitol 2386
12/65	G	12/24/65	1	**Rubber Soul**	Capitol 2442
6/66	G	7/8/66	1	**"Yesterday"…And Today**	Capitol 2553
8/66	G	8/22/66	1	**Revolver**	Capitol 2576
6/67	G	6/15/67	1	**Sgt. Pepper's Lonely Hearts Club Band**	Capitol 2653
11/67	G	12/15/67	1	**Magical Mystery Tour** [S]	Capitol 2835
11/68	G	12/6/68	1	**The Beatles** [a/k/a White Album]	Apple 101
1/69	G	2/5/69	2	Yellow Submarine [S]	Apple 153
10/69	G	10/27/69	1	**Abbey Road**	Apple 383
2/70	G	3/6/70	2	Hey Jude	Apple 385
5/70	G	5/26/70	1	**Let It Be** [S]	Apple 34001
4/73	G	4/13/73	3	The Beatles 1962-1966	Apple 3403
4/73	G	4/13/73	1	**The Beatles 1967-1970**	Apple 3404
6/76	G P	6/14/76 6/14/76	2	Rock 'n' Roll Music	Capitol 11537
5/77	G P	5/5/77 8/12/77	2	The Beatles At The Hollywood Bowl	Capitol 11638
10/77	G	10/24/77	24	Love Songs	Capitol 11711
3/82	G	5/26/82	19	Reel Music	Capitol 12199
10/82	G	10/4/84	50	20 Greatest Hits	Capitol 12245
				JEFF BECK	
3/75	G P	10/8/75 11/21/86	4	Blow By Blow	Epic 33409
6/76	G P	9/14/76 11/21/86	16	Wired	Epic 33849
				THE BEE GEES	
11/70	G	3/30/71	3	Lonely Days Barry, Maurice & Robin Gibb ● Bee Gees/Robert Stigwood	Atco 6795
6/71	G	8/26/71	1	**How Can You Mend A Broken Heart** Barry & Robin Gibb ● Bee Gees/Stigwood	Atco 6824
5/75	G	8/21/75	1	**Jive Talkin'** Bee Gees ● Arif Mardin	RSO 510
6/76	G	9/15/76	1	**You Should Be Dancing** Bee Gees ● Bee Gees/Karl Richardson/Albhy Galuten	RSO 853
9/76	G	12/29/76	3	Love So Right Bee Gees ● Bee Gees/Richardson/Galuten	RSO 859
9/77	G	12/16/77	1	**How Deep Is Your Love**	RSO 882

Release Date	Certification	Date of Certification	Chart Peak	ARTIST/Title Songwriter ● Producer (singles only)	Label & Number
				Bee Gees • Bee Gees/Richardson/Galuten	
12/77	G P	1/26/78 3/13/78	1	**Stayin' Alive** Bee Gees • Bee Gees/Richardson/Galuten	RSO 885
1/78	G P	2/27/78 5/2/78	1	**Night Fever** Bee Gees • Bee Gees/Richardson/Galuten	RSO 889
11/78	G P	11/22/78 2/9/79	1	**Too Much Heaven** Bee Gees • Bee Gees/Richardson/Galuten	RSO 913
1/79	G P	2/5/79 5/14/79	1	**Tragedy** Bee Gees • Bee Gees/Richardson/Galuten	RSO 918
4/79	G	4/10/79	1	**Love You Inside Out** Bee Gees • Bee Gees/Richardson/Galuten	RSO 925
6/69	G	11/10/69	9	Best Of Bee Gees	Atco 292
5/75	G	12/23/75	14	Main Course	RSO 4807
9/76	G P	9/21/76 12/23/76	8	Children Of The World	RSO 3003
10/76	G	1/3/78	50	Gold, Volume One	RSO 3006
5/77	G P	6/24/77 11/22/77	8	Here At Last…Bee Gees…Live	RSO 3901
11/77	G P 11P	11/22/77 1/3/78 11/7/84	1	**Saturday Night Fever** [S]	RSO 4001
1/79	G P	1/30/79 1/30/79	1	**Spirits Having Flown**	RSO 3041
11/79	G P	2/26/80 2/26/80	1	**Bee Gees Greatest**	RSO 4200
6/83	G P	8/30/83 8/30/83	6	Staying Alive [S]	RSO 813 269

HARRY BELAFONTE

Release Date	Certification	Date of Certification	Chart Peak	ARTIST/Title	Label & Number
2/56	G	8/13/63	1	**Belafonte**	RCA 1150
5/56	G	3/12/63	1	**Calypso**	RCA 1248
3/57	G	4/10/67	2	An Evening With Belafonte	RCA 1402
10/59	G	10/16/61	3	Belafonte At Carnegie Hall	RCA 6006
11/60	G	8/13/63	3	Belafonte Returns To Carnegie Hall	RCA 6007
8/61	G	8/23/63	3	Jump Up Calypso	RCA 2388

BELL & JAMES

Release Date	Certification	Date of Certification	Chart Peak	ARTIST/Title	Label & Number
9/78	G	4/6/79	15	Livin' It Up (Friday Night) LeRoy Bell/Casey James • Bell/James	A&M 2069

Release Date	Certification	Date of Certification	Chart Peak	ARTIST/Title Songwriter ● Producer (singles only)	Label & Number
				ARCHIE BELL & THE DRELLS	
1/68	G	5/22/68	1	**Tighten Up** Archie Bell/Billy Butler • Skipper Lee Frazier	Atlantic 2478
				WILLIAM BELL	
10/76	G	4/26/77	10	Tryin' To Love Two William Bell/Paul Mitchell • Bell/Mitchell	Mercury 73839
				THE BELLAMY BROTHERS	
7/82	G	10/10/86	—	Greatest Hits	Warner/Curb 26397
				THE BELLS	
2/71	G	5/27/71	7	Stay Awhile Ken Tobias • Cliff Edwards	Polydor 15023
				PAT BENATAR	
9/80	G	1/26/81	9	Hit Me With Your Best Shot Eddie Schwartz • Keith Olsen	Chrysalis 2464
9/83	G	1/30/89	5	Love Is A Battlefield Mike Chapman/Holly Knight • Neil Geraldo/ Peter Coleman	Chrysalis 42732
9/79	G P	3/25/80 12/8/80	12	In The Heat Of The Night	Chrysalis 1236
8/80	G P 4P	10/21/80 10/30/80 11/6/84	2	Crimes Of Passion	Chrysalis 1275
7/81	G P 2P	9/10/81 9/10/81 11/6/84	1	**Precious Time**	Chrysalis 1346
11/82	G P	3/7/83 3/7/83	4	Get Nervous	Chrysalis 1396
10/83	G P	11/22/83 12/9/83	13	Live From Earth	Chrysalis 41444
11/84	G P	1/9/85 1/9/85	14	Tropico	Chrysalis 41471
11/85	G	3/4/86	26	Seven The Hard Way	Chrysalis 41507
6/88	G	10/12/88	28	Wide Awake In Dreamland	Chrysalis 41628

Release Date	Certification	Date of Certification	Chart Peak	ARTIST/Title Songwriter ● Producer (singles only)	Label & Number
				TONY BENNETT	
6/62	G	7/11/63	5	I Left My Heart In San Francisco	Columbia 8669
8/65	G	10/17/67	20	Tony's Greatest Hits, Volume III	Columbia 9173
				GEORGE BENSON	
3/76	G P 3P	6/4/76 8/10/76 10/22/84	1	**Breezin'**	Warner 2919
1/77	G P	3/15/77 10/6/77	9	In Flight	Warner 2983
1/78	G P	2/28/78 5/3/78	5	Weekend In L.A.	Warner 3139
3/79	G	3/6/79	7	Livin' Inside Your Love	Warner 3277
7/80	G P	9/16/80 10/14/80	3	Give Me The Night	Warner 3453
11/81	G	1/14/82	14	The George Benson Collection	Warner 3577
6/83	G	8/24/83	27	In Your Eyes	Warner 23744
1/85	G	11/13/85	45	20/20	Warner 25178
				GEORGE BENSON & EARL KLUGH	
6/87	G	2/23/88	59	Collaboration	Warner 25580
				BROOK BENTON	
12/69	G	3/18/70	4	Rainy Night In Georgia Tony Joe White • Arif Mardin	Cotillion 44057
				BERLIN	
2/83	G	9/12/84	30	Pleasure Victim	Geffen 2036
3/84	G	4/11/89	28	Love Life	Geffen 4025
				LEONARD BERNSTEIN/NEW YORK PHILHARMONIC ORCHESTRA	
12/59	G	3/21/86	—	Gershwin: An American In Paris/Rhapsody in Blue	Columbia 6091
				CHUCK BERRY	
6/72	G	9/13/72	1	**My Ding-A-Ling** Chuck Berry • Esmond Edwards	Chess 2131

Release Date	Certification	Date of Certification	Chart Peak	ARTIST/Title Songwriter ● Producer (singles only)	Label & Number
5/72	G	10/27/72	8	The London Chuck Berry Sessions	Chess 60020
				DR. MARK BESHARA	
5/81	G	12/2/82	—	Astral Sounds/A Natural High	Dr. Mark Presents
				B-52s	
7/79	G P	11/18/80 5/13/86	59	The B-52s	Warner 3355
9/80	G	10/21/81	18	Wild Planet	Warner 3471
				BIG BROTHER & HOLDING COMPANY **[see also Janis Joplin]**	
8/68	G P	10/15/68 11/21/86	1	**Cheap Thrills**	Columbia 9700
				BIG COUNTRY	
8/83	G	1/19/84	18	The Crossing	Mercury 812870
				BIG DADDY KANE	
6/88	G	8/29/89	116	Long Live The Kane	Cold Chillin' 25731
				MR. ACKER BILK	
1/62	G	6/1/67	1	**Stranger On The Shore** Acker Bilk • Dennis Preston	Atco 6217
4/62	G	6/1/67	3	Stranger On The Shore	Atco 129
				ELVIN BISHOP	
2/76	G	6/23/76	3	Fooled Around And Fell In Love Elvin Bishop • Allan Blazek/Bill Szymczyk	Capricorn 0252
				STEPHEN BISHOP	
9/78	G	12/7/78	35	Bish	ABC 1082

Release Date	Certification	Date of Certification	Chart Peak	ARTIST/Title Songwriter ● Producer (singles only)	Label & Number
				BLACK OAK ARKANSAS	
3/71	G	10/8/74	127	Black Oak Arkansas	Atco 354
3/73	G	11/6/75	90	Raunch 'n' Roll/Live	Atco 7019
11/73	G	1/6/76	52	High On The Hog	Atco 7035
				BLACK SABBATH	
5/70	G P	6/14/71 10/13/86	23	Black Sabbath	Warner 1871
1/71	G P 3P	5/7/71 10/13/86 10/13/86	12	Paranoid	Warner 1887
8/71	G P	9/27/71 10/13/86	8	Master Of Reality	Warner 2562
9/72	G P	11/6/72 10/13/86	13	Black Sabbath, Vol.4	Warner 2602
12/73	G P	3/20/74 10/13/86	11	Sabbath Bloody Sabbath	Warner 2695
2/76	G P	2/7/80 5/13/86	48	We Sold Our Soul For Rock 'n' Roll	Warner 2923
5/80	G P	1/6/81 5/13/86	28	Heaven And Hell	Warner 3372
11/81	G	5/13/86	29	Mob Rules	Warner 3605
				THE BLACKBYRDS	
11/75	G	4/9/76	16	City Life	Fantasy 9490
11/76	G	4/12/77	34	Unfinished Business	Fantasy 9518
9/77	G	12/28/77	43	Action	Fantasy 9535
				BLACKFOOT	
3/79	G P	1/23/80 4/18/86	42	Strikes	Atco 112
				BOBBY BLAND & B.B. KING	
10/74	G	2/28/75	43	Together For The First Time...Live	Dunhill 50190
				BLIND FAITH	
7/69	G	8/19/69	1	**Blind Faith**	Atco 304

Release Date	Certification	Date of Certification	Chart Peak	ARTIST/Title Songwriter ● Producer (singles only)	Label & Number
				BLONDIE	
12/78	G	4/6/79	1	**Heart Of Glass** Debbie Harry/Chris Stein • Mike Chapman	Chrysalis 2295
2/80	G	4/7/80	1	**Call Me** Giorgio Moroder/Harry • Moroder	Chrysalis 2414
10/80	G	1/26/81	1	**The Tide Is High** Duke Reid • Chapman	Chrysalis 2465
1/81	G	3/27/81	1	**Rapture** Harry/Stein • Chapman	Chrysalis 2485
9/78	G P	4/9/79 6/6/79	6	Parallel Lines	Chrysalis 1192
10/79	G P	2/1/80 7/10/80	17	Eat To The Beat	Chrysalis 1225
11/80	G P	1/26/81 1/26/81	7	Autoamerican	Chrysalis 1290
10/81	G	2/9/82	30	The Best Of Blondie	Chrysalis 1337
				BLOOD, SWEAT & TEARS	
2/69	G	6/12/69	2	You've Made Me So Very Happy Berry Gordy/Brenda & Patrice Holloway/Frank Wilson • James William Guercio	Columbia 44776
5/69	G	7/23/69	2	Spinning Wheel David Clayton-Thomas • Guercio	Columbia 44871
10/69	G	1/14/70	2	And When I Die Laura Nyro • Guercio	Columbia 45008
3/68	G	12/2/69	47	Child Is Father To The Man	Columbia 9619
1/69	G P 3P	4/10/69 11/21/86 11/21/86	1	**Blood, Sweat & Tears**	Columbia 9720
7/70	G	7/8/70	1	**Blood, Sweat & Tears 3**	Columbia 30090
7/71	G	8/5/71	10	B, S & T; 4	Columbia 30590
2/72	G P	5/8/72 11/21/86	19	Greatest Hits	Columbia 31170
				BLOODSTONE	
2/73	G	7/19/73	10	Natural High Charles McCormick • Mike Vernon	London 1046

Release Date	Certification	Date of Certification	Chart Peak	ARTIST/Title Songwriter ● Producer (singles only)	Label & Number
				MIKE BLOOMFIELD/AL KOOPER/ STEPHEN STILLS	
8/68	G	12/4/70	12	Super Session	Columbia 9701
				KURTIS BLOW	
6/80	G	8/19/80	87	The Breaks (Part 1) [12-inch single] J.B. Moore/Kurtis Blow/Bob Ford/Russell Simmons/ Lawrence Smith • Moore/Ford	Mercury 4010
				BLUE MAGIC	
4/74	G	8/16/74	8	Sideshow Bobby Eli/Vinnie Barrett • Norman Harris	Atco 6961
				BLUE OYSTER CULT	
3/75	G	7/15/77	22	On Your Feet Or On Your Knees	Columbia 33371
6/76	G P	10/26/76 7/17/78	29	Agents Of Fortune	Columbia 34164
10/77	G	1/19/78	43	Spectres	Columbia 35019
9/78	G P	7/3/80 7/13/88	44	Some Enchanted Evening	Columbia 35563
6/81	G	11/19/82	24	Fire Of Unknown Origin	Columbia 37389
				BLUE SWEDE	
1/74	G	3/28/74	1	**Hooked On A Feeling** Mark James • Bengt Palmers	EMI 3627
				BLUES BROTHERS	
12/78	G P 2P	12/22/78 1/5/79 10/30/84	1	**Briefcase Full Of Blues**	Atlantic 19217
6/80	G	9/10/80	13	The Blues Brothers [S]	Atlantic 16017
				BLUES IMAGE	
3/70	G	8/4/70	4	Ride Captain Ride Blues Image • Richard Polodor	Atco 6746
				CLAUDE BOLLING [see Jean-Pierre Rampal]	

Release Date	Certification	Date of Certification	Chart Peak	ARTIST/Title Songwriter ● Producer (singles only)	Label & Number
				BON JOVI	
1/84	G P	2/4/86 4/14/87	43	Bon Jovi	Mercury 814982
3/85	G P	10/8/85 2/19/87	37	7800° Fahrenheit	Mercury 824509
8/86	G P 2P 3P 4P 5P 6P 7P 8P	10/15/86 10/15/86 11/6/86 12/9/86 1/6/87 1/20/87 2/19/87 4/27/87 8/21/87	1	**Slippery When Wet**	Mercury 830264
9/88	G P 3P 4P 5P	11/18/88 11/18/88 11/18/88 1/11/89 5/25/89	1	**New Jersey**	Mercury 836345
				BOOKER T. & THE M.G.s	

7/62	G	6/1/67	3	Green Onions
				    Booker T. Jones/Steve Cropper/Al Jackson Jr./
				    Lewis Steinberg • Jim Stewart
					Stax 127

				DEBBY BOONE	
8/77	G P	10/19/77 11/22/77	1	**You Light Up My Life** Joe Brooks • Brooks	Warner/Curb 8455
10/77	G P	10/25/77 12/13/77	6	You Light Up My Life	Warner/Curb 3118
				PAT BOONE	
10/57	G	2/12/60	3	Pat's Great Hits	Dot 3071
				BOSTON	
8/76	G P 9P	10/26/76 11/22/76 10/30/86	3	Boston	Epic 34188
8/78	G P 4P	8/25/78 8/25/78 10/30/86	1	**Don't Look Back**	Epic 35050

Release Date	Certification	Date of Certification	Chart Peak	ARTIST/Title Songwriter ● Producer (singles only)	Label & Number
9/86	G P 3P 4P	11/25/86 11/25/86 11/25/86 2/26/87	1	**Third Stage**	MCA 6188
				DAVID BOWIE	
6/75	G	10/17/75	1	**Fame** David Bowie/John Lennon/Carlos Alomar • Bowie/Harry Maslin	RCA 10320
3/83	G	6/16/83	1	**Let's Dance** Bowie • Nile Rodgers/Bowie	EMI America 8158
6/72	G	6/12/74	75	The Rise And Fall Of Ziggy Stardust And The Spiders From Mars	RCA 4702
4/73	G	8/3/83	17	Aladdin Sane	RCA 4852
5/74	G	7/26/74	5	Diamond Dogs	RCA 0576
10/74	G	11/7/74	8	David Live	RCA 0771
3/75	G	7/2/75	9	Young Americans	RCA 0998
1/76	G	2/26/76	3	Station To Station	RCA 1327
5/76	G P	8/2/76 9/15/81	10	Changesonebowie	RCA 1732
4/83	G P	6/9/83 6/27/83	4	Let's Dance	EMI America 17093
9/84	G P	11/21/84 11/21/84	11	Tonight	EMI America 17138
4/87	G	7/8/87	34	Never Let Me Down	EMI America 17267
				THE BOX TOPS	
7/67	G	9/25/67	1	**The Letter** Wayne Carson Thompson • Dan Penn	Mala 565
2/68	G	5/2/68	2	**Cry Like A Baby** Penn/Spooner Oldham • Penn	Mala 593
				THE BOYS	
10/88	G P	4/7/89 6/1/89	33	Messages From The Boys	Motown 6260
				LAURA BRANIGAN	
5/82	G	1/7/83	2	Gloria Umberto Tozzi/Giancarlo Bigazzi/Trevor Veitch • Jack White	Atlantic 4048

1

2

3

4

1. Rocking the planet with the second 12-inch single ever certified gold by the RIAA: Afrika Bambaata & The Soulsonic Force. Kurtis Blow collected the first (for "The Breaks") two years earlier.

2. The Bangles — once upon a time, the Bangs — are the only girl group with a certified pair of gold singles and platinum albums.

3. Summer appears endless for the Beach Boys, who have more gold albums in their sandbox than any other American group except Chicago.

5

4. Anita Baker enjoyed multi-platinum success with *Rapture* and *Giving You The Best That I Got,* for a combined total of 7 million albums back-to-back.

5. The most successful jazz guitarist-turned-pop-vocalist is George Benson, whose debut for Warner Bros. Records (*Breezin'*) outsold all his previous albums combined.

6. The group with the all-time record for gold singles is the act you've known for all these years. So let me introduce to you, the one and only...

7. The Bee Gees have more platinum singles (four) than anyone else, as if being involved with the biggest-selling movie soundtrack in history (*Saturday Night Fever*) wasn't enough.

8. *Crimes Of Passion* was Pat Andrzejewski's most successful album, certified for sales of 4 million. You know her better as Pat Benatar.

9. Scotland's Big Country couldn't beat that sophomore jinx: *The Crossing* was their first and only gold album.

10. The first artist to go gold with that quintessential extravagance of the record industry, the live double album, was...Harry Belafonte.

6

7

8

9

10

Release Date	Certification	Date of Certification	Chart Peak	ARTIST/Title Songwriter ● Producer (singles only)	Label & Number
3/82	G	8/2/84	34	Branigan	Atlantic 19289
3/83	G	9/18/85	29	Branigan 2	Atlantic 80052
4/84	G	8/6/84	23	Self Control	Atlantic 80147
				BRASS CONSTRUCTION	
1/76	G P	3/31/76 12/10/76	10	Brass Construction	United Artists 545
11/76	G	11/12/76	26	Brass Construction II	United Artists 677
11/77	G	1/5/78	66	Brass Construction III	United Artists 775
				BREAD	
5/70	G	8/6/70	1	**Make It With You** David Gates/James Griffin/Robb Royer • Gates	Elektra 45686
10/71	G	1/7/72	3	Baby I'm-A Want You Gates • Gates	Elektra 45751
7/70	G	12/21/72	12	On The Waters	Elektra 74076
3/71	G	12/21/72	21	Manna	Elektra 74086
1/72	G	3/9/72	3	Baby I'm-A Want You	Elektra 75015
11/72	G	11/21/72	18	Guitar Man	Elektra 75047
3/73	G	4/10/73	2	The Best Of Bread	Elektra 75056
5/74	G	12/24/74	32	The Best Of Bread, Volume Two	Elektra 1005
1/77	G	2/17/77	26	Lost Without Your Love	Elektra 1094
				BREATHE	
8/87	G	11/21/88	34	All That Jazz	A&M 5163
				EDIE BRICKELL & THE NEW BOHEMIANS	
8/88	G P	12/20/88 2/1/89	4	Shooting Rubberbands At The Stars	Geffen 24192
				ALICIA BRIDGES	
6/78	G	12/18/78	5	I Love The Nightlife (Disco 'Round) Alicia Bridges/Susan Hutcheson • Steve Buckingham	Polydor 14483

Release Date	Certification	Date of Certification	Chart Peak	ARTIST/Title Songwriter ● Producer (singles only)	Label & Number
				BRIGHTER SIDE OF DARKNESS	20th Century 2002

8/72	G	2/9/73	16	Love Jones
				    Randolph Murph/Clarence Johnson/Ralph Eskridge •
				    Johnson	

				BRITNY FOX	Columbia 44140
6/88	G	12/21/88	39	Britny Fox	
				BROOKLYN BRIDGE	Buddah 75
11/68	G	2/19/69	3	The Worst That Could Happen Jim Webb • Wes Farrell	
				THE BROTHERS JOHNSON	
4/76	G	1/18/77	3	I'll Be Good To You George & Louis Johnson/Senora Sam • Quincy Jones	A&M 1806
6/77	G	10/19/77	5	Strawberry Letter 23 Shuggie Otis • Jones	A&M 1949
2/76	G P	5/12/76 9/13/76	9	Look Out For #1	A&M 4567
5/77	G P	5/24/77 8/2/77	13	Right On Time	A&M 4644
8/78	G P	8/1/78 9/19/78	7	Blam!!	A&M 4717
2/80	G P	4/29/80 9/25/80	5	Light Up The Night	A&M 3716
				THE CRAZY WORLD OF ARTHUR BROWN	Atlantic 2556
8/68	G	12/3/68	2	Fire Arthur Brown/Vincent Crane • Kit Lambert	
				BOBBY BROWN	

5/88	G	1/19/89	4	Don't Be Cruel
				    Antonio "LA" Reid/Kenny "Babyface" Edmonds/
				    Darryl Simmons • LA & Babyface
					MCA 53327

8/88	G	1/10/89	1	**My Prerogative** Bobby Brown/Gene Griffin • Griffin	MCA 53383
3/89	G	6/16/89	3	Every Little Step LA & Babyface • LA & Babyface	MCA 53618

Release Date	Certification	Date of Certification	Chart Peak	ARTIST/Title Songwriter ● Producer (singles only)	Label & Number
5/89	G P	8/1/89 8/25/89	2	On Our Own LA & Babyface/Simmons • LA & Babyface	MCA 53662
6/88	G P 2P 3P 4P 5P	9/6/88 9/28/88 12/2/88 2/7/89 5/5/89 8/17/89	1	**Don't Be Cruel**	MCA 42185
				CHUCK BROWN & THE SOUL SEARCHERS	
1/79	G	3/14/79	34	Bustin' Loose (Part 1) Chuck Brown • James Purdie	Source 40967
1/79	G	8/10/79	31	Bustin' Loose	Source 3076
				JAMES BROWN	
7/72	G	9/19/72	18	Get On The Good Foot (Part 1) James Brown/Fred Wesley/Joe Mims • Brown	Polydor 14139
2/74	G	4/18/74	26	The Payback (Part 1) Brown/Wesley/John Starks • Brown	Polydor 14223
12/73	G	3/18/74	34	The Payback	Polydor 3007
				JACKSON BROWNE	
9/71	G	11/16/76	53	Jackson Browne	Asylum 5051
6/73	G P	10/8/75 5/16/89	43	For Everyman	Asylum 5067
9/74	G P	12/24/74 5/16/89	14	Late For The Sky	Asylum 1017
11/76	G P	11/15/76 4/12/77	5	The Pretender	Asylum 1079
12/77	G P	12/28/77 8/25/78	3	Running On Empty	Asylum 113
7/80	G P	9/15/80 9/15/80	1	**Hold Out**	Asylum 511
8/83	G	11/8/83	8	Lawyers In Love	Asylum 60268
2/86	G	7/8/86	23	Lives In The Balance	Asylum 60457

Release Date	Certification	Date of Certification	Chart Peak	ARTIST/Title Songwriter ● Producer (singles only)	Label & Number
				TOM BROWNE	
7/80	G	2/4/81	18	Love Approach	GRP 5008
				BROWNSVILLE STATION	
9/73	G	1/15/74	3	Smokin' In The Boys Room Michael Lutz/Cub Koda • Doug Morris	Big Tree 16011
				DAVE BRUBECK QUARTET	
10/60	G	4/19/63	2	Time Out Featuring "Take Five"	Columbia 8192
				PEABO BRYSON	
1/78	G	8/18/78	49	Reaching For The Sky	Capitol 11729
11/78	G	2/27/79	35	Crosswinds	Capitol 11875
				PEABO BRYSON & ROBERTA FLACK	
7/83	G	2/8/84	25	Born To Love	Capitol 12284
				B.T. EXPRESS	
6/74	G	11/25/74	2	Do It ('Til You're Satisfied) Billy Nichols • Jeff Lane	Scepter 12395
1/75	G	8/4/75	4	Express B.T. Express • Lane	Roadshow 7001
11/74	G	3/6/75	5	Do It ('Til You're Satisfied)	Roadshow 5117
				BUCKNER & GARCIA	
12/81	G	3/22/82	9	Pac-Man Fever Jerry Buckner/Gary Garcia • Buckner/Garcia	Columbia 02673
2/82	G	4/26/82	24	Pac-Man Fever	Columbia 37941
				BUFFALO SPRINGFIELD	
1/69	G P	4/12/89 4/12/89	42	Retrospective/The Best Of Buffalo Springfield	Atco 283

Release Date	Certification	Date of Certification	Chart Peak	ARTIST/Title Songwriter ● Producer (singles only)	Label & Number
				JIMMY BUFFETT	
1/77	G P	6/20/77 12/14/77	12	Changes In Latitudes, Changes In Attitudes	ABC 990
3/78	G P	4/5/78 5/10/78	10	Son Of A Son Of A Sailor	ABC 1046
10/78	G	11/10/78	72	You Had To Be There	ABC 1008
9/79	G	12/27/79	14	Volcano	MCA 5102
				BULLETBOYS	
9/88	G	4/18/89	34	Bulletboys	Warner Bros. 25782
				JERRY BUTLER	
2/69	G	4/24/69	4	Only The Strong Survive Kenny Gamble/Leon Huff/Jerry Butler • Gamble/Huff	Mercury 72898
				JERRY BUTLER & BRENDA LEE EAGER	
11/71	G	4/6/72	21	Ain't Understanding Mellow Herscholt Polk/Homer Talbert • Butler/Gerald Sims	Mercury 73255
				JONATHAN BUTLER	
5/87	G	3/25/88	50	Jonathan Butler	Jive 1032
				THE BYRDS	
8/67	G P	3/13/68 11/21/86	6	The Byrds' Greatest Hits	Columbia 9516

C

Release Date	Certification	Date of Certification	Chart Peak	ARTIST/Title	Label & Number
				C COMPANY featuring TERRY NELSON	
4/71	G	4/15/71	37	Battle Hymn Of Lt. Calley Julian Wilson/James Smith • Smith	Plantation 73
				THE CABBAGE PATCH KIDS	
8/84	G	6/21/84	—	Cabbage Patch Dreams	Parker Bros. 7216

Release Date	Certification	Date of Certification	Chart Peak	ARTIST/Title Songwriter ● Producer (singles only)	Label & Number
				JOHN CAFFERTY & THE BEAVER BROWN BAND	
9/83	G P 2P	8/31/84 10/5/84 12/16/86	9	Eddie And The Cruisers [S]	Scotti 38929
				THE CALIFORNIA RAISINS	
10/87	G P	1/8/88 6/15/88	60	The California Raisins	Priority 9706
				CAMEO	
7/79	G	12/4/79	46	Secret Omen	Choc. City 2008
5/80	G	7/17/80	25	Cameosis	Choc. City 2011
11/80	G	1/27/81	44	Feel Me	Choc. City 2016
5/81	G	8/6/81	44	Knights Of The Sound Table	Choc. City 2019
4/82	G	7/16/82	23	Alligator Woman	Choc. City 2021
3/84	G	5/30/84	27	She's Strange	Atlanta Art. 814 984
6/85	G	11/11/85	58	Single Life	Atlanta Art. 824 546
8/86	G P	10/29/86 12/9/86	8	Word Up!	Atlanta Art. 830 265
10/88	G	12/19/88	56	Machismo	Atlanta Art. 836 002
				GLEN CAMPBELL **[see also Bobbie Gentry]**	
10/68	G	1/22/69	3	Wichita Lineman Jim Webb • Al De Lory	Capitol 2302
2/69	G	10/14/69	4	Galveston Webb • De Lory	Capitol 2428
5/75	G	9/5/75	1	**Rhinestone Cowboy** Larry Weiss • Dennis Lambert/Brian Potter	Capitol 4095
1/77	G	4/20/77	1	**Southern Nights** Allen Toussaint • Gary Klein	Capitol 4376
9/67	G	10/17/68	5	Gentle On My Mind	Capitol 2809
12/67	G	10/17/68	15	By The Time I Get To Phoenix	Capitol 2851
3/68	G	1/10/69	26	Hey, Little One	Capitol 2878
11/68	G	11/18/68	1	**Wichita Lineman**	Capitol 103

Release Date	Certification	Date of Certification	Chart Peak	ARTIST/Title Songwriter ● Producer (singles only)	Label & Number
11/68	G	12/10/76	—	That Christmas Feeling	Capitol 2978
3/69	G	4/16/69	2	Galveston	Capitol 210
9/69	G	9/19/69	13	Live	Capitol 0268
1/70	G	2/19/70	12	Try A Little Kindness	Capitol 389
3/71	G	5/15/72	39	Glen Campbell's Greatest Hits	Capitol 752
7/75	G	12/31/75	17	Rhinestone Cowboy	Capitol 11430
2/77	G	10/5/77	22	Southern Nights	Capitol 11601
				CANDLE	
8/77	G P	2/26/81 2/14/89	—	The Music Machine	Birdwing 2004
8/78	G	11/8/84	—	Bullfrogs And Butterflies	Birdwing 2010
				CAPTAIN & TENNILLE	
2/75	G	7/1/75	1	**Love Will Keep Us Together** Neil Sedaka/Howard Greenfield • Daryl Dragon	A&M 1672
9/75	G	12/17/75	4	The Way I Want To Touch You Toni Tennille • Morgan Cavett	A&M 1725
1/76	G	4/8/76	3	Lonely Night (Angel Face) Sedaka • Dragon/Tennille	A&M 1782
4/76	G	8/13/76	4	Shop Around Smokey Robinson/Berry Gordy Jr. • Dragon/Tennille	A&M 1817
9/76	G	12/8/76	4	Muskrat Love Willis Allen Ramsey • Dragon/Tennille	A&M 1870
10/79	G	2/11/80	1	**Do That To Me One More Time** Tennille • Dragon	Casablanca 2215
5/75	G	8/1/75	2	Love Will Keep Us Together	A&M 3405
3/76	G P	3/10/76 9/23/76	9	Song Of Joy	A&M 4570
4/77	G	4/11/77	18	Come In From The Rain	A&M 4700
11/77	G	12/13/77	55	Captain & Tennille's Greatest Hits	A&M 4667
10/79	G	8/5/80	23	Make Your Move	Casablanca 7188
				IRENE CARA	
3/83	G	6/17/83	1	**Flashdance...What A Feeling** Giorgio Moroder/Keith Forsey/Irene Cara • Moroder	Casablanca 811 440

Release Date	Certification	Date of Certification	Chart Peak	ARTIST/Title Songwriter ● Producer (singles only)	Label & Number
				GEORGE CARLIN	
1/72	G	9/27/72	13	FM & AM	Little David 7214
10/72	G	6/13/73	22	Class Clown	Little David 1004
10/73	G	12/27/76	35	Occupation: Foole	Little David 1005
11/74	G	5/17/77	19	Toledo Window Box	Little David 3003
				BELINDA CARLISLE	
5/86	G	11/24/86	13	Belinda	IRS 5741
10/87	G	12/7/87	13	Heaven On Earth	MCA 42080
				WALTER CARLOS	
11/68	G P	8/14/69 11/21/86	10	Switched-On Bach	Columbia 7194
				CARL CARLTON	
5/81	G	10/6/81	22	She's A Bad Mama Jama Leon Haywood • Haywood	20th Century 2488
				ERIC CARMEN	
12/75	G	4/21/76	2	All By Myself Eric Carmen • Jimmy Ienner	Arista 0165
10/75	G	10/27/77	21	Eric Carmen	Arista 4057
				KIM CARNES	
3/81	G	6/16/81	1	**Bette Davis Eyes** Donna Weiss/Jackie DeShannon • Val Garay	EMI America 8077
4/81	G	6/16/81	1	**Mistaken Identity**	EMI America 17052
				CARPENTERS	
5/70	G	8/12/70	1	**(They Long To Be) Close To You** Burt Bacharach/Hal David • Jack Daugherty	A&M 1183
8/70	G	11/13/70	2	We've Only Just Begun Paul Williams/Roger Nichols • Daugherty	A&M 1217
1/71	G	4/12/71	3	For All We Know Fred Karlin/Robb Royer/James Griffin • Daugherty	A&M 1243

Release Date	Certification	Date of Certification	Chart Peak	ARTIST/Title Songwriter ● Producer (singles only)	Label & Number
5/71	G	7/21/71	2	Rainy Days And Mondays Williams/Nichols • Daugherty	A&M 1260
8/71	G	10/18/71	2	Superstar Leon Russell/Bonnie Bramlett • Daugherty	A&M 1289
1/72	G	2/29/72	2	Hurting Each Other Gary Geld/Peter Udell • Daugherty	A&M 1322
2/73	G	5/17/73	3	Sing Joe Raposo • Richard & Karen Carpenter	A&M 1413
5/73	G	8/13/73	2	Yesterday Once More Richard Carpenter/John Bettis • Carpenter/Carpenter	A&M 1446
9/73	G	12/11/73	1	**Top Of The World** Carpenter/Bettis • Carpenter/Carpenter/Daugherty	A&M 1468

11/74	G	2/11/75	1	**Please Mr. Postman**
				    Brian Holland/Freddie Gorman/Robert Bateman •
				    Carpenter/Carpenter
					A&M 1646

8/70	G	11/13/70	2	Close To You	A&M 4271
5/71	G	6/7/71	2	Carpenters	A&M 3502
6/72	G	7/10/72	4	A Song For You	A&M 3511
5/73	G	6/7/73	2	Now & Then	A&M 3519
11/73	G	12/11/73	1	**The Singles 1969-1973**	A&M 3601
6/75	G	6/17/75	13	Horizon	A&M 4530
6/76	G	7/14/76	33	A Kind Of Hush	A&M 4581
11/78	G	1/16/81	145	Christmas Portrait	A&M 4726
				THE CARS	
5/78	G P	10/16/78 12/27/78	18	The Cars	Elektra 135
6/79	G P	7/24/79 8/6/79	3	Candy-O	Elektra 507
8/80	G P	10/15/80 10/15/80	5	Panorama	Elektra 514
11/81	G P	1/20/82 1/20/82	9	Shake It Up	Elektra 567
3/84	G P 2P 3P	5/17/84 5/17/84 10/30/84 7/15/85	3	Heartbeat City	Elektra 60296
10/85	G P	1/16/86 1/16/86	12	The Cars' Greatest Hits	Elektra 60464
8/87	G	10/21/87	26	Door To Door	Elektra 60747

Release Date	Certification	Date of Certification	Chart Peak	ARTIST/Title Songwriter ● Producer (singles only)	Label & Number
				JOHNNY CARSON	
11/74	G	12/5/74	30	Here's Johnny/Magic Moments From The Tonight Show	Casablanca 1296
				CLARENCE CARTER	

4/68	G	9/13/68	6	Slip Away
				    William Armstrong/Wilbur Terrell/Marcus Daniel ●
				    Rick Hall
					Atlantic 2508

10/68	G	2/24/69	13	Too Weak To Fight
				    Hall/George Jackson/Clarence Carter/
				    John Keyes ● Hall
					Atlantic 2569

7/70	G	9/11/70	4	Patches Ronald Dunbar/Norman Johnson ● Hall	Atlantic 2748
				JOHNNY CASH **[see also Waylon Jennings]**	
7/69	G	8/14/69	2	A Boy Named Sue Shel Silverstein ● Bob Johnston	Columbia 44944
7/63	G	2/11/65	26	Ring Of Fire (The Best Of Johnny Cash)	Columbia 8853
7/64	G	7/14/67	53	I Walk The Line	Columbia 8990
7/67	G P 2P	7/24/69 11/21/86 11/21/86	82	Johnny Cash's Greatest Hits, Volume 1	Columbia 9478
5/68	G P 2P	10/30/68 11/21/86 11/21/86	13	Johnny Cash At Folsom Prison	Columbia 9639
6/69	G P 2P	8/12/69 11/21/86 11/21/86	1	**Johnny Cash At San Quentin**	Columbia 9827
1/70	G	1/29/70	6	Hello, I'm Johnny Cash	Columbia 9943
5/70	G	12/23/71	54	The World Of Johnny Cash	Columbia 29
10/71	G	10/25/77	94	The Johnny Cash Collection	Columbia 30887
				ROSANNE CASH	
2/81	G	1/6/83	26	Seven Year Ache	Columbia 36965
				DAVID CASSIDY	
10/71	G	12/16/71	9	Cherish Terry Kirkman ● Wes Farrell	Bell 45150

Release Date	Certification	Date of Certification	Chart Peak	ARTIST/Title Songwriter ● Producer (singles only)	Label & Number
1/72	G	6/30/72	15	Cherish	Bell 6070
				SHAUN CASSIDY	

4/77	G	7/19/77	1	**Da Doo Ron Ron**
				    Phil Spector/Jeff Barry/Ellie Greenwich •
				    Michael Lloyd
					Warner/Curb 8365

7/77	G	10/4/77	3	That's Rock 'n' Roll Eric Carmen • Lloyd	Warner/Curb 8423
11/77	G	1/17/78	7	Hey Deanie Carmen • Lloyd	Warner/Curb 8488
6/77	G P	8/9/77 9/20/77	3	Shaun Cassidy	Warner/Curb 3067
10/77	G P	11/22/77 12/13/77	6	Born Late	Warner/Curb 3126
7/78	G P	8/2/78 10/10/78	33	Under Wraps	Warner/Curb 3222
				THE JIMMY CASTOR BUNCH	
4/72	G	6/30/72	6	Troglodyte (Cave Man) Jimmy Castor Bunch • Castor/James Pruitt	RCA 1029
				PETER CETERA **[see also Cher]**	
6/86	G	11/18/86	23	Solitude/Solitaire	Warner 25474
				CHAIRMEN OF THE BOARD	

12/69	G	5/11/70	3	Give Me Just A Little More Time
				    Ronald Dunbar/Edythe Wayne • Brian Holland/
				    Lamont Dozier
					Invictus 9074

				CHAKACHAS	
11/71	G	3/22/72	8	Jungle Fever William Albimoor • Roland Kluger	Polydor 15030
				THE CHAMBERS BROTHERS	
11/67	G	12/4/68	4	The Time Has Come	Columbia 9522

Release Date	Certification	Date of Certification	Chart Peak	ARTIST/Title Songwriter ● Producer (singles only)	Label & Number
				GENE CHANDLER	Mercury 73083
6/70	G	11/11/70	12	Groovy Situation Herman Davis/Russell Lewis • Gene Chandler	
				CHANGE	RFC 3438
5/80	G	10/23/80	29	The Glow Of Love	
				HARRY CHAPIN	
8/74	G	12/31/74	1	**Cat's In The Cradle** Harry & Sandy Chapin • Paul Leka	Elektra 45203
8/74	G	12/17/74	4	Verities & Balderdash	Elektra 1012
4/76	G	6/7/78	48	Greatest Stories—Live	Elektra 2009
				TRACY CHAPMAN	
3/88	G P 2P 3P	6/22/88 7/27/88 9/27/88 3/29/89	1	**Tracy Chapman**	Elektra 60774
				RAY CHARLES	
4/62	G	7/19/62	1	**I Can't Stop Loving You** Don Gibson • Sid Feller	ABC 10330
1/62	G	7/19/62	1	**Modern Sounds In Country And Western Music**	ABC 410
7/62	G	4/6/68	5	Ray Charles' Greatest Hits	ABC 415
10/62	G	4/6/68	2	Modern Sounds In Country And Western Music Volume Two	ABC 435
2/67	G	8/16/68	77	A Man And His Soul	ABC 590
				CHEAP TRICK	
3/79	G	8/13/79	7	I Want You To Want Me Rick Nielsen • Cheap Trick	Epic 50680
8/77	G	8/13/79	73	In Color	Epic 34884
5/78	G	1/16/79	48	Heaven Tonight	Epic 35312
2/79	G P	3/13/79 5/22/79	4	Cheap Trick At Budokan	Epic 35795
9/79	G	2/6/80	6	Dream Police	Epic 35773

1

2

3

4

5

1. Onetime beautician, bunny, and barmaid, Debbie Harry bleached her way to four gold singles and four platinum albums with Blondie.

2. Three of Bobby Brown's four solo gold singles are from his *Don't Be Cruel* album, which is five times platinum — and the largest-selling release in MCA Records' history.

3. The black arts meant platinum for Black Sabbath, whose seven million-selling albums place them among Britain's most popular metal merchants of the past 20 years.

4. The most successful debut album by a group, *Boston* has sold a certified 9 million. Cumulatively, their three albums (in 10 years!) have moved 17 million copies.

7

9

5. The four consecutive platinum albums by the Brothers Johnson (yes, real brothers) were produced by the high priest of widescreen audio, Quincy Jones.

6. The pioneers of '70s soft rock, Bread rose with seven consecutive gold albums and a brace of million-selling singles, "Make It With You" and "Baby I'm-A Want You."

7. Every one of Jackson Browne's albums have gone gold, and most reached platinum. He is Asylum Records' most-certified male solo artist.

8. Glen Campbell appears to have more cities named in the titles of his gold albums than any other artist. Glen, we hope they gave you — and Jim Webb — the keys to Phoenix, Wichita, and Galveston.

9. Certified at 8 million, Bon Jovi's *Slippery When Wet* is Mercury Records' largest-selling album by an American band. It was released in August 1986, and was their third LP.

10. Aladdin Sane Company? David Bowie has 10 gold albums. So does Prince. And, ahem, Tom Jones. And Engelbert Humperdinck.

Release Date	Certification	Date of Certification	Chart Peak	ARTIST/Title Songwriter ● Producer (singles only)	Label & Number
	P	2/6/80			
10/80	G	12/30/80	24	All Shook Up	Epic 36498
3/88	G	7/18/88	16	Lap Of Luxury	Epic 40922
	P	9/28/88			
				CHEECH & CHONG	
8/71	G	7/28/72	28	Cheech & Chong	Ode 77010
6/72	G	8/21/72	2	Big Bambu	Ode 77014
8/73	G	10/2/73	2	Los Cochinos	Ode 77019
10/74	G	10/9/74	5	Cheech & Chong's Wedding Album	Ode 77025
				CHER	
8/71	G	11/19/71	1	**Gypsys, Tramps & Thieves** Robert Stone • Snuff Garrett	Kapp 2146
7/73	G	10/12/73	1	**Half-Breed** Mary Dean/Al Capps • Garrett	MCA 40102
12/73	G	3/22/74	1	**Dark Lady** John Durrill • Garrett	MCA 40161
2/79	G	5/3/79	8	Take Me Home Michele Aller/Bob Esty • Esty	Casablanca 965
8/71	G	4/13/72	16	Gypsys, Tramps & Thieves	Kapp 3649
9/73	G	3/4/74	28	Half-Breed	MCA 2104
2/79	G	5/17/79	25	Take Me Home	Casablanca 7133
11/87	G	5/17/88	32	Cher	Geffen 24164
				CHER & PETER CETERA	
3/89	G	6/1/89	6	After All Tom Snow/Dean Pitchford • Peter Asher	Geffen 27529
				NENEH CHERRY	
3/89	G	6/20/89	3	Buffalo Stance Nina Cherry/Cameron McVey/Philip Ramacon/Jamie Morgan • Tim Simenon/Mark Saunders	Virgin 99231
				CHIC	
10/77	G	2/16/78	6	Dance, Dance, Dance (Yowsah, Yowsah, Yowsah) Nile Rodgers/Bernard Edwards/Kenny Lehman • Rodgers/Edwards	Atlantic 3435
9/78	G	11/15/78	1	**Le Freak**	Atlantic 3519

Release Date	Certification	Date of Certification	Chart Peak	ARTIST/Title Songwriter ● Producer (singles only)	Label & Number
	P	12/7/78		Rodgers/Edwards • Rodgers/Edwards	
1/79	G	3/1/79	7	I Want Your Love Rodgers/Edwards • Rodgers/Edwards	Atlantic 3557
6/79	G	6/26/79	1	**Good Times** Rodgers/Edwards • Rodgers/Edwards	Atlantic 3584
11/77	G	3/29/78	27	Chic	Atlantic 19153
11/78	G P	11/28/78 12/27/78	4	C'est Chic	Atlantic 19209
8/79	G P	8/26/79 12/6/79	5	Risque	Atlantic 16003

CHICAGO

Release Date	Certification	Date of Certification	Chart Peak	ARTIST/Title Songwriter ● Producer (singles only)	Label & Number
7/72	G	11/9/72	3	Saturday In The Park Robert Lamm • James William Guercio	Columbia 45657
9/73	G	1/2/74	4	Just You 'n' Me James Pankow • Guercio	Columbia 45933
7/76	G	10/26/76	1	**If You Leave Me Now** Peter Cetera • Guercio	Columbia 10390
5/82	G	9/15/82	1	**Hard To Say I'm Sorry** Cetera/David Foster • Foster	Full Moon 29979
9/88	G	1/18/89	1	**Look Away** Diane Warren • Ron Nevison	Reprise 27766
4/69	G P 2P	12/17/69 11/21/86 11/21/86	17	Chicago Transit Authority	Columbia 8
2/70	G	4/13/70	4	Chicago II	Columbia 24
1/71	G P	2/4/71 11/21/86	2	Chicago III	Columbia 30110
10/71	G P	11/9/71 11/21/86	3	Chicago At Carnegie Hall	Columbia 30865
7/72	G P 2P	7/31/72 11/21/86 11/21/86	1	**Chicago V**	Columbia 31102
7/73	G P 2P	7/18/73 11/21/86 11/21/86	1	**Chicago VI**	Columbia 32400
3/74	G P	3/18/74 11/21/86	1	**Chicago VII**	Columbia 32810
3/75	G P	3/31/75 11/21/86	1	**Chicago VIII**	Columbia 33100
11/75	G P	11/18/75 11/21/86	1	**Chicago IX/Chicago's Greatest Hits**	Columbia 33900

Release Date	Certification	Date of Certification	Chart Peak	ARTIST/Title Songwriter ● Producer (singles only)	Label & Number
	4P	11/21/86			
6/76	G P 2P	6/21/76 9/14/76 11/21/86	3	Chicago X	Columbia 34200
9/77	G P	9/16/77 10/11/77	6	Chicago XI	Columbia 34860
10/78	G P	10/10/78 10/27/78	12	Hot Streets	Columbia 35512
8/79	G	12/10/79	21	Chicago 13	Columbia 36105
6/82	G P	8/31/82 12/14/82	9	Chicago 16	Full Moon 23689
5/84	G P 2P 3P 4P	9/12/84 10/17/84 12/18/84 2/12/85 5/13/86	4	Chicago 17	Full Moon 25060
9/86	G	12/1/86	35	Chicago 18	Full Moon 25509
6/88	G P	8/23/88 2/1/89	37	Chicago 19	Reprise 25714
				CHICAGO BEARS SHUFFLIN' CREW	

12/85	G	2/11/86	41	Superbowl Shuffle
				   Milton Owens/Lloyd Barry/Richard Meyer/
				   Bobby Daniels ● Daniels/Rich Tufo
					Red Label 71012

				THE CHIPMUNKS	
6/80	G	10/14/80	34	Chipmunk Punk	Excelsior 6008
5/81	G	8/28/81	56	Urban Chipmunk	RCA 4027
10/81	G	1/17/84	72	A Chipmunk Christmas	RCA 4041
				LOU CHRISTIE	
10/65	G	3/3/66	1	**Lightnin' Strikes** Lou Christie/Twyla Herbert ● Charles Calello	MGM 13412
				CINDERELLA	
6/86	G P 2P	10/1/86 12/9/86 2/19/87	3	Night Songs	Mercury 830 076
7/88	G P 2P	9/9/88 9/9/88 11/30/88	10	Long Cold Winter	Mercury 834 612

Release Date	Certification	Date of Certification	Chart Peak	ARTIST/Title Songwriter ● Producer (singles only)	Label & Number
				ERIC CLAPTON	
6/74	G	9/19/74	1	**I Shot The Sheriff** Bob Marley • Tom Dowd	RSO 409
12/77	G	4/17/78	3	Lay Down Sally Eric Clapton/Marcy Levy/George Terry • Glyn Johns	RSO 886
4/72	G	7/14/72	6	History Of Eric Clapton	Atco 803
7/74	G	8/8/74	1	**461 Ocean Boulevard**	RSO 4801
11/77	G P	1/26/78 3/14/78	2	Slowhand	RSO 3030
11/78	G P	11/14/78 11/14/78	8	Backless	RSO 3039
4/80	G	6/23/80	2	Just One Night	RSO 4202
3/81	G	5/12/81	7	Another Ticket	RSO 3095
3/85	G	2/13/87	34	Behind The Sun	Duck 25166
11/86	G	4/21/87	37	August	Duck 25476
4/88	G	6/22/88	34	Crossroads	Polydor 835 261
				THE DAVE CLARK FIVE	
3/64	G	1/21/65	3	Glad All Over	Epic 26093
2/66	G	8/24/66	9	The Dave Clark Five's Greatest Hits	Epic 26185
				LOUIS CLARK/ROYAL PHILHARMONIC ORCHESTRA	
10/81	G P	1/7/82 1/7/82	4	Hooked on Classics	RCA 4194
7/82	G	9/29/82	33	Hooked on Classics II	RCA 4373
				PETULA CLARK	
12/64	G	3/1/65	1	**Downtown** Tony Hatch • Hatch	Warner 5494
				THE CLASH	
5/82	G	11/8/82	7	Combat Rock	Epic 37689
				CLASSICS IV	
9/68	G	2/27/69	5	Stormy Perry Buie/James Cobb Jr. • Buddy Buie	Imperial 66328

Release Date	Certification	Date of Certification	Chart Peak	ARTIST/Title Songwriter ● Producer (singles only)	Label & Number
				VAN CLIBURN	
7/58	G P	11/22/61 7/10/89	1	**Tchaikovsky: Piano Concerto No.1**	RCA 2252
10/61	G	6/19/89	71	My Favorite Chopin	RCA 2576
				CLIMAX	
7/71	G	2/21/72	3	Precious And Few 　Walt Nims ● Larry Cox	Carousel 30055
				PATSY CLINE	
3/67	G .P 2P	7/31/85 11/13/87 7/24/89	—	Greatest Hits	Decca 74854
9/85	G	4/2/87	29	Sweet Dreams [S]	MCA 6149
				CLUB NOUVEAU	
2/87	G	5/5/87	1	**Lean On Me** 　Bill Withers ● Jay King/Thomas McElroy/Denzil Foster	Warner 28430
11/86	G P	3/3/87 4/7/87	6	Life, Love And Pain	Warner 25531
				JOE COCKER	
4/69	G	11/13/70	35	With A Little Help From My Friends	A&M 4182
TK/69	G	4/17/70	11	Joe Cocker!	A&M 4224
8/70	G	8/31/70	2	Mad Dogs & Englishmen [S]	A&M 6002
				JOE COCKER & JENNIFER WARNES	
7/82	G P	1/17/89 1/17/89	1	**Up Where We Belong** 　Jack Nitzsche/Will Jennings/Buffy St. Marie ● 　Stewart Levine	Island 99996
				DAVID ALLAN COE	
10/78	G	11/7/83	—	Greatest Hits	Columbia 35267
				DENNIS COFFEY & THE DETROIT GUITAR BAND	
9/71	G	12/9/71	6	Scorpio 　Dennis Coffey ● Mike Theodore/Coffey	Sussex 226

Release Date	Certification	Date of Certification	Chart Peak	ARTIST/Title Songwriter ● Producer (singles only)	Label & Number
				NAT KING COLE	
11/52	G	9/4/64	30	Unforgettable	Capitol 357
3/57	G	10/24/60	1	**Love Is The Thing**	Capitol 824
8/62	G	1/15/64	3	Ramblin' Rose	Capitol 1793
9/63	G	1/17/69	—	The Christmas Song	Capitol 1967
8/68	G	6/27/79	187	The Best Of Nat "King" Cole	Capitol 2944
				NATALIE COLE	
1/77	G	4/13/77	5	I've Got Love On My Mind Chuck Jackson/Marvin Yancy • Jackson/Yancy	Capitol 4360
10/77	G	4/6/78	10	Our Love Jackson/Yancy • Jackson/Yancy	Capitol 4509
7/75	G	2/11/76	18	Inseparable	Capitol 11429
5/76	G	7/1/76	13	Natalie	Capitol 11517
2/77	G P	3/1/77 8/12/77	8	Unpredictable	Capitol 11600
11/77	G P	12/20/77 6/21/78	16	Thankful	Capitol 11708
7/78	G	7/19/78	31	Natalie…Live!	Capitol 11709
3/79	G	4/2/79	52	I Love You So	Capitol 11928
6/87	G	3/25/88	42	Everlasting	Manhattan 53051
				JUDY COLLINS	
9/66	G	12/21/70	46	In My Life	Elektra 7320
11/67	G	1/20/69	5	Wildflowers	Elektra 74012
11/68	G	10/8/69	29	Who Knows Where The Time Goes	Elektra 74033
11/70	G	4/6/71	17	Whales & Nightingales	Elektra 75010
5/72	G	1/22/74	37	Colors Of The Day/The Best Of Judy Collins	Elektra 75030
3/75	G	11/19/75	17	Judith	Elektra 1032
				PHIL COLLINS **[see also Philip Bailey]**	
2/84	G	5/10/84	1	**Against All Odds (Take A Look At Me Now)** Phil Collins • Arif Mardin	Atlantic 89700

8/88	G	1/10/89	1	**A Groovy Kind Of Love**
				    Toni Wine/Carole Bayer Sager • Collins/
				    Anne Dudley
					Atlantic 89017

Release Date	Certification	Date of Certification	Chart Peak	ARTIST/Title Songwriter ● Producer (singles only)	Label & Number
2/81	G P 2P	6/3/81 9/18/85 1/28/86	7	Face Value	Atlantic 16029
11/82	G P	2/7/83 3/13/85	8	Hello, I Must Be Going!	Atlantic 80035
2/85	G P 2P 3P 4P 5P	4/18/85 4/18/85 6/3/85 8/22/85 12/11/85 6/18/86	1	**No Jacket Required**	Atlantic 81240
				WILLIAM "BOOTSY" COLLINS	
1/77	G	4/13/77	16	Ahh…The Name Is Bootsy, Baby!	Warner 2972
2/78	G	3/8/78	16	Bootsy? Player Of The Year	Warner 3093
				JESSI COLTER **[see Waylon Jennings]**	
				COMMODORES	
5/78	G P	8/22/78 8/22/78	3	Natural High	Motown 902
6/80	G P	2/3/81 2/3/81	7	Heroes	Motown 939
6/81	G P	8/21/81 12/16/81	13	In The Pocket	Motown 955
12/82	G	3/13/85	37	All The Great Hits	Motown 6028
1/85	G	5/8/85	12	Nightshift	Motown 6124
				PERRY COMO	
12/57	G	3/14/58	1	**Catch A Falling Star** Paul Vance/Lee Pockriss	RCA 7128
11/59	G	3/12/63	22	Season's Greetings	RCA 2066
9/61	G	10/27/66	—	Merry Christmas Music	RCA Camden 660
8/68	G	11/19/82	—	The Perry Como Christmas Album	RCA 4016
5/73	G	11/24/76	34	And I Love You So	RCA 0100

Release Date	Certification	Date of Certification	Chart Peak	ARTIST/Title Songwriter ● Producer (singles only)	Label & Number
				CON FUNK SHUN	
9/77	G	5/10/78	51	Secrets	Mercury 1180
5/78	G	8/25/78	32	Loveshine	Mercury 3725
4/79	G	8/23/79	46	Candy	Mercury 3754
3/80	G	6/25/80	30	Spirit Of Love	Mercury 3806
				ARTHUR CONLEY	
2/67	G	6/23/67	2	Sweet Soul Music Otis Redding/Arthur Conley • Redding	Atco 6463
				JOHN CONLEE	
3/83	G	11/6/86	166	John Conlee's Greatest Hits	MCA 5405
				EARL THOMAS CONLEY	
9/85	G	7/25/89	—	Greatest Hits	RCA 7032
				RAY CONNIFF & SINGERS	
11/57	G	7/19/62	10	'S Marvelous	Columbia 1074
9/58	G	7/20/62	9	Concert In Rhythm	Columbia 1163
11/59	G	10/21/63	14	Christmas With Conniff	Columbia 1390
1/61	G	7/20/62	4	Memories Are Made Of This	Columbia 1574
1/62	G	12/4/62	5	So Much In Love	Columbia 1720
10/62	G*	12/15/67	32	We Wish You A Merry Christmas	Columbia 1892
5/66	G P	9/20/66 11/21/86	3	Somewhere My Love	Columbia 9319
1/68	G	3/25/69	25	It Must Be Him	Columbia 9595
4/68	G	12/24/69	22	Honey	Columbia 9661
				NORMAN CONNORS	
4/76	G	1/31/77	39	You Are My Starship	Buddah 5655
				BILL CONTI	
1/77	G	7/7/77	1	**Gonna Fly Now (Theme From "Rocky")** Conti/Carol Connors/Ayn Robbins • Conti	United Art. 940

Release Date	Certification	Date of Certification	Chart Peak	ARTIST/Title Songwriter ● Producer (singles only)	Label & Number
				RITA COOLIDGE **[see also Kris Kristofferson]**	

3/77	G	8/30/77	2	Higher And Higher
				    Carl Smith/Gary Jackson/Raynard Miner/Billy Davis ●
				    Booker T. Jones
					A&M 1922

9/77	G	2/2/78	7	We're All Alone Boz Scaggs ● David Anderle	A&M 1965
3/77	G P	8/18/77 10/19/77	6	Anytime…Anywhere	A&M 4616
6/78	G	6/21/78	32	Love Me Again	A&M 4699
				ALICE COOPER	
6/76	G	4/5/77	12	I Never Cry Alice Cooper/Dick Wagner ● Bob Ezrin	Warner 8228
3/71	G	11/6/72	35	Love It To Death	Warner 1883
11/71	G P	1/28/72 10/13/86	21	Killer	Warner 2567
6/72	G	7/10/72	2	School's Out	Warner 2623
1/73	G P	3/27/73 10/13/86	1	**Billion Dollar Babies**	Warner 2685
11/73	G	12/7/73	10	Muscle Of Love	Warner 2748
8/74	G P	10/15/74 10/13/86	8	Alice Cooper's Greatest Hits	Warner 2803
3/75	G	5/30/75	5	Welcome To My Nightmare	Atlantic 18130
7/76	G	11/23/76	27	Alice Cooper Goes To Hell	Warner 2896
				CORNELIUS BROTHERS & SISTER ROSE	
9/70	G	8/2/71	3	Treat Her Like A Lady Eddie Lee Cornelius ● Bob Archibald	United Art. 50721
5/72	G	8/3/72	2	Too Late To Turn Back Now Cornelius ● Archibald	United Art. 50910
				BILL COSBY	
10/63	G	10/14/66	21	Bill Cosby Is A Very Funny Fellow, Right!	Warner 1518
10/64	G P	10/14/66 10/13/86	32	I Started Out As A Child	Warner 1567
8/65	G	10/14/66	19	Why Is There Air?	Warner 1606
5/66	G	10/14/66	7	Wonderfulness	Warner 1634

Release Date	Certification	Date of Certification	Chart Peak	ARTIST/Title Songwriter ● Producer (singles only)	Label & Number
	P	10/13/86			
4/67	G	6/30/67	2	Revenge	Warner 1691
3/68	G	7/12/68	7	To Russell, My Brother, Whom I Slept With	Warner 1734
10/68	G	3/21/69	16	200 M.P.H.	Warner 1757
8/69	G	10/13/86	51	The Best Of Bill Cosby	Warner 1798
	P	10/13/86			
5/86	G	8/1/86	26	Those Of You With Or Without Children, You'll Understand	Geffen 24104

ELVIS COSTELLO

Release Date	Certification	Date of Certification	Chart Peak	ARTIST/Title	Label & Number
11/77	G	9/4/81	32	My Aim Is True	Columbia 35037
1/79	G	2/23/79	10	Armed Forces	Columbia 35709
2/89	G	6/27/89	32	Spike	Warner 25848

JOHN COUGAR
[see John Cougar Mellencamp]

COWBOY JUNKIES

Release Date	Certification	Date of Certification	Chart Peak	ARTIST/Title	Label & Number
8/88	G	7/19/89	26	The Trinity Session	RCA 8568

THE COWSILLS

Release Date	Certification	Date of Certification	Chart Peak	ARTIST/Title	Label & Number
9/67	G	12/19/67	2	The Rain, The Park And Other Things Artie Kornfeld/Steve Duboff • Kornfeld	MGM 13810
2/69	G	4/24/69	2	Hair James Rado/Gerome Ragni/Galt MacDermot • Bill & Bob Cowsill	MGM 14026

THE ROBERT CRAY BAND

Release Date	Certification	Date of Certification	Chart Peak	ARTIST/Title	Label & Number
11/86	G	3/10/87	13	Strong Persuader	Mercury 830 568
	P	2/10/88			
8/88	G	10/26/88	32	Don't Be Afraid Of The Dark	Mercury 834 923

CREAM

Release Date	Certification	Date of Certification	Chart Peak	ARTIST/Title	Label & Number
12/67	G	9/26/68	5	Sunshine Of Your Love Jack Bruce/Eric Clapton/Pete Brown • Felix Pappalardi	Atco 6544
4/67	G	12/3/68	39	Fresh Cream	Atco 206
12/67	G	5/22/68	4	Disraeli Gears	Atco 232

Release Date	Certification	Date of Certification	Chart Peak	ARTIST/Title Songwriter ● Producer (singles only)	Label & Number
7/68	G	7/22/68	1	**Wheels Of Fire**	Atco 700
1/69	G	4/21/69	2	Goodbye	Atco 7001
7/69	G	11/10/69	3	Best Of Cream	Atco 291
				CREEDENCE CLEARWATER REVIVAL	
12/68	G	1/28/76	2	Proud Mary John Fogerty • Fogerty	Fantasy 619
4/69	G	12/16/70	2	Bad Moon Rising Fogerty • Fogerty	Fantasy 622
10/69	G	12/16/70	3	Down On The Corner Fogerty • Fogerty	Fantasy 634
1/70	G	12/16/70	2	Travelin' Band Fogerty • Fogerty	Fantasy 637
4/70	G	12/16/70	4	Up Around The Bend Fogerty • Fogerty	Fantasy 641
7/70	G	12/16/70	2	Lookin' Out My Back Door Fogerty • Fogerty	Fantasy 645
1/71	G	3/17/71	8	Have You Ever Seen The Rain Fogerty • Fogerty	Fantasy 655
6/68	G	12/16/70	52	Creedence Clearwater Revival	Fantasy 8382
1/69	G	12/16/70	7	Bayou Country	Fantasy 8387
8/69	G	12/16/70	1	**Green River**	Fantasy 8393
12/69	G	12/16/70	3	Willie And The Poor Boys	Fantasy 8397
7/70	G	12/16/70	1	**Cosmo's Factory**	Fantasy 8402
12/70	G	12/18/70	5	Pendulum	Fantasy 8410
4/72	G	6/12/72	12	Mardi Gras	Fantasy 9404
12/72	G	1/26/73	15	Creedence Gold	Fantasy 9418
2/76	G P	3/2/82 2/27/86	100	Chronicle (The 20 Greatest Hits)	Fantasy CCR2
11/80	G	2/27/86	62	The Concert	Fantasy 4501
				PETER CRISS	
9/78	G P	10/2/78 10/2/78	43	Peter Criss	Casablanca 7122
				JIM CROCE	
4/73	G	7/24/73	1	**Bad, Bad Leroy Brown** Jim Croce • Terry Cashman/Tommy West	ABC 11359

Release Date	Certification	Date of Certification	Chart Peak	ARTIST/Title Songwriter ● Producer (singles only)	Label & Number
11/73	G	1/3/74	1	**Time In A Bottle** Croce • Cashman/West	ABC 11405
5/72	G	11/26/73	1	**You Don't Mess Around With Jim**	ABC 756
2/73	G	11/2/73	7	Life And Times	ABC 769
12/73	G	12/6/73	2	I Got A Name	ABC 797
9/74	G	10/22/74	2	Photographs & Memories/His Greatest Hits	ABC 835
				BING CROSBY	
11/45	G	11/13/70	1	**Merry Christmas**	Decca 8128
				DAVID CROSBY **[see also Graham Nash]**	
3/71	G	4/8/71	12	If I Could Only Remember My Name	Atlantic 7203
				CROSBY, STILLS, NASH & YOUNG **[*Crosby, Stills & Nash]**	
6/69	G	9/30/69	6	Crosby, Stills & Nash*	Atlantic 8229
3/70	G	3/25/70	1	**Deja Vu**	Atlantic 7200
3/71	G	4/12/71	1	**4 Way Street**	Atlantic 902
8/74	G	9/19/74	1	**So Far**	Atlantic 18100
6/77	G P	6/28/77 8/18/77	2	CSN*	Atlantic 19104
6/82	G P	8/27/82 1/7/83	8	Daylight Again*	Atlantic 19360
11/88	G P	1/10/89 1/27/89	16	American Dream	Atlantic 81888
				CHRISTOPHER CROSS	
8/81	G	1/7/82	1	**Arthur's Theme (Best That You Can Do)** Christopher Cross/Peter Allen/Burt Bacharach/ Carole Bayer Sager • Michael Omartian	Warner 49787
1/80	G P 4P	5/6/80 8/19/80 10/22/84	6	Christopher Cross	Warner 3383
1/83	G	3/29/83	11	Another Page	Warner 23757

1. You might think the Cars' first six albums were consecutive platinum. You would not be wrong.

2. If you count them as a group, the Carpenters have more gold singles (10) than any other American aggregation. If you count them as a duo, they're top of the world, no matter what nationality.

3. Ode Records owed much of its success to the self-proclaimed "kings of rock comedy," Cheech & Chong. Their first four albums went gold.

4. Would you buy a joke from this man? Actually, George Carlin is the most-certified Caucasian comedian, with four gold albums to Bill Cosby's nine and Richard Pryor's five.

5. After masterminding million-sellers as founding members of Chic, Nile Rodgers and Bernard Edwards bestowed gold on others (Sister Sledge, David Bowie, Robert Palmer) as producers.

1

2

3

4

5

7

8

9

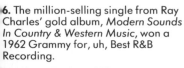

10

6. The million-selling single from Ray Charles' gold album, *Modern Sounds In Country & Western Music*, won a 1962 Grammy for, uh, Best R&B Recording.

7. Johnny Cash: gold for "A Boy Named Sue" and a girl named Rosanne. Other certified parents/offspring include Frank and Nancy Sinatra, Nat and Natalie Cole, Bob and Ziggy Marley, John and Julian Lennon, Hank Williams Sr. and Jr.

8. Chicago has more platinum albums (14) than any other group, and their gold album tally (17) is bested only by the Rolling Stones and the Beatles.

9. Belinda Carlisle spun beauty and the beat into precious metal as a solo artist and with the Go-Go's. She has two gold albums from each career phase.

10. Shaun was the Cassidy family's second golden boy. His triple-play (three million-selling singles and albums) followed brother David's golden streak with the Partridge Family.

Release Date	Certification	Date of Certification	Chart Peak	ARTIST/Title Songwriter ● Producer (singles only)	Label & Number
				CROWDED HOUSE	
7/86	G	5/1/87	12	Crowded House	Capitol 12485
				THE CRUSADERS	
10/74	G	2/17/77	31	Southern Comfort	Blue Thumb 9002
6/78	G	10/10/78	34	Images	Blue Thumb 6030
5/79	G	8/16/79	18	Street Life	MCA 3094
				THE CULT	
4/87	G	3/23/88	38	Electric	Sire 25555
4/89	G	6/13/89	10	Sonic Temple	Sire 25871
				CULTURE CLUB	
11/83	G	2/17/84	1	**Karma Chameleon** Culture Club • Steve Levine	Virgin 04221
11/82	G P	4/18/83 11/7/83	14	Kissing To Be Clever	Virgin 38398
10/83	G P 4P	12/19/83 12/19/83 11/24/86	2	Colour By Numbers	Virgin 39107
10/84	G P	12/28/84 12/28/84	26	Waking Up With The House On Fire	Virgin 39881
				BURTON CUMMINGS	
9/76	G	1/21/77	10	Stand Tall Burton Cummings • Richard Perry	Portrait 70001
				THE MIKE CURB CONGREGATION **[see Sammy Davis, Jr.]**	
				THE CURE	
5/86	G P	2/5/87 5/4/89	48	Standing On A Beach: The Singles	Elektra 60477
5/87	G	8/24/87	35	Kiss Me, Kiss Me, Kiss Me	Elektra 60737
4/89	G*	6/28/89	12	Disintegration	Elektra 60855

Release Date	Certification	Date of Certification	Chart Peak	ARTIST/Title Songwriter ● Producer (singles only)	Label & Number
				CUTTING CREW	
2/87	G	6/3/87	16	Broadcast	Virgin 90573
				D	
				MICHAEL DAMIAN	
3/89	G	7/5/89	1	**Rock On** David Essex • Larry & Tom Weir/Damian	Cypress 1420
				DANA DANE	
7/87	G	1/21/88	46	Dana Dane With Fame	Profile 1233
				THE CHARLIE DANIELS BAND	
6/79	G	8/21/79	3	The Devil Went Down To Georgia Charlie Daniels Band • John Boylan	Epic 50700
11/74	G	6/30/75	38	Fire On The Mountain	Kama Sutra 2603
5/76	G	9/4/81	35	Saddle Tramp	Epic 34150
4/79	G P 2P	6/28/79 8/16/79 11/24/86	5	Million Mile Reflections	Epic 35751
7/80	G P	9/29/80 11/7/80	11	Full Moon	Epic 36571
3/82	G	11/19/82	26	Windows	Epic 37694
7/83	G P	11/1/85 1/23/89	84	A Decade Of Hits	Epic 38795
				TERENCE TRENT D'ARBY	
10/87	G P 2P	3/15/88 4/19/88 11/21/88	4	Introducing The Hardline According To Terence Trent D'Arby	Columbia 40964
				BILLY DAVIS, JR. **[see Marilyn McCoo]**	
				MAC DAVIS	
5/72	G	9/20/72	1	**Baby Don't Get Hooked On Me** Mac Davis • Rick Hall	Columbia 45618

Release Date	Certification	Date of Certification	Chart Peak	ARTIST/Title Songwriter ● Producer (singles only)	Label & Number
9/72	G P	3/7/73 11/21/86	11	Baby Don't Get Hooked On Me	Columbia 31770
3/74	G	9/23/74	13	Stop And Smell The Roses	Columbia 32582
1/75	G	5/21/76	21	All The Love In The World	Columbia 32927
3/80	G	3/4/81	69	It's Hard To Be Humble	Casablanca 7207
				MILES DAVIS	
3/70	G	5/13/76	35	Bitches Brew	Columbia 26
				SAMMY DAVIS JR. with THE MIKE CURB CONGREGATION	
12/71	G	8/21/72	1	**The Candy Man** Anthony Newley/Lesley Bricusse • Mike Curb/Don Costa	MGM 14320
				TYRONE DAVIS	
11/68	G	2/24/69	5	Can I Change My Mind Barry Despenza/Carl Wolfolk • Willie Henderson	Dakar 602
2/70	G	5/4/70	3	Turn Back The Hands Of Time Jack Daniels/Bonnie Thompson • Henderson	Dakar 616
				DAWN featuring TONY ORLANDO	
7/70	G	9/30/70	3	Candida Toni Wine/Irwin Levine • Tokens/Dave Appell	Bell 903
11/70	G	12/16/70	1	**Knock Three Times** Levine/L. Russell Brown • Tokens/Appell	Bell 938
1/73	G	4/2/73	1	**Tie A Yellow Ribbon Round The Ole Oak Tree** Levine/Brown • Tokens/Hank Medress/Appell	Bell 45318
7/73	G	10/9/73	3	Say, Has Anybody Seen My Sweet Gypsy Rose Levine/Brown • Tokens/Medress/Appell	Bell 45374
3/75	G	6/9/75	1	**He Don't Love You (Like I Love You)** Jerry Butler/Curtis Mayfield/Calvin Carter • Medress/Appell	Elektra 45240
3/73	G	4/1/75	30	Tuneweaving	Bell 1112
9/73	G	1/31/75	43	Dawn's New Ragtime Follies	Bell 1130
6/75	G	9/24/75	16	Greatest Hits	Arista 4045
				DORIS DAY	
7/62	G	5/17/68	—	Doris Day's Greatest Hits	Columbia 8635

Release Date	Certification	Date of Certification	Chart Peak	ARTIST/Title Songwriter ● Producer (singles only)	Label & Number
				MORRIS DAY	
10/85	G	12/3/85	37	Color Of Success	Warner 25320
				TAYLOR DAYNE	
7/87	G	2/13/89	7	Tell It To My Heart Seth Swirsky/Ernie Gold • Ric Wake	Arista 9612
5/88	G	2/13/89	3	I'll Always Love You Jimmy George • Wake	Arista 9700
1/88	G P	5/23/88 11/7/88	21	Tell It To My Heart	Arista 8529
				DAZZ BAND	
2/82	G	7/19/82	14	Keep It Live	Motown 6004
				JIMMY DEAN	
9/61	G	12/14/61	1	**Big Bad John** Jimmy Dean • Don Law	Columbia 42175

4/76	G	5/20/76	35	I.O.U.
				    Dean/Lawrence Harkes Jr. •
				    Jack Wiedenmann/Joel Herron
					Casino 052

				DeBARGE	
7/82	G	7/19/83	24	All This Love	Gordy 6012
9/83	G	2/24/84	36	In A Special Way	Gordy 6061
2/85	G	5/8/85	19	Rhythm Of The Night	Gordy 6123
				EL DeBARGE	
5/86	G	9/11/86	24	El DeBarge	Gordy 6181
				CHRIS De BURGH	
6/86	G	7/9/87	25	Into The Light	A&M 5121
				KIKI DEE **[see Elton John]**	

Release Date	Certification	Date of Certification	Chart Peak	ARTIST/Title Songwriter ● Producer (singles only)	Label & Number
				THE DEELE	
7/87	G	6/10/88	54	Eyes Of A Stranger	Solar 72555
				DEEP PURPLE	
5/73	G	8/28/73	4	Smoke On The Water 　　Deep Purple • Deep Purple	Warner 7710
4/72	G P 2P	11/6/72 10/13/86 10/13/86	7	Machine Head	Warner 2607
1/73	G	4/11/73	15	Who Do We Think We Are!	Warner 2678
3/73	G P	5/31/73 10/13/86	6	Made In Japan	Warner 2701
2/74	G	3/20/74	9	Burn	Warner 2766
11/74	G	1/9/75	20	Stormbringer	Warner 2832
10/84	G P	1/15/85 4/9/85	17	Perfect Strangers	Mercury 824 003
				RICK DEES & HIS CAST OF IDIOTS	
7/76	G P	10/6/76 12/13/76	1	**Disco Duck** 　　Rick Dees • Bobby Manuel	RSO 857
				DEF LEPPARD	
3/80	G P	11/18/83 5/9/89	51	On Through The Night	Mercury 3828
7/81	G P	12/17/82 11/18/83	38	High 'n' Dry	Mercury 4021
1/83	G P 6P 7P	3/21/83 4/11/83 10/12/84 9/27/88	2	Pyromania	Mercury 810 308
8/87	G P 2P 3P 4P 5P 6P 7P 8P 9P	10/7/87 10/7/87 11/9/87 1/14/88 6/9/88 7/13/88 8/18/88 9/27/88 11/30/88 1/4/89	1	**Hysteria**	Mercury 830 675

Release Date	Certification	Date of Certification	Chart Peak	ARTIST/Title Songwriter ● Producer (singles only)	Label & Number
				THE DeFRANCO FAMILY featuring TONY DeFRANCO	
6/73	G	11/6/73	3	Heartbeat—It's A Lovebeat William Hudspeth/Michael Kennedy • Walt Meskell	20th Century 2030
				DE LA SOUL	
2/89	G	6/27/89	34	Me, Myself And I De La Soul/George Clinton/Philippe Wynn/ Paul Huston • Huston	Tommy Boy 7926
2/89	G	5/30/89	24	3 Feet High And Rising	Tommy Boy 1019
				THE DELFONICS	
12/69	G	3/18/70	10	Didn't I (Blow Your Mind This Time) Thom Bell/William Hart • Bell/Stan Watson	Philly Groove 161
				THE DELLS	
4/73	G	7/30/73	34	Give Your Baby A Standing Ovation Marv Johnson/Henry Williams • Don Davis	Mercury 5696
				JOHN DENVER	
2/71	G	8/18/71	2	Take Me Home, Country Roads [with FAT CITY] John Denver/Bill Danoff/Taffy Nivert • Milt Okun	RCA 0445
1/74	G	3/28/74	1	**Sunshine On My Shoulders** Denver/Dick Kniss/Mike Taylor • Okun	RCA 0213
7/74	G	7/26/74	1	**Annie's Song** Denver • Okun	RCA 0295
9/74	G	1/3/75	5	Back Home Again Denver • Okun/Kris O'Connor	RCA 10065
3/75	G	6/26/75	1	**Thank God I'm A Country Boy** John Martin Sommers • Okun	RCA 10239
8/75	G	11/18/75	1	**I'm Sorry** Denver • Okun	RCA 10353
3/71	G	9/15/71	15	Poems, Prayers & Promises	RCA 4499
11/71	G	1/5/72	75	Aerie	RCA 4607
8/72	G	12/30/72	4	Rocky Mountain High	RCA 4731
5/73	G	8/27/73	16	Farewell Andromeda	RCA 0101
11/73	G	12/11/73	1	**John Denver's Greatest Hits**	RCA 0374
6/74	G	6/24/74	1	**Back Home Again**	RCA 0548

Release Date	Certification	Date of Certification	Chart Peak	ARTIST/Title Songwriter ● Producer (singles only)	Label & Number
2/75	G	2/19/75	2	An Evening With John Denver	RCA 0764
9/75	G	9/19/75	1	**Windsong**	RCA 1183
10/75	G	10/24/75	14	Rocky Mountain Christmas	RCA 1201
8/76	G P	8/17/76 10/6/76	7	Spirit	RCA 1694
2/77	G P	3/30/77 6/5/81	6	John Denver's Greatest Hits, Volume 2	RCA 2195
11/77	G P	12/1/77 5/12/78	45	I Want To Live	RCA 2521
1/79	G	1/19/79	25	John Denver	RCA 3075
10/79	G P	2/1/80 2/1/80	26	A Christmas Together [with THE MUPPETS]	RCA 3451
5/81	G	12/30/81	32	Some Days Are Diamonds	RCA 4055
2/82	G	12/7/83	39	Seasons Of The Heart	RCA 4256
				DEPECHE MODE	
10/84	G	12/15/86	51	Some Great Reward	Sire 25194
11/85	G	7/26/89	113	Catching Up With Depeche Mode	Sire 25346
4/86	G	8/11/89	90	Black Celebration	Sire 25429
10/87	G	3/8/88	35	Music For The Masses	Sire 25614
				DEREK & THE DOMINOS	
11/70	G	8/26/71	16	Layla	Atco 704
1/73	G	3/23/73	20	In Concert	RSO 8800
				TERI DeSARIO with K.C.	
11/79	G	3/21/80	2	Yes I'm Ready Barbara Mason • Howard Casey	Casablanca 2227
				JACKIE DeSHANNON	

5/69	G	9/29/69	4	Put A Little Love In Your Heart
				    Jackie DeShannon/Randy Myers/Jimmy
				    Holiday • Sam Russell/Irving Hunt
					Imperial 66385

				WILLIAM DeVAUGHN	
3/74	G	5/31/74	4	Be Thankful For What You Got William DeVaughn • Frank Fioravanti/John Davis	Roxbury 0236

Release Date	Certification	Date of Certification	Chart Peak	ARTIST/Title Songwriter ● Producer (singles only)	Label & Number
				DEVO	

8/80	G	12/12/80	14	Whip It
				    Mark Mothersbaugh/Jerry Casale •
				    Devo/Robert Margouleff
					Warner 49550

5/80	G P	11/21/80 5/13/86	22	Freedom Of Choice	Warner 3435
				BARRY DeVORZON & PERRY BOTKIN JR.	
10/76	G	1/18/77	8	Nadia's Theme (The Young And The Restless) Barry DeVorzon/Perry Botkin, Jr. • DeVorzon/Botkin	A&M 1856
				NEIL DIAMOND **[see also Barbra Streisand]**	

6/69	G	8/18/69	4	Sweet Caroline
				    Neil Diamond • Tommy Cogbill/Diamond/
				    Tom Catalano
					Uni 55136

10/69	G	12/31/69	6	Holly Holy Diamond • Catalano/Cogbill	Uni 55175
8/70	G	10/29/70	1	**Cracklin' Rosie** Diamond • Catalano	Uni 55250
4/72	G	7/27/72	1	**Song Sung Blue** Diamond • Diamond/Catalano	Uni 55326
12/69	G	12/7/70	30	Touching You Touching Me	Uni 73071
8/70	G	11/13/70	10	Gold	Uni 73084
11/70	G	1/18/71	13	Tap Root Manuscript	Uni 73092
10/71	G	1/17/72	11	Stones	Uni 93106
7/72	G	8/31/72	5	Moods	Uni 93136
12/72	G	12/23/72	5	Hot August Night	MCA 8000
8/73	G	10/29/81	35	Rainbow	MCA 2103
10/73	G P 2P	10/30/73 11/21/86 11/21/86	2	Jonathan Livingston Seagull [S]	Columbia 32550
5/74	G	9/9/74	29	His 12 Greatest Hits	MCA 2106
10/74	G P	10/30/74 11/21/86	3	Serenade	Columbia 32919
6/76	G P	6/21/76 9/20/76	4	Beautiful Noise	Columbia 33965
2/77	G P	3/1/77 7/5/77	8	Love At The Greek	Columbia 34404

Release Date	Certification	Date of Certification	Chart Peak	ARTIST/Title Songwriter ● Producer (singles only)	Label & Number
11/77	G P 2P	11/17/77 12/13/77 7/6/89	6	I'm Glad You're Here With Me Tonight	Columbia 34990
12/78	G P 2P	12/7/78 12/7/78 10/26/84	4	You Don't Bring Me Flowers	Columbia 35625
1/80	G P	3/13/80 5/9/80	10	September Morn	Columbia 36121
11/80	G P	1/14/81 1/14/81	3	The Jazz Singer [S]	Capitol 12120
11/81	G P	1/12/82 1/12/82	17	On The Way To The Sky	Columbia 37628
5/82	G P 2P	10/19/82 10/5/84 7/6/89	48	12 Greatest Hits, Vol.II	Columbia 38068
9/82	G P	11/29/82 12/16/82	9	Heartlight	Columbia 38359
5/83	G	8/9/89	171	Classics/The Early Years	Columbia 38792
8/84	G	10/5/84	35	Primitive	Columbia 39199
5/86	G	7/21/86	20	Headed For The Future	Columbia 40368
12/88	G	2/16/89	46	The Best Years Of Our Lives	Columbia 45025
				AL DI MEOLA	
3/77	G	7/24/89	58	Elegant Gypsy	Columbia 34461
				DIO	
5/83	G P	9/12/84 3/21/89	56	Holy Diver	Warner 23836
7/84	G P	9/12/84 2/3/87	23	The Last In Line	Warner 25100
8/85	G	10/15/85	29	Sacred Heart	Warner 25292
				DION	
9/68	G	1/13/69	4	Abraham, Martin And John 　Dick Holler ● Phil Gernhard	Laurie 3464
				DIRE STRAITS	
10/78	G P 2P	2/21/79 3/27/79 1/6/87	2	Dire Straits	Warner 3266

Release Date	Certification	Date of Certification	Chart Peak	ARTIST/Title Songwriter ● Producer (singles only)	Label & Number
6/79	G	6/26/79	11	Communique	Warner 3330
11/80	G	4/21/81	19	Making Movies	Warner 3480
9/82	G	4/1/86	19	Love Over Gold	Warner 23828
5/85	G P 2P 3P 4P 5P 6P	7/23/85 8/13/85 9/24/85 11/13/85 1/29/86 5/28/86 1/18/89	1	**Brothers In Arms**	Warner 25264
				D.J. JAZZY JEFF & THE FRESH PRINCE	
2/88	G	2/24/89	12	Parents Just Don't Understand Jeff Townes/Will Smith/Pete Harris • Townes/ Smith/Harris/Bryan New	Jive 1099
2/87	G	12/1/88	83	Rock The House	Jive 1026
3/88	G P 2P	5/31/88 7/21/88 9/30/88	4	He's The DJ, I'm The Rapper	Jive 1091
				DR. BUZZARD'S ORIGINAL SAVANNAH BAND	
6/76	G	12/14/76	22	Dr. Buzzard's Original Savannah Band	RCA 1504
				DR. HOOK **[*Dr. Hook & the Medicine Show]**	
2/72	G	8/2/72	5	Sylvia's Mother* Shel Silverstein • Ron Haffkine	Columbia 45562
11/72	G	4/4/73	6	The Cover Of Rolling Stone* Silverstein • Haffkine	Columbia 45732
10/75	G	5/17/76	6	Only Sixteen Sam Cooke • Haffkine	Capitol 4171
8/78	G	12/26/78	6	Sharing The Night Together Ed Struzick/Ava Aldridge • Haffkine	Capitol 4621
3/79	G	8/22/79	6	When You're In Love With A Beautiful Woman Even Stevens • Haffkine	Capitol 4705
2/80	G	7/10/80	5	Sexy Eyes Robert Mather/Keith Stegall/Chris Waters • Haffkine	Capitol 4831
10/78	G	9/11/79	66	Pleasure & Pain	Capitol 11859

Release Date	Certification	Date of Certification	Chart Peak	ARTIST/Title Songwriter ● Producer (singles only)	Label & Number
				DOKKEN	
9/84	G P	8/13/85 3/16/89	71	Tooth And Nail	Elektra 60376
11/85	G P	3/4/86 4/14/87	32	Under Lock And Key	Elektra 60458
11/87	G P	1/14/88 1/14/88	13	Back For The Attack	Elektra 60735
11/88	G	1/17/89	33	Beast From The East	Elektra 60823
				PLACIDO DOMINGO	
9/81	G P	3/8/82 5/8/89	18	Perhaps Love	CBS 37243
				BO DONALDSON & THE HEYWOODS	
3/74	G	6/5/74	1	**Billy, Don't Be A Hero** Mitch Murray/Peter Callander • Steve Barri	ABC 11435
				DONOVAN	
10/66	G	1/19/67	2	Mellow Yellow Donovan Leitch • Mickie Most	Epic 10098
12/67	G	4/1/70	19	A Gift From A Flower To A Garden	Epic 171
1/69	G	4/22/69	4	Donovan's Greatest Hits	Epic 26439
				THE DOOBIE BROTHERS	
12/74	G	4/14/75	1	**Black Water** Patrick Simmons • Ted Templeman	Warner 8062
1/79	G	4/14/79	1	**What A Fool Believes** Michael McDonald/Kenny Loggins • Templeman	Warner 8725
7/72	G P	8/21/73 10/13/86	21	Toulouse Street	Warner 2634
3/73	G P 2P	7/3/73 10/13/86 10/13/86	7	The Captain And Me	Warner 2694
2/74	G P	4/2/74 10/13/86	4	What Were Once Vices Are Now Habits	Warner 2750
5/75	G	5/28/75	4	Stampede	Warner 2835
3/76	G P	5/11/76 7/27/78	8	Takin' It To The Streets	Warner 2899

Release Date	Certification	Date of Certification	Chart Peak	ARTIST/Title Songwriter ● Producer (singles only)	Label & Number
11/76	G P 5P	11/23/76 12/22/76 10/22/84	5	Best Of The Doobies	Warner 2978
9/77	G	9/14/77	10	Livin' On The Fault Line	Warner 3045
12/78	G P 3P	12/27/78 3/6/79 10/22/84	1	**Minute By Minute**	Warner 3193
9/80	G P	11/18/80 11/18/80	3	One Step Closer	Warner 3452
11/81	G	1/17/82	39	Best Of The Doobies, Volume II	Warner 3612
5/89	G	7/28/89	17	Cycles	Capitol 90371

THE DOORS

Release Date	Certification	Date of Certification	Chart Peak	ARTIST/Title Songwriter ● Producer (singles only)	Label & Number
5/67	G	9/11/67	1	**Light My Fire** The Doors • Paul Rothchild	Elektra 45615
6/68	G	8/28/68	1	**Hello, I Love You** The Doors • Rothchild	Elektra 45635
12/68	G	2/13/69	3	Touch Me The Doors • Rothchild	Elektra 45646
1/67	G P 2P	9/11/67 6/10/87 6/10/87	2	The Doors	Elektra 74007
10/67	G	1/12/68	3	Strange Days	Elektra 74014
7/68	G P	8/6/68 6/10/87	1	**Waiting For The Sun**	Elektra 74024
7/69	G P	8/5/69 6/10/87	6	The Soft Parade	Elektra 75005
2/70	G	2/23/70	4	Morrison Hotel/Hard Rock Cafe	Elektra 75007
7/70	G	7/24/70	8	Absolutely Live	Elektra 9002
11/70	G P	6/20/72 6/10/87	25	13	Elektra 74079
4/71	G P 2P	7/22/71 6/10/87 6/10/87	9	L.A. Woman	Elektra 75011
1/72	G	9/15/80	55	Weird Scenes Inside The Gold Mine	Elektra 6001
9/73	G P	6/10/87 6/10/87	158	The Best Of The Doors	Elektra 5035
9/80	G P 2P	12/30/80 9/18/81 6/10/87	17	Greatest Hits	Elektra 515
10/83	G	6/10/87	23	Alive, She Cried	Elektra 60269

1

2

3

4

1. Clapton is Go(l)d, and he has nine certified albums — preceded by five with Cream — to prove it.

2. This Cinderella (from Pennsylvania) had a ball playing "Night Songs." The outcome was double pumpki...sorry, platinum.

3. Club Nouveau's 1987 hit, "Lean On Me," marked the song's second trip to the golden circle. First time it was writer Bill Withers' original version, in 1972.

4. Ray Conniff arranged hits for Columbia artists Johnnie Ray, Guy Mitchell, and Frankie Laine before he was invited to record his own. When he did, the outcome was nine gold albums.

5. The Clash's one and only gold album was *Combat Rock.* Which probably serves as a handy description of the band's approach to the record industry, too.

6. Blues singer/guitarist Albert Collins may never acquire a platinum album, but his spirit comes close on the Robert Cray Band's million-selling *Strong Persuader.* Way back when, Collins performed at Cray's high school graduation dance.

7. Nat "King" Cole is one of two music giants outcertified by their offspring (the other is Hank Williams). The Cole difference is that both father and progeny went gold for the same record company.

8. Thanks to his throbbing python of love — OK, so it was a boa constrictor — and other theatrics, Alice Cooper accumulated eight gold albums in five years.

9. Perry Como's "Catch A Falling Star" was the first million-selling single certified by the RIAA. It was released by RCA in late 1957.

Release Date	Certification	Date of Certification	Chart Peak	ARTIST/Title Songwriter ● Producer (singles only)	Label & Number
				ANTAL DORATI/THE MINNEAPOLIS SYMPHONY ORCHESTRA	
6/56	G	2/5/63	3	Tchaikovsky: 1812 Festival Overture/ Capriccio Italien	Mercury 50054
				EARLE DOUD/ALEN ROBIN	
11/65	G	11/30/65	3	Welcome To The LBJ Ranch!	Capitol 2423
				CARL DOUGLAS	
9/74	G	11/27/74	1	**Kung Fu Fighting** Carl Douglas • Biddu	20th Century 2140
				THE DRAMATICS	
4/78	G	9/11/78	44	Do What You Wanna Do	ABC 1072
				GEORGE DUKE	
10/77	G	1/18/78	25	Reach For It	Epic 34883
				DURAN DURAN	
6/81	G P	7/22/83 1/4/85	10	Duran Duran	Capitol 12158
5/82	G P	3/1/83 4/26/83	6	Rio	Harvest 12211
11/83	G P	1/16/84 1/16/84	8	Seven And The Ragged Tiger	Capitol 12310
11/84	G P 2P	1/10/85 1/10/85 2/5/85	4	Arena	Capitol 12374
11/86	G P	1/20/87 1/20/87	12	Notorious	Capitol 12540
10/88	G	12/20/88	24	Big Thing	Capitol 90958
				BOB DYLAN	
3/62	G	12/21/73	—	Bob Dylan	Columbia 8579
5/63	G	12/18/70	22	The Freewheelin' Bob Dylan	Columbia 8786
3/65	G	8/25/67	6	Bringing It All Back Home	Columbia 9128
8/65	G	8/25/67	3	Highway 61 Revisited	Columbia 9189
5/66	G	8/25/67	9	Blonde On Blonde	Columbia 841

Release Date	Certification	Date of Certification	Chart Peak	ARTIST/Title Songwriter ● Producer (singles only)	Label & Number
3/67	G P 2P	3/19/68 11/21/86 11/21/86	10	Bob Dylan's Greatest Hits	Columbia 9463
1/68	G	3/19/68	2	John Wesley Harding	Columbia 9604
4/69	G P	5/7/69 11/21/86	3	Nashville Skyline	Columbia 9825
6/70	G	6/22/70	4	Self Portrait	Columbia 30050
10/70	G	12/11/70	7	New Morning	Columbia 30290
11/71	G P	1/3/72 11/21/86	14	Bob Dylan's Greatest Hits, Vol.II	Columbia 31120
1/74	G	1/22/74	1	**Planet Waves**	Asylum 1003
6/74	G	7/8/74	3	Before The Flood	Asylum 201
1/75	G P	2/12/75 8/9/89	1	**Blood On The Tracks**	Columbia 33235
1/76	G P	1/14/76 3/4/76	1	**Desire**	Columbia 33893
9/76	G	9/22/76	17	Hard Rain	Columbia 34349
6/78	G	6/27/78	11	Street Legal	Columbia 35453
8/79	G P	12/26/79 5/9/80	3	Slow Train Coming	Columbia 36120
11/83	G	1/23/84	20	Infidels	Columbia 38819
11/85	G	3/29/89	33	Biograph	Columbia 38830

BOB DYLAN & THE GRATEGUL DEAD

Release Date	Certification	Date of Certification	Chart Peak	ARTIST/Title	Label & Number
1/89	G	8/3/89	37	Dylan & The Dead	Columbia 45056

E

BRENDA LEE EAGER
[see Jerry Butler]

EAGLES

Release Date	Certification	Date of Certification	Chart Peak	Title / Songwriter ● Producer	Label & Number
12/76	G	3/21/77	1	**New Kid In Town** J.D. Souther/Don Henley/Glenn Frey • Bill Szymczyk	Asylum 45373
2/77	G	5/12/77	1	**Hotel California** Don Felder/Henley/Frey • Szymczyk	Asylum 45386
9/79	G	2/1/80	1	**Heartache Tonight** Bob Seger/Henley/Frey/Souther • Szymczyk	Asylum 46545

Release Date	Certification	Date of Certification	Chart Peak	ARTIST/Title Songwriter ● Producer (singles only)	Label & Number
6/72	G	1/22/74	22	Eagles	Asylum 5054
4/73	G	9/23/74	41	Desperado	Asylum 5068
3/74	G	6/5/74	17	On The Border	Asylum 1004
6/75	G	6/30/75	1	**One Of These Nights**	Asylum 1039
2/76	G P	2/24/76 2/24/76	1	**Their Greatest Hits 1971-1975**	Asylum 1052
12/76	G P	12/13/76 12/15/76	1	**Hotel California**	Asylum 1084
9/79	G P	2/1/80 2/1/80	1	**The Long Run**	Asylum 508
11/80	G P	1/7/81 1/7/81	6	Eagles Live	Asylum 705
11/82	G	1/7/83	52	Greatest Hits, Volume 2	Asylum 60205
				EARTH, WIND & FIRE	
1/75	G	6/19/75	1	**Shining Star** Maurice White/Philip Bailey/Larry Dunn • White	Columbia 10090
11/75	G	2/27/76	5	Sing A Song White/Al McKay • White/Charles Stepney	Columbia 10251
6/76	G	10/29/76	12	Getaway Bernard Taylor/Peter Cor • White/Stepney	Columbia 10373
7/78	G	9/14/78	9	Got To Get You Into My Life John Lennon/Paul McCartney • White	Columbia 10796
11/78	G	1/23/79	8	September White/McKay/Allee Willis • White	ARC 10854
4/79	G	5/29/79	6	Boogie Wonderland [with THE EMOTIONS] Jonathan Lind/Willis • White/McKay	ARC 10956
6/79	G	11/19/79	2	After The Love Has Gone David Foster/Bill Champlin/Jay Graydon • White	ARC 11033
9/81	G	1/12/82	3	Let's Groove White/Wayne Vaughn • White	ARC 02536
5/73	G	11/8/73	27	Head To The Sky	Columbia 32194
3/74	G P	5/14/74 11/21/86	15	Open Our Eyes	Columbia 32712
3/75	G P 2P	4/9/75 11/21/86 11/21/86	1	**That's The Way Of The World [S]**	Columbia 33280
12/75	G P 2P	12/5/75 11/21/86 11/21/86	1	**Gratitude**	Columbia 33694

Release Date	Certification	Date of Certification	Chart Peak	ARTIST/Title Songwriter ● Producer (singles only)	Label & Number
9/76	G P 2P	10/7/76 10/13/76 10/26/84	2	Spirit	Columbia 34241
11/77	G P 2P	11/17/77 12/9/77 10/26/84	3	All 'n All	Columbia 34905
11/78	G P 2P	12/7/78 12/7/78 10/26/84	6	The Best Of Earth, Wind & Fire, Vol.I	ARC 35647
6/79	G P 2P	6/7/79 6/7/79 10/26/84	3	I Am	ARC 35730
10/80	G	1/7/81	10	Faces	ARC 36795
10/81	G P	12/13/81 12/30/81	5	Raise!	ARC 37548
2/83	G	4/11/83	12	Powerlight	Columbia 38367
10/87	G	1/18/88	33	Touch The World	Columbia 40596
				SHEENA EASTON	
1/81	G	5/8/81	1	**Morning Train (Nine To Five)** Florrie Palmer • Christopher Neil	EMI America 8071
2/81	G	10/12/81	24	Sheena Easton	EMI America 17049
11/81	G	10/1/84	47	You Could Have Been With Me	EMI America 17061
9/84	G P	11/21/84 3/15/85	15	A Private Heaven	EMI America 17132
10/85	G	12/30/85	40	Do You	EMI America 17173
11/88	G	4/20/89	44	The Lover In Me	MCA 42249
				EAZY-E	
11/88	G P	2/15/89 6/1/89	41	Eazy-Duz-It	Ruthless 57100
				EDISON LIGHTHOUSE	
2/70	G	4/20/70	5	Love Grows (Where My Rosemary Goes) Tony Macauley/Barry Mason • Macauley	Bell 858
				EDWARD BEAR	
11/72	G	3/15/73	3	Last Song Larry Evoy • Gene Martynec	Capitol 3452

Release Date	Certification	Date of Certification	Chart Peak	ARTIST/Title Songwriter ● Producer (singles only)	Label & Number
				JONATHAN EDWARDS	
10/71	G	1/17/72	4	Sunshine Jonathan Edwards • Peter Casperson	Capricorn 8021
				WALTER EGAN	

4/78	G	11/9/78	8	Magnet And Steel
				    Walter Egan • Egan/Lindsey Buckingham/
				    Richard Dashut
					Columbia 10719

				THE 8TH DAY	
4/71	G	9/13/71	11	She's Not Just Another Woman Clyde Wilson/Ron Dunbar • Dunbar	Invictus 9087
				ELECTRIC LIGHT ORCHESTRA **[see also Olivia Newton-John]**	
6/77	G	9/23/77	7	Telephone Line Jeff Lynne • Lynne	United Art. 1000
7/79	G	11/20/79	4	Don't Bring Me Down Lynne • Lynne	Jet 5060
5/80	G	7/15/80	16	I'm Alive Lynne • Lynne	MCA 41246
9/74	G	5/5/75	16	Eldorado	United Art. 339
10/75	G	1/23/76	8	Face The Music	United Art. 546
6/76	G	6/18/76	32	Ole ELO	United Art. 630
10/76	G P	10/25/76 12/6/76	5	A New World Record	United Art. 679
11/77	G P	11/14/77 11/14/77	4	Out Of The Blue	Jet 823
6/79	G P	6/11/79 6/19/79	5	Discovery	Jet 35769
11/79	G P	3/13/80 10/15/80	30	ELO's Greatest Hits	Jet 36310
8/81	G	10/5/81	16	Time	Jet 37371
				LARRY ELGART & HIS MANHATTAN SWING ORCHESTRA	
5/82	G P	7/27/82 1/21/85	24	Hooked On Swing	RCA 4343

Release Date	Certification	Date of Certification	Chart Peak	ARTIST/Title Songwriter ● Producer (singles only)	Label & Number
				YVONNE ELLIMAN	
12/77	G	5/2/78	1	**If I Can't Have You** Barry, Maurice & Robin Gibb • Freddie Perren	RSO 884
				EMERSON, LAKE & PALMER	
1/71	G	8/4/71	18	Emerson, Lake & Palmer	Cotillion 9040
7/71	G	8/26/71	9	Tarkus	Cotillion 9900
1/72	G	4/17/72	10	Pictures At An Exhibition	Cotillion 66666
7/72	G	9/5/72	5	Trilogy	Cotillion 9903
11/73	G	12/12/73	11	Brain Salad Surgery	Manticore 66669

8/74	G	9/19/74	4	Welcome Back, My Friends, To The Show,
				    That Never Ends—Ladies And Gentlemen:
				    Emerson, Lake & Palmer
					Manticore 200

3/77	G	3/29/77	12	Works, Volume 1	Atlantic 7000
11/77	G	12/30/77	37	Works, Volume 2	Atlantic 19147
12/78	G	1/25/79	55	Love Beach	Atlantic 19211
				THE EMOTIONS **[see also Earth, Wind & Fire]**	
5/77	G	8/2/77	1	**Best Of My Love** Maurice White/Al McKay • White	Columbia 10544
7/76	G	1/26/77	45	Flowers	Columbia 34163
6/77	G P	7/12/77 9/1/77	7	Rejoice	Columbia 34762
7/78	G	9/14/78	40	Sunbeam	Columbia 35385
				ENGLAND DAN & JOHN FORD COLEY	
5/76	G	10/12/76	2	I'd Really Love To See You Tonight Parker McGee • Kyle Lehning	Big Tree 16069
7/76	G	12/1/76	17	Nights Are Forever	Big Tree 89517
				ENYA	
1/89	G	4/6/89	25	Watermark	Geffen 24233

Release Date	Certification	Date of Certification	Chart Peak	ARTIST/Title Songwriter ● Producer (singles only)	Label & Number
				E.P.M.D.	
5/88	G	11/9/88	80	Strictly Business	Fresh 82006
				ERASURE	
5/88	G	2/1/89	49	The Innocents	Sire 25730
				ERIC B. & RAKIM	
7/87	G	12/4/87	58	Paid In Full	4th & B'way 4005
7/88	G	9/27/88	22	Follow The Leader	Uni 3
				ESCAPE CLUB	
7/88	G	1/10/89	1	**Wild, Wild West** The Escape Club • Chris Kimsey	Atlantic 89048
7/88	G	12/6/88	27	Wild, Wild West	Atlantic 81871
				DAVID ESSEX	
10/73	G	3/26/74	5	Rock On David Essex • Jeff Wayne	Columbia 45940
				GLORIA ESTEFAN & MIAMI SOUND MACHINE [*Miami Sound Machine]	
8/85	G P	4/28/86 10/8/86	21	Primitive Love*	Epic 40131
5/87	G P 2P	8/11/87 5/9/88 8/5/88	6	Let It Loose	Epic 40769
				MELISSA ETHERIDGE	
5/88	G	3/29/89	22	Melissa Etheridge	Island 90875
				EUROPE	
5/86	G P 2P	4/6/87 8/11/87 10/20/87	8	The Final Countdown	Epic 40241
8/88	G P	11/10/88 2/14/89	19	Out Of This World	Epic 44185

Release Date	Certification	Date of Certification	Chart Peak	ARTIST/Title Songwriter ● Producer (singles only)	Label & Number
				EURYTHMICS	
4/83	G	10/4/83	1	**Sweet Dreams (Are Made Of This)** Annie Lennox/Dave Stewart • Stewart	RCA 13533
5/83	G	11/8/83	15	Sweet Dreams (Are Made Of This)	RCA 4681
1/84	G P	4/2/84 10/4/84	7	Touch	RCA 4917
5/85	G P	7/11/85 9/13/85	9	Be Yourself Tonight	RCA 5429
7/86	G	9/23/86	12	Revenge	RCA 5847
				THE EVERLY BROTHERS	
8/64	G	4/17/86	—	The Very Best Of The Everly Brothers	Warner 1554
				EVIE	
10/77	G	6/16/87	—	Come On Ring Those Bells	Word 8770
				EXILE	
5/78	G	10/4/78	1	**Kiss You All Over** Mike Chapman/Nicky Chinn • Chapman	Warner/Curb 8589
6/78	G	10/10/78	14	Mixed Emotions	Warner/Curb 3205
				EXPOSÉ	
5/89	G	8/10/89	8	What You Don't Know Lewis A. Martinee • Martinee	Arista 9836
1/87	G P	6/8/87 10/22/87	16	Exposure	Arista 8441
6/89	G	8/15/89	33	What You Don't Know	Arista 8532
				F	
				THE FABULOUS THUNDERBIRDS	
2/86	G P	7/25/86 6/1/88	13	Tuff Enuff	CBS Assoc. 40304

Release Date	Certification	Date of Certification	Chart Peak	ARTIST/Title Songwriter ● Producer (singles only)	Label & Number
				FACES	
12/71	G	2/4/72	6	A Nod Is As Good As A Wink…To A Blind Horse	Warner 2574
				DONALD FAGEN	
10/82	G	12/14/82	11	The Nightfly	Warner 23696
				PERCY FAITH & HIS ORCHESTRA	
9/59	G	8/31/62	1	**Theme From "A Summer Place"** Max Steiner • Percy Faith	Columbia 41490
12/57	G	3/22/63	—	Viva—The Music Of Mexico	Columbia 8038
11/59	G	12/4/62	7	Bouquet	Columbia 8124
5/63	G	7/14/67	12	Themes For Young Lovers	Columbia 8823
				FALCO	
1/86	G	4/14/86	3	Falco 3	A&M 5105
				DONNA FARGO	
2/72	G	8/23/72	11	The Happiest Girl In The Whole U.S.A. Donna Fargo • Stan Silver	Dot 17409
8/72	G	1/4/73	5	Funny Face Fargo • Silver	Dot 17429
6/72	G	1/29/73	47	The Happiest Girl In The Whole U.S.A.	Dot 26000
				FAT BOYS	
11/84	G	5/6/85	48	Fat Boys	Sutra 1015
8/85	G	1/9/86	63	The Fat Boys Are Back	Sutra 1016
5/87	G P	7/23/87 9/16/87	8	Crushin'	Tin Pan Apple 831 948
6/88	G	8/24/88	33	Coming Back Hard Again	Tin Pan Apple 835 809
				FATBACK	
5/80	G	8/11/80	44	Hot Box	Spring 6726

Release Date	Certification	Date of Certification	Chart Peak	ARTIST/Title Songwriter ● Producer (singles only)	Label & Number
				JOSE FELICIANO	
4/68	G	10/4/68	2	Feliciano!	RCA 3957
6/69	G	3/20/70	16	Feliciano/10 To 23	RCA 4185
12/69	G	2/9/70	29	Alive Alive-O!	RCA 6021
				FREDDY FENDER	
12/74	G	5/22/75	1	**Before The Next Teardrop Falls** Vivien Keith/Ben Peters • Huey Meaux	ABC/Dot 17540
5/75	G	9/18/75	8	Wasted Days And Wasted Nights Freddy Fender/Wayne Duncan • Meaux	ABC/Dot 17585
4/75	G	8/29/75	20	Before The Next Teardrop Falls	ABC/Dot 2020
				MAYNARD FERGUSON	
3/77	G	12/22/80	22	Conquistador	Columbia 34457
				FERRANTE & TEICHER	
9/69	G	1/19/79	93	10th Anniversary/Golden Piano Hits	United Art. 70
				THE 5TH DIMENSION	
5/68	G	9/17/68	3	Stoned Soul Picnic Laura Nyro • Bones Howe	Soul City 766
2/69	G	4/30/69	1	**Aquarius/Let The Sunshine In** Gerome Ragni/James Rado/Galt MacDermot • Howe	Soul City 772
9/69	G	12/5/69	1	**Wedding Bell Blues** Nyro • Howe	Soul City 779
10/70	G	12/9/70	2	One Less Bell To Answer Burt Bacharach/Hal David • Howe	Bell 940
3/72	G	7/12/72	8	(Last Night) I Didn't Get To Sleep At All Tony Macauley • Howe	Bell 45195
5/67	G	3/26/70	8	Up, Up And Away	Soul City 92000
5/69	G	7/14/69	2	The Age Of Aquarius	Soul City 92005
4/70	G	12/23/70	20	Portrait	Bell 6045
5/70	G	5/22/70	5	Greatest Hits	Soul City 33900
3/71	G	5/26/71	17	Love's Lines, Angles And Rhymes	Bell 6060
10/71	G	12/16/71	32	Live!!	Bell 9000
9/72	G	12/12/72	14	Greatest Hits On Earth	Bell 1106

Release Date	Certification	Date of Certification	Chart Peak	ARTIST/Title Songwriter ● Producer (singles only)	Label & Number
				FINE YOUNG CANNIBALS	IRS 53483
1/89	G	4/18/89	1	**She Drives Me Crazy** David Steele/Roland Gift • David Z/ Fine Young Cannibals	
2/89	G P 2P	4/21/89 4/21/89 8/1/89	1	**The Raw & The Cooked**	IRS 6273
				FIREFALL	
4/76	G	11/3/76	28	Firefall	Atlantic 18174
7/77	G	10/3/77	27	Luna Sea	Atlantic 19101
10/78	G P	10/17/78 1/10/79	27	Elan	Atlantic 19183
				THE FIRM	
2/85	G	4/11/85	17	The Firm	Atlantic 81239
				FIVE MAN ELECTRICAL BAND	
5/71	G	8/30/71	3	Signs Les Emmerson • Dallas Smith	Lionel 3213
				THE FIVE STAIRSTEPS	
2/70	G	8/11/70	8	O-o-h Child Stan Vincent • Vincent	Buddah 165
				THE FIXX	
5/83	G P	8/24/83 1/5/84	8	Reach The Beach	MCA 39001
8/84	G	10/22/84	19	Phantoms	MCA 5507
				ROBERTA FLACK **[see also Peabo Bryson]**	
2/72	G	4/19/72	1	**The First Time Ever I Saw Your Face** Ewan MacColl • Joel Dorn	Atlantic 2864
1/73	G	2/22/73	1	**Killing Me Softly With His Song** Norman Gimbel/Charles Fox • Dorn	Atlantic 2940
6/74	G	8/8/74	1	**Feel Like Makin' Love** Eugene McDaniels • Roberta Flack	Atlantic 3025

Release Date	Certification	Date of Certification	Chart Peak	ARTIST/Title Songwriter ● Producer (singles only)	Label & Number
7/69	G	4/19/72	1	**First Take**	Atlantic 8230
8/70	G	8/26/71	33	Chapter Two	Atlantic 1569
11/71	G	4/19/72	18	Quiet Fire	Atlantic 1594
8/73	G	8/27/73	3	Killing Me Softly	Atlantic 7271
12/77	G	2/27/78	8	Blue Lights In The Basement	Atlantic 19149
				ROBERTA FLACK & DONNY HATHAWAY	

5/72	G	9/5/72	5	Where Is The Love
				    Ralph MacDonald/William Salter • Joel Dorn/
				    Arif Mardin
					Atlantic 2879

2/78	G	5/1/78	2	The Closer I Get To You James Mtume/Reggie Lucas • Mtume/Lucas	Atlantic 3463
4/72	G	7/14/72	3	Roberta Flack & Donny Hathaway	Atlantic 7216
3/80	G	6/4/80	25	Roberta Flack Featuring Donny Hathaway	Atlantic 16013
				FLEETWOOD MAC	

4/77	G	9/14/77	1	**Dreams**
				    Stevie Nicks • Fleetwood Mac/Ken Caillat/
				    Richard Dashut
					Warner 8371

3/72	G P	2/10/76 2/9/88	70	Bare Trees	Reprise 2080
10/73	G	11/9/76	67	Mystery To Me	Reprise 2158
7/75	G P 5P	12/5/75 10/13/86 10/13/86	1	**Fleetwood Mac**	Reprise 2225
2/77	G P 12P 13P	2/15/77 3/9/77 10/22/84 3/1/89	1	**Rumours**	Warner 3010
10/79	G P 2P	2/12/80 2/12/80 10/22/84	4	Tusk	Warner 3350
12/80	G	2/11/81	14	Fleetwood Mac Live	Warner 3500
6/82	G P 2P	8/25/82 8/25/82 10/22/84	1	**Mirage**	Warner 23607
4/87	G P 2P	7/1/87 7/1/87 1/14/88	7	Tango In The Night	Warner 25471
11/88	G P	2/1/89 2/1/89	14	Greatest Hits	Warner 25801

1

2

3

4

1. Good thing Atlantic Records doesn't depend on Crosby, Stills & Nash to make its payroll. Seven albums in 19 years — including one live set and one greatest hits — is rather less than prolific.

2. Bing Crosby's sole gold album, *White Christmas*, showcases the song estimated to have sold more than 30 million singles since its 1942 release.

3. Terence Trent D'Arby's debut album sparked a 1987 Grammy nomination for best new artist, but the singer had to be content with multi-platinum sales. Tracy Chapman won the Grammy.

4. All but one of Creedence Clearwater Revival's 45s between December 1968 and January 1971 reached the million mark, and their first eight albums were consecutive gold.

5. A gold album by any other name? Before they were the Cult, this Northern England band rejoiced under the name of Southern Death Cult.

5

7

10

6. Taylor-made gold: "Tell It To My Heart" and "I'll Always Love You" originated from the same album, the great Dayne's first for Arista Records.

7. Culture Club's premier platinum album, *Kissing To Be Clever*, took its name from a song which never made it past the demo stage.

8. Charlie Daniels' "The Devil Went Down To Georgia" is one of four million-sellers with the state's name in its title. The others are by Brook Benton, Vicki Lawrence, and Gladys Knight.

9. *Bitches Brew* took six years to turn gold for Miles Davis, but the trumpeter remains one of few giants of jazz to acquire a gold album.

10. The Cure's first gold (and platinum) award was for a compilation, released ten years after the British band formed out of high school.

Release Date	Certification	Date of Certification	Chart Peak	ARTIST/Title / Songwriter ● / Producer (singles only)	Label & Number
				THE FLOATERS	
6/77	G	8/25/77	2	Float On / Marvin Willis/Arnold Ingram/James Mitchell Jr. ● / Woody Wilson	ABC 12284
4/77	G / P	7/28/77 / 10/7/77	10	Floaters	ABC 1030
				A FLOCK OF SEAGULLS	
5/82	G	12/2/82	10	A Flock Of Seagulls	Jive 66000
				KING FLOYD	
9/70	G	1/4/71	6	Groove Me / King Floyd III ● Elijah Walker	Chimneyville 435
				THE FLYING MACHINE	
6/69	G	12/12/69	5	Smile A Little Smile For Me / Tony Macauley/Geoff Stevens ● Macauley	Congress 6000
				FOCUS	
12/72	G	6/21/73	8	Moving Waves	Sire 7401
4/73	G	9/26/73	35	Focus 3	Sire 3901
				DAN FOGELBERG	
10/72	G	12/26/79	—	Home Free	Columbia 31751
11/74	G / P / 2P	5/21/76 / 11/21/86 / 11/21/86	17	Souvenirs	Full Moon 33137
9/75	G	11/1/77	23	Captured Angel	Full Moon 33499
5/77	G / P	8/9/77 / 12/26/79	13	Nether Lands	Full Moon 34185
11/79	G / P	3/13/80 / 3/13/80	3	Phoenix	Full Moon 35634
8/81	G / P	11/3/81 / 11/10/81	6	The Innocent Age	Full Moon 37393
10/82	G / P	12/27/82 / 7/18/83	15	Greatest Hits	Full Moon 38308
2/84	G	4/2/84	15	Windows And Walls	Full Moon 39004

Release Date	Certification	Date of Certification	Chart Peak	ARTIST/Title Songwriter ● Producer (singles only)	Label & Number
				DAN FOGELBERG & TIM WEISBERG	Full Moon 35339
8/78	G P	9/29/78 12/12/78	8	Twin Sons Of Different Mothers	
				JOHN FOGERTY	Warner 25203
1/85	G P 2P	3/12/85 3/12/85 9/8/86	1	**Centerfield**	
9/86	G	11/18/86	26	Eye Of The Zombie	Warner 25449
				FOGHAT	
3/73	G	11/11/75	67	Foghat	Bearsville 2136
1/74	G	2/26/75	34	Energized	Bearsville 6950
10/74	G	11/9/76	40	Rock And Roll Outlaws	Bearsville 6956
9/75	G P	3/12/76 10/13/86	23	Fool For The City	Bearsville 6959
11/76	G	2/8/77	36	Night Shift	Bearsville 6962
9/77	G P 2P	10/11/77 12/20/77 10/22/84	11	Foghat Live	Bearsville 6971
5/78	G	6/21/78	25	Stone Blue	Bearsville 6977
				JANE FONDA	Columbia 38054
5/82	G P 2P	9/21/82 1/24/83 10/19/84	15	Jane Fonda's Workout Record	
7/84	G	7/21/86	135	Jane Fonda's Workout Record/New And Improved	Columbia 39287
				FRANK FONTAINE	ABC 442
1/63	G	5/8/68	1	**Songs I Sing On The Jackie Gleason Show**	
				LITA FORD	
2/89	G	8/2/89	8	Close My Eyes Forever [with OZZY OSBOURNE] Lita Ford/Ozzy Osbourne • Mike Chapman	RCA 8899
2/88	G P	5/24/88 6/9/89	29	Lita	RCA 6397

Release Date	Certification	Date of Certification	Chart Peak	ARTIST/Title Songwriter ● Producer (singles only)	Label & Number
				TENNESSEE ERNIE FORD	
10/56	G	2/20/59	2	Hymns	Capitol 756
4/57	G	10/10/61	5	Spirituals	Capitol 818
10/58	G	3/12/62	4	The Star Carol	Capitol 1071
5/59	G	3/22/62	5	Nearer The Cross	Capitol 1005
				FOREIGNER	
6/78	G	9/12/78	3	Hot Blooded Mick Jones/Lou Gramm • Keith Olsen/Jones	Atlantic 3488
9/78	G	11/13/78	2	Double Vision Jones/Gramm • Olsen/Jones/Ian MacDonald	Atlantic 3514
10/81	G	1/20/82	2	Waiting For A Girl Like You Jones/Gramm • Robert Lange/Jones	Atlantic 3868
11/84	G	3/25/85	1	**I Want To Know What Love Is** Jones • Alex Sadkin/Jones	Atlantic 89596
3/77	G P 4P	5/16/77 8/11/77 11/16/84	4	Foreigner	Atlantic 18215
6/78	G P 5P	6/20/78 6/22/78 10/30/84	3	Double Vision	Atlantic 19999
9/79	G P 2P	1/7/80 1/7/80 10/30/84	5	Head Games	Atlantic 29999
7/81	G P 5P	9/18/81 9/18/81 10/30/84	1	4	Atlantic 16999
12/82	G	2/7/83	10	Records	Atlantic 80999
12/85	G P 2P	2/11/85 2/11/85 5/13/85	4	Agent Provocateur	Atlantic 81999
11/87	G P	2/4/88 4/19/88	15	Inside Information	Atlantic 81808
				THE FOUNDATIONS	
11/68	G	3/4/69	3	Build Me Up Buttercup Tony Macauley/Mike D'Abo • Macauley	Uni 55101
				THE 4 SEASONS	
6/64	G	8/24/64	1	**Rag Doll** Bob Crewe/Bob Gaudio • Crewe	Philips 40211

Release Date	Certification	Date of Certification	Chart Peak	ARTIST/Title Songwriter ● Producer (singles only)	Label & Number
12/75	G	3/29/76	1	**December, 1963 (Oh What A Night)** Gaudio/Judy Parker • Gaudio	Warner/Curb 8168
11/65	G	8/4/66	10	The 4 Seasons' Gold Vault Of Hits	Philips 196
11/66	G	9/13/67	22	2nd Vault Of Golden Hits	Philips 221
11/68	G	10/8/70	37	Edizione D'Oro	Philips 6501
				FOUR TOPS	
1/73	G	4/2/73	4	Ain't No Woman (Like The One I've Got) Dennis Lambert/Brian Potter • Steve Barri/ Lambert/Potter	Dunhill 4339
				SAMANTHA FOX	
10/88	G	2/24/89	8	I Wanna Have Some Fun Full Force • Full Force	Jive 1154
11/86	G	4/9/87	24	Touch Me	Jive 1012
9/87	G	8/19/88	51	Samantha Fox	Jive 1061
10/88	G	2/24/89	37	I Wanna Have Some Fun	Jive 1150
				PETER FRAMPTON	
3/75	G	9/13/76	32	Frampton	A&M 4512
1/76	G P 6P	2/27/76 4/8/76 11/14/84	1	**Frampton Comes Alive!**	A&M 3703
6/77	G P	6/13/77 6/13/77	2	I'm In You	A&M 4704
6/79	G	7/3/79	19	Where I Should Be	A&M 3710
				CONNIE FRANCIS	
10/63	G	6/11/69	68	The Very Best Of Connie Francis	MGM 4167
				FRANKIE GOES TO HOLLYWOOD	
1/84	G	1/17/89	10	Relax Peter Gill/Holly Johnson/Mark O'Toole • Trevor Horn	Island 99805
10/84	G	3/4/85	33	Welcome To The Pleasuredome	Island 90232

Release Date	Certification	Date of Certification	Chart Peak	ARTIST/Title Songwriter ● Producer (singles only)	Label & Number
				ARETHA FRANKLIN	
2/67	G	6/13/67	9	I Never Loved A Man (The Way I Love You) Ronnie Shannon • Jerry Wexler	Atlantic 2386
4/67	G	6/1/67	1	**Respect** Otis Redding • Wexler	Atlantic 2403
7/67	G	9/5/67	4	Baby I Love You Shannon • Wexler	Atlantic 2427
11/67	G	1/10/68	2	Chain Of Fools Don Covay • Wexler	Atlantic 2464
2/68	G	4/1/68	5	(Sweet, Sweet Baby) Since You've Been Gone Aretha Franklin/Ted White • Wexler	Atlantic 2486
5/68	G	7/22/68	7	Think Franklin/White • Wexler	Atlantic 2518
7/68	G	10/11/68	10	I Say A Little Prayer Burt Bacharach/Hal David • Wexler	Atlantic 2546
11/68	G	1/13/69	14	See Saw Covay/Steve Cropper • Wexler	Atlantic 2574
7/70	G	10/23/70	11	Don't Play That Song Ahmet Ertegun/Betty Nelson • Wexler/Tom Dowd/Arif Mardin	Atlantic 2751
3/71	G	5/13/71	6	Bridge Over Troubled Water Paul Simon • Wexler/Dowd/Mardin	Atlantic 2796
7/71	G	8/26/71	2	Spanish Harlem Jerry Leiber/Phil Spector • Wexler/Dowd/Mardin	Atlantic 2817
10/71	G	12/13/71	9	Rock Steady Franklin • Wexler/Dowd/Mardin	Atlantic 2838
2/72	G	4/19/72	5	Day Dreaming Franklin • Wexler/Dowd/Mardin	Atlantic 2866
10/73	G	2/20/74	3	Until You Come Back To Me Stevie Wonder/Clarence Paul/Morris Broadnax • Wexler/Mardin/Franklin	Atlantic 2995
3/67	G	6/13/67	2	I Never Loved A Man The Way I Love You	Atlantic 8139
1/68	G	8/23/68	2	Lady Soul	Atlantic 8176
7/68	G	12/3/68	3	Aretha Now	Atlantic 8186
5/71	G	7/14/71	7	Aretha Live At Fillmore West	Atlantic 7205
2/72	G	4/19/72	11	Young, Gifted & Black	Atlantic 7213
6/72	G	7/14/72	7	Amazing Grace	Atlantic 906
6/76	G	7/6/76	18	Sparkle [S]	Atlantic 18176
7/82	G	2/1/83	23	Jump To It	Arista 9602
6/85	G P	8/26/85 12/10/85	13	Who's Zoomin' Who?	Arista 8286

Release Date	Certification	Date of Certification	Chart Peak	ARTIST/Title Songwriter ● Producer (singles only)	Label & Number
10/86	G	12/16/86	32	Aretha	Arista 8442
				MICHAEL FRANKS	
2/76	G	9/1/87	131	The Art Of Tea	Reprise 2230
				JOHN FRED & HIS PLAYBOY BAND	
11/67	G	1/31/68	1	**Judy In Disguise (With Glasses)** John Fred/Andrew Bernard • Fred/Bernard	Paula 282
				ACE FREHLEY	
9/78	G P	10/2/78 10/2/78	26	Ace Frehley	Casablanca 7121
				DOUG E. FRESH & THE GET FRESH CREW	
7/85	G	2/27/86	—	The Show Douglas Davis/Ricky Walters • Dennis Bell/Ollie Cotton	Reality 960
				GLENN FREY	
5/82	G	12/8/82	32	No Fun Aloud	Asylum 60129
7/84	G	8/6/85	22	The Allnighter	MCA 5501
				THE FRIENDS OF DISTINCTION	
2/69	G	6/19/69	3	Grazing In The Grass Philemon Hou/Harry Elston • John Florez	RCA 0107
7/69	G	12/12/69	15	Going In Circles Jerry Peters/Anita Poree • Florez	RCA 0204
				FRIJID PINK	
1/70	G	5/4/70	7	House Of The Rising Sun Traditional/Arr: Alan Price • Mike Valvano	Parrot 341
				FUNKADELIC	
7/78	G	11/21/78	28	One Nation Under A Groove George Clinton/Gary Shider/Junie Morrison • Clinton	Warner 8618
9/78	G P	10/4/78 12/19/78	16	One Nation Under A Groove	Warner 3209

Release Date	Certification	Date of Certification	Chart Peak	ARTIST/Title Songwriter ● Producer (singles only)	Label & Number
9/79	G	1/22/80	18	Uncle Jam Wants You	Warner 3371

G

Release Date	Certification	Date of Certification	Chart Peak	ARTIST/Title	Label & Number
				KENNY G	
7/86	G P 2P*	5/1/87 6/12/87 11/9/87	6	Duotones	Arista 8427
9/88	G P 2P	11/29/88 11/29/88 2/23/89	8	Silhouette	Arista 8457
				PETER GABRIEL	
9/82	G	5/14/87	28	Security	Geffen 2011
5/86	G P 2P	7/22/86 8/13/86 7/21/87	2	So	Geffen 24088
				GALLERY	
2/72	G	6/20/72	4	Nice To Be With You Jim Gold • Mike Theodore/Dennis Coffey	Sussex 232
				THE GAP BAND	
11/79	G	4/21/80	42	The Gap Band II	Mercury 3804
12/80	G P	2/12/81 4/23/81	16	Gap Band III	Mercury 4003
5/82	G P	7/21/82 12/17/82	14	Gap Band IV	Total Experience 3001
9/83	G	12/9/83	28	Gap Band V—Jammin'	Total Experience 3004
				ART GARFUNKEL	
9/73	G	10/24/73	5	Angel Clare	Columbia 31474
10/75	G P	12/5/75 11/21/86	7	Breakaway	Columbia 33700
10/77	G	3/2/78	19	Watermark	Columbia 34975

Release Date	Certification	Date of Certification	Chart Peak	ARTIST/Title Songwriter ● Producer (singles only)	Label & Number
				JUDY GARLAND	
6/61	G	6/27/62	1	Judy At Carnegie Hall	Capitol 1569
				LEIF GARRETT	
11/77	G	1/31/78	37	Leif Garrett	Atlantic 19152
11/78	G	11/8/78	34	Feel The Need	Scotti 7100
				LARRY GATLIN	
10/78	G	9/9/81	171	Larry Gatlin's Greatest Hits Vol. 1	Monument 7628
9/79	G	6/6/80	102	Straight Ahead	Columbia 36250
				MARVIN GAYE	
10/82	G	12/16/82	3	Sexual Healing Marvin Gaye/Ollie Brown • Gaye	Columbia 03302
10/82	G P 2P	12/30/82 12/30/82 7/6/89	7	Midnight Love	Columbia 38197
				CRYSTAL GAYLE	
7/77	G	11/14/77	2	Don't It Make My Brown Eyes Blue Richard Leigh • Allen Reynolds	United Art. 1016
7/77	G P	11/14/77 2/15/78	12	We Must Believe In Magic	United Art. 771
6/78	G P	9/15/78 5/11/82	52	When I Dream	United Art. 858
9/79	G	1/10/80	36	Miss The Mississippi	Columbia 36203
10/79	G	3/7/80	62	Classic Crystal	United Art. 982
				GLORIA GAYNOR	
12/78	G P	2/12/79 4/16/79	1	**I Will Survive** Freddie Perren/Dino Fekaris • Perren/Fekaris	Polydor 14508
12/78	G P	2/5/79 3/27/79	4	Love Tracks	Polydor 6184

Release Date	Certification	Date of Certification	Chart Peak	ARTIST/Title Songwriter ● Producer (singles only)	Label & Number
				THE J. GEILS BAND	
10/81	G	1/25/82	1	**Centerfold** Seth Justman • Justman	EMI America 8102
2/82	G	6/9/82	4	Freeze-Frame Peter Wolf/Justman • Justman	EMI America 8108
10/72	G	2/8/74	54	"Live"/Full House	Atlantic 7241
4/73	G	9/14/73	10	Bloodshot	Atlantic 7260
11/78	G	2/6/79	49	Sanctuary	EMI America 17006
1/80	G	4/22/80	18	Love Stinks	EMI America 17016
10/81	G P	12/30/81 1/11/82	1	**Freeze-Frame**	EMI America 17062
11/82	G	1/11/83	23	Showtime!	EMI America 17087
				GENESIS	
3/78	G P	5/31/78 2/11/88	14	And Then There Were Three...	Atlantic 19173
3/80	G P	7/21/80 2/11/88	11	Duke	Atlantic 16014
9/81	G P 2P	12/11/81 5/3/82 2/11/88	7	Abacab	Atlantic 19313
6/82	G	10/4/82	10	Three Sides Live	Atlantic 2000
10/83	G P	12/19/83 12/16/83	9	Genesis	Atlantic 80116
6/86	G P 2P 3P	8/7/86 8/7/86 10/21/86 4/14/87	3	Invisible Touch	Atlantic 81641
				BOBBIE GENTRY	
7/67	G	9/11/67	1	**Ode To Billie Joe** Bobbie Gentry • Kelly Gordon/Bobby Paris	Capitol 5950
8/67	G	10/9/67	1	**Ode To Billie Joe**	Capitol 2830
				BOBBIE GENTRY & GLEN CAMPBELL	
9/68	G	1/29/69	11	Bobbie Gentry & Glen Campbell	Capitol 2928

Release Date	Certification	Date of Certification	Chart Peak	ARTIST/Title Songwriter ● Producer (singles only)	Label & Number
				GEORGIA SATELLITES	
9/86	G P	2/5/87 8/24/87	5	Georgia Satellites	Elektra 60496
				STAN GETZ/JOAO GILBERTO	
3/64	G	6/16/65	2	Getz/Gilberto	Verve 8545
				ANDY GIBB	
4/77	G	8/9/77	1	**I Just Want To Be Your Everything** Barry Gibb • Gibb/Albhy Galuten/Karl Richardson	RSO 872
10/77	G	2/16/78	1	**(Love Is) Thicker Than Water** Barry & Andy Gibb • Gibb/Galuten/Richardson	RSO 883
4/78	G P	5/19/78 7/12/78	1	**Shadow Dancing** Andy Gibb/Bee Gees • Gibb/Galuten/Richardson	RSO 893
7/78	G	8/15/78	5	An Everlasting Love Barry Gibb • Gibb/Galuten/Richardson	RSO 904
10/78	G	1/3/79	9	(Our Love) Don't Throw It All Away Barry Gibb/Blue Weaver • Gibb/Galuten/Richardson	RSO 911
5/77	G P	11/22/77 8/4/78	19	Flowing Rivers	RSO 3019
5/78	G P	5/30/78 6/17/78	7	Shadow Dancing	RSO 3034
1/80	G	5/7/80	21	After Dark	RSO 3069
				BARRY GIBB **[see Barbra Streisand]**	
				DEBBIE GIBSON	
2/87	G	1/17/89	4	Only In My Dreams Debbie Gibson • Fred Zarr	Atlantic 89322
9/87	G	1/17/89	4	Shake Your Love Gibson • Zarr	Atlantic 89187
1/89	G	3/9/89	1	**Lost In Your Eyes** Gibson • Gibson	Atlantic 88970
3/89	G	5/24/89	11	Electric Youth Gibson • Zarr	Atlantic 88919
8/87	G P 2P	12/17/87 2/4/88 5/24/88	7	Out Of The Blue	Atlantic 81780

Release Date	Certification	Date of Certification	Chart Peak	ARTIST/Title Songwriter ● Producer (singles only)	Label & Number
1/89	3P G P 2P	12/6/88 3/16/89 3/16/89 3/29/89	1	**Electric Youth**	Atlantic 81932
				NICK GILDER	
5/78	G P	9/29/78 1/4/79	1	**Hot Child In The City** Nick Gilder/James McCullough • Mike Chapman	Chrysalis 2226
				JIMMY GILMER & THE FIREBALLS	
7/63	G	11/29/63	1	**Sugar Shack** Keith McCormack/Faye Voss • Norman Petty	Dot 16487
				TOMPALL GLASER **[see Waylon Jennings]**	
				GLASS TIGER	
5/86	G	3/2/87	27	The Thin Red Line	Manhattan 53032
				JACKIE GLEASON	
11/52	G	6/27/62	1	**Music For Lovers Only**	Capitol 352
8/54	G	6/27/62	1	**Music, Martinis And Memories**	Capitol 509
				GO-GO'S	
1/82	G	5/25/82	2	We Got The Beat Charlotte Caffey • Richard Gottehrer/Rob Freeman	IRS 9903
7/81	G P 2P	12/15/81 3/2/82 11/14/84	1	**Beauty And The Beat**	IRS 70021
7/82	G	10/4/82	8	Vacation	IRS 70031
				GOLDEN EARRING	
3/74	G	9/20/74	12	Moontan	Track 396
				BOBBY GOLDSBORO	
2/68	G	4/4/68	1	**Honey** Bobby Russell • Bob Montgomery/Goldsboro	United Art. 50283

Release Date	Certification	Date of Certification	Chart Peak	ARTIST/Title Songwriter ● Producer (singles only)	Label & Number
4/68	G	11/27/68	5	Honey	United Art. 6642
				DICKIE GOODMAN	
8/75	G	9/19/75	4	Mr. Jaws Dickie Goodman/Bill Ramal ● Goodman/Ramal	Cash 451
				ROBERT GOULET	
12/64	G	10/30/68	5	My Love Forgive Me	Columbia 9096
				G.Q.	
1/79	G	4/23/79	12	Disco Nights (Rock-Freak) E. Raheim LeBlanc ● Jimmy Simpson/Beau Ray Fleming	Arista 0388
3/79	G P	5/8/79 10/19/79	13	Disco Nights	Arista 4225
				GRAHAM CENTRAL STATION	
7/75	G	10/15/75	22	Ain't No 'Bout-A-Doubt It	Warner 2876
				LARRY GRAHAM	
4/80	G	9/24/80	9	One In A Million You Sam Dees ● Larry Graham	Warner 49221
6/80	G	9/16/80	26	One In A Million You	Warner 3447
				GRAND FUNK RAILROAD **[*Grand Funk]**	
7/73	G	10/9/73	1	**We're An American Band*** Don Brewer ● Todd Rundgren	Capitol 3660
2/74	G	4/24/74	1	**The Loco-Motion*** Carole King/Gerry Goffin ● Rundgren	Capitol 3840
9/69	G	10/12/70	27	On Time	Capitol 307
1/70	G	7/6/70	11	Grand Funk	Capitol 406
6/70	G	8/12/70	6	Closer To Home	Capitol 471
11/70	G	11/23/70	5	Live Album	Capitol 633
4/71	G	4/30/71	6	Survival	Capitol 764

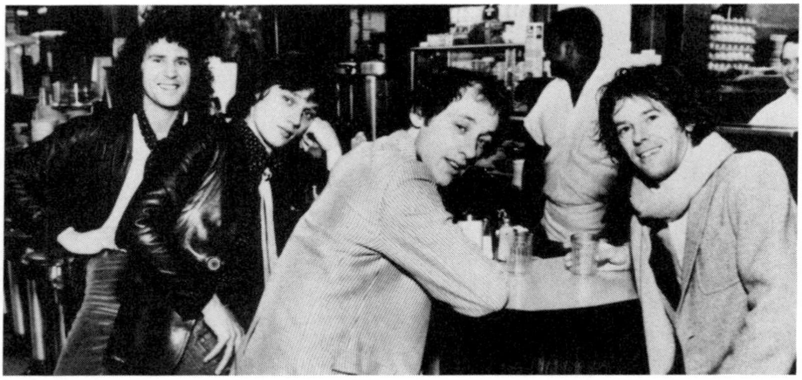

1

2

3

4

1. Certified at six million, Dire Straits' *Brothers In Arms* has sold more copies than any other Warner Bros. album released in 1985 — or since.

2. Mohandas Dewese (Kool Moe Dee to the rest of us) acquired platinum status with his second album. He arrived at Jive via an independent single on Rooftop Records.

3. The rocky mountain altitude was obviously good for John Denver, whose accumulation of 16 gold albums places him in the top 10 most-certified solo singers.

4. Depeche Mode's fourth album was their first to go gold, two years after its release and ten years after the band (whose name means "fast fashion") was first formed.

5. Earth, Wind & Fire has more platinum and gold albums than any other R&B group, and tie with Kool & The Gang for the most gold singles.

6. All six of Dr. Hook's gold 45s were produced by their manager, Ron Haffkine, who discovered the band while searching for musicians for the soundtrack of a Dustin Hoffman movie.

5

6

7

8

9

10

7. The U.S. male — living, that is — with the largest gold album collection is Neil Diamond. Nine of his total of 23 were released in the '80s, 13 in the '70s, and one in the '60s.

8. The Doobie Brothers share (with Simon & Garfunkel) the claim on the music industry's top-selling greatest hits album. *Best Of The Doobies* and Paul & Artie's *Greatest Hits* are both certified at 5 million.

9. The Eagles' first greatest-hits package was the recording industry's first certified platinum album. The date was February 24, 1976, when the compilation was also certified gold.

10. Bob Dylan was not well-regarded around Columbia Records when A&R legend John Hammond first signed him. But "Hammond's Folly" subsequently made 19 albums which went gold for the label.

Release Date	Certification	Date of Certification	Chart Peak	ARTIST/Title Songwriter ● Producer (singles only)	Label & Number
11/71	G	11/29/71	5	E Pluribus Funk	Capitol 853
5/72	G	6/8/72	17	Mark, Don & Mel 1969-71	Capitol 11042
9/72	G	10/12/72	7	Phoenix	Capitol 11099
8/73	G	8/21/73	2	We're An American Band*	Capitol 11207
3/74	G	3/29/74	5	Shinin' On*	Capitol 11278
12/74	G	12/18/74	10	All The Girls In The World Beware!!*	Capitol 11356
				AMY GRANT	
4/79	G	4/21/87	—	My Father's Eyes	Myrrh 6625
4/82	G P	11/21/83 6/24/85	—	Age To Age	Myrrh 6697
10/83	G*	11/25/85	—	A Christmas Album	Myrrh 6768
2/84	G	5/2/85	133	Straight Ahead	Myrrh/A&M 5058
5/85	G P	9/5/85 6/16/86	35	Unguarded	Myrrh/A&M 5060
7/86	G P	2/10/87 8/23/89	66	The Collection	Myrrh/A&M 3900
6/88	G	12/22/88	71	Lead Me On	Myrrh/A&M 5199
				EARL GRANT	
7/61	G	8/24/67	7	Ebb Tide	Decca 74165
				EDDY GRANT	
3/83	G	7/11/83	2	Electric Avenue 　　Eddy Grant • Grant	Portrait 03793
3/83	G	8/29/83	10	Killer On The Rampage	Portrait 38554
				THE GRASS ROOTS	
6/68	G	12/3/68	5	Midnight Confessions 　　Lou Josie • Steve Barri	Dunhill 4144
11/68	G	7/14/70	25	Golden Grass	Dunhill 50047
9/71	G	8/9/72	58	Their 16 Greatest Hits	Dunhill 50107

Release Date	Certification	Date of Certification	Chart Peak	ARTIST/Title Songwriter ● Producer (singles only)	Label & Number
				GRATEFUL DEAD **[see also Bob Dylan]**	
4/67	G	11/15/71	73	The Grateful Dead	Warner 1689
5/70	G P	7/11/74 10/13/86	27	Workingman's Dead	Warner 1869
10/70	G P	7/11/74 10/13/86	30	American Beauty	Warner 1893
11/72	G	12/14/72	24	Europe '72	Warner 2668
2/74	G P	3/14/80 12/15/86	75	The Best Of/Skeletons From The Closet	Warner 2764
8/77	G	9/4/87	28	Terrapin Station	Arista 7001
11/78	G	9/4/87	41	Shakedown Street	Arista 4198
7/87	G P	9/4/87 9/18/87	6	In The Dark	Arista 8452
				DOBIE GRAY	
1/73	G	7/5/73	5	Drift Away 　Mentor Williams • Williams	Decca 33057
				GREAT WHITE	
4/89	G	7/26/89	5	Once Bitten Twice Shy 　Ian Hunter • Alan Niven/Michael Lardie	Capitol 44366
6/87	G P	10/12/87 4/27/88	23	Once Bitten	Capitol 12565
4/89	G P*	6/13/89 7/26/89	9	…Twice Shy	Capitol 90640
				R.B. GREAVES	
9/69	G	12/11/69	2	Take A Letter Maria 　R.B. Greaves • Ahmet Ertegun	Atco 6714
				AL GREEN	
6/71	G	10/26/71	11	Tired Of Being Alone 　Al Green • Green/Willie Mitchell	Hi 2194
11/71	G	1/6/72	1	**Let's Stay Together** 　Green/Mitchell/Al Jackson Jr. • Mitchell	Hi 2202
3/72	G	4/28/72	4	Look What You Done For Me 　Green/Mitchell/Jackson • Mitchell	Hi 2211
6/72	G	8/29/72	3	I'm Still In Love With You 　Green/Mitchell/Jackson • Mitchell	Hi 2216

Release Date	Certification	Date of Certification	Chart Peak	ARTIST/Title Songwriter ● Producer (singles only)	Label & Number
10/72	G	12/15/72	3	You Ought To Be With Me Green/Mitchell/Jackson • Mitchell	Hi 2227
2/73	G	4/23/73	10	Call Me (Come Back Home) Green/Mitchell/Jackson • Mitchell	Hi 2235
6/73	G	8/28/73	10	Here I Am (Come And Take Me) Green/Mabon Hodges • Mitchell/Green	Hi 2247
9/74	G	1/22/75	7	Sha-La-La (Make Me Happy) Green • Mitchell	Hi 2274
1/72	G	4/28/72	8	Let's Stay Together	Hi 32070
10/72	G	11/29/72	4	I'm Still In Love With You	Hi 32074
5/73	G	7/12/73	10	Call Me	Hi 32077
12/73	G	1/22/74	24	Livin' For You	Hi 32082
11/74	G	1/10/75	15	Al Green Explores Your Mind	Hi 32087
				NORMAN GREENBAUM	
11/69	G	4/23/70	3	Spirit In The Sky Norman Greenbaum/Erik Jacobsen • Jacobsen	Reprise 0885
				LEE GREENWOOD	
4/82	G	11/6/86	—	Inside Out	MCA 5305
3/83	G	2/24/84	73	Somebody's Gonna Love You	MCA 5403
5/84	G	2/15/85	150	You've Got A Good Love Comin'	MCA 5488
4/85	G	11/7/85	163	Greatest Hits	MCA 5582
				HENRY GROSS	
2/76	G	6/18/76	6	Shannon Henry Gross • Terry Cashman/Tommy West	Lifesong 45002
				GTR	
4/86	G	7/22/86	11	GTR	Arista 8400
				THE GUESS WHO	
2/69	G	6/25/69	6	These Eyes Randy Bachman/Burton Cummings • Jack Richardson	RCA 0102
6/69	G	10/28/69	10	Laughing Bachman/Cummings • Richardson	RCA 0195
3/70	G	5/22/70	1	**American Woman**	RCA 0325

Release Date	Certification	Date of Certification	Chart Peak	ARTIST/Title Songwriter ● Producer (singles only)	Label & Number
				Bachman/Cummings/Garry Peterson/Jim Kale • Richardson	
1/70	G	5/22/70	9	American Woman	RCA 4266
10/70	G	11/13/70	14	Share The Land	RCA 4359
4/71	G	6/15/71	12	The Best Of The Guess Who	RCA 1004
				GUNS N' ROSES	
6/88	G	6/27/89	1	**Sweet Child O' Mine** Guns n' Roses • Mike Clink	Geffen 27963
3/89	G	6/13/89	4	Patience Guns n' Roses • Clink	Geffen 22996
7/87	G P 2P 3P 4P 5P 6P 7P 8P	2/17/88 4/19/88 7/12/88 8/16/88 9/13/88 10/4/88 12/6/88 2/1/89 7/26/89	1	**Appetite For Destruction**	Geffen 24148
11/88	G P 2P 3P	3/1/89 3/1/89 3/1/89 8/29/89	2	GN'R Lies	Geffen 24198
				ARLO GUTHRIE	
10/67	G P	9/29/69 10/13/86	17	Alice's Restaurant	Reprise 6267
				GUY	
6/88	G P	11/18/88 3/7/89	27	Guy	Uptown 42176
				H	
				SAMMY HAGAR	
1/82	G	1/28/83	28	Standing Hampton	Geffen 2006
12/82	G	5/25/83	17	Three Lock Box	Geffen 2021
9/84	G P	11/13/84 11/19/85	32	VOA	Geffen 24043

Release Date	Certification	Date of Certification	Chart Peak	ARTIST/Title Songwriter ● Producer (singles only)	Label & Number
6/87	G	9/15/87	14	Sammy Hagar	Geffen 24144
				MERLE HAGGARD	
7/68	G	11/2/72	—	The Best Of Merle Haggard	Capitol 2951
1/70	G	10/2/70	46	Okie From Muskogee	Capitol 384
7/70	G	3/11/71	68	The Fightin' Side Of Me	Capitol 451
9/72	G	4/30/74	137	The Best Of The Best Of Merle Haggard	Capitol 11082
10/81	G	7/11/83	161	Big City	Epic 37593
9/84	G	8/7/89	—	His Epic Hits: The First 11	Epic 39545
				MERLE HAGGARD & WILLIE NELSON	
1/83	G P	7/11/83 8/7/84	37	Poncho & Lefty	Epic 37958
				DARYL HALL & JOHN OATES	
1/76	G	6/30/76	4	Sara Smile Daryl Hall & John Oates • Christopher Bond/ Hall & Oates	RCA 10530
1/77	G	4/1/77	1	**Rich Girl** Hall • Bond	RCA 10860
1/81	G	5/22/81	1	**Kiss On My List** Janna Allen/Hall • Hall & Oates	RCA 12142
8/81	G	12/15/81	1	**Private Eyes** Hall & Oates • Hall & Oates	RCA 12296
10/81	G	1/7/82	1	**I Can't Go For That (No Can Do)** Hall & Oates/Sara Allen • Hall & Oates	RCA 12357
10/82	G	1/14/83	1	**Maneater** Hall & Oates/Sara Allen • Hall & Oates	RCA 13354
10/73	G	10/5/76	33	Abandoned Luncheonette	Atlantic 7269
8/75	G	12/14/76	17	Daryl Hall & John Oates	RCA 1144
8/76	G	11/4/76	13	Bigger Than Both Of Us	RCA 1467
9/77	G	9/16/77	30	Beauty On A Back Street	RCA 2300
8/78	G	10/25/78	27	Along The Red Ledge	RCA 2804
7/80	G P	5/6/81 1/22/82	17	Voices	RCA 3646
9/81	G P	11/4/81 12/22/81	5	Private Eyes	RCA 4028
10/82	G	12/14/82	3	H2O	RCA 4383

Release Date	Certification	Date of Certification	Chart Peak	ARTIST/Title Songwriter ● Producer (singles only)	Label & Number
	P 2P	12/16/82 4/1/85			
10/83	G P 2P	12/20/83 12/20/83 4/1/85	7	Rock 'n Soul, Part 1	RCA 4858
10/84	G P 2P	12/3/84 12/3/84 4/1/85	5	Big Bam Boom	RCA 5309
8/85	G	10/29/85	21	Live At The Apollo With David Ruffin & Eddie Kendrick	RCA 7035
4/88	G P	6/30/88 11/30/88	24	Ooh Yeah!	Arista 8539
				HAMILTON, JOE FRANK & REYNOLDS	
5/71	G	8/10/71	4	Don't Pull Your Love Dennis Lambert/Brian Potter • Steve Barri	Dunhill 4276
5/75	G	9/12/75	1	**Fallin' In Love** Dan Hamilton/Ann Hamilton • Jim Price	Playboy 6024
				MARVIN HAMLISCH	
1/74	G	6/7/74	3	The Entertainer Scott Joplin • Marvin Hamlisch	MCA 40174
				ALBERT HAMMOND	
9/72	G	1/9/73	5	It Never Rains In Southern California Albert Hammond/Mike Hazelwood • Hammond/ Don Altfeld	Mums 6011
				HERBIE HANCOCK	
10/73	G P	4/23/74 11/21/86	13	Head Hunters	Columbia 32731
8/83	G	4/2/84	43	Future Shock	Columbia 38814
				EMMYLOU HARRIS **[see also Dolly Parton]**	
2/75	G	10/13/86	45	Pieces Of The Sky	Reprise 2213
1/76	G	7/27/78	25	Elite Hotel	Reprise 2236
1/77	G	2/11/81	21	Luxury Liner	Warner 3115
1/78	G	3/23/88	29	Quarter Moon In A Ten Cent Town	Warner 3141
11/78	G	2/18/81	81	Profile/Best Of Emmylou Harris	Warner 3258

Release Date	Certification	Date of Certification	Chart Peak	ARTIST/Title Songwriter ● Producer (singles only)	Label & Number
4/79	G	2/18/81	43	Blue Kentucky Girl	Warner 3318
5/80	G	4/1/81	26	Roses In The Snow	Warner 3422
2/81	G	10/9/81	22	Evangeline	Warner 3508
				MAJOR HARRIS	
2/75	G	6/25/75	5	Love Won't Let Me Wait Bobby Eli/Vinnie Barrett • Eli	Atlantic 3248
				SAM HARRIS	
8/84	G	11/8/84	35	Sam Harris	Motown 6103
				GEORGE HARRISON	
11/70	G	12/14/70	1	**My Sweet Lord** George Harrison • Harrison/Phil Spector	Apple 2995
12/70	G	12/17/70	1	**All Things Must Pass**	Apple 639
12/71	G	1/4/72	2	The Concert For Bangla Desh	Apple 3385
6/73	G	6/1/73	1	**Living In The Material World**	Apple 3410
12/74	G	12/16/74	4	Dark Horse	Apple 3418
9/75	G	11/11/75	8	Extra Texture (Read All About It)	Apple 3420
11/76	G	2/15/77	31	The Best Of George Harrison	Capitol 11578
12/76	G	1/19/77	11	Thirty-Three & 1/3	Dark Horse 3005
3/79	G	5/8/79	14	George Harrison	Dark Horse 3255
11/87	G P	1/12/88 1/12/88	8	Cloud Nine	Dark Horse 25643
				DEBBIE HARRY	
8/81	G	10/19/81	25	KooKoo	Chrysalis 1347
				COREY HART	
5/84	G	1/20/87	31	First Offense	EMI America 17117
6/85	G	8/21/85	20	Boy In The Box	EMI America 17161
9/86	G	12/29/86	55	Fields Of Fire	EMI America 17217
				FREDDIE HART	
6/71	G	11/29/71	17	Easy Loving Freddie Hart • George Richey	Capitol 3115

Release Date	Certification	Date of Certification	Chart Peak	ARTIST/Title Songwriter ● Producer (singles only)	Label & Number
9/71	G	10/23/72	37	Easy Loving	Capitol 838
8/78	G	1/23/79	29	**DAN HARTMAN** Instant Replay Dan Hartman • Hartman	Blue Sky 2772
2/72	G	8/10/72	18	**DONNY HATHAWAY** **[see also Roberta Flack]** Donny Hathaway Live	Atco 386
4/69	G	6/3/69	4	**THE EDWIN HAWKINS SINGERS** Oh Happy Day Edwin Hawkins • Lamont Bench	Pavilion 20001
				ISAAC HAYES	
5/69	G	12/12/69	8	Hot Buttered Soul	Enterprise 1001
5/73	G	7/3/73	14	Live At The Sahara Tahoe	Enterprise 5005
9/73	G	11/28/73	16	Joy	Enterprise 5007
6/75	G	7/15/75	18	Chocolate Chip	H.B.S. 874
9/79	G	1/21/80	39	Don't Let Go	Polydor 6224
				LEE HAZLEWOOD **[see Nancy Sinatra]**	
				HEAD EAST	
6/75	G	9/19/78	126	Flat As A Pancake	A&M 4537
				JEFF HEALEY BAND	
9/88	G	8/28/89	22	See The Light	Arista 8553
				HEART	
3/76	G P	9/8/76 11/5/76	7	Dreamboat Annie	Mushroom 5005
5/77	G P 2P	6/2/77 8/2/77 11/24/86	9	Little Queen	Portrait 34799

Release Date	Certification	Date of Certification	Chart Peak	ARTIST/Title Songwriter ● Producer (singles only)	Label & Number
4/78	G P	6/2/78 6/2/78	17	Magazine	Mushroom 5008
9/78	G P	9/27/78 10/27/78	17	Dog & Butterfly	Portrait 3555
3/80	G	5/5/80	5	Bebe Le Strange	Epic 36371
11/80	G	1/23/81	13	Greatest Hits/Live	Epic 36888
6/85	G P 2P 3P 4P	8/21/85 9/30/85 12/12/85 3/27/86 8/28/86	1	**Heart**	Capitol 12410
5/87	G P 2P	7/14/87 7/14/87 10/1/87	2	Bad Animals	Capitol 12546
				HEATWAVE	
5/77	G P	10/17/77 12/22/77	2	Boogie Nights 　Rod Temperton • Barry Blue	Epic 50370
12/77	G	3/17/78	18	Always And Forever 　Temperton • Blue	Epic 50490
3/78	G	7/17/78	7	The Groove Line 　Temperton • Blue	Epic 50524
7/77	G P	10/10/77 12/22/77	11	Too Hot To Handle	Epic 34761
4/78	G P	4/10/78 6/21/78	10	Central Heating	Epic 35260
5/79	G	7/20/79	38	Hot Property	Epic 35970
				HEAVY D & THE BOYZ	
6/89	G*	8/17/89	19	Big Tyme	MCA 42302
				BOBBY HEBB	
5/66	G	10/4/66	2	Sunny 　Bobby Hebb • Jerry Ross	Philips 40356
				MICHAEL HENDERSON	
6/78	G	11/20/78	38	In The Night-Time	Buddah 5712

Release Date	Certification	Date of Certification	Chart Peak	ARTIST/Title / Songwriter ● / Producer (singles only)	Label & Number
				JIMI HENDRIX	
8/67	G / P / 2P	3/19/68 / 10/13/86 / 10/13/86	5	Are You Experienced?	Reprise 6261
1/68	G / P	10/10/68 / 10/13/86	3	Axis: Bold As Love	Reprise 6281
9/68	G / P	11/18/68 / 10/13/86	1	**Electric Ladyland**	Reprise 6307
6/69	G / P / 2P	10/14/69 / 10/13/86 / 10/13/86	6	Smash Hits	Reprise 2025
4/70	G	6/3/70	5	Band Of Gypsys	Capitol 472
9/70	G	11/22/70	16	Monterey International Pop Festival [with OTIS REDDING]	Reprise 2029
1/71	G	4/1/71	3	The Cry Of Love	Reprise 2034
10/71	G	12/9/71	15	Rainbow Bridge [S]	Reprise 2040
2/72	G	5/26/72	12	Hendrix In The West	Reprise 2049
2/75	G	11/8/83	5	Crash Landing	Reprise 2204
				DON HENLEY	
10/82	G	3/28/83	3	Dirty Laundry / Don Henley/Danny Kortchmar ● Henley/ Kortchmar/Greg Ladanyi	Asylum 69894
8/82	G	12/8/82	24	I Can't Stand Still	Asylum 60048
11/84	G / P / 2P	1/29/85 / 4/9/85 / 4/11/89	13	Building The Perfect Beast	Geffen 24026
				HERMAN'S HERMITS	
4/65	G	6/16/65	1	**Mrs. Brown You've Got A Lovely Daughter** / Trevor Peacock ● Mickie Most	MGM 13341
6/65	G	8/31/65	1	**I'm Henry VIII, I Am** / R.P. Weston/Fred Murray ● Most	MGM 13367
1/67	G	4/14/67	4	There's A Kind Of Hush / Geoff Stevens/Les Reed ● Most	MGM 13681
2/65	G	8/31/65	2	Introducing Herman's Hermits	MGM 4282
5/65	G	8/31/65	2	Herman's Hermits On Tour	MGM 4295
11/65	G	1/11/66	5	The Best Of Herman's Hermits	MGM 4315
11/66	G	6/13/69	20	The Best Of Herman's Hermits, Volume 2	MGM 4416

Release Date	Certification	Date of Certification	Chart Peak	ARTIST/Title Songwriter ● Producer (singles only)	Label & Number
2/67	G	6/13/69	13	There's A Kind Of Hush All Over The World	MGM 4438
				PATRICK HERNANDEZ	
5/79	G	11/13/79	16	Born To Be Alive Patrick Hernandez • Jean Vanlou	Columbia 10986
				DAN HILL	
10/77	G	2/28/78	3	Sometimes When We Touch Dan Hill/Barry Mann • Matthew McCauley/ Fred Mollin	20th Century 2355
10/77	G	3/17/78	21	Longer Fuse	20th Century 547
				AL HIRT	
8/63	G	4/4/64	3	Honey In The Horn	RCA 2733
5/64	G	12/16/64	8	Cotton Candy	RCA 2917
8/64	G	2/20/65	9	Sugar Lips	RCA 2965
1/65	G	10/11/66	13	The Best Of Al Hirt	RCA 3309
				THE HOLLIES	
5/72	G	9/11/72	2	Long Cool Woman (In A Black Dress) Roger Cook/Allan Clarke/Roger Greenaway • Ron Richards/Hollies	Epic 10871
3/74	G	8/22/74	6	The Air That I Breathe Albert Hammond/Mike Hazelwood • Richards/Hollies	Epic 11100
				BUDDY HOLLY **[*Buddy Holly & The Crickets]**	
5/57	G	12/30/69	1	**That'll Be The Day*** Buddy Holly/Norman Petty/Jerry Allison • Petty	Brunswick 55009
2/59	G	12/24/69	11	The Buddy Holly Story	Coral 57279
8/78	G	11/14/83	55	20 Golden Greats	MCA 3040
				DALLAS HOLM & PRAISE	
11/82	G	3/27/84	—	Dallas Holm & Praise Live	Greentree 3441

Release Date	Certification	Date of Certification	Chart Peak	ARTIST/Title Songwriter ● Producer (singles only)	Label & Number
				EDDIE HOLMAN	
8/69	G	3/17/70	2	Hey There Lonely Girl Earl Shuman/Leon Carr • Peter DeAngelis	ABC 11240
				CLINT HOLMES	
8/72	G	7/3/73	2	Playground In My Mind Paul Vance/Lee Pockriss • Vance/Pockriss	Epic 10891
				RUPERT HOLMES	
9/79	G	1/7/80	1	**Escape (The Pina Colada Song)** Rupert Holmes • Holmes/Jim Boyer	Infinity 50035
9/79	G	5/27/80	33	Partners In Crime	Infinity 9020
				THE HONEY CONE	
3/71	G	5/14/71	1	**Want Ads** Norman Johnson/Greg Perry/Barney Perkins • Perry	Hot Wax 7011
7/71	G	9/23/71	11	Stick Up Johnson/Perry/Angelo Bond • Perry/Johnson	Hot Wax 7106
				THE HONEYDRIPPERS	
10/84	G P	12/13/84 12/13/84	4	Volume One	Es Paranza 90220
				HOOTERS	
5/85	G P	10/18/85 3/12/86	12	Nervous Night	Columbia 39912
7/87	G	9/28/87	27	One Way Home	Columbia 40659
				MARY HOPKIN	
9/68	G	11/20/68	2	Those Were The Days Gene Raskin • Paul McCartney	Apple 1801
				BRUCE HORNSBY & THE RANGE	
4/86	G P 2P	11/12/86 12/9/86 4/8/87	3	The Way It Is	RCA 5904
5/88	G P	7/6/88 7/6/88	5	Scenes From The Southside	RCA 6686

1

2

3

4

1. The Fat Boys are rap's largest trio, with four gold albums and one platinum. That's presumably what happens when you enlist the help of Chubby Checker and the Beach Boys.

2. A girl group for the late '80s: Exposé, with two gold albums and one gold single on their career resumé.

3. Thanks to four gold and two platinum albums in three years, the Eurythmics were RCA Records' most popular British import of the '80s.

4. The man behind the Electric Light Orchestra's substantial gold and platinum legacy, Jeff Lynne, has other precious metal achievements, including George Harrison's *Cloud Nine* and *Traveling Wilburys Vol.1*.

5. Fine Young Cannibals arrived with a splash in 1989: a Number 1 gold single in ''She Drives Me Crazy,'' and a Number 1 double-platinum album in *The Raw & The Cooked.*

5

6. The 5th Dimension were once turned down by Motown. Five gold singles and seven gold albums later, it was obvious that the "Don't call us..." didn't kill their career.

7. The Emotions' 1977 gold "Best Of My Love" was masterminded by Earth, Wind & Fire's Maurice White. The girls returned the favor two years later with featured vocals on EW&F's "Boogie Wonderland."

8. The only female artist on Island Records with a gold album, Melissa Etheridge was one of the late '80s singer/songwriters helped to prominence by Tracy Chapman's multi-platinum success.

7

8

Release Date	Certification	Date of Certification	Chart Peak	ARTIST/Title Songwriter ● Producer (singles only)	Label & Number
				JOHNNY HORTON	
3/59	G	12/20/66	1	**The Battle Of New Orleans** Jimmy Driftwood	Columbia 41339
1/61	G P	11/2/64 11/21/86	8	Johnny Horton's Greatest Hits	Columbia 8396
				HOT	
12/76	G	7/11/77	6	Angel In Your Arms Terry Woodford/Clayton Ivey/Tom Brasfield • Woodford/Ivey	Big Tree 16085
				HOT CHOCOLATE	
9/75	G	1/13/76	3	You Sexy Thing Errol Brown/Tony Wilson • Mickie Most	Big Tree 16047
11/78	G	2/2/79	6	Every 1's A Winner Brown • Most	Infinity 50002
				WHITNEY HOUSTON	
4/87	G P	7/27/87 2/13/89	1	**I Wanna Dance With Somebody (Who Loves Me)** George Merrill/Shannon Rubicam • Narada Michael Walden	Arista 9598
2/85	G P 2P 3P 4P 5P 6P 7P 8P 9P	6/24/85 8/26/85 11/1/85 2/14/86 3/24/86 5/1/86 6/12/86 9/18/86 2/24/87 10/6/88	1	**Whitney Houston**	Arista 8212
5/87	G P 2P 3P 4P 5P 6P	7/28/87 7/28/87 7/28/87 8/4/87 9/30/87 11/20/87 4/18/88	1	**Whitney**	Arista 8405
				THE HUES CORPORATION	
2/74	G	6/24/74	1	**Rock The Boat** Wally Holmes • John Florez	RCA 0232

Release Date	Certification	Date of Certification	Chart Peak	ARTIST/Title Songwriter ● Producer (singles only)	Label & Number
				THE HUMAN LEAGUE	
2/82	G	7/26/82	1	**Don't You Want Me** Jo Callis/Phil Oakey/Philip Wright • Martin Rushent/Human League	A&M 2397
2/82	G	7/14/82	3	Dare	A&M 4892
				HUMBLE PIE	
10/71	G	2/23/72	21	Performance/Rockin' The Fillmore	A&M 3506
3/72	G	9/8/72	6	Smokin'	A&M 4342
				ENGELBERT HUMPERDINCK	
8/76	G	2/15/77	8	After The Lovin' Alan Bernstein/Richard Ziegler • Joel Diamond/Charles Calello	Epic 50270
5/67	G	12/6/67	7	Release Me	Parrot 71012
11/67	G	2/27/69	10	The Last Waltz	Parrot 71015
7/68	G	2/27/69	12	A Man Without Love	Parrot 71022
2/69	G	1/14/70	12	Engelbert	Parrot 71026
12/69	G	1/14/70	5	Engelbert Humperdinck	Parrot 71030
6/70	G	12/18/70	19	We Made It Happen	Parrot 71038
1/71	G	5/13/71	22	Sweetheart	Parrot 71043
8/71	G	3/31/72	25	Another Time, Another Place	Parrot 71048
10/76	G P	1/4/77 5/23/77	17	After The Lovin'	Epic 34381
10/77	G	12/23/81	156	Christmas Tyme	Epic 35031
				BRIAN HYLAND	
6/70	G	1/6/71	3	Gypsy Woman Curtis Mayfield • Del Shannon	Uni 55240
				JANIS IAN	
3/75	G P	9/11/75 11/21/86	1	**Between The Lines**	Columbia 33394

Release Date	Certification	Date of Certification	Chart Peak	ARTIST/Title Songwriter ● Producer (singles only)	Label & Number
				ICE-T	
9/88	G	11/22/88	35	Power	Sire 25765
				BILLY IDOL	
6/82	G	6/28/84	45	Billy Idol	Chrysalis 41377
11/83	G P 2P	4/6/84 6/20/84 1/14/85	6	Rebel Yell	Chrysalis 41450
10/86	G P	1/13/87 1/13/87	6	Whiplash Smile	Chrysalis 41514
9/87	G P	11/17/87 1/19/88	10	Vital Idol	Chrysalis 41620
				JULIO IGLESIAS	
3/83	G P	10/11/83 8/17/84	32	Julio	Columbia 38640
8/84	G P 2P 3P	10/22/84 10/22/84 10/22/84 2/1/87	5	1100 Bel Air Place	Columbia 39157
				JULIO IGLESIAS & WILLIE NELSON	
2/84	G	5/14/84	5	To All The Girls I've Loved Before Albert Hammond/Hal David • Richard Perry	Columbia 04217
				THE INDEPENDENTS	
1/73	G	5/23/73	21	Leaving Me Chuck Jackson/Marvin Yancy • Jackson/Yancy	Wand 11252
				INFORMATION SOCIETY	
7/88	G	1/18/89	3	What's On Your Mind (Pure Energy) Paul Robb/Kurt Valaquen • Fred Maher	Tommy B. 27826
6/88	G	12/6/88	25	Information Society	Tommy B. 25691
				JAMES INGRAM [see also Patti Austin]	
10/83	G	12/3/84	46	It's Your Night	Qwest 23970

Release Date	Certification	Date of Certification	Chart Peak	ARTIST/Title Songwriter ● Producer (singles only)	Label & Number
				INSTANT FUNK	Salsoul 2078
12/78	G	4/2/79	20	Got My Mind Made Up 　Kim & Scotty Miller/Raymond Earl • Bunny Sigler	
1/79	G	4/18/79	12	Instant Funk	Salsoul 8513
				THE INTRUDERS	Gamble 214
3/68	G	5/14/68	6	Cowboys To Girls 　Kenny Gamble/Leon Huff • Gamble/Huff	
				INXS	
2/83	G	1/26/88	46	Shabooh Shoobah	Atco 90072
5/84	G	4/14/87	52	The Swing	Atco 90160
10/85	G P	3/14/86 1/26/88	11	Listen Like Thieves	Atlantic 81277
10/87	G P 2P 3P*	12/22/87 12/22/87 3/11/88 9/2/88	3	Kick	Atlantic 81796
				IRON BUTTERFLY	
7/68	G	12/3/68	4	In-A-Gadda-Da-Vida	Atco 250
1/69	G	7/22/69	3	Ball	Atco 280
				IRON MAIDEN	
5/81	G	1/20/87	78	Killers	Harvest 12141
3/82	G P	10/4/83 10/2/86	33	The Number Of The Beast	Harvest 12202
5/83	G P	7/28/83 11/5/86	14	Piece Of Mind	Capitol 12274
9/84	G	11/7/84	21	Powerslave	Capitol 12321
9/85	G	12/18/85	19	Live After Death	Capitol 12441
9/86	G	11/18/86	11	Somewhere In Time	Capitol 12524
4/88	G	6/6/88	12	Seventh Son Of A Seventh Son	Capitol 90258
				THE ISLEY BROTHERS	
3/69	G	4/9/69	2	It's Your Thing 　Isleys • Isleys	T-Neck 901

Release Date	Certification	Date of Certification	Chart Peak	ARTIST/Title Songwriter ● Producer (singles only)	Label & Number
6/73	G	10/2/73	6	That Lady (Part 1) Isleys • Isleys	T-Neck 2251
5/75	G	9/11/75	4	Fight The Power (Part 1) Isleys/Chris Jasper • Isleys	T-Neck 2256
8/73	G	11/9/73	8	3 + 3	T-Neck 32453
8/74	G	11/4/74	14	Live It Up	T-Neck 33070
5/75	G	6/30/75	1	**The Heat Is On**	T-Neck 33536
5/76	G	6/3/76	9	Harvest For The World	T-Neck 33809
4/77	G P	4/19/77 6/2/77	6	Go For Your Guns	T-Neck 34432
4/78	G P	4/10/78 5/3/78	4	Showdown	T-Neck 34930
5/79	G	6/7/79	14	Winner Takes All	T-Neck 36077
4/80	G P	6/4/80 6/4/80	8	Go All The Way	T-Neck 36305
3/81	G	5/5/81	28	Grand Slam	T-Neck 37080
5/83	G	7/18/83	19	Between The Sheets	T-Neck 38674
				IT'S A BEAUTIFUL DAY	
6/69	G	11/27/72	47	It's A Beautiful Day	Columbia 9768

J

Release Date	Certification	Date of Certification	Chart Peak	ARTIST/Title	Label & Number
				TERRY JACKS	
12/73	G	2/14/74	1	**Seasons In The Sun** Jacques Brel/Rod McKuen • Jacks	Bell 45432
				FREDDIE JACKSON	
5/85	G P	7/23/85 9/26/85	10	Rock Me Tonight	Capitol 12404
10/86	G P	12/16/86 1/20/87	23	Just Like The First Time	Capitol 12495
7/88	G	9/20/88	48	Don't Let Love Slip Away	Capitol 48987

Release Date	Certification	Date of Certification	Chart Peak	ARTIST/Title Songwriter ● Producer (singles only)	Label & Number
				JANET JACKSON	
1/86	G P 2P 3P 4P*	4/18/86 6/13/86 8/7/86 12/8/86 4/6/87	1	**Control**	A&M 5106
				JERMAINE JACKSON	
3/80	G	9/3/81	6	Let's Get Serious	Motown 928
5/84	G	7/10/84	19	Jermaine Jackson	Arista 8203
				JOE JACKSON	
3/79	G	9/11/79	20	Look Sharp!	A&M 4743
6/82	G	11/17/82	4	Night And Day	A&M 4906
				MICHAEL JACKSON	
7/79	G P	11/29/79 2/14/89	1	**Don't Stop 'Til You Get Enough** Greg Phillinganes/Michael Jackson • Quincy Jones	Epic 50742
10/79	G P	2/14/80 2/14/89	1	**Rock With You** Rod Temperton • Jones	Epic 50797
1/80	G	2/14/89	10	Off The Wall Temperton • Jones	Epic 50838
4/80	G	2/14/89	10	She's Out Of My Life Tom Bahler • Jones	Epic 50871
1/83	G P	4/4/83 2/14/89	1	**Billie Jean** Jackson • Jones	Epic 03509
2/83	G P	5/9/83 2/14/89	1	**Beat It** Jackson • Jones	Epic 03759
7/87	G	9/28/87	1	**I Just Can't Stop Loving You** [with SIEDAH GARRETT] Jackson • Jones	Epic 07253
8/79	G P 5P 6P	12/10/79 12/10/79 6/24/85 6/1/88	3	Off The Wall	Epic 35745
11/82	G P 20P	1/31/83 1/31/83 10/30/84	1	**Thriller**	Epic 38112
8/87	G P 3P 4P	11/9/87 11/9/87 11/9/87 12/31/87	1	Bad	Epic 40600

Release Date	Certification	Date of Certification	Chart Peak	ARTIST/Title Songwriter ● Producer (singles only)	Label & Number
	5P 6P	3/21/88 6/1/88			
				MICHAEL JACKSON & PAUL McCARTNEY	
10/82	G	1/13/83	2	The Girl Is Mine Michael Jackson • Quincy Jones	Epic 03288
10/83	G	12/12/83	1	Say, Say, Say Paul McCartney/Jackson • George Martin	Columbia 04168
				MILLIE JACKSON	
10/74	G	1/20/75	21	Caught Up	Spring 6703
8/77	G	12/19/77	34	Feelin' Bitchy	Spring 6715
7/78	G	8/28/78	55	Get It Out'cha System	Spring 6719
				THE JACKSONS	
9/76	G P	2/10/77 2/14/89	6	Enjoy Yourself Kenny Gamble/Leon Huff • Gamble/Huff	Epic 50289
1/79	G P	4/12/79 6/11/79	7	Shake Your Body (Down To The Ground) The Jacksons • The Jacksons	Epic 50656
6/84	G	8/31/84	3	State Of Shock [with MICK JAGGER] Michael Jackson/Randy Hansen • Jackson	Epic 04503
11/76	G	4/5/77	36	The Jacksons	Epic 34229
11/78	G P	3/13/79 5/8/79	11	Destiny	Epic 35552
9/80	G P	12/10/80 12/10/80	10	Triumph	Epic 36424
6/84	G P 2P	8/31/84 8/31/84 10/30/84	4	Victory	Epic 38946
				MICK JAGGER	
3/85	G P	5/6/85 6/24/85	13	She's The Boss	Columbia 39940
				THE JAGGERZ	
1/70	G	3/27/70	2	The Rapper Donnie Iris • The Jaggerz	Kama Sutra 502

Release Date	Certification	Date of Certification	Chart Peak	ARTIST/Title Songwriter ● Producer (singles only)	Label & Number
				THE JAMES GANG	
6/70	G	10/26/71	20	James Gang Rides Again	ABC 711
4/71	G	7/12/72	27	Thirds	ABC 721
9/71	G	6/26/72	24	Live In Concert	ABC 733
				BOB JAMES	
12/78	G	12/22/80	37	Touchdown	Tappan Zee 35594
				BOB JAMES & EARL KLUGH	
10/79	G	5/24/82	23	One On One	Tappan Zee 36241
				BOB JAMES & DAVID SANBORN	
5/86	G	1/6/87	50	Double Vision	Warner 25393
				RICK JAMES	
4/78	G	8/22/78	13	Come Get It!	Gordy 981
4/81	G P	7/7/81 7/7/81	3	Street Songs	Gordy 1002
5/82	G	7/19/82	13	Throwin' Down	Gordy 6005
8/83	G	12/12/83	16	Cold Blooded	Gordy 6043
				TOMMY JAMES & THE SHONDELLS	
4/66	G	8/24/66	1	**Hanky Panky** Jeff Barry/Ellie Greenwich • Henry Glover	Roulette 4686
				AL JARREAU	
6/80	G	5/14/82	27	This Time	Warner 3434
8/81	G P	10/28/81 10/1/82	9	Breakin' Away	Warner 3576
3/83	G	5/25/83	13	Jarreau	Warner 23801
10/84	G	2/11/86	49	High Crime	Warner 25106
				JAY & THE AMERICANS	
11/68	G	5/16/69	6	**This Magic Moment** Doc Pomus/Mort Shuman • Kenny Vance	United Art. 50475

Release Date	Certification	Date of Certification	Chart Peak	ARTIST/Title Songwriter ● Producer (singles only)	Label & Number
				JEFFERSON AIRPLANE	
2/67	G	7/24/67	3	Surrealistic Pillow	RCA 3766
9/68	G	1/23/70	6	Crown Of Creation	RCA 4058
11/69	G	1/21/70	13	Volunteers	RCA 4238
11/70	G	2/12/71	12	The Worst Of Jefferson Airplane	RCA 4459
9/71	G	9/3/71	11	Bark	Grunt 1001
8/72	G	1/4/73	20	Long John Silver	Grunt 1007
1/77	G	9/30/83	37	Flight Log (1966-1976)	Grunt 1255
				JEFFERSON STARSHIP **[*Starship]**	
8/85	G	2/24/89	1	**We Built This City*** Bernie Taupin/Martin Page/Dennis Lambert/Peter Wolf • Lambert/Wolf/ Jeremy Smith	Grunt 14170
12/86	G	2/24/89	1	**Nothing's Gonna Stop Us Now*** Diane Warren/Albert Hammond • Narada Michael Walden	Grunt 5109
12/70	G	8/18/81	20	Blows Against The Empire [PAUL KANTNER/JEFFERSON STARSHIP]	RCA 4448
10/74	G	2/19/75	11	Dragon Fly	Grunt 0717
7/75	G	8/22/75	1	**Red Octopus**	Grunt 0999
6/76	G P	6/30/76 9/28/76	3	Spitfire	Grunt 1557
2/78	G P	2/28/78 5/4/78	5	Earth	Grunt 2515
1/79	G	2/9/79	20	Gold	Grunt 3247
11/79	G	3/10/80	10	Freedom At Point Zero	Grunt 3452
3/81	G	7/16/81	26	Modern Times	Grunt 3848
5/84	G	1/11/85	28	Nuclear Furniture	Grunt 4921
9/85	G P	11/15/85 12/27/85	7	Knee Deep In The Hoopla*	Grunt 5488
6/87	G	11/5/87	12	No Protection*	Grunt 6413
				WAYLON JENNINGS	
8/80	G	12/9/80	21	Theme From "The Dukes Of Hazzard" Waylon Jennings • Ritchie Albright	RCA 12067

Release Date	Certification	Date of Certification	Chart Peak	ARTIST/Title Songwriter ● Producer (singles only)	Label & Number
6/75	G	3/24/77	49	Dreaming My Dreams	RCA 1062
7/76	G	8/1/77	34	Are You Ready For The Country	RCA 1816
11/76	G	1/13/78	46	Waylon Live	RCA 1108
4/77	G P	6/14/77 10/7/77	15	Ol' Waylon	RCA 2317
9/78	G	9/26/78	48	I've Always Been Crazy	RCA 2979
4/79	G P 3P	5/16/79 9/7/79 1/21/85	28	Greatest Hits	RCA 3378
11/79	G	3/3/80	49	What Goes Around Comes Around	RCA 3493
5/80	G	8/22/80	36	Music Man	RCA 3602
				WAYLON JENNINGS & JESSI COLTER	
2/81	G	9/15/81	43	Leather And Lace	RCA 3931
				WAYLON JENNINGS & WILLIE NELSON	
1/78	G P 2P	2/3/78 4/11/78 1/21/85	12	Waylon & Willie	RCA 2686
10/82	G	3/21/83	57	WWII	RCA 4455
				WAYLON JENNINGS/WILLIE NELSON/ JOHNNY CASH/KRIS KRISTOFFERSON	
5/85	G	2/10/86	92	Highwayman	Columbia 40056
				WAYLON JENNINGS/WILLIE NELSON/ JESSI COLTER/TOMPALL GLASER	
1/76	G P 2P	3/30/76 11/24/76 1/21/85	10	Wanted: The Outlaws	RCA 1321
				JETHRO TULL	
9/69	G	11/6/72	20	Stand Up	Reprise 6360
4/70	G	11/13/70	11	Benefit	Reprise 6400
5/71	G*	7/1/71	7	Aqualung	Reprise 2035
4/72	G	5/25/72	1	**Thick As A Brick**	Reprise 2072
10/72	G	11/6/72	3	Living In The Past	Chrysalis 2106

Release Date	Certification	Date of Certification	Chart Peak	ARTIST/Title Songwriter ● Producer (singles only)	Label & Number
7/73	G	7/27/73	1	**A Passion Play**	Chrysalis 1040
10/74	G	11/8/74	2	War Child	Chrysalis 1067
9/75	G	11/13/75	7	Minstrel In The Gallery	Chrysalis 1082
1/76	G P	2/25/76 5/3/78	13	M.U.—The Best Of Jethro Tull	Chrysalis 1078
2/77	G	2/15/77	8	Songs From The Wood	Chrysalis 1132
4/78	G	4/18/78	19	Heavy Horses	Chrysalis 1175
9/78	G	9/29/78	21	Live—Bursting Out	Chrysalis 1201
9/79	G	2/1/80	22	Stormwatch	Chrysalis 1238
9/87	G	5/2/88	32	Crest Of A Knave	Chrysalis 41590
				THE JETS	
10/85	G P	9/18/86 7/30/87	21	The Jets	MCA 5667
10/87	G	12/22/87	35	Magic	MCA 42085
				J.J. FAD	
4/88	G	1/17/89	30	Supersonic Juana Burns/Dania Birks/Juanita Lee/Fatima Shaheed • Dr. Dre/DJ Yella/Arabian Prince	Ruthless 99328
6/88	G	9/30/88	49	Supersonic—The Album	Ruthless 90959
				JOAN JETT & THE BLACKHEARTS	
12/81	G P	4/12/82 9/20/92	1	**I Love Rock 'n Roll** Jake Hooker/Alan Merrill • Ritchie Cordell/ Kenny Laguna	Boardwalk 135
12/81	G P	4/12/82 4/12/82	2	I Love Rock 'n Roll	Boardwalk 33243
6/83	G	8/23/83	20	Album	Blackheart 5437
5/88	G P	9/28/88 2/17/89	19	Up Your Alley	CBS Assoc. 44147
				BILLY JOEL	
11/77	G	3/6/78	3	Just The Way You Are Billy Joel • Phil Ramone	Columbia 10646
10/78	G	1/16/79	3	My Life Joel • Ramone	Columbia 10853

Release Date	Certification	Date of Certification	Chart Peak	ARTIST/Title Songwriter ● Producer (singles only)	Label & Number
5/80	G	7/23/80	1	**It's Still Rock And Roll To Me** Joel • Ramone	Columbia 11276
9/83	G	1/16/84	3	Uptown Girl Joel • Ramone	Columbia 04149
11/73	G P 2P*	11/11/75 11/21/86 11/21/86	27	Piano Man	Columbia 32544
10/74	G	12/22/80	35	Streetlife Serenade	Columbia 33146
5/76	G P	5/28/80 7/6/89	122	Turnstiles	Columbia 33848
9/77	G P 6P	12/1/77 1/18/78 10/19/84	2	The Stranger	Columbia 34987
10/78	G P 5P	10/23/78 10/23/78 10/19/84	1	**52nd Street**	Columbia 35609
3/80	G P 5P	5/5/80 5/5/80 10/19/84	1	**Glass Houses**	Columbia 36384
9/81	G P	12/8/81 12/30/81	8	Songs In The Attic	Columbia 37461
9/82	G P	11/29/82 12/7/82	7	The Nylon Curtain	Columbia 38200
8/83	G P 4P 5P	10/3/83 10/3/83 10/19/84 7/6/89	4	An Innocent Man	Columbia 38837
6/85	G P 2P 3P	10/18/85 10/18/85 1/27/86 8/9/89	6	Greatest Hits, Volume I & Volume II	Columbia 40121
7/86	G P 2P	10/8/86 10/8/86 4/6/87	7	The Bridge	Columbia 40402
10/87	G	1/18/88	38	Kohuept (Live In Leningrad)	Columbia 40996
				ELTON JOHN **[see also Dionne Warwick]**	
11/72	G	2/5/73	1	**Crocodile Rock** Elton John/Bernie Taupin • Gus Dudgeon	MCA 40000
10/73	G	1/4/74	2	Goodbye Yellow Brick Road John/Taupin • Dudgeon	MCA 40148
2/74	G	4/8/74	1	**Bennie And The Jets**	MCA 40198

1

2

3

5

4

1. Crystal Gayle and older sister Loretta Lynn have an equal number of gold albums (four) to their credit, although Loretta claims an additional three by way of her duets with Conway Twitty.

2. At 13 million copies, Fleetwood Mac's *Rumours* has sold more than any album by any other group. It's also the second-largest LP in recording industry history, behind Michael Jackson's *Thriller*.

3. Peter Frampton has at least two claims to fame: *Frampton Comes Alive!* is the biggest-selling live album in music history (6 million) and the biggest-selling double-album by one artist.

4. Tennessee Ernie Ford was the first artist to receive an RIAA gold album, for his 1956 release, *Hymns*. First LP to go gold under the program was the *Oklahoma!* soundtrack.

5. Aretha Franklin's 14 gold singles outnumber all her female competitors — as if Lady Soul had any competitors. All were produced or coproduced by Jerry Wexler.

6. The first Peter Gabriel album to go gold was actually the fourth consecutive release to be titled *Peter Gabriel*. To minimize the confusion, Geffen Records stickered the jacket as *Security*.

7. The combination of Genesis and solo Phil Collins is mighty potent, with cumulative sales of more than 16 million albums across the two acts.

6

8. Back-to-back double-platinum albums make Kenny G the top-selling saxman of the past 30 years. *Duotones* reached two million 16 months after release; *Silhouette* did the trick in less than one-third the time.

9. Critics accused Foreigner of playing "corporate rock," but certified album sales close to 20 million must help offset that problem.

10. Marvin Gaye's sole certified million-selling single, "Sexual Healing," also produced his first Grammy: for best male R&B vocal performance in 1982.

7

8

9

10

Release Date	Certification	Date of Certification	Chart Peak	ARTIST/Title Songwriter ● Producer (singles only)	Label & Number
				John/Taupin • Dudgeon	
6/74	G	9/6/74	2	Don't Let The Sun Go Down On Me John/Taupin • Dudgeon	MCA 40259
11/74	G	1/29/75	1	**Lucy In The Sky With Diamonds** John Lennon/Paul McCartney • Dudgeon	MCA 40344
3/75	G	4/23/75	1	**Philadelphia Freedom** John/Taupin • Dudgeon	MCA 40364
6/75	G	9/10/75	4	Someone Saved My Life Tonight John/Taupin • Dudgeon	MCA 40421
10/75	G	12/4/75	1	**Island Girl** John/Taupin • Dudgeon	MCA 40461
10/76	G	1/25/77	6	Sorry Seems To Be The Hardest Word John/Taupin • Dudgeon	MCA 40645
6/79	G	8/17/79	9	Mama Can't Buy You Love LeRoy Bell/Casey James • Thom Bell	MCA 41042
4/80	G	8/12/80	3	Little Jeannie John/Gary Osborne • John/Clive Franks	MCA 41236
8/70	G	2/17/71	4	Elton John	Uni 73090
1/71	G	3/22/71	5	Tumbleweed Connection	Uni 73096
2/71	G	4/6/71	36	Friends [S]	Paramount 6004
11/71	G	2/19/72	8	Madman Across The Water	Uni 93120
5/72	G	7/24/72	1	**Honky Chateau**	Uni 93135
1/73	G	2/12/73	1	**Don't Shoot Me, I'm Only The Piano Player**	MCA 2100
10/73	G	10/12/73	1	**Goodbye Yellow Brick Road**	MCA 10003
6/74	G	7/5/74	1	**Caribou**	MCA 2116
11/74	G	11/8/74	1	**Greatest Hits**	MCA 2128
5/75	G	5/21/75	1	**Captain Fantastic And The Brown Dirt Cowboy**	MCA 2142
10/75	G	10/21/75	1	**Rock Of The Westies**	MCA 2163
5/76	G	5/6/76	4	Here And There	MCA 2197
10/76	G P	10/29/76 12/9/76	3	Blue Moves	Rocket 11004
9/77	G P	9/30/77 11/9/77	21	Elton John's Greatest Hits, Volume II	MCA 3027
10/78	G P	10/24/78 11/15/78	15	A Single Man	MCA 3065
5/80	G	9/22/80	13	21 At 33	MCA 5121
4/82	G	11/22/82	17	Jump Up!	Geffen 2013
5/83	G	1/18/84	25	Too Low For Zero	Geffen 4006
7/84	G	9/12/84	20	Breaking Hearts	Geffen 24031

Release Date	Certification	Date of Certification	Chart Peak	ARTIST/Title Songwriter ● Producer (singles only)	Label & Number
11/85	G	6/26/86	48	Ice On Fire	Geffen 24077
6/87	G	1/5/88	24	Live In Australia With The Melbourne Symphony Orchestra	MCA 8022
9/87	G	2/14/89	84	Greatest Hits Vol.III 1979-1987	Geffen 24153
6/88	G	8/19/88	16	Reg Strikes Back	MCA 6240
				ELTON JOHN & KIKI DEE	
6/76	G	8/17/76	1	**Don't Go Breaking My Heart** Elton John/Bernie Taupin • Gus Dudgeon	Rocket 40585
				ROBERT JOHN	

12/71	G	3/15/72	3	The Lion Sleeps Tonight
				  Solomon Linda/Paul Campbell/Luigi Creatore/Hugo
				  Peretti/George Weiss/Albert Stanton • Hank Medress/
				  Dave Appell
					Atlantic 2846

4/79	G	9/11/79	1	**Sad Eyes** Robert John • George Tobin	EMI America 8015
				SAMMY JOHNS	
1/75	G	5/5/75	5	Chevy Van Sammy Johns • Jay Senter/Larry Knechtel	GRC 2046
				DON JOHNSON	
8/86	G	11/10/86	17	Heartbeat	Epic 40366
				JESSE JOHNSON'S REVUE	
2/85	G	8/29/85	43	Jesse Johnson's Revue	A&M 5024
				THE JONES GIRLS	
3/79	G	8/30/79	38	You Gonna Make Me Love Somebody Else Kenny Gamble/Leon Huff • Gamble/Huff	Phil. Int. 3680
				GEORGE JONES	
8/80	G P	9/18/81 12/29/83	132	I Am What I Am	Epic 36586

Release Date	Certification	Date of Certification	Chart Peak	ARTIST/Title Songwriter ● Producer (singles only)	Label & Number
				HOWARD JONES	
3/85	G P	6/17/85 3/25/88	10	Dream Into Action	Elektra 60390
				QUINCY JONES	
5/74	G	10/9/74	6	Body Heat	A&M 3617
2/77	G	2/23/77	21	Roots	A&M 4626
6/78	G P	6/21/78 11/10/78	15	Sounds…And Stuff Like That!	A&M 4685
3/81	G P	6/16/81 2/24/82	10	The Dude	A&M 3721
				RICKIE LEE JONES	
3/79	G P	5/22/79 8/7/79	3	Rickie Lee Jones	Warner 3296
7/81	G	9/30/81	5	Pirates	Warner 3432
				TOM JONES	
8/67	G	10/3/69	6	I'll Never Fall In Love Again Lonnie Donegan/Jim Currie • Peter Sullivan	Parrot 40018
12/69	G	2/18/70	5	Without Love Danny Small • Sullivan	Parrot 40045
1/71	G	3/25/71	2	She's A Lady Paul Anka • Gordon Mills	Parrot 40058
2/67	G	11/24/69	65	Green, Green Grass Of Home	Parrot 71009
10/67	G	7/3/69	13	Tom Jones Live!	Parrot 71014
5/68	G	5/7/69	14	The Tom Jones Fever Zone	Parrot 71019
12/68	G	5/7/69	5	Help Yourself	Parrot 71025
5/69	G	6/4/69	4	This Is Tom Jones	Parrot 71028
10/69	G	10/27/69	3	Live In Las Vegas	Parrot 71031
4/70	G	4/24/70	6	Tom	Parrot 71037
10/70	G	1/15/71	23	I (Who Have Nothing)	Parrot 71039
5/71	G	1/12/72	17	She's A Lady	Parrot 71046
9/71	G	3/31/72	43	Live At Caesar's Palace	Parrot 71049

Release Date	Certification	Date of Certification	Chart Peak	ARTIST/Title Songwriter ● Producer (singles only)	Label & Number
				JANIS JOPLIN **[see also Big Brother & the Holding Co.]**	
9/69	G	12/3/69	5	I Got Dem Ol' Kozmic Blues Again Mama!	Columbia 9913
2/71	G P 3P	2/24/71 11/21/86 11/21/86	1	**Pearl**	Columbia 30322
5/72	G	6/21/72	4	Joplin In Concert	Columbia 31160
7/73	G P	6/12/75 11/21/86	37	Janis Joplin's Greatest Hits	Columbia 32168
				JOURNEY	
1/78	G P 2P 3P	5/3/78 10/10/78 10/19/84 7/6/89	21	Infinity	Columbia 34912
3/79	G P 2P	4/12/79 10/19/79 10/19/84	20	Evolution	Columbia 35797
2/80	G P 2P	5/5/80 7/3/80 7/24/89	8	Departure	Columbia 36339
2/81	G P	4/29/81 12/23/81	9	Captured	Columbia 37016
7/81	G P 6P 7P	9/18/81 9/18/81 10/19/84 7/6/89	1	**Escape**	Columbia 37408
1/83	G P 3P 4P	4/4/83 4/4/83 10/19/84 7/24/89	2	Frontiers	Columbia 38504
4/86	G P 2P	6/23/86 6/23/86 7/24/89	4	Raised On Radio	Columbia 39936
11/88	G P 2P	1/23/89 1/23/89 6/13/89	10	Journey's Greatest Hits	Columbia 44493
				JUDAS PRIEST	
5/80	G P	7/23/82 8/9/89	34	British Steel	Columbia 36443
7/82	G P	10/29/82 4/18/83	17	Screaming For Vengeance	Columbia 38160
1/84	G	3/26/84	18	Defenders Of The Faith	Columbia 39219

Release Date	Certification	Date of Certification	Chart Peak	ARTIST/Title Songwriter ● Producer (singles only)	Label & Number
	P	9/26/88			
3/86	G	6/10/86	17	Turbo	Columbia 40158
	P	7/24/89			
5/88	G	7/18/88	31	Ram It Down	Columbia 44244

THE JUDDS

Release Date	Certification	Date of Certification	Chart Peak	ARTIST/Title	Label & Number
10/84	G	4/4/85	71	Why Not Me	RCA/Curb 5319
	P	4/25/86			
10/85	G	2/12/86	66	Rockin' With The Rhythm	RCA/Curb 7042
	P	10/7/86			
2/87	G	4/9/87	52	Heartland	RCA/Curb 5916
	P	1/25/89			
8/88	G	10/5/88	76	Greatest Hits	RCA/Curb 8318
	P	5/23/89			
4/89	G	6/9/89	51	Rivers Of Time	RCA/Curb 9595

K

BERT KAEMPFERT & HIS ORCHESTRA

Release Date	Certification	Date of Certification	Chart Peak	Title	Label & Number
11/60	G	3/4/69	1	**Wonderland By Night**	Decca 74101
11/64	G	8/24/67	5	Blue Midnight	Decca 74569
9/66	G	3/4/69	30	Bert Kaempfert's Greatest Hits	Decca 74810

KANSAS

Release Date	Certification	Date of Certification	Chart Peak	Title	Label & Number
1/78	G	7/14/78	6	Dust In The Wind Kerry Livgren • Jeff Glixman	Kirshner 4274
3/75	G	6/20/80	57	Song For America	Kirshner 33385
11/75	G	12/16/77	70	Masque	Kirshner 33806
10/76	G	1/25/77	5	Leftoverture	Kirshner 34224
	P	3/15/77			
	3P	11/24/86			
9/77	G	10/11/77	4	Point Of Know Return	Kirshner 34929
	P	11/29/77			
	3P	11/24/86			
11/78	G	11/16/78	32	Two For The Show	Kirshner 35660
	P	3/14/79			
5/79	G	6/18/79	10	Monolith	Kirshner 36008
9/80	G	12/12/80	26	Audio-Visions	Kirshner 36588

Release Date	Certification	Date of Certification	Chart Peak	ARTIST/Title Songwriter ● Producer (singles only)	Label & Number
				PAUL KANTNER/JEFFERSON STARSHIP [see Jefferson Starship]	
8/77	G	11/30/82	—	**THE KENDALLS** Heaven's Just A Sin Away	Ovation 1719
11/63	G	1/15/64	18	**PRESIDENT JOHN F. KENNEDY** John Fitzgerald Kennedy—A Memorial Album	Premier 402099
8/84	G	11/30/84	3	**CHAKA KHAN** I Feel For You Prince • Arif Mardin	Warner 29195
10/78	G	11/14/78	12	Chaka	Warner 3245
5/81	G	7/1/81	17	What Cha' Gonna Do For Me	Warner 3526
10/84	G P	12/13/84 12/18/84	14	I Feel For You	Warner 25162
10/88	G	4/18/89	96	**KID 'N PLAY** 2 Hype	Select 21628
4/69	G	10/14/69	9	**ANDY KIM** Baby I Love You Jeff Barry/Ellie Greenwich/Phil Spector • Barry	Steed 716
6/74	G	10/3/74	1	**Rock Me Gently** Andy Kim • Kim	Capitol 3895
11/69	G	3/29/77	28	**KING CRIMSON** In The Court Of The Crimson King	Atlantic 8245
				B.B. KING [see Bobby Bland]	
4/71	G	7/21/71	1	**CAROLE KING** **It's Too Late** Carole King/Toni Stern • Lou Adler	Ode 66015

Release Date	Certification	Date of Certification	Chart Peak	ARTIST/Title Songwriter ● Producer (singles only)	Label & Number
3/71	G	6/7/71	1	**Tapestry**	Ode 77009
12/71	G	12/9/71	1	**Music**	Ode 77013
11/72	G	11/1/72	2	Rhymes & Reasons	Ode 77016
6/73	G	6/26/73	6	Fantasy	Ode 77018
9/74	G	10/16/74	1	**Wrap Around Joy**	Ode 77024
1/76	G	3/25/76	3	Thoroughbred	Ode 77034
7/77	G	9/23/77	17	Simple Things	Capitol 11667
3/78	G	4/4/78	47	Her Greatest Hits	Ode 34967
				EVELYN "CHAMPAGNE" KING	
9/77	G	8/11/78	9	Shame John Fitch/Reuben Cross • Theodore Life	RCA 11122
9/78	G	2/22/79	23	I Don't Know If It's Right Life/Fitch • Life	RCA 11386
9/77	G	9/6/78	14	Smooth Talk	RCA 2466
3/79	G	4/25/79	35	Music Box	RCA 3033
8/82	G	12/14/82	27	Get Loose	RCA 4337
				KINGDOM COME	
2/88	G	4/29/88	12	Kingdom Come	Polydor 835 368
				THE KINGSTON TRIO	
9/58	G	1/21/59	1	**Tom Dooley** Dave Guard • Voyle Gilmore	Capitol 4049
6/58	G	4/18/60	1	**The Kingston Trio**	Capitol 996
1/59	G	10/24/60	2	From The Hungry i	Capitol 1107
6/59	G	4/18/60	1	**The Kingston Trio At Large**	Capitol 1199
10/59	G	10/24/60	1	**Here We Go Again!**	Capitol 1258
4/60	G	6/22/61	1	**Sold Out**	Capitol 1352
7/60	G	6/27/62	1	**String Along**	Capitol 1407
4/62	G	9/4/64	7	The Best Of The Kingston Trio	Capitol 1705
				THE KINKS	
8/66	G	11/25/68	9	Greatest Hits!	Reprise 6217

Release Date	Certification	Date of Certification	Chart Peak	ARTIST/Title Songwriter ● Producer (singles only)	Label & Number
7/79	G	1/7/80	11	Low Budget	Arista 4240
6/80	G	12/8/80	14	One For The Road	Arista 8401
8/81	G	1/27/82	15	Give The People What They Want	Arista 9567
				KISS	
8/76	G	1/5/77	7	Beth Peter Criss/Stanley Pendridge/Bob Ezrin • Ezrin	Casablanca 863
5/79	G	8/16/79	11	I Was Made For Lovin' You Paul Stanley/Vini Poncia/Desmond Child • Poncia	Casablanca 983
2/74	G	6/8/77	87	Kiss	Casablanca 9001
10/74	G	6/23/77	100	Hotter Than Hell	Casablanca 7006
3/75	G	2/28/77	32	Dressed To Kill	Casablanca 7016
9/75	G	12/4/75	9	Alive!	Casablanca 7020
3/76	G P	4/22/76 11/11/76	11	Destroyer	Casablanca 7025
11/76	G P	11/11/76 1/5/77	11	Rock And Roll Over	Casablanca 7037
6/77	G P	6/30/77 6/30/77	4	Love Gun	Casablanca 7057
10/77	G P	11/28/77 11/28/77	7	Alive II	Casablanca 7076
4/78	G P	5/16/78 5/16/78	22	Double Platinum	Casablanca 7100
5/79	G P	6/6/79 7/10/79	9	Dynasty	Casablanca 7152
5/80	G	7/30/80	35	Unmasked	Casablanca 7225
9/83	G	12/22/83	24	Lick It Up	Mercury 814 297
9/84	G P	12/3/84 12/12/84	19	Animalize	Mercury 822 495
9/85	G	11/13/85	20	Asylum	Mercury 826 099
9/87	G P	11/17/87 2/18/88	18	Crazy Nights	Mercury 832 626
11/88	G P	2/1/89 2/1/89	21	Smashes, Thrashes & Hits	Mercury 836 427
				EARL KLUGH **[see George Benson; Bob James]**	

Release Date	Certification	Date of Certification	Chart Peak	ARTIST/Title Songwriter ● Producer (singles only)	Label & Number
				KLYMAXX	
11/84	G	11/25/85	18	Meeting In The Ladies Room	Constell. 5529
				THE KNACK	
6/79	G	8/16/79	1	**My Sharona** Doug Fieger/Berton Avarre • Mike Chapman	Capitol 4731
6/79	G P	7/11/79 8/3/79	1	**Get The Knack**	Capitol 11948
2/80	G	4/14/80	15	But The Little Girls Understand	Capitol 12045
				GLADYS KNIGHT & THE PIPS [see also Dionne Warwick]	
8/73	G	10/18/73	1	**Midnight Train To Georgia** Jim Weatherly • Tony Camillo	Buddah 383
11/73	G	1/30/74	4	I've Got To Use My Imagination Gerry Goffin/Barry Goldberg • Kenny Kerner/ Richie Wise	Buddah 393
2/74	G	4/15/74	3	Best Thing That Ever Happened To Me Weatherly • Kerner/Wise	Buddah 403
4/74	G	7/15/74	5	On And On Curtis Mayfield • Mayfield	Buddah 423
10/73	G	11/5/73	9	Imagination	Buddah 5141
3/74	G	6/7/74	35	Claudine [S]	Buddah 5602
11/74	G	11/12/74	17	I Feel A Song	Buddah 5612
10/75	G	4/12/76	24	2nd Anniversary	Buddah 5639
5/83	G	8/29/83	34	Visions	Columbia 38205
11/87	G	3/8/88	39	All Our Love	MCA 42004
				KOOL & THE GANG	
10/73	G	2/21/74	4	Jungle Boogie Ronald Bell/Kool & The Gang • Kool & The Gang	De-Lite 559
3/74	G	6/21/74	6	Hollywood Swinging Ricky West/Kool & The Gang • Kool & The Gang	De-Lite 561
8/79	G	12/10/79	8	Ladies' Night George Brown/Kool & The Gang • Eumir Deodato	De-Lite 801
12/79	G	5/9/89	5	Too Hot Brown/Kool & The Gang • Deodato	De-Lite 802

Release Date	Certification	Date of Certification	Chart Peak	ARTIST/Title Songwriter ● Producer (singles only)	Label & Number
9/80	G P	1/14/81 3/19/81	1	**Celebration** Bell/Kool & The Gang • Deodato/Kool & The Gang	De-Lite 807
2/82	G	5/9/89	10	Get Down On It Bell/James Taylor/Kool & The Gang • Deodato	De-Lite 818
10/83	G	5/9/89	2	Joanna Charles Smith/Taylor/Kool & The Gang • Bell/ Jim Bonnefond/Kool & The Gang	De-Lite 829
6/85	G	5/9/89	2	Cherish Bell/Taylor/Kool & The Gang • Bell/Bonnefond/ Kool & The Gang	De-Lite 880 869
8/73	G	5/10/74	33	Wild And Peaceful	De-Lite 2013
9/74	G	8/18/75	63	Light Of Worlds	De-Lite 2014
7/79	G P	1/21/80 1/21/80	13	Ladies' Night	De-Lite 9513
9/80	G P	12/16/80 2/25/81	10	Celebrate!	De-Lite 9518
9/81	G P	12/3/81 12/28/81	12	Something Special	De-Lite 8502
9/82	G	11/10/82	29	As One	De-Lite 8505
12/83	G	2/24/84	29	In The Heart	De-Lite 8508
11/84	G P 2P	3/1/85 7/12/85 3/21/86	13	Emergency	De-Lite 822 943
10/86	G	1/12/87	25	Forever	Mercury 830 398
				KOOL MOE DEE	
11/87	G P	4/14/88 11/14/88	35	How Ya Like Me Now?	Jive 1079
5/89	G	8/22/89	25	Knowledge Is King	Jive 1182
				AL KOOPER **[see Mike Bloomfield]**	
				ANDRE KOSTELANETZ & HIS ORCHESTRA	
4/63	G	2/11/65	—	Wonderland Of Golden Hits	Columbia 8839

Release Date	Certification	Date of Certification	Chart Peak	ARTIST/Title Songwriter ● Producer (singles only)	Label & Number
				KRIS KRISTOFFERSON **[see also Waylon Jennings;** **Barbra Streisand]**	
3/73	G	11/8/73	16	Why Me Kris Kristofferson • Fred Foster	Monument 8571
7/71	G	11/9/73	21	The Silver Tongued Devil And I	Monument 30679
9/71	G	12/18/74	43	Me And Bobby McGhee	Monument 30817
11/72	G	11/29/73	31	Jesus Was A Capricorn	Monument 31909
4/77	G	11/9/78	45	Songs Of Kristofferson	Monument 34687
				KRIS KRISTOFFERSON & RITA COOLIDGE	
9/73	G	10/20/75	26	Full Moon	A&M 4403
				KROKUS	
3/83	G	3/27/84	25	Headhunter	Arista 9623
8/84	G	12/3/84	31	The Blitz	Arista 8243
				L	
				LaBELLE	
11/74	G	3/25/75	1	**Lady Marmalade** Bob Crewe/Kenny Nolan • Allen Toussaint	Epic 50048
11/74	G	5/6/75	7	Nightbirds	Epic 33075
				PATTI LaBELLE	
12/83	G	5/29/84	40	I'm In Love Again	Phil. Int. 38539
4/86	G P	6/27/86 6/27/86	1	**Winner In You**	MCA 5737
				PATTI LaBELLE & MICHAEL McDONALD	
3/86	G	5/23/86	1	**On My Own** Burt Bacharach/Carole Bayer Sager • Bacharach/Sager	MCA 52770

Release Date	Certification	Date of Certification	Chart Peak	ARTIST/Title Songwriter ● Producer (singles only)	Label & Number
				LAKESIDE	
10/80	G	1/28/81	16	Fantastic Voyage	Solar 3720
				MARIO LANZA	
4/51	G	3/28/68	1	**The Great Caruso**	RCA 1127
5/54	G	1/19/60	1	**Songs From The Student Prince** **& Other Great Musical Comedies**	RCA 1837
				NICOLETTE LARSON	
11/78	G	2/27/79	15	Nicolette	Warner 3243
				DENISE LaSALLE	
7/71	G	11/30/71	13	Trapped By A Thing Called Love Denise LaSalle • LaSalle/Bill Jones	Westbound 182
				CYNDI LAUPER	
10/83	G P	4/2/84 4/17/89	2	Girls Just Want To Have Fun Robert Hazard • Rick Chertoff	Portrait 04120
3/84	G	4/17/89	1	**Time After Time** Cyndi Lauper/Rob Hyman • Chertoff	Portrait 04432
7/84	G	4/17/89	3	She Bop Lauper/Steven Lunt/Gary Corbett/Chertoff • Chertoff	Portrait 04516
10/83	G P 2P 4P	3/26/84 5/7/84 10/30/84 3/12/85	4	She's So Unusual	Portrait 38930
9/86	G P	11/12/86 11/24/86	4	True Colors	Portrait 40313
				VICKI LAWRENCE	
11/72	G	4/2/73	1	**The Night The Lights Went Out In Georgia** Bobby Russell • Snuff Garrett	Bell 45303
				RONNIE LAWS	
4/77	G	12/9/77	37	Friends And Strangers	Blue Note 730
				LED ZEPPELIN	
11/69	G	4/13/70	4	Whole Lotta Love Led Zeppelin • Jimmy Page	Atlantic 2690

1. Columbia Records has claimed Herbie Hancock's platinum *Head Hunters* to be the biggest-selling jazz album in the label's history.

2. Freddie Hart's self-penned "Easy Loving" was country music's top hit in 1971. Little wonder he parlayed that into a gold album.

3. The Georgia Satellites lifted off to platinum with their 1986 debut album, but couldn't maintain that orbit for their next release.

4. Black music's most-certified solo singer — we're talking consecutive hit singles here — is the Reverend Al Green, with seven: from "Tired Of Being Alone" to "Sha-La-La."

5. Marvin Hamlisch owes his golden moment to Paul Newman and Robert Redford. His interpretation of the Scott Joplin melody was featured in the soundtrack of *The Sting*.

7

9

6. A quartet of gold albums made Lee Greenwood one of country music's more successful male stars of the '80s. His fastest certification: 1985's *Greatest Hits*.

7. In the first half of the '70s, Grand Funk Railroad was America's most-wanted heavy metal band, with no fewer than 11 consecutive gold albums.

8. The titles of Great White's two platinum albums make up the title of their one gold single, "Once Bitten Twice Shy." That must be some kind of first.

9. Merle Haggard's best-known songs are "Okie From Muskogee" and "The Fightin' Side Of Me," which lead off two of his six gold albums.

10. Twelve gold (and six platinum) albums make Daryl Hall & John Oates the most successful duo in rock history. Ooh yeah, don't forget their six gold singles, too.

10

Release Date	Certification	Date of Certification	Chart Peak	ARTIST/Title Songwriter ● Producer (singles only)	Label & Number
1/69	G	7/22/69	10	Led Zeppelin	Atlantic 8216
10/69	G	11/10/69	1	**Led Zeppelin II**	Atlantic 8236
10/70	G	10/8/70	1	**Led Zeppelin III**	Atlantic 7201
11/71	G	11/16/71	2	Untitled	Atlantic 7208
4/73	G	4/10/73	1	**Houses Of The Holy**	Atlantic 7255
3/75	G	3/6/75	1	**Physical Graffiti**	Swan Song 200
4/76	G P	4/1/76 4/12/76	1	**Presence**	Swan Song 8416
10/76	G P 2P	11/3/76 11/15/76 10/30/84	2	The Song Remains The Same [S]	Swan Song 201
9/79	G P 3P	1/7/80 1/7/80 10/30/84	1	**In Through The Out Door**	Swan Song 16002
12/82	G P	2/7/83 2/7/83	6	Coda	Swan Song 90051

JOHNNY LEE

Release Date	Certification	Date of Certification	Chart Peak	ARTIST/Title Songwriter ● Producer (singles only)	Label & Number

7/80	G	11/18/80	5	Lookin' For Love
				  Wanda Mallette/Patti Ryan/Bob Morrison •
				  John Boylan
					Asylum 47004

10/80	G	5/12/82	132	Lookin' For Love	Asylum 309

THE LEMON PIPERS

Release Date	Certification	Date of Certification	Chart Peak	ARTIST/Title Songwriter ● Producer (singles only)	Label & Number
11/67	G	2/14/68	1	**Green Tambourine** Paul Leka/Shelley Pinz • Leka	Buddah 23

JOHN LENNON

Release Date	Certification	Date of Certification	Chart Peak	ARTIST/Title Songwriter ● Producer (singles only)	Label & Number
2/70	G	12/14/70	3	Instant Karma (We All Shine On) John Lennon • Phil Spector	Apple 1818
10/80	G	12/24/80	1	**(Just Like) Starting Over** Lennon • Lennon/Yoko Ono/Jack Douglas	Geffen 49604
1/81	G	4/1/81	2	Woman Lennon • Lennon/Ono/Douglas	Geffen 49644
1/70	G	3/17/70	10	Live Peace In Toronto 1969 [with PLASTIC ONO BAND]	Apple 3362
12/70	G	1/28/71	6	John Lennon/Plastic Ono Band	Apple 3372
9/71	G	10/1/71	1	**Imagine**	Apple 3379
11/73	G	11/30/73	9	Mind Games	Apple 3414

Release Date	Certification	Date of Certification	Chart Peak	ARTIST/Title Songwriter ● Producer (singles only)	Label & Number
9/74	G	10/22/74	1	**Walls And Bridges**	Apple 3416
9/88	G	1/5/89	31	Imagine: John Lennon [S]	Capitol 90803
				JOHN LENNON & YOKO ONO	
11/80	G P 3P	1/10/81 1/10/81 10/22/84	1	**Double Fantasy**	Geffen 2001
1/84	G	4/13/84	11	Milk And Honey	Polydor 817 160
				JULIAN LENNON	
10/84	G P	1/9/85 3/13/85	17	Valotte	Atlantic 80184
3/86	G	5/22/86	32	The Secret Value Of Daydreaming	Atlantic 81640
				THE LETTERMEN	
9/66	G	5/5/69	17	The Best Of The Lettermen	Capitol 2554
11/67	G	1/17/69	10	The Lettermen!!!...And "Live!"	Capitol 2758
3/68	G	3/20/70	13	Goin' Out Of My Head	Capitol 2865
8/69	G	6/5/70	17	Hurt So Bad	Capitol 269
				LEVERT	
6/87	G	3/16/89	5	Casanova Reggie Calloway • Calloway	Atlantic 89217
7/87	G	10/15/87	32	The Big Throwdown	Atlantic 81773
10/88	G	3/21/89	79	Just Coolin'	Atlantic 81926
				GARY LEWIS & THE PLAYBOYS	
12/64	G	4/28/67	1	**This Diamond Ring** Al Kooper/Bobby Brass/Irwin Levine • Snuff Garrett	Liberty 55756
9/66	G	9/29/69	10	Golden Greats	Liberty 7468
				HUEY LEWIS & THE NEWS	
1/84	G	1/30/89	6	I Want A New Drug Huey Lewis/Chris Hayes • Lewis & The News	Chrysalis 42766
6/85	G	1/30/89	1	**The Power Of Love** Lewis/Hayes • Lewis & The News	Chrysalis 42876

Release Date	Certification	Date of Certification	Chart Peak	ARTIST/Title Songwriter ● Producer (singles only)	Label & Number
2/82	G	10/16/85	13	Picture This	Chrysalis 1340
9/83	G P 5P 6P 7P	2/13/84 2/29/84 11/9/84 8/19/85 7/20/87	1	**Sports**	Chrysalis 41412
8/86	G P 2P 3P	12/4/86 12/4/86 12/4/86 7/25/88	1	**Fore!**	Chrysalis 41534
7/88	G P	9/27/88 9/27/88	11	Small World	Chrysalis 41622
				RAMSEY LEWIS	
11/74	G	5/12/75	12	Sun Goddess	Columbia 33194
				ENOCH LIGHT & THE LIGHT BRIGADE	
10/59	G	5/8/68	1	**Persuasive Percussion**	Command 800
				GORDON LIGHTFOOT	
3/74	G	6/18/74	1	**Sundown** Gordon Lightfoot • Lenny Waronker	Reprise 1194
4/70	G	6/14/71	12	Sit Down Young Stranger [a/k/a If You Could Read My Mind]	Reprise 6392
12/73	G P	5/31/74 10/13/86	1	**Sundown**	Reprise 2177
11/75	G P	4/19/77 10/13/86	34	Gord's Gold	Reprise 2237
6/76	G P	10/26/76 2/7/80	12	Summertime Dream	Reprise 2246
1/78	G	4/25/78	22	Endless Wire	Warner 3149
				MARK LINDSAY	
11/69	G	4/13/70	10	Arizona Kenny Young • Jerry Fuller	Columbia 45037
				LIPPS, INC.	
1/80	G P	5/23/80 7/17/80	1	**Funkytown** Steve Greenberg • Greenberg	Casablanca 2233

Release Date	Certification	Date of Certification	Chart Peak	ARTIST/Title Songwriter ● Producer (singles only)	Label & Number
1/80	G	5/27/80	5	Mouth To Mouth	Casablanca 7197
				LISA LISA AND CULT JAM	
8/85	G P	10/8/86 7/24/89	52	Lisa Lisa And Cult Jam With Full Force	Columbia 40135
4/87	G P	8/11/87 8/11/87	7	Spanish Fly	Columbia 40477
				LITTLE FEAT	
8/74	G	4/17/86	36	Feets Don't Fail Me Now	Warner 2784
2/78	G*	6/13/79	18	Waiting For Columbus	Warner 3140
8/88	G	2/14/89	36	Let It Roll	Warner 25750
				LITTLE RIVER BAND	
6/77	G	1/9/78	49	Diamantina Cocktail	Harvest 11645
5/78	G P	8/29/78 5/9/79	16	Sleep Catcher	Harvest 11783
7/79	G P	11/20/79 11/20/79	10	First Under The Wire	Capitol 11954
8/81	G	11/18/81	21	Time Exposure	Capitol 12163
11/82	G	10/19/83	33	Greatest Hits	Capitol 12247
				LIVING COLOUR	
5/88	G P	2/14/89 4/17/89	6	Vivid	Epic 44099
				L.L. COOL J.	
5/89	G	7/24/89	15	I'm That Type Of Guy L.L. Cool J./Dwayne Simon/Steve Ett • L.L. Cool J.	Def Jam 68902
11/85	G P	4/14/86 4/19/88	46	Radio	Def Jam 40239
5/87	G P 2P	8/11/87 8/11/87 11/9/87	3	Bigger And Deffer	Def Jam 40793
6/89	G P	8/9/89 8/9/89	6	Walking With A Panther	Def Jam 45172

Release Date	Certification	Date of Certification	Chart Peak	ARTIST/Title Songwriter ● Producer (singles only)	Label & Number
				LOBO	
9/72	G	11/29/72	2	I'd Love You To Want Me Lobo • Phil Gernhard	Big Tree 147
				LOGGINS & MESSINA	
10/72	G	3/7/73	4	Your Mama Don't Dance Kenny Loggins/Jim Messina • Messina	Columbia 45719
1/72	G	5/11/73	70	Sittin' In	Columbia 31044
10/72	G P	2/2/73 11/21/86	16	Loggins & Messina	Columbia 31748
10/73	G P	12/7/73 11/21/86	10	Full Sail	Columbia 32540
4/74	G	6/18/74	5	On Stage	Columbia 32848
10/74	G	11/25/74	8	Mother Lode	Columbia 33175
1/76	G	8/19/76	16	Native Sons	Columbia 33578
11/76	G P	5/10/77 12/30/81	61	The Best Of Friends	Columbia 34388
				KENNY LOGGINS	
1/84	G	4/9/84	1	**Footloose** Kenny Loggins/Dean Pitchford • Loggins/Lee DeCarlo	Columbia 04310
4/77	G P	9/20/77 12/22/80	27	Celebrate Me Home	Columbia 34655
6/78	G P	9/14/78 10/13/78	7	Nightwatch	Columbia 35387
9/80	G	11/14/80	11	Alive	Columbia 36738
10/80	G P	2/6/80 11/1/85	16	Keep The Fire	Columbia 36172
9/82	G	11/22/82	13	High Adventure	Columbia 38127
3/85	G	7/24/89	41	Vox Humana	Columbia 39174
				LONDON SYMPHONY ORCHESTRA/VARIOUS ARTISTS	
11/72	G	12/13/72	5	Tommy	Ode 99001
				LAURIE LONDON	
2/58	G	7/8/58	1	**He's Got The Whole World In His Hands** Traditional/Arr: Geoff Love	Capitol 3891

Release Date	Certification	Date of Certification	Chart Peak	ARTIST/Title Songwriter ● Producer (singles only)	Label & Number
				CLAUDINE LONGET	
3/67	G	4/17/70	11	Claudine	A&M 4121
				LOOKING GLASS	
5/72	G	8/9/72	1	**Brandy (You're A Fine Girl)** Elliot Lurie • Mike Gershman/Bob Liston/Looking Glass	Epic 10874
				TRINI LOPEZ	
6/63	G	4/26/65	2	Trini Lopez At PJ's	Reprise 6093
				LOVE AND ROCKETS	
3/89	G	8/2/89	14	Love And Rockets	Big Time 9715
				LOVE UNLIMITED	
2/72	G	7/24/72	14	Walkin' In The Rain With The One I Love Barry White • White	Uni 55319
7/73	G	2/7/74	3	Under The Influence Of…	20th Century 414
				LOVE UNLIMITED ORCHESTRA	
11/73	G	2/7/74	1	**Love's Theme** Barry White • White	20th Century 2069
1/74	G	4/29/74	8	Rhapsody In White	20th Century 433
10/74	G	4/8/75	28	White Gold	20th Century 458
				LOVERBOY	
9/80	G P*	5/8/81 2/8/82	13	Loverboy	Columbia 36762
10/81	G P 3P	12/30/81 3/12/82 10/19/84	7	Get Lucky	Columbia 36738
6/83	G P*	8/12/83 8/12/83	7	Keep It Up	Columbia 38703
9/85	G P	11/1/85 11/1/85	13	Lovin' Every Minute Of It	Columbia 39953
8/87	G	11/9/87	42	Wildside	Columbia 40893

Release Date	Certification	Date of Certification	Chart Peak	ARTIST/Title Songwriter ● Producer (singles only)	Label & Number
				THE LOVIN' SPOONFUL	
7/66	G	9/19/66	1	**Summer In The City** John & Mark Sebastian/Steve Boone • Erik Jacobsen	Kama Sutra 211
2/67	G	7/7/67	3	The Best Of The Lovin' Spoonful	Kama Sutra 8056
				L.T.D.	
8/77	G	12/22/77	4	Back In Love Again Len Ron Hanks/Zane Gray • Bobby Martin	A&M 1974
7/77	G	11/9/77	21	Something To Love	A&M 4646
6/78	G P	6/21/78 9/19/78	18	Togetherness	A&M 4705
6/79	G	10/30/79	29	Devotion	A&M 4771
				LULU	
6/67	G	11/2/67	1	**To Sir With Love** Don Black/Mark London • Mickie Most	Epic 10187
				RAY LYNCH	
12/84	G	4/7/89	—	Deep Breakfast	Music West 102
				CHERYL LYNN	
8/78	G	1/16/79	12	Got To Be Real Cheryl Lynn/David Paich/David Foster • Marty & David Paich	Columbia 10808
10/78	G	2/23/79	23	Cheryl Lynn	Columbia 35486
				LORETTA LYNN **[see also Conway Twitty]**	
2/67	G	4/13/70	80	Don't Come Home A Drinkin'	Decca 74842
6/68	G	1/18/72	—	Loretta Lynn's Greatest Hits	Decca 75000
1/71	G	6/15/83	81	Coal Miner's Daughter	Decca 75253
5/74	G	10/29/81	—	Greatest Hits Volume II	MCA 420

Release Date	Certification	Date of Certification	Chart Peak	ARTIST/Title Songwriter ● Producer (singles only)	Label & Number
				LYNYRD SKYNYRD	
8/73	G P 2P	12/18/74 7/21/87 7/21/87	27	Lynyrd Skynyrd (Pronounced Leh-nerd Skin-nerd)	MCA 363
4/74	G P 2P	9/20/74 7/21/87 7/21/87	12	Second Helping	MCA 413
3/75	G P	6/27/75 7/21/87	9	Nuthin' Fancy	MCA 2137
2/76	G	1/20/81	20	Gimme Back My Bullets	MCA 2170
9/76	G P 3P	10/26/76 12/30/76 7/21/87	9	One More From The Road	MCA 6001
10/77	G P 2P	10/27/77 12/12/77 7/21/87	5	Street Survivors	MCA 3029
9/78	G P	9/8/78 11/10/78	15	Skynyrd's First And…Last	MCA 3047
11/79	G P 3P	3/25/80 4/18/80 7/21/87	12	Gold & Platinum	MCA 11008

M

Release Date	Certification	Date of Certification	Chart Peak	ARTIST/Title Songwriter ● Producer (singles only)	Label & Number
				M	
8/79	G	12/5/79	1	**Pop Muzik** Robin Scott • Scott	Sire 49033
				JEANETTE MacDONALD & NELSON EDDY	
2/59	G	10/27/66	40	Favorites In Hi-Fi	RCA 1738
				BYRON MacGREGOR	
12/73	G	1/8/74	4	Americans Gordon Sinclair • Peter Scheurmier	Westbound 222
				MARY MacGREGOR	
10/76	G	2/10/77	1	**Torn Between Two Lovers** Peter Yarrow/Phil Jarrell • Yarrow/Barry Beckett	Ariola Am. 7638

Release Date	Certification	Date of Certification	Chart Peak	ARTIST/Title Songwriter ● Producer (singles only)	Label & Number
				MADONNA	
10/84	G	1/10/85	1	**Like A Virgin** Billy Steinberg/Tom Kelly • Nile Rodgers	Sire 29210
2/85	G	7/16/85	1	**Crazy For You** John Bettis/Jon Lind • John "Jellybean" Benitez	Geffen 29051
5/85	G	7/30/85	—	Angel/Into The Groove [12-inch single] Madonna/Steve Bray • Rodgers	Sire 20335
3/89	G P	5/16/89 5/16/89	1	**Like A Prayer** Madonna/Patrick Leonard • Madonna/Leonard	Sire 27539
5/89	G	8/11/89	2	Express Yourself Madonna/Bray • Madonna/Bray	Sire 22948
7/83	G P 2P 3P 4P	5/31/84 8/14/84 12/5/84 10/15/85 3/23/88	8	Madonna	Sire 23867
11/84	G P 2P 3P 4P 5P 6P 7P	1/23/85 1/23/85 1/23/85 2/5/85 4/23/85 7/22/85 11/6/85 7/14/87	1	**Like A Virgin**	Sire 25157
6/86	G P 2P 3P 4P 5P	9/8/86 9/8/86 9/8/86 11/18/86 2/3/87 8/11/87	1	**True Blue**	Sire 25442
7/87	G P	9/29/87 9/29/87	7	Who's That Girl [S]	Sire 25611
11/87	G P	1/20/88 1/20/88	14	You Can Dance	Sire 25535
3/89	G P 2P	5/23/89 5/23/89 5/23/89	1	**Like A Prayer**	Sire 25844
				THE MAIN INGREDIENT	
6/72	G	9/20/72	3	Everybody Plays The Fool Ken Williams/**Rudy Clark**/J.R. Bailey • Tony Sylvester/Luther Simmons	RCA 0731
1/74	G	5/10/74	10	Just Don't Want To Be Lonely Vinnie Barrett/John Freeman/Bobby Eli • Sylvester/Simmons/Cuba Gooding	RCA 0205

Release Date	Certification	Date of Certification	Chart Peak	ARTIST/Title Songwriter ● Producer (singles only)	Label & Number
				THE MAMAS & THE PAPAS	
12/65	G	6/10/66	4	California Dreamin' John Phillips • Lou Adler	Dunhill 4020
3/66	G	6/10/66	1	**Monday, Monday** Phillips • Adler	Dunhill 4026
2/66	G	6/10/66	1	**If You Can Believe Your Eyes And Ears**	Dunhill 50006
9/66	G	12/1/66	4	The Mamas & The Papas	Dunhill 50010
3/67	G	4/20/67	2	The Mamas & The Papas Deliver	Dunhill 50014
10/67	G	2/9/68	5	Farewell To The First Golden Era	Dunhill 50025
				MELISSA MANCHESTER	
1/75	G	6/24/77	12	Melissa	Arista 4031
1/83	G	6/28/89	43	Greatest Hits	Arista 9611
				HENRY MANCINI	
4/69	G	6/25/69	1	**Love Theme From Romeo & Juliet** Nino Rota • Joe Reisman	RCA 0131
12/58	G	12/31/59	1	**The Music From Peter Gunn**	RCA 1956
8/61	G	10/30/62	1	**Breakfast At Tiffany's [S]**	RCA 2362
3/64	G	10/5/65	8	The Pink Panther [S]	RCA 2795
7/64	G	4/10/67	42	The Best Of Mancini	RCA 2693
9/66	G	12/14/82	—	A Merry Mancini Christmas	RCA 3612
4/69	G	9/12/69	5	A Warm Shade Of Ivory	RCA 4140
				BARBARA MANDRELL	
1/79	G	1/26/81	170	The Best Of Barbara Mandrell	ABC 1119
8/81	G	2/22/82	86	Barbara Mandrell Live	MCA 5243
				CHUCK MANGIONE	
3/75	G	9/29/82	47	Chase The Clouds Away	A&M 4518
10/77	G P 2P	3/27/78 5/18/78 11/14/84	2	Feels So Good	A&M 4658
9/78	G	10/10/78	14	Children Of Sanchez [S]	A&M 6700
2/80	G	4/29/80	8	Fun And Games	A&M 3715

Release Date	Certification	Date of Certification	Chart Peak	ARTIST/Title Songwriter ● Producer (singles only)	Label & Number
				THE MANHATTAN TRANSFER	
4/75	G	10/7/87	33	The Manhattan Transfer	Atlantic 18133
11/81	G	10/7/87	103	The Best Of The Manhattan Transfer	Atlantic 19319
				THE MANHATTANS	
3/76	G P	6/17/76 8/23/76	1	**Kiss And Say Goodbye** Winfred Lovett • Bobby Martin	Columbia 10310
2/80	G	7/18/80	5	Shining Star Leo Graham/Paul Richmond • Graham	Columbia 11222
4/76	G	10/7/76	16	The Manhattans	Columbia 33820
2/77	G	3/10/78	68	It Feels So Good	Columbia 34450
4/80	G	7/10/80	24	After Midnight	Columbia 36411
				BARRY MANILOW	
10/74	G	1/31/75	1	**Mandy** Scott English/Richard Kerr • Barry Manilow/ Ron Dante	Bell 45613
11/75	G	1/6/76	1	**I Write The Songs** Bruce Johnston • Manilow/Dante	Arista 0157
4/77	G	9/7/77	1	**Looks Like We Made It** Kerr/Will Jennings • Manilow/Dante	Arista 0244
1/78	G	4/6/78	3	Can't Smile Without You Chris Arnold/David Martin/Geoff Morrow • Manilow/Dante	Arista 0305
6/78	G	9/7/78	8	Copacabana (At The Copa) Manilow/Bruce Sussman/Jack Feldman • Manilow/Dante	Arista 0339
9/73	G	10/22/76	28	Barry Manilow I	Arista 4007
10/74	G P	7/18/75 9/2/87	9	Barry Manilow II	Arista 4016
10/75	G P 2P	12/30/75 9/2/87 9/2/87	5	Tryin' To Get The Feeling	Arista 4060
8/76	G P 2P	8/17/76 1/6/77 9/2/87	6	This One's For You	Arista 4090
5/77	G P 3P	6/16/77 6/16/77 9/2/87	1	**Barry Manilow Live**	Arista 8500
2/78	G	2/15/78	3	Even Now	Arista 4164

Release Date	Certification	Date of Certification	Chart Peak	ARTIST/Title Songwriter ● Producer (singles only)	Label & Number
	P 3P	2/22/78 9/2/87			
11/78	G P 3P	11/27/78 11/27/78 9/2/87	7	Greatest Hits	Arista 8601
10/79	G P	1/28/80 1/28/80	9	One Voice	Arista 9505
12/80	G P	2/4/81 2/4/81	15	Barry	Arista 9537
9/81	G	11/24/81	14	If I Should Love Again	Arista 9573
11/82	G	1/17/83	32	Here Comes The Night	Arista 9610
11/83	G	1/4/84	30	Greatest Hits, Vol.II	Arista 8102
11/84	G	1/14/85	28	2:00 AM Paradise Cafe	Arista 8254
5/85	G	9/2/87	100	The Barry Manilow Collection/20 Classic Hits	Arista 8274
				MANFRED MANN'S EARTH BAND	
8/76	G	3/1/77	1	**Blinded By The Light** Bruce Springsteen • Manfred Mann/Earth Band	Warner 8252
8/76	G	4/5/77	10	The Roaring Silence	Warner 2965
				MANNHEIM STEAMROLLER	
10/84	G P	3/17/88 11/1/88	50	Mannheim Steamroller Christmas	Am. Grama. 1984
9/88	G	11/30/88	36	A Fresh Aire Christmas	Am. Grama. 1988
				MANTOVANI & HIS ORCHESTRA	
1/53	G	9/18/61	7	Strauss Waltzes	London 685
11/53	G	9/18/61	3	Christmas Carols	London 913
6/55	G	9/18/61	8	Song Hits From Theatreland	London 1219
5/57	G	9/18/61	1	**Film Encores**	London 1700
4/58	G	9/18/61	5	Gems Forever…	London 3032
11/60	G	9/3/63	2	Great Theme Music	London 3231
1/67	G	2/18/70	53	Mantovani's Golden Hits	London 483
				TEENA MARIE	
5/81	G	8/6/81	23	It Must Be Magic	Gordy 1004
11/84	G	4/1/85	31	Starchild	Epic 39528

1. *Heart* is the largest-selling album by a group for Capitol Records. The 1985 release has been certified at 4 million — twice as many as the band's previous high, *Little Queen* from 1977.

2. The enduring legacy of Jimi Hendrix includes ten gold albums, two of which (*Are You Experienced?* and *Electric Ladyland*) have sold 2 million copies.

3. Buddy Holly's "That'll Be The Day" (with the Crickets) became a certified million-seller ten years after he died. Two compilations of Holly's music also went gold posthumously.

4. Herman's Hermits squirreled away five gold albums during their '60s heyday, more than such British Invasion contemporaries as the Dave Clark Five, the Animals, Freddie & the Dreamers, and the Kinks.

6

8

5. Bruce Hornsby's career has been helped considerably by Huey Lewis, who recorded Bruce and brother John's song, "Jacob's Ladder." Hornsby's second platinum album included his version.

6. Powered by his interpretation of Curtis Mayfield's "Pusher Man," among other raps, Ice-T reached gold first time out with his Sire debut.

7. *Whitney Houston* stands as the biggest-selling album to date by a female artist, as well as the most successful debut album by a solo singer.

8. Billy Idol's gold and platinum streak began with his second solo album, released in 1982. Before that, he fronted British punk band Generation X.

9. In the time-honored tradition of one-hit-wonder girl groups was Hot, fronted by Gwen Owens, former backup singer for Marvin Gaye and Stevie Wonder.

9

Release Date	Certification	Date of Certification	Chart Peak	ARTIST/Title Songwriter ● Producer (singles only)	Label & Number
				BOB MARLEY & THE WAILERS	
7/84	G P	6/22/88 6/22/88	54	Legend	Island 90169
				ZIGGY MARLEY & THE MELODY MAKERS	
3/88	G	6/30/88	23	Conscious Party	Virgin 90878
				M/A/R/R/S	
10/87	G	4/8/88	13	Pump Up The Volume Martyn Young/Steve Young • Martyn Young	4th & B'way 7452
				THE MARSHALL TUCKER BAND	
5/73	G	8/14/75	29	The Marshall Tucker Band	Capricorn 0112
2/74	G	8/16/77	37	A New Life	Capricorn 0124
11/74	G	11/7/75	54	Where We All Belong	Capricorn 0145
8/75	G	2/4/76	15	Searchin' For A Rainbow	Capricorn 0161
2/77	G P	6/2/77 5/23/78	23	Carolina Dreams	Capricorn 0180
4/78	G	5/2/78	22	Together Forever	Capricorn 0205
10/78	G	10/30/78	67	Greatest Hits	Capricorn 0214
				MARTIKA	
4/89	G	7/10/89	1	**Toy Soldiers** Martika/Michael Jay • Jay	Columbia 68747
10/88	G	8/3/89	15	Martika	Columbia 44290
				DEAN MARTIN	
5/64	G	8/19/64	1	**Everybody Loves Somebody** Irving Taylor/Ken Lane • Jimmy Bowen	Reprise 0281
8/64	G	2/2/68	15	Dream With Dean	Reprise 6123
8/64	G	1/29/65	2	Everybody Loves Somebody	Reprise 6130
10/64	G	12/2/65	9	The Door Is Still Open To My Heart	Reprise 6140
1/65	G	11/7/66	13	Dean Martin Hits Again	Reprise 6146
8/65	G	4/25/66	13	(Remember Me) I'm The One Who Loves You	Reprise 6170
10/65	G	3/19/68	11	Houston	Reprise 6181
2/66	G	5/2/68	40	Somewhere There's A Someone	Reprise 6201

Release Date	Certification	Date of Certification	Chart Peak	ARTIST/Title Songwriter ● Producer (singles only)	Label & Number
10/66	G	11/27/68	—	The Dean Martin Christmas Album	Reprise 6222
8/67	G	3/19/68	20	Welcome To My World	Reprise 6250
5/68	G	2/3/69	26	Dean Martin's Greatest Hits! Vol.1	Reprise 6301
7/68	G	12/23/70	83	Dean Martin's Greatest Hits! Vol.2	Reprise 6320
12/68	G	8/30/69	14	Gentle On My Mind	Reprise 6330
				STEVE MARTIN	
5/78	G	8/23/78	17	King Tut Steve Martin • William McEuen	Warner 8577
9/77	G P	11/29/77 5/9/78	10	Let's Get Small	Warner 3090
10/78	G P	11/1/78 11/21/78	2	A Wild And Crazy Guy	Warner 3238
9/79	G	1/22/80	25	Comedy Is Not Pretty!	Warner 3392
				AL MARTINO	
1/66	G	12/30/66	8	Spanish Eyes	Capitol 2435
				RICHARD MARX	
6/89	G*	8/21/89	1	**Right Here Waiting** Richard Marx • Marx/David Cole	EMI 50219
5/87	G P 2P	11/11/87 2/24/88 8/24/88	8	Richard Marx	EMI Manhattan 53049
4/89	G P 2P*	7/17/89 7/17/89 8/28/89	1	**Repeat Offender**	EMI 90380
				MARY JANE GIRLS	
2/85	G	6/20/85	18	Only Four You	Gordy 6092
				HUGH MASAKELA	
5/68	G	7/18/68	1	**Grazing In The Grass** Philemon Hou • Stewart Levine	Uni 55066

Release Date	Certification	Date of Certification	Chart Peak	ARTIST/Title Songwriter ● Producer (singles only)	Label & Number
				DAVE MASON	
6/70	G	2/7/74	22	Alone Together	Blue Thumb 19
10/74	G	10/7/76	25	Dave Mason	Columbia 33096
4/77	G	11/4/77	37	Let It Flow	Columbia 34680
6/78	G	9/14/78	41	Mariposa de Oro	Columbia 35285
				JOHNNY MATHIS	
12/57	G	5/5/60	2	Warm	Columbia 1078
3/58	G P	6/1/59 11/21/86	1	**Johnny's Greatest Hits**	Columbia 1133
8/58	G	12/4/62	6	Swing Softly	Columbia 1165
10/58	G P*	12/7/60 11/21/86	3	Merry Christmas	Columbia 1195
1/59	G	12/4/62	4	Open Fire, Two Guitars	Columbia 1270
6/59	G	1/12/62	2	More Johnny's Greatest Hits	Columbia 1344
9/59	G P	4/21/60 11/21/86	1	**Heavenly**	Columbia 1351
1/60	G	12/4/62	2	Faithfully	Columbia 8219
9/69	G	12/26/79	—	Give Me Your Love For Christmas	Columbia 9923
6/72	G P	7/9/76 11/21/86	141	Johnny Mathis' All-Time Greatest Hits	Columbia 31345
10/75	G	12/30/80	97	Feelings	Columbia 33887
3/78	G P	5/2/78 7/6/78	9	You Light Up My Life	Columbia 35259
				JOHNNY MATHIS & DENIECE WILLIAMS	
2/78	G	5/2/78	1	**Too Much, Too Little, Too Late** Nat Kipner/John Vallins • Jack Gold	Columbia 10693
7/78	G	7/20/78	19	That's What Friends Are For	Columbia 35435
				PAUL MAURIAT & HIS ORCHESTRA	
10/67	G	2/27/68	1	**Love Is Blue** Andre Popp/Pierre Cour	Philips 40495
7/67	G	2/27/68	1	**Blooming Hits**	Philips 248

Release Date	Certification	Date of Certification	Chart Peak	ARTIST/Title Songwriter ● Producer (singles only)	Label & Number
				JOHN MAYALL	
8/69	G	11/29/77	32	The Turning Point	Polydor 4004
				CURTIS MAYFIELD	
7/72	G	10/31/72	4	Freddie's Dead Curtis Mayfield • Mayfield	Curtom 1975
11/72	G	1/18/73	8	Superfly Mayfield • Mayfield	Curtom 1978
9/70	G	6/6/73	19	Curtis	Curtom 8005
7/72	G	9/7/72	1	**Superfly [S]**	Curtom 8014
5/73	G	6/6/73	16	Back To The World	Curtom 8015
				MAZE featuring FRANKIE BEVERLY	
1/77	G	8/1/77	52	Maze Featuring Frankie Beverly	Capitol 11607
1/78	G	3/10/78	27	Golden Time Of Day	Capitol 11710
3/79	G	5/1/79	33	Inspiration	Capitol 11912
7/80	G	1/6/81	31	Joy And Pain	Capitol 12087
6/81	G	10/15/81	34	Live In New Orleans	Capitol 12156
3/85	G	6/11/85	45	Can't Stop The Love	Capitol 12377
				M.C. HAMMER	
9/88	G P	4/17/89 7/26/89	30	Let's Get It Started	Capitol 90924
				C.W. McCALL	
11/75	G	12/19/75	1	**Convoy** C.W. McCall/Bill Fries/Chip Davis • Davis/Don Sears	MGM 14839
10/75	G	1/29/76	12	Black Bear Road	MGM 5008
				PETER McCANN	
3/77	G	8/17/77	5	Do You Wanna Make Love Peter McCann • Hal Yoergler	20th Century 2335

Release Date	Certification	Date of Certification	Chart Peak	ARTIST/Title Songwriter ● Producer (singles only)	Label & Number
				PAUL McCARTNEY **[*Wings]** **[see also Michael Jackson]**	
8/71	G	9/21/71	1	**Uncle Albert/Uncle Halsey** Paul & Linda McCartney • McCartney/McCartney	Apple 1837
4/73	G	7/6/73	1	**My Love*** Paul McCartney • McCartney	Apple 1861
6/73	G	8/31/73	2	Live And Let Die* McCartney • George Martin	Apple 1863
3/74	G	6/4/74	1	**Band On The Run*** McCartney • McCartney	Apple 1873
5/75	G	9/5/75	1	**Listen To What The Man Said*** McCartney • McCartney	Capitol 4091
4/76	G	6/11/76	1	**Silly Love Songs*** McCartney • McCartney	Capitol 4256
6/76	G	10/25/76	3	Let 'Em In* McCartney • McCartney	Capitol 4293
3/79	G	5/15/79	5	Good Night Tonight* McCartney • McCartney	Columbia 10939
4/80	G	7/21/80	1	**Coming Up (Live At Glasgow)** McCartney • McCartney	Columbia 11263
4/70	G	4/30/70	1	**Paul McCartney**	Apple 3363
5/71	G	6/9/71	2	Ram [PAUL & LINDA McCARTNEY]	Apple 3375
12/71	G	1/13/72	10	Wild Life*	Apple 3386
4/73	G	5/25/73	1	**Red Rose Speedway***	Apple 3409
12/73	G	12/7/73	1	**Band On The Run***	Apple 3415
6/75	G	6/2/75	1	**Venus And Mars***	Capitol 11419
3/76	G P	3/25/76 5/3/76	1	**Wings At The Speed Of Sound***	Capitol 11525
12/76	G P	12/13/76 12/20/76	1	**Wings Over America***	Capitol 11593
3/78	G P	3/20/78 3/30/78	2	London Town*	Capitol 11777
12/78	G P	12/6/78 12/6/78	29	Wings Greatest*	Capitol 11905
6/79	G P	6/18/79 7/18/79	8	Back To The Egg*	Columbia 36057
5/80	G	7/25/80	3	Paul McCartney II	Columbia 36511
4/82	G P	6/29/82 6/29/82	1	**Tug Of War**	Columbia 37462
11/83	G	1/9/84	15	Pipes Of Peace	Columbia 39149

Release Date	Certification	Date of Certification	Chart Peak	ARTIST/Title Songwriter ● Producer (singles only)	Label & Number
	P	2/17/84			
10/84	G	12/26/84	21	Give My Regards To Broad Street [S]	Columbia 39613
5/89	G	8/7/89	21	Flowers In The Dirt	Capitol 91653
				PAUL McCARTNEY & STEVIE WONDER	
4/82	G	6/7/82	1	**Ebony And Ivory** Paul McCartney • George Martin	Columbia 02860
				MARILYN McCOO & BILLY DAVIS, JR.	
8/76	G	11/30/76	1	**You Don't Have To Be A Star** James Dean/John Glover • Don Davis	ABC 12208
8/76	G	2/17/77	30	I Hope We Get To Love In Time	ABC 952
				VAN McCOY	
4/75	G	6/26/75	1	**The Hustle** Van McCoy • Hugo Peretti/Luigi Creatore	Avco 4653
				MICHAEL McDONALD **[see also Patti LaBelle]**	
8/82	G	10/13/82	6	If That's What It Takes	Warner 23703
				RONNIE McDOWELL	
8/77	G	9/8/77	13	The King Is Gone Ronnie McDowell/Lee Morgan • McDowell/Morgan	Scorpion 135
				REBA McENTIRE	
2/86	G	1/23/87	—	Whoever's In New England	MCA 5691
9/86	G	4/21/87	—	What Am I Gonna Do About You	MCA 5807
4/87	G P	12/9/87 5/16/89	139	Reba McEntire's Greatest Hits	MCA 5979
9/87	G	4/20/88	102	The Last One To Know	MCA 42030
4/88	G	12/13/88	118	Reba	MCA 42134
5/89	G	8/23/89	78	Sweet Sixteen	MCA 6294
				McFADDEN & WHITEHEAD	
3/79	G P	5/8/79 7/27/79	13	Ain't No Stoppin' Us Now Gene McFadden/John Whitehead/Jerry Cohen • McFadden/Whitehead/Cohen	Phil. Int. 3681

Release Date	Certification	Date of Certification	Chart Peak	ARTIST/Title Songwriter ● Producer (singles only)	Label & Number
5/79	G	8/16/79	23	McFadden & Whitehead	Phil. Int. 35800
				BOBBY McFERRIN	
7/88	G	1/4/89	1	**Don't Worry, Be Happy** Bobby McFerrin • Linda Goldstein	EMI Manhattan 50146
3/88	G P	8/31/88 9/26/88	5	Simple Pleasures	EMI Manhattan 48059
				MAUREEN McGOVERN	
4/73	G	8/14/73	1	**The Morning After** Al Kasha/Joel Hirschhorn • Carl Maduri	20th Century 2010
				BOB & DOUG McKENZIE	
1/82	G	3/15/82	8	Great White North	Mercury 4034
				ROD McKUEN [see San Sebastian Strings]	
				MAHAVISHNU JOHN McLAUGHLIN/ CARLOS SANTANA	
6/73	G	9/17/73	14	Love Devotion Surrender	Columbia 32034
				DON McLEAN	
11/71	G	1/3/72	1	**American Pie** Don McLean • Ed Freeman	United Art. 50856
10/71	G	1/3/72	1	**American Pie**	United Art. 5535
				SISTER JANET MEAD	
1/74	G	4/8/74	4	The Lord's Prayer Adaptation/Arnold Strals • Martin Erdman	A&M 1491
				VAUGHN MEADER	
11/62	G	12/18/62	1	**The First Family**	Cadence 3060

Release Date	Certification	Date of Certification	Chart Peak	ARTIST/Title Songwriter ● Producer (singles only)	Label & Number
				MEAT LOAF	
2/78	G	7/20/78	11	Two Out Of Three Ain't Bad Jim Steinman • Todd Rundgren	Cleve. Int. 50513
10/77	G P 4P	5/22/78 8/25/78 11/24/86	14	Bat Out Of Hell	Cleve. Int. 34974
				MECO	
7/77	G P	9/28/77 6/8/78	1	**Star Wars Theme/Cantina Band** John Williams • Meco Monardo/Harold Wheeler/ Tony Bongiovi	Millennium 604
7/77	G P	9/28/77 6/8/78	13	Star Wars And Other Galactic Funk	Millennium 8001
				BILL MEDLEY & JENNIFER WARNES	
5/87	G	2/24/89	1	**(I've Had) The Time Of My Life** Frank Previte/John DeNicola/Don Markowitz • Michael Lloyd	RCA 5224
				MEGADETH	
9/86	G	11/28/88	76	Peace Sells…But Who's Buying?	Capitol 12526
				MEL & TIM	
9/69	G	12/23/69	10	Backfield In Motion Hubert McPherson/Melvin Harden • Karl Tarleton	Bamboo 107
				MELANIE	
9/71	G	12/16/71	1	**Brand New Key** Melanie Safka • Peter Schekeryk	Neighborhood 4201
4/70	G	12/13/71	17	Candles In The Rain	Buddah 5060
10/71	G	6/13/72	15	Gather Me	Neighborhood 47001
				JOHN COUGAR MELLENCAMP [*John Cougar]	
4/82	G	10/8/82	2	Hurts So Good* John Cougar Mellencamp/George Green • Don Gehman/ Mellencamp	Riva 209
7/82	G	10/29/82	1	**Jack And Diane***	Riva 210

Release Date	Certification	Date of Certification	Chart Peak	ARTIST/Title Songwriter ● Producer (singles only)	Label & Number
				Mellencamp • Mellencamp/Gehman	
4/82	G P 2P 3P	7/6/82 8/26/82 10/12/84 4/7/86	1	**American Fool***	Riva 7501
10/83	G P 2P	12/16/83 12/16/83 10/25/84	9	Uh-Huh	Riva 7504
7/85	G P 2P 3P	10/24/85 10/24/85 12/30/85 4/7/86	2	Scarecrow	Riva 824 865
8/87	G P 2P	10/22/87 10/22/87 1/14/88	6	The Lonesome Jubilee	Mercury 832 465
5/89	G P	7/10/89 7/10/89	7	Big Daddy	Mercury 838 220

HAROLD MELVIN & THE BLUE NOTES

Release Date	Certification	Date of Certification	Chart Peak	ARTIST/Title Songwriter ● Producer (singles only)	Label & Number
9/72	G	11/21/72	3	If You Don't Know Me By Now Kenny Gamble/Leon Huff • Gamble/Huff	Phil. Int. 3520
9/73	G	12/28/73	7	The Love I Lost Gamble/Huff • Gamble/Huff	Phil. Int. 3533
2/75	G	6/30/75	26	To Be True	Phil. Int. 33148
11/75	G	1/12/76	9	Wake Up Everybody	Phil. Int. 33808

MEN AT WORK

Release Date	Certification	Date of Certification	Chart Peak	ARTIST/Title Songwriter ● Producer (singles only)	Label & Number
10/82	G	2/25/83	1	**Down Under** Colin Hay/Ron Strykert • Peter McIan	Columbia 03303
5/82	G P 4P	10/22/82 11/22/82 10/19/84	1	**Business As Usual**	Columbia 37978
4/83	G P 2P	6/20/83 6/20/83 10/19/84	1	**Cargo**	Columbia 38660
6/85	G	9/11/85	50	Two Hearts	Columbia 40078

MEN WITHOUT HATS

Release Date	Certification	Date of Certification	Chart Peak	ARTIST/Title Songwriter ● Producer (singles only)	Label & Number
7/83	G	10/7/83	13	Rhythm Of Youth	Backstreet 39002

Release Date	Certification	Date of Certification	Chart Peak	ARTIST/Title Songwriter ● Producer (singles only)	Label & Number
				SERGIO MENDES & BRASIL '66	
8/66	G	8/25/67	7	Sergio Mendes & Brasil '66	A&M 4116
3/67	G	5/26/69	24	Equinox	A&M 4122
2/68	G	9/4/68	5	Look Around	A&M 4137
11/68	G	5/26/69	3	Fool On The Hill	A&M 4160
				MERCY	
3/69	G	7/15/69	2	Love (Can Make You Happy) Jack Sigler Jr. ● Jamie/Guyden	Sundi 6811
				METALLICA	
11/84	G P	11/5/87 5/16/89	100	Ride The Lightning	Elektra 60396
2/86	G P	11/4/86 7/27/88	29	Master Of Puppets	Elektra 60439
8/87	G	12/8/87	28	Garage Days Re-Revisited	Elektra 60757
1/88	G	5/16/89	120	Kill 'Em All	Elektra 60766
8/88	G P 2P	10/31/88 10/31/88 7/19/89	6	…And Justice For All	Elektra 60812
				MFSB	
2/74	G	4/1/74	1	**TSOP (The Sound Of Philadelphia)** Kenny Gamble/Leon Huff ● Gamble/Huff	Phil. Int. 3540
1/74	G	4/16/74	4	Love Is The Message	Phil. Int. 32707
				MIAMI SOUND MACHINE [see Gloria Estefan]	
				GEORGE MICHAEL	
10/87	G P 2P 3P 4P 5P 6P 7P	1/18/88 1/18/88 1/18/88 2/8/88 5/9/88 7/13/88 9/26/88 2/16/89	1	**Faith**	Columbia 40867

Release Date	Certification	Date of Certification	Chart Peak	ARTIST/Title Songwriter ● Producer (singles only)	Label & Number
				BETTE MIDLER	
3/80	G	7/25/80	3	The Rose Amanda McBroom • Paul Rothchild	Atlantic 3656
1/89	G	5/24/89	1	**Wind Beneath My Wings** Larry Henley/Jeff Silbar • Arif Mardin	Atlantic 88972
11/72	G	4/25/73	9	The Divine Miss M	Atlantic 7238
11/73	G	12/12/73	6	Bette Midler	Atlantic 7270
12/79	G P	4/10/80 6/11/80	12	The Rose [S]	Atlantic 16010
11/88	G P	3/21/89 5/16/89	2	Beaches [S]	Atlantic 81933
				MIDNIGHT OIL	
1/88	G P	7/13/88 11/21/88	21	Diesel And Dust	Columbia 40967
				MIDNIGHT STAR	
7/83	G P 2P	10/17/83 12/14/83 2/5/85	27	No Parking On The Dance Floor	Solar 60241
11/84	G	1/17/85	32	Planetary Invasion	Solar 60384
5/86	G	8/25/86	56	Headlines	Solar 60454
				MIKE + THE MECHANICS	
10/85	G	5/27/86	26	Mike + The Mechanics	Atlantic 81287
10/88	G	3/16/89	13	Living Years	Atlantic 81923
				BUDDY MILES **[see Carlos Santana]**	
				GLENN MILLER & HIS ORCHESTRA	
1/54	G	6/28/61	1	**The Glenn Miller Story**	RCA 3057
1/62	G	7/2/68	—	Glenn Miller Plays Selections From The Glenn Miller Story And Other Hits	RCA 1192
10/69	G	1/28/86	—	A Memorial 1944-1969	RCA 6019
3/75	G	7/25/84	—	Pure Gold	RCA 0974

Release Date	Certification	Date of Certification	Chart Peak	ARTIST/Title Songwriter ● Producer (singles only)	Label & Number
				MITCH MILLER & THE GANG	
6/58	G	11/16/59	1	**Sing Along With Mitch**	Columbia 1160
10/58	G	12/7/60	1	**Christmas Sing-Along With Mitch**	Columbia 1205
11/58	G	4/21/60	4	More Sing Along With Mitch	Columbia 1243
3/59	G	12/7/60	4	Still More! Sing Along With Mitch	Columbia 1283
5/59	G	11/6/63	11	Folk Songs Sing Along With Mitch	Columbia 1316
8/59	G	1/12/62	7	Party Sing Along With Mitch	Columbia 1331
3/60	G	3/8/62	8	Saturday Night Sing Along With Mitch	Columbia 1414
6/60	G	3/7/62	5	Sentimental Sing Along With Mitch	Columbia 1457
10/60	G	3/7/62	5	Memories Sing Along With Mitch	Columbia 8342
2/61	G	7/6/62	5	Happy Times! Sing Along With Mitch	Columbia 8368
10/61	G	1/12/62	1	**Holiday Sing Along With Mitch**	Columbia 8501
				ROGER MILLER	
1/65	G	5/19/65	4	King Of The Road Roger Miller • Jerry Kennedy	Smash 1965
4/64	G	8/4/66	37	Dang Me	Smash 67049
1/65	G	9/1/65	4	The Return Of Roger Miller	Smash 67061
10/65	G	2/11/66	6	Golden Hits	Smash 67073
				STEVE MILLER BAND	
9/73	G	1/11/74	1	**The Joker** Steve Miller • Miller	Capitol 3732
12/76	G	4/18/77	2	Fly Like An Eagle Miller • Miller	Capitol 4372
5/82	G	8/23/82	1	**Abracadabra** Miller • Miller/Gary Mallaber	Capitol 5126
11/72	G	11/4/77	56	Anthology	Capitol 11114
9/73	G P	12/6/73 7/8/87	2	The Joker	Capitol 11235
5/76	G P	7/28/76 9/27/76	3	Fly Like An Eagle	Capitol 11497
5/77	G P	5/11/77 6/10/77	2	Book Of Dreams	Capitol 11630
11/78	G P	11/27/78 11/27/78	18	Greatest Hits 1974-78	Capitol 11872
10/81	G	12/30/81	26	Circle Of Love	Capitol 12121

153

1

2

3

4

5

1. The man with the biggest-selling album in music history, Michael Jackson also has a handy collection of gold singles: 12, including two with Paul McCartney and three with the Jacksons.

2. The Jeffersons (Airplane and Starship) cruised to 16 gold albums between 1967 and 1984, making them one of America's four most popular bands. They tie with Kiss and the Beach Boys, behind Chicago's 17 gold LPs.

3. Is she really going gold with him? Joe Jackson's debut album — and his fifth — joined the winners' circle. He and Sweden's Roxette have a title in common, too.

4. Jeff Townes (he's the DJ) and Will Smith (the rapper) met at a party in January 1986, and released their first album, *Rock The House,* 13 months later. You know them better as DJ Jazzy Jeff and the Fresh Prince.

5. Billy Joel is one of only two singers to have three albums reach (or pass) the 5 million mark. And, yes, the competition's initials are MJ.

6

7

8

9

10

6. All of the Jacksons' post-Motown top 10 hits went gold, and two ("Enjoy Yourself," "Shake Your Body") undulated to platinum. Three of their six Epic albums sold a million, too.

7. This parrot is alive. Tom Jones collected his first gold single with "I'll Never Fall In Love Again" only upon its re-release. Credit for the resuscitation goes to Parrot Records.

8. Waylon Jennings was hot as a pistol between 1975 and 1982, when all but two of his solo albums — plus duet LPs with Willie Nelson and Jessi Colter — turned gold. So did *Wanted: The Outlaws* with Willie, Jessi, and Tompall Glaser.

9. Journey's *Escape* is the largest-selling album on Columbia Records by an American band. It was released in July 1981, and hit the 7 million mark eight years later.

10. Elton John is Britain's most popular solo artist, judging by his collection of 23 gold albums. Nearest rival from his homeland: Paul McCartney, with 16.

Release Date	Certification	Date of Certification	Chart Peak	ARTIST/Title Songwriter ● Producer (singles only)	Label & Number
6/82	G P	8/9/82 11/16/82	3	Abracadabra	Capitol 12216
				MILLI VANILLI	Arista 9781

12/88	G
	P
		2/23/89
		4/4/89
			2	Girl You Know It's True
				    Bill Pettaway/Sean Spencer/Kevin Lyles/Rodney
				    Hollaman/Ky Adeyemo • Frank Farian
					Arista 9781

4/89	G	6/22/89	1	**Baby Don't Forget My Number** Farian/Roger Dalton/Franz Reuter/Berndt Nail • Farian	Arista 9832
3/89	G P 2P*	5/2/89 6/8/89 8/22/89	1	**Girl You Know It's True**	Arista 8592
				FRANK MILLS	Polydor 14517
12/78	G	3/29/79	3	Music Box Dancer Frank Mills • Mills	Polydor 14517
3/79	G	4/16/79	21	Music Box Dancer	Polydor 6192
				STEPHANIE MILLS	20th Century 2460
7/80	G	1/16/81	6	Never Knew Love Like This Before James Mtume/Reggie Lucas • Mtume/Lucas	20th Century 2460
8/79	G	8/21/79	22	Whatcha Gonna Do With My Lovin'?	20th Century 583
4/80	G	7/20/80	16	Sweet Sensation	20th Century 603
4/81	G	9/15/81	30	Stephanie	20th Century 700
6/87	G	8/28/87	30	If I Were Your Woman	MCA 5996
				RONNIE MILSAP	RCA 2043
11/76	G	10/16/79	—	Live	RCA 2043
8/77	G	2/10/78	97	It Was Almost Like A Song	RCA 2439
6/78	G	10/13/78	109	Only One Love In My Life	RCA 2780
9/80	G P 2P	2/12/81 7/14/81 4/25/86	36	Greatest Hits	RCA 3772
8/81	G	12/8/81	31	There's No Gettin' Over Me	RCA 4060
4/85	G P	10/2/85 5/5/89	102	Greatest Hits Vol.2	RCA 5425

Release Date	Certification	Date of Certification	Chart Peak	ARTIST/Title Songwriter ● Producer (singles only)	Label & Number
				KYLIE MINOGUE	
7/88	G	3/1/89	53	Kylie	Geffen 24195
				JUDI SHEPPARD MISSETT	
11/81	G	6/22/82	117	Jazzercise	MCA 5272
				MISSING PERSONS	
10/82	G	1/20/83	17	Spring Session M	Capitol 12228
				MR. MISTER	
6/85	G P	11/26/85 1/16/86	1	**Welcome To The Real World**	RCA 8045
				JONI MITCHELL	
4/70	G P	12/23/70 10/13/86	27	Ladies Of The Canyon	Reprise 6376
6/71	G P	11/15/71 10/13/86	15	Blue	Reprise 2038
11/72	G	12/22/72	11	For The Roses	Asylum 5057
1/74	G	2/27/74	2	Court And Spark	Asylum 1001
11/74	G	11/27/74	2	Miles Of Aisles [with TOM SCOTT & THE L.A. EXPRESS]	Asylum 202
11/75	G	12/4/75	4	The Hissing Of Summer Lawns	Asylum 1051
12/76	G	12/23/76	13	Hejira	Asylum 1087
12/77	G	2/13/78	25	Don Juan's Reckless Daughter	Asylum 701
				MODERN ENGLISH	
2/83	G	8/29/89	70	After The Snow	Sire 23821
				MOLLY HATCHETT	
9/78	G P	6/28/79 12/30/80	64	Molly Hatchett	Epic 35347
9/79	G P 2P	1/10/80 2/22/80 11/24/86	19	Flirtin' With Disaster	Epic 36110
9/80	G	11/7/80	25	Beatin' The Odds	Epic 36572

Release Date	Certification	Date of Certification	Chart Peak	ARTIST/Title Songwriter ● Producer (singles only)	Label & Number
				THE MOMENTS	
3/70	G	6/5/70	3	Love On A Two-Way Street Sylvia Robinson/Bert Keyes • Robinson	Stang 5102
				EDDIE MONEY	
10/77	G P 2P	7/6/78 11/13/79 7/6/89	37	Eddie Money	Columbia 34909
1/79	G	1/23/79	17	Life For The Taking	Columbia 35598
6/82	G P	11/19/82 8/11/87	20	No Control	Columbia 37960
8/86	G P	12/8/86 8/11/87	20	Can't Hold Back	Columbia 40096
				THE MONKEES	
8/66	G	10/27/66	1	**Last Train To Clarksville** Tommy Boyce/Bobby Hart • Boyce/Hart	Colgems 1001
11/66	G	11/28/66	1	**I'm A Believer** Neil Diamond • Jeff Barry	Colgems 1002
3/67	G	3/8/67	2	A Little Bit Me, A Little Bit You Diamond • Barry	Colgems 1004
7/67	G	7/14/67	3	Pleasant Valley Sunday Carole King/Gerry Goffin • Chip Douglas	Colgems 1007
10/67	G	11/14/67	1	**Daydream Believer** John Stewart • Douglas	Colgems 1012
2/68	G	2/26/68	3	Valleri Boyce/Hart • Monkees	Colgems 1019
9/66	G	10/27/66	1	**The Monkees**	Colgems 101
1/67	G	1/6/67	1	**More Of The Monkees**	Colgems 102
5/67	G	5/19/67	1	**Headquarters**	Colgems 103
11/67	G	11/2/67	1	**Pisces, Aquarius, Capricorn & Jones Ltd.**	Colgems 104
4/68	G	4/17/68	3	The Birds, The Bees & The Monkees	Colgems 109
7/76	G	8/28/86	58	Greatest Hits	Arista 4089
6/86	G P	8/28/86 1/15/87	21	Then & Now…The Best Of The Monkees	Arista 8432
				HUGO MONTENEGRO & HIS ORCHESTRA	
12/67	G	9/9/69	9	Music From "A Fistful Of Dollars," "For A Few Dollars More," & "The Good, The Bad And The Ugly"	RCA 3927

Release Date	Certification	Date of Certification	Chart Peak	ARTIST/Title Songwriter ● Producer (singles only)	Label & Number
				WES MONTGOMERY	
9/67	G	5/26/69	13	A Day In The Life	A&M 3001
				MONTROSE	
10/73	G P	4/13/77 10/13/86	133	Montrose	Warner 2740
				THE MOODY BLUES	
1/68	G	12/18/72	2	Nights In White Satin Justin Hayward • Tony Clarke	Deram 85023
3/68	G	10/2/70	3	Days Of Future Passed	Deram 18012
8/68	G	12/9/70	23	In Search Of The Lost Chord	Deram 18017
5/69	G	10/2/70	20	On The Threshold Of A Dream	Deram 18025
12/69	G	7/22/70	14	To Our Children's Children's Children	Threshold 1
9/70	G	11/2/70	3	A Question Of Balance	Threshold 3
8/71	G	9/10/71	2	Every Good Boy Deserves Favour	Threshold 5
11/72	G	11/21/72	1	**Seventh Sojourn**	Threshold 7
11/74	G	12/2/74	11	This Is The Moody Blues	Threshold 12/13
6/78	G P	6/19/78 1/26/79	13	Octave	London 708
5/81	G P	7/21/81 8/18/81	1	**Long Distance Voyager**	Threshold 2901
4/86	G	7/2/86	9	The Other Side Of Life	Threshold 829 179
				JACKIE MOORE	
11/69	G	3/10/71	30	Precious, Precious Jackie Moore/Dave Crawford • Crawford	Atlantic 2681
				THE MORMON TABERNACLE CHOIR	
9/59	G	10/21/63	1	**The Lord's Prayer**	Columbia 6068
10/64	G	10/23/79	—	The Joy Of Christmas	Columbia 6499
10/65	G	1/15/85	—	The Mormon Tabernacle Choir Sings Christmas Carols	Columbia 67777
9/70	G	1/15/85	—	Joy To The World	Columbia 30077
				VAN MORRISON	
2/70	G	11/19/76	29	Moondance	Warner 1835

Release Date	Certification	Date of Certification	Chart Peak	ARTIST/Title Songwriter ● Producer (singles only)	Label & Number
	P	10/13/86			
10/71	G	12/13/77	27	Tupelo Honey	Warner 1950
				THE MOTELS	
4/82	G	10/13/82	16	All Four One	Capitol 12177
10/83	G	12/21/83	22	Little Robbers	Capitol 12288
				THE MOTHERS OF INVENTION **[see also Frank Zappa]**	
9/73	G	11/9/76	32	Over-nite Sensation	DiscReet 2149
				MOTLEY CRUE	
8/82	G P	9/27/84 7/27/87	77	Too Fast For Love	Elektra 60174
10/83	G P 2P*	1/12/84 2/7/84 1/9/85	17	Shout At The Devil	Elektra 60289
6/85	G P 2P	8/22/85 8/22/85 11/9/85	6	Theatre Of Pain	Elektra 60418
5/87	G P 2P	7/15/87 7/15/87 9/16/87	2	Girls, Girls, Girls	Elektra 60725
				MOUNTAIN	
2/70	G	8/28/70	17	Mountain Climbing!	Windfall 4501
1/71	G	5/26/71	16	Nantucket Sleighride	Windfall 5500
				MOUTH & MacNEAL	
2/72	G	8/2/72	8	How Do You Do? Henry Van Hoof/Hans Van Hemart • Van Hemart	Philips 40715
				MTUME	
2/83	G	7/25/83	45	Juicy Fruit James Mtume • Mtume	Epic 03578
				MARIA MULDAUR	
8/73	G	5/13/74	3	Maria Muldaur	Reprise 2148

Release Date	Certification	Date of Certification	Chart Peak	ARTIST/Title Songwriter ● Producer (singles only)	Label & Number
				MUNGO JERRY	
6/70	G	8/31/70	3	In The Summertime Ray Dorset • Barry Murray	Janus 125
				MUPPETS	
7/70	G	10/23/70	23	The Sesame Street Book And Record	Columbia 1069
8/78	G	11/21/78	75	Sesame Street Fever	Sesame St. 79005
7/79	G	12/6/79	32	The Muppet Movie [S]	Atlantic 16001
				SHIRLEY MURDOCK	
2/86	G	5/7/87	44	Shirley Murdock!	Elektra 60443
				MICHAEL MURPHEY	
2/75	G	7/21/75	3	Wildfire Michael Murphey/Larry Cansler • Bob Johnston	Epic 50084
1/75	G	11/17/75	18	Blue Sky—Night Thunder	Epic 33290
				EDDIE MURPHY	
8/85	G	12/23/85	2	Party All The Time Rick James • James	Columbia 05609
7/82	G*	1/9/84	52	Eddie Murphy	Columbia 38180
11/83	G P	1/9/84 4/16/85	35	Eddie Murphy: Comedian	Columbia 39005
9/85	G	12/23/85	26	How Could It Be?	Columbia 39952
				WALTER MURPHY	
5/76	G	9/8/76	1	**A Fifth Of Beethoven** Adapted/Walter Murphy • Murphy	Private S. 45073
8/76	G	10/26/76	15	A Fifth Of Beethoven	Private S. 2015
				ANNE MURRAY	
2/70	G	11/6/70	8	Snowbird Gene MacLellan • Brian Ahern	Capitol 2738
4/78	G	10/26/78	1	**You Needed Me** Randy Goodrum • Jim Ed Norman	Capitol 4574

Release Date	Certification	Date of Certification	Chart Peak	ARTIST/Title Songwriter ● Producer (singles only)	Label & Number
8/70	G	12/21/73	41	Snowbird	Capitol 579
8/74	G	3/17/87	32	Country	Capitol 11324
1/78	G P	10/12/78 12/19/78	12	Let's Keep It That Way	Capitol 11743
1/79	G P	2/5/79 8/19/87	23	New Kind Of Feeling	Capitol 11849
10/79	G	2/7/80	24	I'll Always Love You	Capitol 12012
9/80	G P 3P	11/10/80 11/26/80 10/16/87	16	Anne Murray's Greatest Hits	Capitol 12110
4/81	G	6/29/81	55	Where Do You Go When You Dream	Capitol 12144
10/81	G P	10/25/82 8/19/87	54	Christmas Wishes	Capitol 16232
10/83	G	3/15/85	72	A Little Good News	Capitol 12301
10/84	G	6/11/85	92	Heart Over Mind	Capitol 12363
1/86	G	9/23/87	68	Something To Talk About	Capitol 12466
				THE MUSIC EXPLOSION	
4/67	G	7/26/67	2	Little Bit O' Soul John Carter/Ken Lewis • Jerry Kasenetz/Jeff Katz	Laurie 3380

N

Release Date	Certification	Date of Certification	Chart Peak	ARTIST/Title	Label & Number
				JIM NABORS	
9/66	G	1/5/68	24	Jim Nabors Sings Love Me With All Your Heart	Columbia 9358
10/67	G	12/4/70	—	Jim Nabors' Christmas Album	Columbia 9531
10/68	G	1/15/74	173	The Lord's Prayer And Other Sacred Songs	Columbia 9716
				NAJEE	
11/87	G	2/23/88	56	Najee's Theme	EMI America 17241
				GRAHAM NASH	
5/71	G	8/26/71	15	Songs For Beginners	Atlantic 7204
				GRAHAM NASH & DAVID CROSBY	
3/72	G	5/30/72	4	Graham Nash/David Crosby	Atlantic 7220

Release Date	Certification	Date of Certification	Chart Peak	ARTIST/Title Songwriter ● Producer (singles only)	Label & Number
9/75	G	11/7/75	6	Wind On The Water	ABC 902
7/76	G	10/19/76	26	Whistling Down The Wire	ABC 956
				JOHNNY NASH	
7/72	G	11/17/72	1	**I Can See Clearly Now** Johnny Nash • Nash	Epic 50902
				DAVID NAUGHTON	
1/79	G	7/31/79	5	Makin' It Freddie Perren/Dino Fekaris • Perren	RSO 916
				NAZARETH	
3/75	G	4/8/76	8	Love Hurts Nazareth • Manny Charlton	A&M 1671
4/75	G	4/8/76	17	Hair Of The Dog	A&M 4511
				RICKY NELSON	
4/61	G	8/10/77	1	**Travellin' Man** Jerry Fuller • Nelson	Imperial 5741
6/72	G	11/24/72	6	Garden Party [RICK NELSON & THE STONE CANYON BAND] Nelson • Nelson	Decca 32980
				WILLIE NELSON **[see also Merle Haggard; Julio Iglesias; Waylon Jennings]**	
5/75	G P 2P	3/11/76 11/21/86 11/21/86	28	Red Headed Stranger	Columbia 33482
3/76	G	5/5/78	48	The Sound In Your Mind	Columbia 34092
9/76	G	12/16/86	60	The Troublemaker	Columbia 34112
4/78	G P 3P	7/20/78 12/26/78 10/19/84	30	Stardust	Columbia 35305
11/78	G P	2/13/79 3/6/80	32	Willie And Family Live	Columbia 35642
10/79	G	3/6/80	42	Willie Nelson Sings Kristofferson	Columbia 36188
10/79	G*	11/22/82	73	Pretty Paper	Columbia 36189
12/79	G	7/3/80	52	The Electric Horseman [S]	Columbia 36327

Release Date	Certification	Date of Certification	Chart Peak	ARTIST/Title Songwriter ● Producer (singles only)	Label & Number
8/80	G P	10/15/80 11/12/80	11	Honeysuckle Rose [S]	Columbia 36752
3/81	G P	5/5/81 8/13/81	31	Somewhere Over The Rainbow	Columbia 36883
9/81	G P 2P	11/3/81 6/15/82 12/8/86	27	Willie Nelson's Greatest Hits (& Some That Will Be)	Columbia 37542
2/82	G P 3P	4/30/82 6/15/82 10/19/84	2	Always On My Mind	Columbia 37951
11/83	G	1/9/84	54	Without A Song	Columbia 39110
7/84	G	12/18/84	69	City Of New Orleans	Columbia 39145
9/85	G	4/6/87	178	Half Nelson	Columbia 39990
				WILLIE NELSON & RAY PRICE	
5/80	G	10/3/83	70	San Antonio Rose	Columbia 36476
				WILLIE NELSON & LEON RUSSELL	
6/79	G	8/2/79	25	One For The Road	Columbia 36064
				NENA	
9/83	G	3/26/84	2	99 Luftballons Joem Fahrenkrog-Petersen/Carlo Karges ● Reinhold Heil/Manne Praeker	Epic 04108
				PETER NERO	
11/71	G	12/20/72	23	Summer Of '42	Columbia 31105
				NEW BIRTH	
11/73	G	5/31/74	50	It's Been A Long Time	RCA 0285
				THE NEW CHRISTY MINSTRELS	
7/63	G	10/16/64	15	Ramblin'	Columbia 8855
				NEW EDITION	
8/84	G	1/4/85	4	Cool It Now Vincent Brantley/Rick Timas ● Brantley/Timas	MCA 52455

Release Date	Certification	Date of Certification	Chart Peak	ARTIST/Title Songwriter ● Producer (singles only)	Label & Number
9/84	G P	12/5/84 1/17/85	6	New Edition	MCA 5515
11/85	G P	1/3/86 6/2/86	32	All For Love	MCA 5679
11/86	G	1/23/87	43	Under The Blue Moon	MCA 5912
6/88	G P	8/19/88 9/28/88	12	Heart Break	MCA 42207
				NEW KIDS ON THE BLOCK	
11/88	G	3/29/89	3	You Got It (The Right Stuff) Maurice Starr • Starr/Michael Jonzun	Columbia 08092
3/89	G	6/13/89	1	**I'll Be Loving You (Forever)** Starr • Starr/Jonzun	Columbia 68671
6/89	G	8/22/89	1	**Hangin' Tough** Starr • Starr	Columbia 68960
3/88	G P 2P 3P*	11/21/88 3/29/89 6/13/89 7/28/89	1	**Hangin' Tough**	Columbia 40985
				NEW ORDER	
8/87	G	2/17/88	36	Substance	Qwest 25621
				NEW RIDERS OF THE PURPLE SAGE	
9/73	G	11/19/79	55	The Adventures Of Panama Red	Columbia 32450
				THE NEW SEEKERS	
11/71	G	1/27/72	7	I'd Like To Teach The World To Sing Billy Backer/Billy Davis/Roger Cook/Roger Greenaway • David Mackay	Elektra 45762
				THE NEW VAUDEVILLE BAND	
10/66	G	11/28/66	1	**Winchester Cathedral** Geoff Stevens • Stevens	Fontana 1562
11/66	G	12/21/66	5	Winchester Cathedral	Fontana 27560
				BOB NEWHART	
4/60	G	3/1/62	1	**The Button-Down Mind Of Bob Newhart**	Warner 1379

Release Date	Certification	Date of Certification	Chart Peak	ARTIST/Title Songwriter ● Producer (singles only)	Label & Number
10/60	G	12/21/67	1	**The Button-Down Mind Strikes Back!**	Warner 1393
				RANDY NEWMAN	
11/77	G	1/24/78	2	Short People Randy Newman • Lenny Waronker/Russ Titelman	Warner 8492
10/77	G	1/24/78	9	Little Criminals	Warner 3079
				JUICE NEWTON	
2/81	G	7/1/81	4	Angel Of The Morning Chip Taylor • Richard Landis	Capitol 4976
5/81	G	9/2/81	2	Queen Of Hearts Hank DeVito • Landis	Capitol 4997
2/81	G P	8/13/81 1/5/82	22	Juice	Capitol 12136
5/82	G	7/16/82	20	Quiet Lies	Capitol 12210
				WAYNE NEWTON	
3/72	G	7/19/72	4	Daddy Don't You Walk So Fast Peter Callander/Geoff Stevens • Wes Farrell	Chelsea 0100
				OLIVIA NEWTON-JOHN	
7/73	G	2/8/74	6	Let Me Be There John Rostill • Bruce Welch/John Farrar	MCA 40101
3/74	G	6/26/74	5	If You Love Me (Let Me Know) Rostill • Farrar	MCA 40209
8/74	G	10/9/74	1	**I Honestly Love You** Peter Allen/Jeff Barry • Barry	MCA 40280
1/75	G	3/5/75	1	**Have You Never Been Mellow** Farrar • Farrar	MCA 40349
5/75	G	9/16/75	3	Please Mr. Please Welch/ Rostill • Farrar	MCA 40418
6/78	G	8/31/78	3	Hopelessly Devoted To You Farrar • Farrar	RSO 903
11/78	G	2/12/79	3	A Little More Love Farrar • Farrar	MCA 40975
5/80	G	7/15/80	1	**Magic** Farrar • Farrar	MCA 41247
9/81	G	12/3/81	1	**Physical**	MCA 51182

Release Date	Certification	Date of Certification	Chart Peak	ARTIST/Title Songwriter ● Producer (singles only)	Label & Number
	P	1/5/82		Stephen A. Kipner/April/Terry Shaddick • Farrar	
12/73	G	10/14/74	54	Let Me Be There	MCA 389
5/74	G	9/9/74	1	**If You Love Me, Let Me Know**	MCA 411
2/75	G	2/26/75	1	**Have You Never Been Mellow**	MCA 2133
9/75	G	9/29/75	12	Clearly Love	MCA 2148
3/76	G	4/27/76	13	Come On Over	MCA 2186
10/76	G	12/8/76	30	Don't Stop Believin'	MCA 2223
10/77	G P 2P	10/21/77 12/15/77 10/12/84	13	Olivia Newton-John's Greatest Hits	MCA 3028
11/78	G P	11/15/78 12/5/78	7	Totally Hot	MCA 3067
10/81	G P 2P	12/16/81 12/16/81 10/12/84	6	Physical	MCA 5229
9/82	G P 2P	11/15/82 11/29/82 10/12/84	16	Olivia's Greatest Hits, Vol. 2	MCA 5347
10/85	G	12/19/85	29	Soul Kiss	MCA 6151
				OLIVIA NEWTON-JOHN & ELO	
6/80	G P 2P	8/19/80 8/19/80 10/12/84	4	Xanadu [S]	MCA 6100
				OLIVIA NEWTON-JOHN & JOHN TRAVOLTA	
3/78	G P	4/12/78 7/18/78	1	**You're The One That I Want** John Farrar • Farrar	RSO 891
7/78	G	8/31/78	5	Summer Nights Jim Jacobs/Warren Casey • Louis St. Louis	RSO 906
11/83	G P	1/16/84 1/16/84	26	Two Of A Kind [S]	MCA 6127
				PAUL NICHOLAS	
7/77	G	12/22/77	6	Heaven On The 7th Floor Dominic Bugatti/Frank Musker • Christopher Neil	RSO 878

1

2

3

4

1. British steel merchants Judas Priest took their name from a song on Bob Dylan's *John Wesley Harding* album. Gold begets gold.

2. The queen of Ode Records is a King. Carole's *Tapestry* was the first of seven gold albums she made for the label.

3. The movie soundtrack of *Oklahoma!* — featuring singer Gordon MacRae and the songs of Rodgers & Hammerstein — was the first album certified gold by the RIAA.

4. Not content with their group popularity, Kiss members Peter Criss, Ace Frehley, Gene Simmons, and Paul Stanley gave the world simultaneous solo albums in 1978. Each was simultaneously certified gold and platinum.

5. Kid 'n' Play's gold album, *2 Hype*, featured the skills of the producer also responsible for Salt-N-Pepa's precious metal acquisitions, Hurby "Luv Bug" Azor.

6. Paul McCartney is the most-certified ex-Beatle, which won't surprise you. His precious metal count is seven platinum and 16 gold albums, and 12 gold singles.

5

6

7

8

10

9

7. The only Oxford University scholar with gold and platinum to his name? Kris Kristofferson graduated to million-selling status with a little help from Sammi Smith, Rita Coolidge, Barbra Streisand, and Waylon Jennings.

8. The Kingston Trio was the first group to receive an RIAA gold award, for their 1958 chart-topper, "Tom Dooley." Theirs was also the first live album certified gold, *From The Hungry i.*

9. Two of John Lennon's three million-selling singles were certified gold after his December 1980 murder: "(Just Like) Starting Over" and "Woman," both from the triple platinum *Double Fantasy* album.

10. Every one of Led Zeppelin's ten albums has gone gold, of course, and most were certified platinum. The band's one and only top 10 single, "Whole Lotta Love," sold a million, too.

Release Date	Certification	Date of Certification	Chart Peak	ARTIST/Title Songwriter ● Producer (singles only)	Label & Number
				STEVIE NICKS	
8/81	G P 3P	10/7/81 10/7/81 10/30/84	1	**Bella Donna**	Modern 139
6/83	G P	9/12/83 9/12/83	5	The Wild Heart	Modern 90048
11/85	G P	1/21/86 1/21/86	12	Rock A Little	Modern 90479
5/89	G	7/11/89	10	The Other Side Of The Mirror	Modern 91245
				NIGHT RANGER	
10/83	G P	4/24/84 6/19/84	15	Midnight Madness	MCA 5456
5/85	G P	7/22/85 11/15/85	10	7 Wishes	Camel 5593
3/87	G	10/14/87	28	Big Life	MCA 5839
				MAXINE NIGHTINGALE	
12/75	G	4/27/76	2	Right Back Where We Started From Pierre Tubbs/Vince Edwards • Tubbs/Edwards	United Art. 752
3/79	G	9/18/79	5	Lead Me On Allee Willis/David Lasley • Denny Diante	Windsong 11530
				NILSSON	
11/71	G	3/3/72	1	**Without You** Peter Ham/Tom Evans • Richard Perry	RCA 0604
11/71	G	3/3/72	3	Nilsson Schmilsson	RCA 4515
7/72	G	12/30/72	12	Son Of Schmilsson	RCA 4717
				1910 FRUITGUM COMPANY	
12/67	G	3/5/68	4	Simon Says Elliot Chipraut • Jerry Kasenetz/Jeff Katz	Buddah 24
6/68	G	9/20/68	5	1, 2, 3, Red Light Sal & Bobby Trimachi • Kasenetz/Katz	Buddah 54
1/69	G	3/31/69	5	Indian Giver Bo Gentry/Ritchie Cordell/Bobby Bloom • Kasenetz/Katz	Buddah 91

Release Date	Certification	Date of Certification	Chart Peak	ARTIST/Title Songwriter ● Producer (singles only)	Label & Number
				NITTY GRITTY DIRT BAND	United Art. 9801
10/72	G	5/25/73	68	Will The Circle Be Unbroken	
				CLIFF NOBLES & CO.	Phil-L.A. 313
5/68	G	7/29/68	2	The Horse Jesse James • James	
				KENNY NOLAN	20th Century 2287
7/76	G	3/21/77	3	I Like Dreamin' Kenny Nolan • Nolan/Charles Calello	
				CHRIS NORMAN **[see Suzi Quatro]**	
				ALDO NOVA	Portrait 37498
1/82	G P	5/14/82 2/14/89	8	Aldo Nova	
				NU SHOOZ	Atlantic 81647
5/86	G	10/2/86	27	Poolside	
				TED NUGENT	
9/75	G P 2P	7/26/76 11/21/86 11/21/86	28	Ted Nugent	Epic 33692
9/76	G P	11/11/76 9/27/77	24	Free-For-All	Epic 34121
6/77	G P	7/11/77 9/27/77	17	Cat Scratch Fever	Epic 34700
1/78	G P	2/14/78 7/20/78	13	Double Live Gonzo!	Epic 35069
10/78	G P	10/30/78 11/16/78	24	Weekend Warriors	Epic 35551
5/79	G	6/7/79	18	State Of Shock	Epic 36000
5/80	G	7/23/80	13	Scream Dream	Epic 36404
				N.W.A.	Ruthless 57102
1/89	G P	4/13/89 7/18/89	37	Straight Outta Compton	

Release Date	Certification	Date of Certification	Chart Peak	ARTIST/Title Songwriter ● Producer (singles only)	Label & Number
				# O	
				THE OAK RIDGE BOYS	
3/81	G P	6/16/81 3/8/82	5	Elvira Dallas Frazier • Ron Chancey	MCA 51084
9/77	G	3/21/80	120	Y'All Come Back Saloon	ABC/Dot 2093
6/78	G	4/13/83	164	Room Service	ABC 1065
3/79	G	8/29/80	—	The Oak Ridge Boys Have Arrived	MCA 1135
2/80	G	10/10/80	154	Together	MCA 3220
10/80	G P	2/4/81 4/16/82	99	Greatest Hits	MCA 5150
5/81	G P 2P	7/23/81 7/29/81 10/12/84	14	Fancy Free	MCA 5209
2/82	G	4/6/82	20	Bobbie Sue	MCA 5294
10/82	G	12/27/82	73	Christmas	MCA 5365
2/83	G	4/3/83	51	American Made	MCA 5390
10/83	G	6/15/84	121	Deliver	MCA 5455
8/84	G	11/21/84	71	Greatest Hits 2	MCA 5496
				OCEAN	
2/71	G	5/3/71	2	Put Your Hand In The Hand Gene MacLellan • Greg Brown/Bill Gilliland	Kama Sutra 519
				BILLY OCEAN	
6/84	G	10/31/84	1	**Caribbean Queen (No More Love On The Run)** Keith Diamond/Billy Ocean • Diamond	Jive 9199
6/84	G P 2P	10/24/84 1/2/85 9/5/85	9	Suddenly	Jive 8213
4/86	G P 2P	6/23/86 6/25/86 12/23/86	6	Love Zone	Jive 8409
2/88	G P	4/26/88 7/21/88	18	Tear Down These Walls	Jive 8495

Release Date	Certification	Date of Certification	Chart Peak	ARTIST/Title Songwriter ● Producer (singles only)	Label & Number
				ALAN O'DAY	
2/77	G	6/28/77	1	**Undercover Angel** Alan O'Day • Steve Barri/Michael Omartian	Pacific 001
				OHIO EXPRESS	
4/68	G	6/17/68	4	Yummy Yummy Yummy Artie Resnick/Joey Levine • Jerry Kasanetz/Jeff Katz	Buddah 38
10/68	G	1/7/69	15	Chewy Chewy Resnick/Levine • Kasanetz/Katz	Buddah 70
				OHIO PLAYERS	
1/73	G	5/14/73	15	Funky Worm Ohio Players • Ohio Players	Westbound 214
8/74	G	10/25/74	13	Skin Tight Ohio Players • Ohio Players	Mercury 73609
11/74	G	1/23/75	1	**Fire** Ohio Players • Ohio Players	Mercury 73643
11/75	G	1/5/76	1	**Love Rollercoaster** Ohio Players • Ohio Players	Mercury 73734
4/74	G	6/28/74	11	Skin Tight	Mercury 705
11/74	G	12/13/74	1	**Fire**	Mercury 1013
8/75	G	8/15/75	2	Honey	Mercury 1038
6/76	G	6/7/76	12	Contradiction	Mercury 1088
10/76	G	1/20/77	31	Gold	Mercury 1122
				O'JAYS	
6/72	G	9/1/72	3	Backstabbers Gene McFadden/John Whitehead/Leon Huff • Kenny Gamble/Huff	Phil. Int. 3517
1/73	G	2/9/73	1	**Love Train** Gamble/Huff • Gamble/Huff	Phil. Int. 3524
3/74	G	6/12/74	9	For The Love Of Money Gamble/Huff/Anthony Jackson • Gamble/Huff	Phil. Int. 3544
10/75	G	1/12/76	5	I Love Music Gamble/Huff • Gamble/Huff	Phil. Int. 3577
3/78	G	6/16/78	4	Use Ta Be My Girl Gamble/Huff • Gamble/Huff	Phil. Int. 3542
8/72	G	5/8/73	10	Backstabbers	Phil. Int. 31712

Release Date	Certification	Date of Certification	Chart Peak	ARTIST/Title Songwriter ● Producer (singles only)	Label & Number
10/73	G	1/21/74	11	Ship Ahoy	Phil. Int. 32408
6/74	G	6/19/75	17	Live In London	Phil. Int. 32953
4/75	G	6/12/75	11	Survival	Phil. Int. 33150
11/75	G P	12/5/75 11/21/86	7	Family Reunion	Phil. Int. 33807
9/76	G	10/21/76	20	Message In The Music	Phil. Int. 34245
5/77	G	7/12/77	27	Travellin' At The Speed Of Thought	Phil. Int. 34684
4/78	G P	5/2/78 5/31/78	6	So Full Of Love	Phil. Int. 35355
8/79	G P	12/26/79 12/26/79	16	Identify Yourself	Phil. Int. 36027
				THE O'KAYSIONS	
6/68	G	12/3/68	5	Girl Watcher Buck Trail/Wayne Pittman • North State Music	ABC 11094
				MIKE OLDFIELD	
10/73	G	3/26/74	3	Tubular Bells	Virgin 105
				OLIVER	
7/69	G	10/10/69	2	Jean Rod McKuen • Bob Crewe	Crewe 334
				ALEXANDER O'NEAL	
7/87	G	10/20/87	29	Hearsay	Tabu 40320
				100 PROOF AGED IN SOUL	
7/70	G	11/14/70	8	Somebody's Been Sleeping Greg Perry/General Johnson/Angelo Bond • Perry	Hot Wax 7004
				YOKO ONO [see John Lennon]	
				ROY ORBISON	
8/64	G	10/30/64	1	**Oh Pretty Woman** Roy Orbison/Bill Dees • Wesley Rose	Monument 851
8/62	G	3/24/66	14	Roy Orbison's Greatest Hits	Monument 4009

Release Date	Certification	Date of Certification	Chart Peak	ARTIST/Title Songwriter ● Producer (singles only)	Label & Number
5/87	G	7/11/89	95	In Dreams: The Greatest Hits	Virgin 90604
1/89	G P	3/29/89 3/29/89	5	Mystery Girl	Virgin 90158
				TONY ORLANDO **[see Dawn]**	
				EUGENE ORMANDY/PHILADELPHIA **ORCHESTRA**	
11/62	G	1/7/63	109	The Glorious Sound Of Christmas	Columbia 6369
11/69	G	10/21/63	—	Handel: Messiah [with THE MORMON TABERNACLE CHOIR]	Columbia 607
				JEFFREY OSBORNE	
8/83	G	12/27/83	25	Stay With Me Tonight	A&M 4940
10/84	G	12/20/84	39	Don't Stop	A&M 5017
5/86	G	8/11/86	26	Emotional	A&M 5103
				OZZY OSBOURNE	
3/81	G P	7/31/81 6/18/82	21	Blizzard Of Oz	Jet 36812
11/81	G P	1/4/82 5/10/82	16	Diary Of A Madman	Jet 37492
11/82	G	1/24/83	14	Speak Of The Devil	Jet 38350
11/83	G P	1/23/84 4/14/86	19	Bark At The Moon	CBS Assoc. 38987
1/86	G P	4/14/86 4/14/86	6	The Ultimate Sin	CBS Assoc. 40026
9/88	G P	12/19/88 4/17/89	13	No Rest For The Wicked	CBS Assoc. 44245
				OZZY OSBOURNE & RANDY RHOADS	
4/87	G	8/11/87	6	Tribute	CBS Assoc. 40714
				K.T. OSLIN	
6/87	G P	3/22/88 5/23/89	68	80's Ladies	RCA 5924
8/88	G*	12/21/88	75	This Woman	RCA 8369

Release Date	Certification	Date of Certification	Chart Peak	ARTIST/Title Songwriter ● Producer (singles only)	Label & Number
				DONNY OSMOND	
2/71	G	8/30/71	7	Sweet And Innocent Rick Hall/Billy Sherrill • Hall	MGM 14227
7/71	G	10/13/71	1	**Go Away Little Girl** Gerry Goffin/Carole King • Hall	MGM 14285
11/71	G	7/28/72	9	Hey Girl Goffin/King • Hall	MGM 14322
2/72	G	3/24/72	3	Puppy Love Paul Anka • Mike Curb/Don Costa	MGM 14367

2/73	G	9/14/73	8	The Twelfth Of Never
				    Paul Francis Webster/Jerry Livingston •
				    Curb/Costa
					MGM 14503

6/71	G	12/13/71	13	The Donny Osmond Album	MGM 4782
10/71	G	1/26/72	12	To You With Love, Donny	MGM 4797
5/72	G	12/30/72	6	Portrait of Donny	MGM 4820
7/72	G	1/24/73	11	Too Young	MGM 4854
12/72	G	9/14/73	29	My Best To You	MGM 4872
				DONNY & MARIE OSMOND	
6/74	G	9/20/74	4	I'm Leaving It (All) Up To You Don Harris/Dewey Terry Jr • Mike Curb	MGM 14735
8/74	G	2/21/75	35	I'm Leaving It All Up To You	MGM 4968
3/76	G	12/23/76	60	Donny & Marie/Featuring Songs From Their Television Show	Polydor 6068
10/76	G	1/12/78	85	New Season	Polydor 6083
10/78	G	11/6/78	98	Goin' Coconuts [S]	Polydor 6169
				MARIE OSMOND	
8/73	G	12/7/73	5	Paper Roses Janice Torre/Fred Spielman • Sonny James	MGM 14609
				THE OSMONDS	
11/70	G	2/4/71	1	**One Bad Apple** George Jackson • Rick Hall	MGM 14193
8/71	G	11/17/71	3	Yo-Yo Joe South • Hall	MGM 14295

1/72	G	3/24/72	4	Down By The Lazy River
				    Alan Osmond/Merrill Osmond •
				    Michael Lloyd/Alan Osmond
					MGM 13324

Release Date	Certification	Date of Certification	Chart Peak	ARTIST/Title Songwriter ● Producer (singles only)	Label & Number
1/71	G	9/13/71	14	Osmonds	MGM 4724
6/71	G	1/20/72	22	Homemade	MGM 4770
1/72	G	5/29/72	10	Phase-III	MGM 4796
6/72	G	12/30/72	13	Live	MGM 4826
10/72	G	1/24/73	14	Crazy Horses	MGM 4851
				GILBERT O'SULLIVAN	
3/72	G	8/9/72	1	**Alone Again (Naturally)** Gilbert O'Sullivan • Gordon Mills	MAM 3619
10/72	G	3/22/73	2	Clair O'Sullivan • Mills	MAM 3626
6/73	G	9/18/73	7	Get Down O'Sullivan • Mills	MAM 3629
				THE OUTFIELD	
7/85	G P 2P	4/14/86 6/23/86 2/16/89	9	Play Deep	Columbia 40027
6/87	G	9/28/87	18	Bangin'	Columbia 40619
				OUTLAWS	
7/75	G	9/20/77	13	Outlaws	Arista 4042
3/78	G	9/14/79	29	Bring It Back Alive	Arista 8300
11/80	G	7/20/81	25	Ghost Riders	Arista 9542
				BUCK OWENS	
6/64	G	3/6/68	46	The Best Of Buck Owens	Capitol 2105
				OZARK MOUNTAIN DAREDEVILS	
11/73	G	9/6/77	26	Ozark Mountain Daredevils	A&M 4411

P

Release Date	Certification	Date of Certification	Chart Peak	ARTIST/Title	Label & Number
				PABLO CRUISE	
2/77	G P	8/25/77 4/29/80	19	A Place In The Sun	A&M 4625

Release Date	Certification	Date of Certification	Chart Peak	ARTIST/Title Songwriter ● Producer (singles only)	Label & Number
6/78	G P	6/21/78 9/19/78	6	Worlds Away	A&M 4697
				JIMMY PAGE	
6/88	G	8/23/88	26	Outrider	Geffen 24188
				ROBERT PALMER	
1/86	G	1/17/89	1	**Addicted To Love** Robert Palmer • Bernard Edwards	Island 99570
11/85	G P	4/18/86 9/17/86	8	Riptide	Island 90471
6/88	G P	8/24/88 11/3/88	13	Heavy Nova	EMI Manhattan 48057
				PAPER LACE	
5/74	G	8/9/74	1	**The Night Chicago Died** Mitch Murray/Pete Callander • Murray/Callander	Mercury 73492
				RAY PARKER JR. **[*Raydio]**	
11/77	G	4/26/78	8	Jack And Jill* Ray Parker Jr • Ray Parker Jr	Arista 0283
6/84	G	8/7/84	1	Ghostbusters Parker Jr. • Parker Jr.	Arista 9212
1/78	G	9/22/78	27	Raydio*	Arista 4163
4/79	G	8/13/79	45	Rock On*	Arista 4212
3/80	G	7/2/80	33	Two Places At The Same Time [RAY PARKER JR. & RAYDIO]	Arista 9515
3/81	G	5/27/81	13	A Woman Needs Love [RAY PARKER JR. & RAYDIO]	Arista 9543
4/82	G	6/10/82	11	The Other Woman	Arista 9590
11/84	G	8/8/85	60	Chartbusters	Arista 8266
				PARLIAMENT	
5/76	G	10/19/76	15	Tear The Roof Off The Sucker George Clinton/Bootsy Collins/Jerome Brailey • Clinton	Casablanca 856

Release Date	Certification	Date of Certification	Chart Peak	ARTIST/Title Songwriter ● Producer (singles only)	Label & Number

1/78	G	4/20/78	16	Flash Light
				    Clinton/Bernie Worrell/Collins •
				    Clinton
					Casablanca 909

1/76	G P	4/26/76 9/20/76	13	Mothership Connection	Casablanca 7022
10/76	G	10/19/76	20	The Clones Of Dr. Funkenstein	Casablanca 7034
5/77	G	6/8/77	29	Parliament Live/P-Funk Earth Tour	Casablanca 7053
12/77	G P	1/10/78 5/4/78	13	Funkentelechy Vs. The Placebo Syndrome	Casablanca 7084
12/78	G	12/13/78	23	Motor-Booty Affair	Casablanca 7125
11/79	G	3/11/80	44	Gloryhallastoopid (Or Pin The Tale On The Funky)	
				THE ALAN PARSONS PROJECT	
6/77	G P	9/16/77 10/25/78	9	I Robot	Arista 7002
6/78	G	7/24/78	26	Pyramid	Arista 4180
9/79	G	2/11/80	13	Eve	Arista 9504
11/80	G P	2/18/81 8/12/81	13	The Turn Of A Friendly Card	Arista 9518
6/82	G P	9/21/82 2/4/83	7	Eye In The Sky	Arista 9599
2/84	G	4/24/84	15	Ammonia Avenue	Arista 8204
				DOLLY PARTON **[see also Kenny Rogers]**	
10/77	G	2/1/78	3	Here You Come Again Barry Mann/Cynthia Weil • Gary Klein	RCA 11123
11/80	G	2/19/81	1	**9 To 5** Dolly Parton • Gregg Perry	RCA 12133
7/75	G	6/12/78	—	The Best Of Dolly Parton	RCA 1117
10/77	G P	12/27/77 4/28/78	20	Here You Come Again	RCA 2544
7/78	G	8/16/78	27	Heartbreaker	RCA 2797
5/79	G	11/13/79	40	Great Balls Of Fire	RCA 3361
11/80	G	3/6/81	11	9 To 5 And Odd Jobs	RCA 3852
9/82	G P	10/31/83 10/7/86	77	Greatest Hits	RCA 4422

Release Date	Certification	Date of Certification	Chart Peak	ARTIST/Title Songwriter ● Producer (singles only)	Label & Number
				DOLLY PARTON/LINDA RONSTADT/EMMYLOU HARRIS	
3/87	G P	7/14/87 7/14/87	6	Trio	Warner 25491
				THE PARTRIDGE FAMILY	
8/70	G	11/11/70	1	**I Think I Love You** Tony Romeo • Wes Farrell	Bell 910
1/71	G	3/11/71	6	Doesn't Somebody Want To Be Wanted Mike Appell/Jim Cretecos/Farrell • Farrell	Bell 963
10/70	G	12/16/70	4	The Partridge Family Album	Bell 6050
3/71	G	3/25/71	3	Up To Date	Bell 6059
8/71	G	9/27/71	9	The Partridge Family Sound Magazine	Bell 6064
10/71	G	11/2/71	—	A Partridge Family Christmas Card	Bell 6066
3/72	G	5/24/72	18	The Partridge Family Shopping Bag	Bell 6072
9/72	G	12/13/72	21	At Home With Their Greatest Hits	Bell 1107
				SANDI PATTI	
3/83	G	6/25/85	—	More Than Wonderful/Live	Impact 3818
9/83	G	12/14/88	—	The Gift Goes On	Impact 3874
8/84	G	3/30/87	—	Songs From The Heart	Impact 3884
9/85	G P	12/18/86 7/5/89	—	Hymns Just For You	Benson 3910
2/86	G	2/10/87	—	Morning Like This	Word/A&M 8325
2/88	G	8/23/89	—	Make His Praise Glorious	Word/A&M 9064
				PAUL & PAULA	
12/62	G	2/26/63	1	**Hey! Paula** Ray Hildebrand • Major Bill Smith	Philips 40084
				BILLY PAUL	
9/72	G	12/4/72	1	**Me And Mrs. Jones** Kenny Gamble/Leon Huff/Cary Gilbert • Gamble/Huff	Phil. Int. 3521
10/72	G	2/9/73	17	360 Degrees Of Billy Paul	Phil. Int. 31793

Release Date	Certification	Date of Certification	Chart Peak	ARTIST/Title Songwriter ● Producer (singles only)	Label & Number
				LUCIANO PAVAROTTI	
10/76	G P	12/15/81 10/10/85	—	O Holy Night	London 26473
11/79	G	8/9/84	77	O Sole Mio/Favourite Neapolitan Songs	London 26560
				JOHNNY PAYCHECK	
10/77	G	12/18/78	72	Take This Job And Shove It	Epic 35045
				FREDA PAYNE	
2/70	G	7/22/70	3	Band Of Gold Ronald Dunbar/Edythe Wayne • Eddie Holland/ Lamont Dozier	Invictus 9075
5/71	G	8/27/71	12	Bring The Boys Home Greg Perry/Angelo Bond/Norman Johnson • Perry	Invictus 9092
				PEACHES & HERB	
10/78	G	2/16/79	5	Shake Your Groove Thing Freddie Perren/Dino Fekaris • Perren	Polydor 14514
3/79	G P	4/6/79 5/11/79	1	**Reunited** Perren/Fekaris • Perren	Polydor 14547
10/78	G P	2/16/79 3/28/79	2	2 Hot!	Polydor 6172
10/79	G	2/7/80	31	Twice The Fire	Polydor 6239
				PEBBLES	
11/87	G P	4/26/88 7/18/88	14	Pebbles	MCA 42094
				TEDDY PENDERGRASS	
5/78	G	10/25/78	25	Close The Door Kenny Gamble/Leon Huff • Gamble/Huff	Phil. Int. 3648
3/77	G P	5/23/77 6/21/78	17	Teddy Pendergrass	Phil. Int. 34390
6/78	G P	6/16/78 8/25/78	11	Life Is A Song Worth Singing	Phil. Int. 35095
6/79	G P	6/11/79 7/27/79	5	Teddy	Phil. Int. 36003

1

2

3

4

1. Who's that girl with the multi-platinum moves? Madonna's first three albums sold 16 million copies, including 7 million of *Like A Virgin*.

2. The Manhattans were the first group with a platinum single. "Kiss And Say Goodbye," written by Winfred (Blue) Lovett, was certified for sales of two million in August 1976.

3. Another overnight success: Midnight Oil went platinum for the first time in 1988 with *Diesel And Dust*, a mere 14 years after the band began in Australia.

4. Without even the slightest hint of a Top 40 hit, Frankie Beverly guided Maze to six gold albums — five of them consecutive — between 1977 and 1985. No other R&B act has done so well without some crossover action.

5. Rick ("Super Freak") James masterminded Teena Marie's first recordings for Motown, but by the time she reached gold — with her fourth album — she was producing herself.

6. In his heyday, British orchestra leader Mantovani hit the concert trail as dutifully as any rock band to promote a new release. And he made more than four dozen albums...

5

6

7

8

9

7. Six gold albums make Reba McEntire country music's Queen of the '80s. No other female singer — in country, that is — has done better that decade.

8. Barry Manilow's five gold singles (from "Mandy" to "Copacabana") were coproduced by Ron Dante — whose voice also helped sell a million of the Archies' "Sugar, Sugar."

9. In the history of the recording industry, George Michael's *Faith* (seven times platinum) is the most successful debut album by a male soloist.

10. Dean Martin accumulated 12 gold albums while on Reprise Records. The man who founded the company, one Francis Albert Sinatra, managed 11.

Release Date	Certification	Date of Certification	Chart Peak	ARTIST/Title Songwriter ● Producer (singles only)	Label & Number
11/79	G	3/13/80	33	Teddy Live! Coast To Coast	Phil. Int. 36294
7/80	G P	9/29/80 11/12/80	14	TP	Phil. Int. 36745
9/81	G	12/23/81	19	It's Time For Love	Phil. Int. 37491
5/84	G	9/17/84	38	Love Language	Asylum 60317
4/88	G	8/23/88	54	Joy	Asylum 60775
				PEOPLE'S CHOICE	
6/75	G	11/15/75	11	Do It Anyway You Wanna Leon Huff • Huff	TSOP 4769
				STEVE PERRY	
4/84	G P	6/13/84 7/13/84	12	Street Talk	Columbia 39334
				THE PERSUADERS	
6/71	G	10/29/71	15	Thin Line Between Love And Hate Richard Poindexter/Robert Poindexter/Jackie Members • Poindexter Bros.	Atco 6822
				PET SHOP BOYS	
3/86	G P	5/20/86 9/29/86	7	Please	EMI America 17193
9/87	G	11/23/87	25	Actually	EMI Manhattan 46972
10/88	G	12/22/88	34	Introspective	EMI 90868
				PETER, PAUL & MARY	
10/69	G	12/30/69	1	**Leaving On A Jet Plane** John Denver • Albert Grossman/Milt Okun	Warner 7340
3/62	G P 2P	12/10/62 10/13/86 10/13/86	1	**Peter, Paul & Mary**	Warner 1449
1/63	G	8/27/63	2	(Moving)	Warner 1473
10/63	G	11/13/63	1	**In The Wind**	Warner 1507
7/64	G	1/21/65	4	In Concert	Warner 1555
3/65	G	4/30/70	8	A Song Will Rise	Warner 1589
10/65	G	1/29/70	11	See What Tomorrow Brings	Warner 1615

Release Date	Certification	Date of Certification	Chart Peak	ARTIST/Title Songwriter ● Producer (singles only)	Label & Number
7/67	G	1/27/69	15	Album 1700	Warner 1700
5/70	G P	10/16/70 10/13/86	15	10 Years Together/The Best Of Peter, Paul & Mary	Warner 2552
				TOM PETTY & THE HEARTBREAKERS **[*Tom Petty]**	
9/77	G	1/25/88	55	Tom Petty & The Heartbreakers	Shelter 52006
5/78	G	7/7/78	23	You're Gonna Get It!	Shelter 52029
10/79	G P 2P	2/25/80 2/27/80 10/12/84	2	Damn The Torpedoes	Backstreet 5105
5/81	G P	7/14/81 8/10/81	5	Hard Promises	Backstreet 5160
11/82	G	1/4/83	9	Long After Dark	Backstreet 5360
3/85	G P	5/24/85 9/20/85	7	Southern Accents	MCA 5486
4/87	G	7/21/87	20	Let Me Up (I've Had Enough)	MCA 5836
4/89	G P*	6/23/89 7/21/89	3	Full Moon Fever*	MCA 6253
				BOBBY "BORIS" PICKETT & THE CRYPT-KICKERS	
8/70	G	8/28/73	10	Monster Mash Bobby Pickett/Leonard Capizzi • Gary Paxton	Parrot 348
				WILSON PICKETT	
1/71	G	3/22/71	17	Don't Let The Green Grass Fool You Jerry Akines/Johnnie Bellmon/Victor Drayton/ Reginald Turner • Rick Hall	Atlantic 2781
4/71	G	6/22/71	13	Don't Knock My Love (Part 1) Brad Shapiro/Wilson Pickett • Dave Crawford/Shapiro	Atlantic 2797
				PILOT	
11/74	G	8/13/75	5	Magic David Paton/William Lyall • Alan Parsons	EMI 3992
				PINK FLOYD	
1/80	G	3/24/80	1	**Another Brick In The Wall** Roger Waters • Waters/Bob Ezrin/Dave Gilmour	Columbia 11187
11/69	G	2/28/74	74	Ummagumma	Harvest 388

Release Date	Certification	Date of Certification	Chart Peak	ARTIST/Title Songwriter ● Producer (singles only)	Label & Number
10/71	G	10/29/73	70	Meddle	Harvest 832
3/73	G	4/17/73	1	**The Dark Side Of The Moon**	Harvest 11163
9/75	G P 3P 4P	9/17/75 11/21/86 11/21/86 8/9/89	1	**Wish You Were Here**	Columbia 33453
2/77	G P 2P 3P	2/12/77 3/10/77 10/26/84 8/9/89	3	Animals	Columbia 34474
11/79	G P 4P 7P	3/13/80 3/13/80 10/26/84 8/9/89	1	**The Wall**	Columbia 36183
11/81	G P	1/29/82 7/6/89	31	A Collection Of Great Dance Songs	Columbia 37680
3/83	G P	5/23/83 5/23/83	6	The Final Cut	Columbia 38243
9/87	G P 2P	11/9/87 11/9/87 1/18/88	3	A Momentary Lapse Of Reason	Columbia 40599
11/88	G P	1/23/89 1/23/89	11	Delicate Sound Of Thunder	Columbia 44484
				ROBERT PLANT	
6/82	G	8/27/82	5	Pictures At Eleven	Swan Song 8512
7/83	G P	10/17/83 1/12/84	8	The Principle Of Moments	Es Paranza 90101
5/85	G	7/18/85	20	Shaken 'n' Stirred	Es Paranza 90265
2/88	G P	4/19/88 5/9/88	6	Now And Zen	Es Paranza 90863
				PLASTIC ONO BAND **[see John Lennon]**	
				THE PLATTERS	
2/60	G	12/7/61	6	Encore Of Golden Hits	Mercury 60472
10/60	G	9/1/65	20	More Encore Of Golden Hits	Mercury 60591
				PLAYER	
9/77	G	1/12/78	1	**Baby Come Back**	RSO 879

Release Date	Certification	Date of Certification	Chart Peak	ARTIST/Title Songwriter ● Producer (singles only)	Label & Number
				Peter Beckett/John Crowley • Dennis Lambert/ Brian Potter	
10/77	G	4/24/78	26	Player	RSO 3026
8/78	G	10/17/78	37	Danger Zone	RSO 3036
				POCO	
11/78	G	4/12/79	14	Legend	ABC 1099
				POINTER SISTERS	
11/78	G	2/5/79	2	Fire Bruce Springsteen • Richard Perry	Planet 45901
6/80	G	11/25/80	3	He's So Shy Tom Snow/Cynthia Weil • Perry	Planet 47916
5/81	G	9/2/81	2	Slow Hand Michael Clark/John Bettis • Perry	Planet 47929
5/73	G	2/7/74	13	The Pointer Sisters	Blue Thumb 48
2/74	G	7/25/74	82	That's A Plenty	Blue Thumb 6009
10/78	G	2/13/79	13	Energy	Planet 1
6/81	G	9/16/81	12	Black & White	Planet 18
11/83	G P 2P 3P	6/1/84 10/4/84 2/25/85 12/5/85	8	Break Out	Planet 4705
7/85	G P	9/3/85 9/3/85	24	Contact	RCA 5487
				POISON	
10/88	G	1/26/89	1	**Every Rose Has Its Thorn** Poison • Tom Werman	Enigma 44203
5/86	G P 2P	3/17/87 4/23/87 9/9/87	3	Look What The Cat Dragged In	Enigma 12523
4/88	G P 2P 3P 4P	6/28/88 6/28/88 9/20/88 11/18/88 1/5/89	2	Open Up And Say…Ahh!	Enigma 48493

Release Date	Certification	Date of Certification	Chart Peak	ARTIST/Title Songwriter ● Producer (singles only)	Label & Number
				POLICE	
5/83	G	8/15/83	1	**Every Breath You Take** Sting • Hugh Padgham/Police	A&M 2542
2/79	G P	3/31/81 8/15/84	23	Outlandos D'Amour	A&M 4753
10/79	G	6/10/81	25	Regatta De Blanc	A&M 4792
10/80	G P	12/12/80 2/27/81	5	Zenyatta Mondatta	A&M 4831
10/81	G P 2P	12/15/81 12/15/81 11/14/84	2	Ghost In The Machine	A&M 3730
6/83	G P 4P	8/30/83 8/30/83 11/14/84	1	**Synchronicity**	A&M 3735
10/86	G P	1/13/87 1/13/87	7	Every Breath You Take/The Singles	A&M 3902
				THE POPPY FAMILY	
10/69	G	6/22/70	2	Which Way You Goin' Billy? Terry Jacks • Jacks	London 129
				THE POWER STATION	
3/85	G P	5/21/85 8/8/85	6	The Power Station	Capitol 12380
				PEREZ PRADO	
5/58	G	8/18/58	1	**Patricia** Perez Prado/Bob Marcus	RCA 7245
				ELVIS PRESLEY	
1/58	G	4/15/83	1	**Don't** Jerry Leiber/Mike Stoller • Steve Sholes	RCA 7150
4/58	G	8/3/83	2	Wear My Ring Around Your Neck Bert Carroll/Russell Moody/Marilyn Schack/ Freddy Friday • Sholes	RCA 7240
6/58	G	8/11/58	1	**Hard Headed Woman** Claude DeMetrius • Sholes	RCA 7280
10/58	G	4/15/83	8	I Got Stung Aaron Schroeder/David Hill • Sholes/Chet Atkins	RCA 7410
3/59	G	8/3/83	2	A Fool Such As I Bill Trader • Sholes/Atkins	RCA 7506

Release Date	Certification	Date of Certification	Chart Peak	ARTIST/Title Songwriter ● Producer (singles only)	Label & Number
7/60	G	4/15/83	1	**It's Now Or Never** Aaron Schroeder/Wally Gold • Sholes/Atkins	RCA 7777
11/60	G	4/15/83	1	**Are You Lonesome Tonight?** Roy Turk/Lou Handman • Sholes/Atkins	RCA 7810
11/61	G	3/30/62	2	Can't Help Falling In Love Hugo Peretti/Luigi Creatore/George David Weiss • Sholes	RCA 7968
10/62	G	4/15/83	2	Return To Sender Otis Blackwell/Winfield Scott • Sholes/Atkins	RCA 8100
4/65	G	3/31/86	3	Crying In The Chapel Artie Glenn • Sholes	RCA 0643
4/69	G	6/25/69	3	In The Ghetto Mac Davis • Chips Moman	RCA 9741
8/69	G	10/28/69	1	**Suspicious Minds** Mark James • Moman/Felton Jarvis/Presley	RCA 9764
11/69	G	1/21/70	6	Don't Cry Daddy Mac Davis/Billy Strange • Moman	RCA 9768
4/70	G	8/14/70	9	The Wonder Of You Baker Knight	RCA 9835
8/72	G	10/27/72	2	Burning Love Dennis Linde • Jarvis	RCA 0769
6/77	G	9/12/77	18	Way Down Layng Martine Jr • Presley/Jarvis	RCA 10998
11/77	G	1/13/78	22	My Way Paul Anka/Jacques Revaux/Claude Francois • Jarvis	RCA 11165
3/56	G	11/1/66	1	**Elvis Presley**	RCA 1254
10/56	G	2/17/60	1	**Elvis**	RCA 1382
7/57	G	4/9/68	1	**Loving You [S]**	RCA 1515
11/57	G	8/13/63	1	**Elvis' Christmas Album**	RCA 1035
3/58	G P	10/17/61 5/20/88	3	Elvis' Golden Records	RCA 1707
12/59	G	11/1/66	31	Elvis' Gold Records, Volume 2	RCA 2075
10/60	G	3/12/63	1	**G.I. Blues [S]**	RCA 2256
12/60	G	4/9/69	13	His Hand In Mine	RCA 2328
10/61	G	12/21/61	1	**Blue Hawaii [S]**	RCA 2426
11/62	G	8/13/63	3	Girls! Girls! Girls! [S]	RCA 2621
9/63	G	11/1/66	3	Elvis' Golden Records, Volume 3	RCA 2765
11/64	G	5/20/88	1	**Roustabout [S]**	RCA 2999
3/67	G	2/16/68	18	How Great Thou Art	RCA 3758

Release Date	Certification	Date of Certification	Chart Peak	ARTIST/Title Songwriter ● Producer (singles only)	Label & Number
12/68	G	7/22/69	8	Elvis	RCA 4088
5/69	G	1/28/70	13	From Elvis In Memphis	RCA 4155
11/69	G	12/12/69	12	From Memphis To Vegas/From Vegas To Memphis	RCA 6020
6/70	G	2/23/71	13	On Stage/February 1970	RCA 4362
8/70	G	2/13/73	45	Worldwide 50 Gold Award Hits, Vol. 1	RCA 6401
12/70	G	6/28/73	21	Elvis — That's The Way It Is [S]	RCA 4445
1/71	G	12/1/77	12	Elvis Country	RCA 4460
10/71	G P 2P	11/4/77 12/1/77 5/20/88	—	Elvis Sings The Wonderful World Of Christmas	RCA 4579
7/72	G P	8/4/72 5/20/88	11	Elvis As Recorded At Madison Square Garden	RCA 4776
2/73	G P 2P	2/13/73 5/20/88 5/20/88	1	**Aloha From Hawaii Via Satellite**	RCA 6089
1/74	G	1/8/75	43	Elvis — A Legendary Performer Volume 1	RCA 0341
3/75	G P	9/12/77 5/20/88	—	Pure Gold	RCA 0971
1/76	G	10/25/77	46	Elvis — A Legendary Performer Volume 2	RCA 1349
3/76	G	12/1/77	—	His Hand In Mine	RCA 1319
5/76	G	10/7/77	41	From Elvis Presley Boulevard, Memphis, Tennessee	RCA 1506
3/77	G P	9/30/77 1/14/83	44	Welcome To My World	RCA 2274
7/77	G P	9/12/77 9/12/77	3	Moody Blue	RCA 2428
10/77	G P	10/14/77 10/14/77	5	Elvis In Concert	RCA 2587
12/78	G	12/18/78	113	Elvis — A Legendary Performer Volume 3	RCA 3082
				BILLY PRESTON	
12/71	G	6/21/72	2	Outa Space Billy Preston/Joseph Greene • Preston	A&M 1320
3/73	G	6/26/73	1	**Will It Go Round In Circles** Preston/Bruce Fisher • Preston	A&M 1411
9/73	G	12/18/73	4	Space Race Preston • Preston	A&M 1463
6/74	G	10/16/74	1	**Nothing From Nothing** Preston/Fisher • Preston	A&M 1544

Release Date	Certification	Date of Certification	Chart Peak	ARTIST/Title Songwriter ● Producer (singles only)	Label & Number
				THE PRETENDERS	
1/80	G P	6/2/80 8/11/82	9	Pretenders	Sire 6083
1/84	G P	4/18/84 4/18/84	5	Learning To Crawl	Sire 23980
10/86	G	12/22/86	25	Get Close	Sire 25488
				PRETTY POISON	
8/87	G	3/9/89	8	Catch Me (I'm Falling) Jade Starling/Whey Cooler • Kae Williams Jr./ Kurt Shore	Virgin 99416
				RAY PRICE **[see also Willie Nelson]**	
8/70	G	3/3/71	28	For The Good Times	Columbia 30106
8/72	G	12/28/82	165	Ray Price's All-Time Greatest Hits	Columbia 31364
				CHARLEY PRIDE	
10/71	G	3/8/72	21	Kiss An Angel Good Mornin' Ben Peters • Jack Clement	RCA 0550
10/66	G	1/9/75	—	Country	RCA 3645
12/67	G	6/14/73	199	The Country Way	RCA 3895
1/69	G	2/23/71	78	In Person	RCA 4094
6/69	G	6/14/73	44	The Sensational Charley Pride	RCA 4153
10/69	G	1/19/70	24	The Best Of Charley Pride	RCA 4223
2/70	G	2/23/71	22	Just Plain Charley	RCA 4290
7/70	G	2/23/71	30	Charley Pride's 10th Album	RCA 4367
1/71	G	6/14/73	42	From Me To You	RCA 4468
3/71	G	1/9/75	76	Did You Think To Pray	RCA 4513
11/71	G	2/15/72	38	Charley Pride Sings Heart Songs	RCA 4617
3/72	G	10/19/72	50	The Best Of Charley Pride, Volume 2	RCA 4682
				PRINCE **[* Prince & The Revolution]**	
8/79	G	3/18/80	11	I Wanna Be Your Lover Prince • Prince	Warner 49050
5/84	G P	7/24/84 8/21/84	1	**When Doves Cry*** Prince & The Revolution • Prince & The Revolution	Warner 29286

Release Date	Certification	Date of Certification	Chart Peak	ARTIST/Title Songwriter ● Producer (singles only)	Label & Number
7/84	G	11/7/84	1	**Let's Go Crazy*** Prince & The Revolution • Prince & The Revolution	Warner 29216
9/84	G	12/5/84	2	Purple Rain* Prince & The Revolution • Prince & The Revolution	Warner 29174
2/86	G	5/5/86	1	**Kiss*** Prince & The Revolution • Prince & The Revolution	Paisley Park 28751
5/89	G P	8/11/89 8/11/89	1	**Batdance** Prince • Prince	Warner 22924
10/79	G P	2/15/80 2/21/80	22	Prince	Warner 3366
10/80	G	6/20/84	45	Dirty Mind	Warner 3478
11/81	G P	1/14/82 1/11/85	21	Controversy	Warner 3601
11/82	G P 2P 3P	1/11/83 5/17/83 10/22/84 7/22/85	9	1999	Warner 23720
6/84	G P 8P 9P 10P	8/29/84 8/29/84 11/13/84 1/16/85 2/22/89	1	**Purple Rain*** [S]	Warner 25110
5/85	G P 2P	7/2/85 7/2/85 7/2/85	1	**Around The World In A Day***	Paisley Park 25286
3/86	G P	6/3/86 6/3/86	3	Parade [S]	Paisley Park 25395
3/87	G P	7/2/87 7/2/87	6	Sign O' The Times	Paisley Park 25577
5/88	G	12/5/88	11	Lovesexy	Paisley Park 25720
6/89	G P 2P	8/29/89 8/29/89 8/29/89	1	**Batman [S]**	Warner 25936
				PROCOL HARUM	
5/72	G	8/28/72	5	Live In Concert With The Edmonton Symphony Orchestra	A&M 4335
				RICHARD PRYOR	
7/75	G P	9/29/75 10/13/86	12	Is It Something I Said?	Reprise 2227
11/75	G	10/13/86	29	That Nigger's Crazy	Partee/Reprise 2404

Release Date	Certification	Date of Certification	Chart Peak	ARTIST/Title Songwriter ● Producer (singles only)	Label & Number
9/76	G	12/7/76	22	Bicentennial Nigger	Warner 2960
5/77	G P	3/14/80 5/13/86	68	Richard Pryor's Greatest Hits	Warner 3057
12/78	G	3/6/79	32	Wanted Live In Concert	Warner 3364
				PUBLIC ENEMY	
6/88	G P	9/26/88 8/22/89	42	It Takes A Nation Of Millions To Hold Us Back	Def Jam 44303
				GARY PUCKETT & THE UNION GAP	
9/67	G	2/8/68	4	Woman, Woman Jim Glaser/Jimmy Payne • Jerry Fuller	Columbia 44297
2/68	G	4/5/68	2	Young Girl Fuller • Fuller	Columbia 44450
5/68	G	7/18/68	2	Lady Willpower Fuller • Fuller	Columbia 44547
8/68	G	12/19/68	7	Over You Fuller • Fuller	Columbia 44644
4/68	G	3/25/69	21	Young Girl	Columbia 9664
6/70	G P	3/17/71 11/21/86	50	Gary Puckett & The Union Gap's Greatest Hits	Columbia 1042
				PURE PRAIRIE LEAGUE	
9/72	G	3/16/76	34	Bustin' Out	RCA 4769
				Q	
				QUARTERFLASH	
10/81	G P	2/5/82 6/29/82	8	Quarterflash	Geffen 2003
				SUZI QUATRO & CHRIS NORMAN	
1/79	G	6/7/79	4	Stumblin' In Mike Chapman/Nicky Chinn • Chapman	RSO 917
				QUEEN	
12/75	G	6/3/76	9	Bohemian Rhapsody Freddie Mercury • Roy Thomas Baker/Queen	Elektra 45297

Release Date	Certification	Date of Certification	Chart Peak	ARTIST/Title Songwriter ● Producer (singles only)	Label & Number
10/77	G P	1/25/78 4/25/78	4	We Are The Champions Mercury • Queen	Elektra 45441
12/79	G	5/12/80	1	**Crazy Little Thing Called Love** Mercury • Queen	Elektra 46579
8/80	G P	10/1/80 11/25/80	1	**Another One Bites The Dust** John Deacon • Queen/Mack	Elektra 47031
9/73	G	3/29/77	83	Queen	Elektra 75064
11/74	G	11/18/75	12	Sheer Heart Attack	Elektra 1026
12/75	G	3/9/76	4	A Night At The Opera	Elektra 1053
12/76	G	12/29/76	5	A Day At The Races	Elektra 101
11/77	G P	11/14/77 12/28/77	3	News Of The World	Elektra 112
11/78	G P	11/28/78 11/28/78	6	Jazz	Elektra 166
6/79	G	7/24/79	16	Live Killers	Elektra 702
7/80	G P	9/15/80 10/1/80	1	**The Game**	Elektra 513
10/81	G P	12/30/81 12/30/81	14	Greatest Hits	Elektra 564
5/82	G	7/12/82	22	Hot Space	Elektra 60128
2/84	G	4/24/84	23	The Works	Capitol 12322

QUEENSRYCHE

Release Date	Certification	Date of Certification	Chart Peak	ARTIST/Title	Label & Number
4/88	G	4/14/89	50	Operation: Mindcrime	EMI Manhattan 48640

? & THE MYSTERIANS

Release Date	Certification	Date of Certification	Chart Peak	ARTIST/Title	Label & Number
8/66	G	11/11/66	1	**96 Tears** Rudy Martinez	Cameo 428

QUIET RIOT

Release Date	Certification	Date of Certification	Chart Peak	ARTIST/Title	Label & Number
7/83	G	12/12/83	5	Cum On Feel The Noize Noddy Holder/Jimmy Lea • Spencer Proffer	Pasha 04005
2/83	G P 4P	9/12/83 10/11/83 11/24/86	1	**Metal Health**	Pasha 38443
7/84	G P	9/17/84 9/17/84	15	Condition Critical	Pasha 39516

Release Date	Certification	Date of Certification	Chart Peak	ARTIST/Title Songwriter ● Producer (singles only)	Label & Number
				# R	
				EDDIE RABBITT	
6/80	G	3/25/81	1	**Drivin' My Life Away** Eddie Rabbitt/Even Stevens/David Malloy • Malloy	Elektra 46656
10/80	G	3/10/81	5	I Love A Rainy Night Rabbitt/Stevens/Malloy • Malloy	Elektra 47066
10/79	G	10/24/80	151	The Best Of Eddie Rabbitt	Elektra 235
6/80	G P	10/24/80 2/23/81	19	Horizon	Elektra 276
8/81	G	10/5/81	23	Step By Step	Elektra 532
				GERRY RAFFERTY	
3/78	G	7/18/78	2	Baker Street Gerry Rafferty • Hugh Murphy/Rafferty	United Art. 1192
3/78	G P	5/26/78 6/20/78	1	**City To City**	United Art. 840
5/79	G	6/1/79	29	Night Owl	United Art. 958
				RAFFI	
11/84	G	5/23/89	—	Singable Songs For The Very Young	Shoreline 0202
				RAIDERS **[see Paul Revere & The Raiders]**	
				BONNIE RAITT	
9/72	G	12/3/85	138	Give It Up	Warner 2643
4/77	G	10/24/80	25	Sweet Forgiveness	Warner 2990
3/89	G	7/26/89	22	Nick Of Time	Capitol 91268
				JEAN-PIERRE RAMPAL/ **CLAUDE BOLLING**	
1/76	G	11/19/80	173	Suite For Flute And Jazz Piano	Columbia 33233

1

2

3

4

1. The brainchild of music publisher Don Kirshner, the Monkees were America's most successful pop group in the '60s. Proof? Half-a-dozen gold singles and five gold albums that decade.

2. Willie Nelson has friends. His tally of 22 gold and nine platinum albums (the most by any country music artist) includes projects with Waylon Jennings, Leon Russell, Kris Kristofferson, Ray Price, Jessi Colter, Julio Iglesias, Johnny Cash, and Tompall Glaser.

3. Mitch Miller's singalong stash of 11 gold albums puts him in the same certification league as Grand Funk Railroad and the Who, among others. Poetic justice?

4. Mtume's "Juicy Fruit" (a subtle piece of work) is one of the few gold singles which didn't reach the top 40 of *Billboard*'s pop charts. It did spend eight weeks at the R&B summit.

5

6

7

8

5. Boston's New Edition owe their rise to fame to producer Maurice Starr — the Don Kirshner of the '80s? — who has since delivered New Kids On The Block.

6. The first RIAA gold award for Warner Bros. Records came from comedian Bob Newhart, whose *Button-Down Mind* albums struck the nation's funny bone in 1960.

7. After Motley Crue's first album for Elektra *(Shout At The Devil)* sold a million, the band's debut *(Too Fast For Love)* was reissued. The result: more platinum.

8. Midnight Star's double-platinum *No Parking On The Dance Floor,* released in July 1983, is the largest-selling album in the history of Solar Records.

Release Date	Certification	Date of Certification	Chart Peak	ARTIST/Title Songwriter ● Producer (singles only)	Label & Number
				BOOTS RANDOLPH	
5/63	G	2/7/67	79	Boots Randolph's Yakety Sax	Monument 18002
12/66	G	2/18/69	36	Boots With Strings	Monument 18066
				THE RASCALS **[*The Young Rascals]**	
4/67	G	6/13/67	1	**Groovin'*** Felix Cavaliere/Eddie Brigati • The Rascals	Atlantic 2401
3/68	G	6/28/68	3	A Beautiful Morning Cavaliere/Brigati • The Rascals	Atlantic 2493
7/68	G	8/23/68	1	**People Got To Be Free** Cavaliere/Brigati • The Rascals	Atlantic 2537
4/66	G	9/4/68	15	The Young Rascals*	Atlantic 8123
12/66	G	7/29/68	14	Collections*	Atlantic 8134
7/67	G	7/22/68	5	Groovin'*	Atlantic 8148
7/68	G	9/4/68	1	**Time Peace/The Rascals' Greatest Hits**	Atlantic 8190
1/69	G	4/21/69	17	Freedom Suite	Atlantic 901
				RASPBERRIES	
6/72	G	11/6/72	5	Go All The Way Eric Carmen • Jimmy Ienner	Capitol 3348
				RATT	
2/84	G P 2P	6/27/84 8/6/84 12/13/84	7	Out Of The Cellar	Atlantic 80143
5/85	G P	7/31/85 7/31/85	7	Invasion Of Your Privacy	Atlantic 81257
9/86	G P	11/25/86 2/26/87	26	Dancin' Undercover	Atlantic 81683
10/88	G	1/10/89	17	Reach For The Sky	Atlantic 81929
				LOU RAWLS	
4/76	G	8/19/76	2	You'll Never Find Another Love Like Mine Kenny Gamble/Leon Huff • Gamble/Huff	Phil. Int. 3592
4/66	G	2/16/67	4	Lou Rawls Live!	Capitol 2459
8/66	G	4/24/69	7	Soulin'	Capitol 2566
5/76	G	8/23/76	7	All Things In Time	Phil. Int. 33957

Release Date	Certification	Date of Certification	Chart Peak	ARTIST/Title Songwriter ● Producer (singles only)	Label & Number
	P	1/25/77			
4/77	G	7/5/77	41	Unmistakably Lou	Phil. Int. 34488
11/77	G	2/14/78	41	When You Hear Lou, You've Heard It All	Phil. Int. 35036
				RAY, GOODMAN & BROWN	

10/79	G	5/13/80	5	Special Lady
				  Harry Ray/Al Goodman/Lee Walter •
				  Vincent Castellano
					Polydor 2033

1/80	G	4/2/80	17	Ray, Goodman & Brown	Polydor 6240
				RAYDIO **[see Ray Parker Jr.]**	
				CHRIS REA	
7/78	G	10/26/78	49	Whatever Happened To Benny Santini?	United Art. 879
				READY FOR THE WORLD	
5/85	G P	10/2/85 1/30/86	17	Ready For The World	MCA 5594
11/86	G	1/23/87	32	Long Time Coming	MCA 5829
				REDBONE	
10/73	G	4/22/74	5	Come And Get Your Love Lolly Vegas • Pat & Lolly Vegas	Epic 11035
				OTIS REDDING **[see also Jimi Hendrix]**	
1/68	G	3/11/68	1	**(Sittin' On) The Dock Of The Bay** Steve Cropper/Otis Redding • Cropper	Volt 157
				HELEN REDDY	
5/72	G	12/18/72	1	**I Am Woman** Helen Reddy/Ray Burton • Jay Senter	Capitol 3350
6/73	G	8/30/73	1	**Delta Dawn** Alex Harvey/Larry Collins • Tom Catalano	Capitol 3645
10/73	G	1/8/74	3	Leave Me Alone (Ruby Red Dress) Linda Laurie • Catalano	Capitol 3768
10/74	G	1/13/75	1	**Angie Baby** Alan O'Day • Joe Wissert	Capitol 3972

Release Date	Certification	Date of Certification	Chart Peak	ARTIST/Title Songwriter ● Producer (singles only)	Label & Number
5/71	G	11/27/74	100	I Don't Know How To Love Him	Capitol 762
11/72	G	3/7/73	14	I Am Woman	Capitol 11068
7/73	G	9/19/73	8	Long Hard Climb	Capitol 11213
3/74	G	6/6/74	11	Love Song For Jeffrey	Capitol 11284
10/74	G	12/18/74	8	Free And Easy	Capitol 11348
6/75	G	1/19/76	11	No Way To Treat A Lady	Capitol 11418
12/75	G	12/3/75	5	Helen Reddy's Greatest Hits	Capitol 11467
8/76	G	8/2/76	16	Music, Music	Capitol 11547
				JERRY REED	
9/70	G	3/29/71	8	Amos Moses Jerry Reed • Chet Atkins	RCA 9904
				LOU REED	
1/74	G	5/1/78	45	Rock 'n' Roll Animal	RCA 0472
				JIM REEVES	
7/64	G	7/20/66	9	The Best Of Jim Reeves	RCA 2890
5/66	G	2/26/68	21	Distant Drums	RCA 3542
				R.E.M.	
7/86	G	1/23/87	21	Lifes Rich Pageant	IRS 5783
8/87	G P	11/2/87 1/25/88	10	Document	IRS 42059
11/88	G P	1/10/89 2/14/89	12	Green	Warner 25795
				RENE & ANGELA	
6/85	G	7/15/86	64	Street Called Desire	Mercury 824607
				REO SPEEDWAGON	

11/80	G
	P
		3/16/81
		4/17/89
			1	**Keep On Loving You**
				   Kevin Cronin • Cronin/Gary Richrath/
				   Kevin Beamish
					Epic 50953

3/81	G	4/17/89	5	Take It On The Run Richrath • Cronin/Richrath/Beamish	Epic 01054

Release Date	Certification	Date of Certification	Chart Peak	ARTIST/Title Songwriter ● Producer (singles only)	Label & Number
12/84	G	4/17/89	1	**Can't Fight This Feeling** Cronin • Cronin/Richrath/Alan Gratzer	Epic 04713
10/72	G	8/13/81	—	R.E.O./T.W.O.	Epic 31745
11/73	G P	5/28/80 4/17/89	171	Ridin' The Storm Out	Epic 32378
7/77	G P	8/9/77 12/14/78	72	Live/You Get What You Play For	Epic 34494
4/78	G P	6/26/78 11/7/80	29	You Can Tune A Piano, But You Can't Tuna Fish	Epic 35082
8/79	G	12/5/79	33	Nine Lives	Epic 35988
3/80	G	2/6/81	55	A Decade Of Rock And Roll 1970 To 1980	Epic 36444
11/80	G P 7P	2/2/81 2/2/81 11/24/86	1	**Hi Infidelity**	Epic 36844
6/82	G P	9/21/82 10/1/82	7	Good Trouble	Epic 38100
10/84	G P	3/11/85 3/11/85	7	Wheels Are Turnin'	Epic 39593
2/87	G	8/11/87	28	Life As We Know It	Epic 40444
5/88	G	9/28/88	56	The Hits	Epic 44202
				RESTLESS HEART	
10/86	G	3/22/88	73	Wheels	RCA 5648
				PAUL REVERE & THE RAIDERS **[*The Raiders]**	
2/71	G	6/30/71	1	**Indian Reservation*** John D. Loudermilk • Mark Lindsay	Columbia 45332
1/66	G	1/6/67	5	Just Like Us!	Columbia 9251
5/66	G	3/20/67	9	Midnight Ride	Columbia 9308
11/66	G	4/17/67	9	The Spirit Of '67	Columbia 9395
4/67	G	8/25/67	15	Greatest Hits	Columbia 9462
				RANDY RHOADS **[see Ozzy Osbourne]**	

Release Date	Certification	Date of Certification	Chart Peak	ARTIST/Title Songwriter ● Producer (singles only)	Label & Number
				RHYTHM HERITAGE	
10/75	G	2/11/76	1	**Theme From "S.W.A.T."** Barry DeVorzon • Steve Barri/Michael Omartian	ABC 12135
				CHARLIE RICH	
1/73	G	9/4/73	15	Behind Closed Doors Kenny O'Dell • Billy Sherrill	Epic 10950
9/73	G	12/10/73	1	**The Most Beautiful Girl** Norro Wilson/Sherrill/Rory Bourke • Sherrill	Epic 11040
4/73	G P	11/27/73 11/21/86	8	Behind Closed Doors	Epic 32247
1/74	G	10/23/74	36	There Won't Be Anymore	RCA 0433
3/74	G	4/22/74	24	Very Special Love Songs	Epic 32531
				CLIFF RICHARD	
6/76	G	10/20/76	6	Devil Woman Christine Authors/Terry Britten • Bruce Welch	Rocket 40574
				KEITH RICHARDS	
9/88	G	6/20/89	24	Talk Is Cheap	Virgin 90973
				LIONEL RICHIE **[see also Diana Ross]**	
10/82	G	12/9/82	1	**Truly** Lionel Richie • Richie/James Anthony Carmichael	Motown 1644
9/83	G	12/12/83	1	**All Night Long (All Night)** Richie • Richie/Carmichael	Motown 1698
2/84	G	5/30/84	1	**Hello** Richie • Richie/Carmichael	Motown 1722
10/85	G	1/21/86	1	**Say You, Say Me** Richie • Richie/Carmichael	Motown 1819
10/82	G P 4P	12/9/82 12/9/82 10/19/84	3	Lionel Richie	Motown 6007
10/83	G P 8P 10P	12/12/83 12/12/83 10/19/84 12/19/85	1	**Can't Slow Down**	Motown 6059
8/86	G	10/16/86	1	**Dancing On The Ceiling**	Motown 6158

Release Date	Certification	Date of Certification	Chart Peak	ARTIST/Title Songwriter ● Producer (singles only)	Label & Number
	P 3P 4P	10/16/86 10/16/86 5/21/87			
				THE RIGHTEOUS BROTHERS	Verve 10383
2/66	G	5/9/66	1	**(You're My) Soul And Inspiration** Barry Mann/Cynthia Weil • Bill Medley	
4/66	G	11/28/66	7	Soul & Inspiration	Verve 5001
5/67	G	5/29/69	21	Greatest Hits	Verve 5020
				JEANNIE C. RILEY	Plantation 3
8/68	G	8/26/68	1	**Harper Valley P.T.A.** Tom T. Hall • Shelby Singleton	
9/68	G	12/20/68	12	Harper Valley P.T.A.	Plantation 1
				MINNIE RIPERTON	Epic 50057
12/74	G	4/8/75	1	**Lovin' You** Minnie Riperton/Richard Rudolph • Stevie Wonder	
5/74	G	3/21/75	4	Perfect Angel	Epic 32561
				JOHNNY RIVERS	United Art. 50960
9/72	G	1/29/73	6	Rockin' Pneumonia — Boogie Woogie Flu Huey P Smith/John Vincent • Johnny Rivers	
4/77	G	11/29/77	10	Swayin' To The Music (Slow Dancin') Jack Tempchin • Rivers	Big Tree 16094
9/66	G	3/6/75	29	Johnny Rivers' Golden Hits	Imperial 12324
6/68	G	9/29/69	5	Realization	Imperial 12372
6/69	G	3/6/75	26	A Touch Of Gold	Imperial 12427
				MARTY ROBBINS	Columbia 1349
11/59	G P	9/21/65 11/21/86	6	Gunfighter Ballads And Trail Songs	
8/72	G	12/28/82	—	Marty Robbins' All-Time Greatest Hits	Columbia 31361

Release Date	Certification	Date of Certification	Chart Peak	ARTIST/Title Songwriter ● Producer (singles only)	Label & Number
				ROBBIE ROBERTSON	
10/87	G	10/21/88	38	Robbie Robertson	Geffen 24160
				SMOKEY ROBINSON	
1/81	G	7/7/81	2	Being With You Smokey Robinson • George Tobin	Tamla 54321
2/81	G	7/7/81	10	Being With You	Tamla 375
2/87	G	9/8/87	26	One Heartbeat	Motown 6226
				ROCKWELL	
1/84	G	3/29/84	2	Somebody's Watching Me Rockwell • Curtis Anthony Nolen/Rockwell	Motown 1702
1/84	G	3/29/84	15	Somebody's Watching Me	Motown 6052
				TOMMY ROE	
5/62	G	3/25/69	1	**Sheila** Tommy Roe • Felton Jarvis	ABC 10329
1/66	G	3/25/69	8	Sweet Pea Roe • Steve Barri	ABC 10762
11/68	G	3/7/69	1	**Dizzy** Roe/Fred Weller • Barri	ABC 11164
11/69	G	1/19/70	8	Jam Up Jelly Tight Roe/Weller • Barri	ABC 11247
				ROGER	
9/81	G	11/20/81	26	The Many Facets of Roger	Warner 3594
11/87	G	2/9/88	35	Unlimited	Reprise 25496
				KENNY ROGERS **[*Kenny Rogers & The First Edition]**	
1/77	G	6/22/77	5	Lucille Roger Bowling/Hal Rynum • Larry Butler	United Art. 929
4/79	G	8/6/79	5	She Believes In Me Steve Gibb • Butler	United Art. 1273
11/79	G	3/7/80	3	Coward Of The County Bowling/Billy Edd Wheeler • Butler	United Art. 1327

Release Date	Certification	Date of Certification	Chart Peak	ARTIST/Title Songwriter ● Producer (singles only)	Label & Number
9/80	G	11/25/80	1	**Lady** Lionel Richie • Richie	United Art. 1380
1/71	G	3/27/73	57	Greatest Hits*	Reprise 6437
10/76	G	8/10/77	30	Kenny Rogers	United Art. 689
7/77	G	12/15/77	39	Daytime Friends	United Art. 754
1/78	G P	2/15/78 7/20/78	33	Ten Years Of Gold	United Art. 835
7/78	G	9/15/78	53	Love Or Something Like It	United Art. 903
11/78	G P	11/30/78 2/27/79	12	The Gambler	United Art. 934
9/79	G P	1/16/80 1/16/80	5	Kenny	United Art. 979
3/80	G P	5/28/80 5/28/80	12	Gideon	United Art. 1035
9/80	G P	12/2/80 12/2/80	1	**Kenny Rogers' Greatest Hits**	Liberty 1072
6/81	G P	8/28/81 8/28/81	6	Share Your Love	Liberty 1108
11/81	G P	1/5/82 1/5/82	34	Christmas	Liberty 51115
6/82	G	8/30/82	34	Love Will Turn You Around	Liberty 51124
2/83	G	4/14/83	18	We've Got Tonight	Liberty 51143
8/83	G P	10/31/83 10/31/83	6	Eyes That See In The Dark	RCA 4697
10/83	G P	12/21/83 12/21/83	22	Twenty Greatest Hits	Liberty 51152
9/84	G P	12/3/84 12/3/84	31	What About Me?	RCA 5043
10/85	G	12/5/85	51	The Heart Of The Matter	RCA 7023
				KENNY ROGERS & DOLLY PARTON	
8/83	G P	10/18/83 12/7/83	1	**Islands In The Stream** Barry, Maurice & Robin Gibb • Barry Gibb/Karl Richardson/Albhy Galuten	RCA 13615
10/84	G P*	12/3/84 12/3/84	31	Once Upon A Christmas	RCA 15307
				KENNY ROGERS & DOTTIE WEST	
4/79	G	7/2/79	82	Classics	United Art. 946

Release Date	Certification	Date of Certification	Chart Peak	ARTIST/Title Songwriter ● Producer (singles only)	Label & Number
				THE ROLLING STONES	
5/65	G	7/19/65	1	**(I Can't Get No) Satisfaction** Mick Jagger/Keith Richards • Andrew Loog Oldham	London 9766
1/67	G	5/1/67	1	**Ruby Tuesday** Jagger/Richards • Oldham	London 904
7/69	G	8/26/69	1	**Honky Tonk Women** Jagger/Richards • Jimmy Miller	London 910
9/73	G	11/15/73	1	**Angie** Jagger/Richards • Jimmy Miller	Rolling S. 19105
5/78	G	7/26/78	1	**Miss You** Jagger/Richards • The Glimmer Twins	Rolling S. 19307
7/65	G*	10/12/65	1	**Out Of Our Heads**	London 429
11/65	G	1/15/66	4	December's Children (And Everybody's)	London 451
3/66	G*	4/27/66	3	Big Hits (High Tide And Green Grass)	London 1
6/66	G*	8/9/66	2	Aftermath	London 476
11/66	G	1/19/67	6	Got Live If You Want It!	London 493
1/67	G	2/24/67	2	Between The Buttons	London 499
6/67	G	8/16/67	3	Flowers	London 509
11/67	G	12/6/67	2	Their Satanic Majesties Request	London 2
11/68	G*	12/23/68	5	Beggars Banquet	London 539
9/69	G*	9/9/69	2	Through The Past, Darkly (Big Hits Vol. 2)	London 3
11/69	G*	11/24/69	3	Let It Bleed	London 4
10/70	G*	11/2/70	6	Get Yer Ya-Ya's Out!	London 5
4/71	G	5/11/71	1	**Sticky Fingers**	Rolling S. 59100
12/71	G*	1/20/72	4	Hot Rocks 1964-1971	London 606/7
5/72	G	5/30/72	1	**Exile On Main St.**	Rolling S. 2900
12/72	G	1/17/73	9	More Hot Rocks (Big Hits And Fazed Cookies)	London 626/7
9/73	G	9/25/73	1	**Goats Head Soup**	Rolling S. 59101
10/74	G	10/31/74	1	**It's Only Rock 'N Roll**	Rolling S. 79101
6/75	G	8/7/75	6	Made In The Shade	Rolling S. 79102
4/76	G P	4/26/76 6/23/76	1	**Black And Blue**	Rolling S. 79104
10/77	G	10/4/77	5	Love You Live	Rolling S. 9001
6/78	G P 4P	6/12/78 6/22/78 10/30/84	1	**Some Girls**	Rolling S. 39108
7/80	G P	9/10/80 9/10/80	1	**Emotional Rescue**	Rolling S. 16015

Release Date	Certification	Date of Certification	Chart Peak	ARTIST/Title Songwriter ● Producer (singles only)	Label & Number
3/81	G	6/3/81	15	Sucking In The Seventies	Rolling S. 16028
8/81	G P 3P	10/30/81 10/30/81 10/30/84	1	**Tattoo You**	Rolling S. 16052
6/82	G	1/18/83	5	Still Life (American Concert 1981)	Rolling S. 39113
11/83	G P	1/4/84 1/4/84	4	Undercover	Rolling S. 90120
3/86	G P	6/10/86 6/10/86	4	Dirty Work	Rolling S. 40250
				THE ROMANTICS	
10/83	G	1/23/84	14	In Heat	Nemperor 38880
				LINDA RONSTADT **[see also Dolly Parton]**	
8/77	G	1/23/78	3	Blue Bayou Roy Orbison/Joe Melson • Peter Asher	Elektra 45431
9/73	G	8/25/75	45	Don't Cry Now	Asylum 5064
11/74	G	1/31/75	1	**Heart Like A Wheel**	Capitol 11358
9/75	G*	10/8/75	4	Prisoner In Disguise	Asylum 1045
8/76	G P	8/30/76 10/28/76	3	Hasten Down The Wind	Asylum 1072
12/76	G P*	12/8/76 1/19/77	6	Greatest Hits	Asylum 1092
5/77	G	11/13/78	46	A Retrospective	Capitol 11629
9/77	G P	9/19/77 10/12/77	1	**Simple Dreams**	Asylum 104
9/78	G P	9/22/78 9/22/78	1	**Living In The USA**	Asylum 155
2/80	G P	5/12/80 5/12/80	3	Mad Love	Asylum 510
10/80	G*	12/5/80	26	Greatest Hits, Volume 2	Asylum 516
9/82	G	11/23/82	31	Get Closer	Asylum 60185
9/83	G P 2P	11/17/83 12/14/83 10/30/84	3	What's New	Asylum 60260
11/84	G P	1/17/85 1/17/85	13	Lush Life	Asylum 60387
9/86	G	12/8/86	46	For Sentimental Reasons	Elektra 60474

Release Date	Certification	Date of Certification	Chart Peak	ARTIST/Title Songwriter ● Producer (singles only)	Label & Number
11/87	G	2/17/88	42	Canciones De Mi Padre	Elektra 60765
				ROSE ROYCE	
8/76	G P	12/21/76 2/22/77	1	**Car Wash** Norman Whitfield • Whitfield	MCA 40615
8/76	G	12/21/76	14	Car Wash [S]	MCA 6000
8/77	G P	10/4/77 12/6/77	9	Rose Royce II/In Full Bloom	Whitfield 3074
8/78	G	9/20/78	28	Rose Royce III/Strikes Again!	Whitfield 3227
				DAVID ROSE & HIS ORCHESTRA	
5/62	G	6/13/69	3	The Stripper And Other Fun Songs For The Family	MGM 4062
				DIANA ROSS	
6/80	G	12/16/81	1	Upside Down Nile Rodgers/Bernard Edwards • Rodgers/Edwards	Motown 1494
5/74	G	1/21/86	66	Anthology [DIANA ROSS & THE SUPREMES]	Motown 794
5/79	G	7/17/80	14	The Boss	Motown 923
5/80	G P	2/3/81 2/3/81	2	Diana	Motown 936
10/81	G	3/15/83	37	All The Great Hits	Motown 960
10/81	G P	1/22/82 1/22/82	15	Why Do Fools Fall In Love	RCA 4153
10/82	G	12/14/82	27	Silk Electric	RCA 4384
9/84	G	11/5/84	26	Swept Away	RCA 5009
				DIANA ROSS & LIONEL RICHIE	
7/81	G P	8/21/81 10/16/81	1	**Endless Love** Lionel Richie • Richie	Motown 1519
				ROSSINGTON COLLINS BAND	
6/80	G	8/19/80	13	Anytime, Anyplace, Anywhere	MCA 5130
				DAVID LEE ROTH	
1/85	G P	4/2/85 6/11/85	15	Crazy From The Heat	Warner 25222

Release Date	Certification	Date of Certification	Chart Peak	ARTIST/Title Songwriter ● Producer (singles only)	Label & Number
7/86	G P	9/9/86 9/9/86	4	Eat 'Em And Smile	Warner 25470
1/88	G P	3/29/88 3/29/88	6	Skyscraper	Warner 25671
				ROXETTE	
2/89	G	4/4/89	1	**The Look** Per Gessle • Clarence Ofwerman	EMI 50190
4/89	G	6/2/89	28	Look Sharp!	EMI 91098
				ROXY MUSIC	
5/82	G	12/5/86	53	Avalon	Warner 23686
				THE ROYAL GUARDSMEN	
12/66	G	1/12/67	2	Snoopy Vs. The Red Baron Phil Gernhard/Dick Holler • Gernhard	Laurie 3366
				RUFUS featuring Chaka Khan	
3/74	G	8/9/74	3	Tell Me Something Good Stevie Wonder • Bob Monaco/Rufus	ABC 11427
12/75	G	3/2/76	5	Sweet Thing Tony Maiden/Chaka Khan • Rufus	ABC 12149
3/74	G	9/5/74	4	Rags To Rufus	ABC 809
12/74	G	12/27/74	7	Rufusized	ABC 837
11/75	G	1/14/76	7	Rufus Featuring Chaka Khan	ABC 909
1/77	G P	1/27/77 4/13/77	12	Ask Rufus	ABC 975
1/78	G	2/24/78	14	Street Player	ABC 1049
11/79	G	3/11/80	14	Masterjam	MCA 5103
				RUN–D.M.C.	
5/84	G	12/17/84	53	Run-DMC	Profile 1202
1/85	G P	6/30/85 2/18/87	52	King Of Rock	Profile 1205
5/86	G P 2P	7/15/86 7/15/86 9/15/86	3	Raising Hell	Profile 1217

1

2

3

4

5

1. Peaches & Herb were among several acts for whom producer Freddie Perren spun gold. The others: Yvonne Elliman, Gloria Gaynor, David Naughton, the Sylvers, and Tavares.

2. All five O'Jays gold singles were produced by Philadelphia hotshots Kenny Gamble and Leon Huff, who also worked magic for Teddy Pendergrass, Joe Simon, Billy Paul, the Three Degrees, and the Jacksons, among others.

3. Four years before "Caribbean Queen" was crowned gold for Billy Ocean, he had a couple of songs recorded by La Toya Jackson. She'd like some more now, Bill.

4. Juice Newton tasted platinum three years before her first gold. The country-pop singer can be heard on Bob Welch's *French Kiss* album, a 1978 million-seller.

5. K.T. Oslin is one of country music's new wave of platinum stars. She wrote most of the songs on her debut album, *'80s Ladies,* which reached a million two years after release.

6. In gold and platinum, the Oak Ridge Boys are second to Alabama as country music's most popular group. But the Oaks have what their rivals don't: a gold single.

7. Olivia Newton-John has more gold 45s (11) than any other white female singer. She's runner-up to Aretha Franklin (14) and Donna Summer (12) but leads both of them in gold albums.

8. After 15 years of country recordings, Dolly Parton turned to pop songsmiths Barry Mann and Cynthia Weil ("Here You Come Again") and gained her first gold.

9. As lead vocalist for Harold Melvin & The Blue Notes, Teddy Pendergrass reached a million hearts and minds with "If You Don't Know Me By Now." Sixteen years later, the song went gold again, for Simply Red.

10. The son of a baker, classical music giant Luciano Pavarotti was inspired to follow a singing career by seeing Mario Lanza in *The Great Caruso.*

Release Date	Certification	Date of Certification	Chart Peak	ARTIST/Title Songwriter ● Producer (singles only)	Label & Number
5/88	3P G P	4/24/87 7/19/88 7/19/88	9	Tougher Than Leather	Profile 1265
				TODD RUNDGREN	
2/72	G	2/26/75	29	Something/Anything?	Bearsville 2066
				RUSH	
3/76	G P	11/16/77 2/25/81	61	2112	Mercury 1079
10/76	G P	11/16/77 3/4/81	40	All The World's A Stage	Mercury 7508
8/77	G	11/16/77	33	A Farewell To Kings	Mercury 1184
10/78	G	12/14/78	47	Hemispheres	Mercury 3743
1/80	G P	3/17/80 11/9/87	4	Permanent Waves	Mercury 4001
1/81	G P 2P	4/13/81 4/27/81 10/12/84	3	Moving Pictures	Mercury 4013
10/81	G P	1/5/82 11/9/87	10	Exit…Stage Left	Mercury 7001
9/82	G P	11/10/82 11/10/82	10	Signals	Mercury 4063
4/84	G P	6/26/84 6/26/84	10	Grace Under Pressure	Mercury 818476
10/85	G P	12/18/85 1/27/86	10	Power Windows	Mercury 826098
9/87	G	11/9/87	13	Hold Your Fire	Mercury 832464
1/89	G	3/9/89	21	A Show Of Hands	Mercury 836346
				LEON RUSSELL **[see also Willie Nelson]**	
5/71	G	2/3/72	17	Leon Russell & The Shelter People	Shelter 8903
7/72	G	9/19/72	2	Carney	Shelter 8911
6/73	G	6/26/73	9	Leon Live	Shelter 8917
4/75	G	3/9/76	30	Will O' The Wisp	Shelter 2138
10/76	G	12/29/76	40	Best Of Leon	Shelter 52004

Release Date	Certification	Date of Certification	Chart Peak	ARTIST/Title Songwriter ● Producer (singles only)	Label & Number
				S	
				SADE	
1/85	G P	5/6/85 5/6/85	5	Diamond Life	Portrait 39581
11/85	G P 2P	1/27/86 1/27/86 3/12/86	1	**Promise**	Portrait 40263
4/88	G P	8/5/88 8/5/88	7	Stronger Than Pride	Epic 44210
				STAFF SGT. BARRY SADLER	
1/66	G	2/17/66	1	**The Ballad Of The Green Berets** Barry Sadler/Robin Moore • Andy Wiswell	RCA 8739
2/66	G	2/17/66	1	**Ballads Of The Green Berets**	RCA 3547
				SAGA	
10/82	G	7/11/83	29	Worlds Apart	Portrait 38246
				SALT-N-PEPA	
11/87	G	3/23/88	19	Push It Hurvy "Luv Bug" Azor • Azor	Next Plateau 315
12/86	G P	1/8/88 3/23/88	26	Hot, Cool & Vicious	Next Plateau 1007
7/88	G	12/1/88	38	A Salt With A Deadly Pepa	Next Plateau 1011
				SAM & DAVE	
8/67	G	11/22/67	2	Soul Man Isaac Hayes/David Porter • Hayes/Porter	Stax 231
				SAM THE SHAM & THE PHARAOHS	
2/65	G	8/5/65	2	Wooly Bully Sam Samudio • Stan Kesler	MGM 13322
5/66	G	8/11/66	2	Lil' Red Riding Hood Ronald Blackwell • Kesler	MGM 13506

Release Date	Certification	Date of Certification	Chart Peak	ARTIST/Title Songwriter ● Producer (singles only)	Label & Number
				SAN SEBASTIAN STRINGS/ROD McKUEN	
4/67	G	12/30/68	52	The Sea	Warner 1670
				DAVID SANBORN [see also Bob James]	
1/87	G	1/14/88	74	A Change Of Heart	Warner 25479
6/88	G	8/29/89	59	Close-Up	Reprise 25715
				THE SANDPIPERS	
9/66	G	2/7/68	13	Guantanamera	A&M 4117
				SAMANTHA SANG	

11/77	G
	P
		2/9/78
		4/21/78
			3	Emotion
				    Barry & Robin Gibb ● Barry Gibb/
				    Albhy Galuten/Karl Richardson
					Private S. 178

2/78	G	3/28/78	29	Emotion	Private S. 7009
				SANTA ESMERALDA	
10/77	G	6/8/78	25	Don't Let Me Be Misunderstood	Casablanca 7080
				SANTANA [see also Mahavishnu John McLaughlin]	
8/69	G P 2P	12/2/69 11/21/86 11/21/86	4	Santana	Columbia 9781
10/70	G P 4P	10/20/70 11/21/86 11/21/86	1	**Abraxas**	Columbia 30130
10/71	G P 2P	10/5/71 11/21/86 11/21/86	1	**Santana III**	Columbia 30595
11/72	G P	11/9/72 11/21/86	8	Caravanserai	Columbia 31610
11/73	G	11/29/73	25	Welcome	Columbia 32445
7/74	G P	10/3/74 11/21/86	17	Santana's Greatest Hits	Columbia 33050
10/74	G	8/9/89	20	Borboletta	Columbia 33135

Release Date	Certification	Date of Certification	Chart Peak	ARTIST/Title Songwriter ● Producer (singles only)	Label & Number
3/76	G	6/11/76	10	Amigos	Columbia 33576
1/77	G	4/26/77	27	Festival	Columbia 34423
10/77	G	12/1/77	10	Moonflower	Columbia 34914
10/78	G	10/27/78	27	Inner Secrets	Columbia 35600
3/81	G	6/22/81	9	Zebop!	Columbia 37158
				CARLOS SANTANA & BUDDY MILES	
7/72	G P	8/8/72 11/21/86	8	Carlos Santana & Buddy Miles! Live!	Columbia 31308
				JOE SATRIANI	
10/87	G	2/17/89	29	Surfing With The Alien	Relativity 8193
				LEO SAYER	
10/76	G	12/28/76	1	**You Make Me Feel Like Dancing** Leo Sayer/Vini Poncia • Richard Perry	Warner 8283
2/77	G	5/10/77	1	**When I Need You** Carole Bayer Sager/Albert Hammond • Perry	Warner 8332
9/80	G	12/24/80	2	More Than I Can Say Sonny Curtis/Jerry Allison • Alan Tarney	Warner 49565
11/76	G P	4/26/77 9/19/77	10	Endless Flight	Warner 2962
				BOZ SCAGGS	
6/76	G	10/29/76	3	Lowdown Boz Scaggs/David Paich • Joe Wissert	Columbia 10367
2/76	G P 4P	7/16/76 9/22/76 10/26/84	2	Silk Degrees	Columbia 33920
11/77	G P	11/17/77 12/9/77	11	Down Two Then Left	Columbia 34729
4/80	G P	6/4/80 2/6/81	8	Middle Man	Columbia 36106
11/80	G	2/2/81	24	Hits!	Columbia 36841
				SCANDAL featuring PATTY SMYTH	
7/84	G P	9/17/84 4/16/85	17	Warrior	Columbia 39173

Release Date	Certification	Date of Certification	Chart Peak	ARTIST/Title Songwriter ● Producer (singles only)	Label & Number
				JOEY SCARBURY	
4/81	G	8/11/81	2	Theme From "Greatest American Hero" Mike Post/Stephen Geyer • Post	Elektra 47147
				SCORPIONS	
6/79	G	5/28/86	55	Lovedrive	Mercury 3795
5/80	G	3/8/84	52	Animal Magnetism	Mercury 3825
3/82	G P	6/24/82 3/8/84	10	Blackout	Mercury 4039
2/84	G P 2P	4/30/84 4/30/84 10/25/84	6	Love At First Sting	Mercury 814 981
6/85	G P	8/19/85 9/4/86	14	World Wide Live	Mercury 824 344
4/88	G P	6/20/88 6/20/88	5	Savage Amusement	Mercury 832 963
				TOM SCOTT & THE L.A. EXPRESS **[see Joni Mitchell]**	
				SEALS & CROFTS	
7/72	G	12/14/72	7	Summer Breeze	Warner 2629
4/73	G	6/25/73	4	Diamond Girl	Warner 2699
2/74	G	3/12/74	14	Unborn Child	Warner 2761
3/75	G	9/29/75	30	I'll Play For You	Warner 2848
10/75	G P 2P	12/5/75 10/13/86 10/13/86	11	Greatest Hits	Warner 2886
4/76	G	8/25/76	37	Get Closer	Warner 2907
				DAN SEALS	
8/85	G	2/5/87	59	Won't Be Blue Anymore	EMI America 17166
				JOHN SEBASTIAN	
3/76	G	5/19/76	1	**Welcome Back** John Sebastian • Sebastian/Steve Barri	Reprise 1349

Release Date	Certification	Date of Certification	Chart Peak	ARTIST/Title Songwriter ● Producer (singles only)	Label & Number
				NEIL SEDAKA	
9/75	G	11/25/75	1	**Bad Blood** Neil Sedaka/Phil Cody • Sedaka/Robert Appere	Rocket 40460
11/74	G	11/11/75	23	Sedaka's Back	Rocket 463
9/75	G	12/18/75	16	The Hungry Years	Rocket 2157
				THE SEEKERS	
10/66	G	8/14/67	2	Georgy Girl Tom Springfield/Jim Dale • W.H. Miller	Capitol 5756
				BOB SEGER & THE SILVER BULLET BAND	
3/75	G P	4/17/89 5/10/89	131	Beautiful Loser	Capitol 11378
4/76	G P	12/22/76 12/16/77	34	'Live' Bullet	Capitol 11523
10/76	G P	1/25/77 3/25/77	8	Night Moves	Capitol 11557
5/78	G P	5/30/78 5/30/78	4	Stranger In Town	Capitol 11698
2/80	G P	4/29/80 4/29/80	1	**Against The Wind**	Capitol 12041
9/81	G P	11/4/81 11/4/81	3	Nine Tonight	Capitol 12182
12/82	G P	2/11/83 2/11/83	5	The Distance	Capitol 12254
3/86	G P	5/28/86 5/28/86	3	Like A Rock	Capitol 12398
				THE SEX PISTOLS	
11/77	G	12/2/87	106	Never Mind The Bollocks, Here's The Sex Pistols	Warner 3147
				SHA NA NA	
3/73	G	11/1/73	38	The Golden Age Of Rock 'N' Roll	Kama Sutra 2073
				SHALAMAR	
8/79	G	2/7/80	8	The Second Time Around Leon Sylvers/William Shelby • Sylvers/Dick Griffey	Solar 11709

Release Date	Certification	Date of Certification	Chart Peak	ARTIST/Title Songwriter ● Producer (singles only)	Label & Number
9/79	G	4/7/80	23	Big Fun	Solar 3479
12/80	G	4/27/81	40	Three For Love	Solar 3577
1/82	G	6/16/82	35	Friends	Solar 28
				SHANNON	

10/83	G	6/7/84	8	Let The Music Play
				    Chris Barbosa/Ed Chisholm • Mark Liggett/
				    Barbosa/Rod Hui
					Mirage 99810

1/84	G	6/11/84	32	Let The Music Play	Mirage 90134
				ROBERT SHAW CHORALE	
11/57	G	8/19/64	5	Christmas Hymns And Carols	RCA 2139
				SHEILA E.	
6/84	G	1/10/85	28	The Glamorous Life	Warner 25107
8/85	G	1/28/86	50	Romance 1600	Paisley Park 25317
				SHERIFF	
11/88	G	3/15/89	1	**When I'm With You** Arnold Lanni • Stacy Heydon	Capitol 44302
				ALLAN SHERMAN	
10/62	G	12/10/62	1	**My Son, The Folk Singer**	Warner 1475
				BOBBY SHERMAN	
5/69	G	10/7/69	3	Little Woman Daniel Janssen • Jackie Mills	Metromedia 121
11/69	G	1/20/70	9	La La La (If I Had You) Janssen • Mills	Metromedia 150
1/70	G	4/2/70	9	Easy Come, Easy Go Jack Keller/Diane Hilderbrand • Mills	Metromedia 177
7/70	G	9/3/70	5	Julie, Do Ya Love Me Tom Bahler • Mills	Metromedia 194
10/69	G	2/10/70	11	Bobby Sherman	Metromedia 1014
3/70	G	7/8/70	10	Here Comes Bobby	Metromedia 1028

Release Date	Certification	Date of Certification	Chart Peak	ARTIST/Title Songwriter ● Producer (singles only)	Label & Number
10/70	G	10/30/70	20	With Love, Bobby (The Scrapbook Album)	Metromedia 1032
				SHOCKING BLUE	
11/69	G	1/28/70	1	**Venus** Robbie Van Leeuwen • Van Leeuwen	Colossus 108
				SILVER CONVENTION	
9/75	G	12/2/75	1	**Fly, Robin, Fly** Silvester Levay/Stephan Prager • Michael Kunze	Midland Int. 10339
2/76	G	6/7/76	2	Get Up And Boogie Levay/Prager • Kunze	Midland Int. 10571
7/75	G	12/10/75	10	Save Me	Midland Int. 1129
				HARRY SIMEONE CHORALE	
12/61	G	3/10/69	119	Sing We Now Of Christmas [a/k/a The Little Drummer Boy]	20th Century 3002
				GENE SIMMONS	
9/78	G P	10/2/78 10/2/78	22	Gene Simmons	Casablanca 7120
				RICHARD SIMMONS	
5/82	G P	7/12/82 7/12/82	44	Reach	Elektra 60122
				SIMON & GARFUNKEL	
9/65	G	2/14/66	1	**The Sounds Of Silence** Paul Simon • Tom Wilson	Columbia 43396
4/68	G	6/10/68	1	**Mrs. Robinson** Simon • Roy Halee/Simon & Garfunkel	Columbia 44511
1/70	G	2/27/70	1	**Bridge Over Troubled Water** Simon • Halee/Simon & Garfunkel	Columbia 45079
3/70	G	6/12/70	4	Cecilia Simon • Halee/Simon & Garfunkel	Columbia 45133
10/64	G	3/4/69	30	Wednesday Morning, 3 AM	Columbia 9049
1/66	G	8/25/67	21	Sounds Of Silence	Columbia 9269
9/66	G P 3P	7/6/67 11/21/86 11/21/86	4	Parsley, Sage, Rosemary And Thyme	Columbia 9363

Release Date	Certification	Date of Certification	Chart Peak	ARTIST/Title Songwriter ● Producer (singles only)	Label & Number
2/68	G	3/27/68	1	**The Graduate [S]**	Columbia 3180
3/68	G P 2P	4/18/68 11/21/86 11/21/86	1	**Bookends**	Columbia 9529
2/70	G P 5P	2/9/70 11/21/86 11/21/86	1	**Bridge Over Troubled Water**	Columbia 9914
6/72	G P 5P	7/6/72 11/21/86 11/21/86	5	Simon & Garfunkel's Greatest Hits	Columbia 31350
2/82	G P	5/12/82 5/13/86	6	The Concert In Central Park	Warner 3654
				CARLY SIMON	
11/72	G	1/8/73	1	**You're So Vain** Carly Simon • Richard Perry	Elektra 45824
7/77	G	11/9/77	2	Nobody Does It Better Carole Bayer Sager/Marvin Hamlisch • Perry	Elektra 45413
7/80	G	12/5/80	11	Jesse Simon/Mike Mainieri • Mainieri	Warner 49518
11/71	G	9/5/73	30	Anticipation	Elektra 75016
12/72	G	12/8/72	1	**No Secrets**	Elektra 75049
1/74	G	1/22/74	3	Hotcakes	Elektra 1002
11/75	G	12/18/75	17	The Best Of Carly Simon	Elektra 1048
4/78	G P	5/15/78 8/7/78	10	Boys In The Trees	Elektra 128
3/87	G P	8/19/87 2/1/88	25	Coming Around Again	Arista 8443
				CARLY SIMON & JAMES TAYLOR	
1/74	G	5/14/74	5	Mockingbird Inez & Charlie Foxx • Richard Perry	Elektra 45880
				JOE SIMON	
2/69	G	6/16/69	13	The Chokin' Kind Harlan Howard • John Richbourg	Sound Stage 7 2628
10/71	G	1/6/72	11	Drowning In The Sea Of Love Kenny Gamble/Leon Huff • Gamble/Huff	Spring 120
6/72	G	8/29/72	11	Power Of Love Gamble/Huff/Joe Simon • Gamble/Huff	Spring 128

Release Date	Certification	Date of Certification	Chart Peak	ARTIST/Title Songwriter ● Producer (singles only)	Label & Number
				PAUL SIMON	
7/73	G	10/9/73	2	Loves Me Like A Rock Paul Simon • Simon/Phil Ramone	Columbia 45907
12/75	G	3/11/76	1	**50 Ways To Leave Your Lover** Simon • Simon/Ramone	Columbia 10270
2/72	G P	3/1/72 11/21/86	4	Paul Simon	Columbia 30750
5/73	G P	6/15/73 11/21/86	2	There Goes Rhymin' Simon	Columbia 32280
2/74	G	6/11/74	33	Paul Simon In Concert/Live Rhymin'	Columbia 32855
10/75	G	11/17/75	1	**Still Crazy After All These Years**	Columbia 33540
11/77	G P	11/17/77 2/1/78	18	Greatest Hits, Etc.	Columbia 35032
8/80	G	10/14/80	12	One-Trick Pony [S]	Warner 3472
8/86	G P 2P 3P	10/29/86 12/22/86 5/5/87 1/14/88	3	Graceland	Warner 25447
				SIMPLE MINDS	
10/85	G	1/31/86	10	Once Upon A Time	A&M 5092
				SIMPLY RED	
4/89	G	7/19/89	1	**If You Don't Know Me By Now** Kenny Gamble/Leon Huff • Stewart Levine	Elektra 69297
10/85	G	7/22/86	16	Picture Book	Elektra 60452
2/89	G	6/28/89	22	A New Flame	Elektra 60828
				FRANK SINATRA	
3/56	G	6/21/62	2	Songs For Swingin' Lovers!	Capitol 653
11/56	G	11/7/62	8	This Is Sinatra!	Capitol 768
9/57	G	5/20/80	18	A Jolly Christmas From Frank Sinatra [a/k/a The Sinatra Christmas Album]	Capitol 894
9/58	G	6/21/62	1	**Frank Sinatra Sings For Only The Lonely**	Capitol 1053
2/59	G	6/22/61	2	Come Dance With Me!	Capitol 1069
7/60	G	6/21/62	1	**Nice 'n' Easy**	Capitol 1417
9/63	G	11/15/65	8	Sinatra's Sinatra	Reprise 1010

Release Date	Certification	Date of Certification	Chart Peak	ARTIST/Title Songwriter ● Producer (singles only)	Label & Number
8/65	G	2/6/66	5	September Of My Years	Reprise 1014
11/65	G	2/6/66	9	A Man And His Music	Reprise 1016
5/66	G*	8/16/66	1	**Strangers In The Night**	Reprise 1017
8/66	G	11/27/67	9	Sinatra At The Sands	Reprise 1019
12/66	G	2/7/67	6	That's Life	Reprise 1020
7/68	G P	11/19/70 10/13/86	55	Frank Sinatra's Greatest Hits!	Reprise 1025
11/68	G	12/12/69	18	Cycles	Reprise 1027
4/69	G	3/12/70	11	My Way	Reprise 1029
10/73	G	11/17/76	13	Ol' Blue Eyes Is Back	Reprise 2155
3/80	G	10/21/81	17	Trilogy: Past, Present, Future	Reprise 2300
				NANCY SINATRA	
12/65	G	2/25/66	1	**These Boots Are Made For Walkin'** Lee Hazlewood • Hazlewood	Reprise 0432
10/66	G	4/3/67	5	Sugar Town Hazlewood • Hazlewood	Reprise 0527
2/66	G	11/7/66	5	Boots	Reprise 6202
				NANCY & FRANK SINATRA	
3/67	G	4/19/67	1	**Somethin' Stupid** C. Carson Parks • Jimmy Bowen/Lee Hazlewood	Reprise 0561
				NANCY SINATRA & LEE HAZLEWOOD	
3/68	G	11/19/70	13	Nancy & Lee	Reprise 6273
				THE SINGING NUN	
10/63	G	12/17/63	1	**The Singing Nun**	Philips 203
				SIR MIX-A-LOT	
2/88	G	2/21/89	82	Swass	Nastymix 70123
				SISTER SLEDGE	
4/79	G	6/18/79	2	We Are Family Nile Rodgers/Bernard Edwards • Rodgers/Edwards	Cotillion 44251

Release Date	Certification	Date of Certification	Chart Peak	ARTIST/Title Songwriter ● Producer (singles only)	Label & Number
1/79	G P	4/10/79 5/23/79	3	We Are Family	Cotillion 5209
				RICKY SKAGGS	
3/82	G	3/7/83	77	Waitin' For The Sun To Shine	Epic 37193
9/82	G	10/3/83	61	Highways & Heartaches	Epic 37996
10/83	G	10/5/84	—	Don't Cheat In Our Hometown	Sugar Hill/ Epic 38954
				SKID ROW	
1/89	G P*	3/29/89 7/11/89	7	Skid Row	Atlantic 81936
				SKYY	
11/81	G	3/4/82	18	Skyy Line	Salsoul 8548
				SLAVE	
2/77	G	6/14/77	22	Slave	Cotillion 9914
10/80	G	3/30/81	53	Stone Jam	Cotillion 5224
				PERCY SLEDGE	
3/66	G	7/15/66	1	**When A Man Loves A Woman** Calvin Lewis/Andrew Wright • Quin Ivy/ Marlin Greene	Atlantic 2326
				SLICK RICK	
12/88	G*	4/17/89	31	The Great Adventures Of Slick Rick	Def Jam 40513
				SLY & THE FAMILY STONE	
11/68	G	2/13/69	1	**Everyday People** Sylvester Stewart [a/k/a Sly Stone] • Stone	Epic 10407
12/69	G	2/9/70	1	**Thank You (Falettinme Be Mice Elf Again)** Stone • Stone	Epic 10555
10/71	G	11/30/71	1	**Family Affair** Stone • Stone	Epic 10805
6/73	G	9/12/73	12	If You Want Me To Stay Stone • Stone	Epic 11017
4/69	G	12/4/69	13	Stand!	Epic 26456

1

2

3

4

5

1. Peter, Paul & Mary provided John Denver with his first gold disc, as writer of ''Leaving On A Jet Plane.'' The record's producer, Milt Okun, later masterminded all six of Denver's million-selling singles.

2. Charley Pride was money in the bank during the first half of the '70s, with 11 consecutive gold albums. No other country star matched that performance until Willie Nelson's gold deposits hit a consecutive 12 in the '80s.

3. Pink Floyd's *The Wall* is Columbia Records' largest-selling album by a British group. It's certified at 7 million copies, and was released in November 1979.

4. The Pointer Sisters have good reason to thank producer Richard Perry: they're the only girl group with a triple-platinum album. *Break Out* was released on Perry's own Planet Records.

5. Simply stated, the man from Memphis has the most gold albums (32) in recording industry history and more gold singles (17) than any other solo performer. As if numbers do justice to Elvis' stature in rock & roll...

6

7

8

9

6. Tom Petty enjoyed twin platinum albums in 1989, one for his sans-Heartbreakers *Full Moon Fever* and the other for his Traveling Wilburys excursion.

7. The fourth R.E.M. album, *Lifes Rich Pageant,* was the Atlanta band's first to go gold. Platinum followed more easily with *Document* and *Green.*

8. The provocative sleeve of Poison's *Open Up And Say...Aah!* did not arrest the album's ascent to four million in sales.

9. Richard Pryor is second to Bill Cosby in the gold album comedy stakes: his five to Dr. Huxtable's nine. Eddie Murphy's score is three, but he does have a gold single for consolation.

10. No movie soundtrack of original music has sold more than Prince's *Purple Rain,* at 10 million copies. He did rather well, too, with a little thing called *Batman.*

10

Release Date	Certification	Date of Certification	Chart Peak	ARTIST/Title Songwriter ● Producer (singles only)	Label & Number
	P	11/21/86			
10/70	G	11/16/70	2	Greatest Hits	Epic 30325
	P	11/21/86			
	3P	11/21/86			
10/71	G	11/8/71	1	**There's A Riot Goin' On**	Epic 30986
6/73	G	8/17/73	7	Fresh	Epic 32134
7/74	G	11/8/74	15	Small Talk	Epic 32930
				FRANKIE SMITH	
10/80	G	6/19/81	—	Double Dutch Bus [12-inch single] Frankie Smith/Bill Bloom • Smith/Bloom	WMOT 5351
2/81	G	9/22/81	30	Double Dutch Bus [7-inch single] Frankie Smith/Bill Bloom • Smith/Bloom	WMOT 5356
				O.C. SMITH	
8/68	G	11/1/68	2	Little Green Apples Bobby Russell • Jerry Fuller	Columbia 44616
				REX SMITH	
2/79	G	7/20/79	10	You Take My Breath Away Stephen Lawrence/Bobby Hart • Charles Calello/Lawrence	Columbia 10908
3/79	G	5/29/79	19	Sooner Or Later	Columbia 35813
				SAMMI SMITH	
11/70	G	4/26/71	8	Help Me Make It Through The Night Kris Kristofferson • Jim Malloy	Mega 0015
				THE SMOTHERS BROTHERS	
10/61	G	11/13/68	45	The Songs And Comedy Of The Smothers Brothers!	Mercury 20611
9/62	G	2/22/67	26	The Two Sides Of The Smothers Brothers	Mercury 20675
3/63	G	8/16/66	27	The Funny Side Of The Smothers Brothers (Think Ethnic!)	Mercury 20777
				PHOEBE SNOW	
7/74	G	4/9/75	4	Phoebe Snow	Shelter 2109
1/76	G	7/9/76	13	Second Childhood	Columbia 33952

Release Date	Certification	Date of Certification	Chart Peak	ARTIST/Title Songwriter ● Producer (singles only)	Label & Number
				SONNY & CHER	
6/65	G	9/17/65	1	**I Got You Babe** Sonny Bono • Bono	Atco 6359
8/65	G	9/30/65	2	Look At Us	Atco 177
9/71	G	7/27/72	35	Sonny & Cher Live	Kapp 3654
2/72	G	5/6/72	14	All I Ever Need Is You	Kapp 3660
				THE S.O.S. BAND	
3/80	G P	6/20/80 9/29/80	3	Take Your Time (Do It Right) Harold Clayton/Sigidi Abdallah • Abdallah	Tabu 5522
6/80	G	8/11/80	12	S.O.S.	Tabu 36332
7/83	G	1/16/84	47	On The Rise	Tabu 38697
4/86	G	4/6/87	44	Sands Of Time	Tabu 40279
				DAVID SOUL	
12/76	G	4/6/77	1	**Don't Give Up On Us** Tony Macauley • Macauley	Private S. 129
				SOUL II SOUL	
5/89	G	7/11/89	11	Keep On Movin' Beresford Romeo • Jazzie B./Nellee Hooper	Virgin 99205
6/89	G*	8/10/89	14	Keep On Movin'	Virgin 91267
				SOUTHER, HILLMAN, FURAY BAND	
7/74	G	9/23/74	11	The Souther, Hillman, Furay Band	Asylum 1006
				RED SOVINE	
6/76	G	11/16/76	40	Teddy Bear Red Sovine/Billy Joe Burnette/Dale Royal/ Tommy Hill • Hill	Starday 142
				SPINNERS **[see also Dionne Warwick]**	
7/72	G	10/30/72	3	I'll Be Around Thom Bell/Phil Hurtt • Bell	Atlantic 2904

Release Date	Certification	Date of Certification	Chart Peak	ARTIST/Title Songwriter ● Producer (singles only)	Label & Number
12/72	G	2/13/73	4	Could It Be I'm Falling In Love Melvin & Mervin Steals • Bell	Atlantic 2927
4/73	G	7/13/73	11	One Of A Kind (Love Affair) Joseph Jefferson • Bell	Atlantic 2962
7/75	G	11/14/75	5	They Just Can't Stop It (The Games People Play) Jefferson/Bruce Hawes/Charles Simmons • Bell	Atlantic 3284
8/76	G	12/8/76	2	The Rubberband Man Bell/Linda Creed • Bell	Atlantic 3355
11/79	G	4/10/80	2	Working My Way Back To You Sandy Linzer/Denny Randell • Michael Zager	Atlantic 3637
4/73	G	7/13/73	14	Spinners	Atlantic 7256
2/74	G	5/21/74	16	Mighty Love	Atlantic 7296
11/74	G	12/18/74	9	New And Improved	Atlantic 18118
7/75	G	9/18/75	8	Pick Of The Litter	Atlantic 18141
7/76	G	10/12/76	25	Happiness Is Being With The Detroit Spinners	Atlantic 18181
				SPIRIT	
12/70	G	6/18/76	63	Twelve Dreams Of Dr. Sardonicus	Epic 30267
				RICK SPRINGFIELD	
3/81	G	8/4/81	1	**Jessie's Girl** Rick Springfield • Keith Olsen	RCA 12201
1/81	G P	8/4/81 12/2/81	7	Working Class Dog	RCA 3697
3/82	G P	5/11/82 5/11/82	2	Success Hasn't Spoiled Me Yet	RCA 4125
4/83	G P	6/15/83 9/30/83	12	Living In Oz	RCA 4660
3/84	G P	7/10/84 7/10/84	16	Hard To Hold [S]	RCA 4935
4/85	G	6/13/85	21	Tao	RCA 5370
				BRUCE SPRINGSTEEN	
1/73	G	11/21/78	60	Greetings From Asbury Park, N.J.	Columbia 31903
11/73	G	5/2/77	59	The Wild, The Innocent & The E Street Shuffle	Columbia 32432
9/75	G	10/8/75	3	Born To Run	Columbia 33795

Release Date	Certification	Date of Certification	Chart Peak	ARTIST/Title Songwriter ● Producer (singles only)	Label & Number
	P 3P	11/21/86 11/21/86			
6/78	G P 2P	6/16/78 6/27/78 7/6/89	5	Darkness On The Edge Of Town	Columbia 35318
10/80	G P	12/12/80 12/12/80	1	**The River**	Columbia 36854
9/82	G P	12/19/82 7/6/89	3	Nebraska	Columbia 38358
6/84	G P 3P 6P 7P 8P 10P 11P	8/7/84 8/7/84 10/19/84 5/6/85 7/8/85 9/11/85 11/1/85 8/9/89	1	**Born In The U.S.A.**	Columbia 38653
11/86	G P 3P	2/2/87 2/2/87 2/2/87	1	**Live 1975-1985**	Columbia 40558
10/87	G P 2P 3P	12/31/87 12/31/87 12/31/87 4/19/88	1	**Tunnel Of Love**	Columbia 40999
				SPYRO GYRA	
3/79	G P	9/19/79 6/1/87	27	Morning Dance	Infinity 9004
3/80	G	6/5/85	19	Catching The Sun	MCA 5108
10/80	G	6/1/87	49	Carnaval	MCA 5149
				SQUEEZE	
11/82	G	1/26/88	47	Singles—45's And Under	A&M 4922
				BILLY SQUIER	
4/81	G P	7/23/81 9/18/81	5	Don't Say No	Capitol 12146
7/82	G P	9/21/82 10/26/82	5	Emotions In Motion	Capitol 12217
7/84	G P	10/1/84 10/1/84	11	Signs Of Life	Capitol 12361

Release Date	Certification	Date of Certification	Chart Peak	ARTIST/Title Songwriter ● Producer (singles only)	Label & Number
				JIM STAFFORD	
10/73	G	3/6/74	3	Spiders And Snakes Jim Stafford/David Bellamy • Phil Gernhard/Lobo	MGM 14648
				PAUL STANLEY	
9/78	G P	10/2/78 10/2/78	40	Paul Stanley	Casablanca 7123
				THE STAPLE SINGERS	

10/73	G	12/19/73	9	If You're Ready (Come Go With Me)
				  Homer Banks/Carl Hampton/Raymond Jackson •
				  Al Bell
					Stax 0179

9/75	G	11/24/75	1	**Let's Do It Again** Curtis Mayfield • Mayfield	Curtom 0109
				STARLAND VOCAL BAND	
3/76	G	7/15/76	1	**Afternoon Delight** Bill Danoff • Milt Okun	Windsong 10588
				STARPOINT	
7/85	G	7/1/86	60	Restless	Elektra 60424
				RINGO STARR	
4/71	G	8/3/71	4	It Don't Come Easy Ringo Starr • George Harrison	Apple 1831
9/73	G	12/28/73	1	**Photograph** Starr/Harrison • Richard Perry	Apple 1865
12/73	G	1/31/74	1	**You're Sixteen** Richard & Robert Sherman • Perry	Apple 1870
11/73	G	11/8/73	2	Ringo	Apple 3413
11/74	G	12/9/74	8	Goodnight Vienna	Apple 3417
				STARS ON...	
4/81	G	7/2/81	1	**Stars On 45** Various • Jaap Eggermont	Radio 3810
5/81	G	7/2/81	9	Stars On Long Play	Radio 16044

Release Date	Certification	Date of Certification	Chart Peak	ARTIST/Title Songwriter ● Producer (singles only)	Label & Number
				STARSHIP [see Jefferson Starship]	
				THE STATLER BROTHERS	
7/75	G	3/10/77	121	The Best Of The Statler Bros.	Mercury 1037
4/78	G	12/19/78	155	Entertainers…On And Off The Record	Mercury 5007
10/78	G	10/20/82	183	The Statler Brothers Christmas Card	Mercury 5012
4/79	G	6/26/81	183	The Originals	Mercury 5016
12/79	G	2/25/81	153	The Best Of The Statler Bros. Rides Again, Volume II	Mercury 5024
				STEAM	
9/69	G	12/8/69	1	Na Na Hey Hey Kiss Him Goodbye Gary De Carlo/Dale Frashuer/Paul Leka • Leka	Fontana 1667
				STEELY DAN	
10/72	G	5/31/73	17	Can't Buy A Thrill	ABC 758
7/73	G	3/2/78	35	Countdown To Ecstasy	ABC 779
3/74	G	5/14/74	8	Pretzel Logic	ABC 808
3/75	G	5/12/75	13	Katy Lied	ABC 846
5/76	G	9/15/76	15	The Royal Scam	ABC 931
9/77	G P	10/4/77 12/27/77	3	Aja	ABC 1006
11/78	G P	12/7/78 12/7/78	30	Greatest Hits	ABC 1107
11/80	G P	1/22/81 1/22/81	9	Gaucho	MCA 6102
				STEPPENWOLF	
5/68	G	9/19/68	2	Born To Be Wild Mars Bonfire • Gabriel Mekler	Dunhill 4138
9/68	G	3/25/69	3	Magic Carpet Ride John Kay/Rushton Moreve • Mekler	Dunhill 4161
2/68	G	11/27/68	6	Steppenwolf	Dunhill 50029
9/68	G	2/12/69	3	The Second	Dunhill 50037
10/69	G	3/18/70	17	Monster	Dunhill 50066
4/70	G	7/14/70	7	Live	Dunhill 50075
11/70	G	4/12/71	19	Steppenwolf 7	Dunhill 50090

Release Date	Certification	Date of Certification	Chart Peak	ARTIST/Title Songwriter ● Producer (singles only)	Label & Number
2/71	G	4/12/71	24	Steppenwolf Gold/Their Great Hits	Dunhill 50099
2/73	G	12/4/86	152	16 Greatest Hits	Dunhill 50135
				CAT STEVENS	
7/70	G	1/15/76	164	Mona Bone Jakon	A&M 4260
11/70	G	5/12/71	8	Tea For The Tillerman	A&M 4280
10/71	G	10/18/71	2	Teaser And The Firecat	A&M 4313
10/72	G	10/12/72	1	**Catch Bull At Four**	A&M 4365
8/73	G	8/1/73	3	Foreigner	A&M 4391
4/74	G	4/8/74	2	Buddha And The Chocolate Box	A&M 3623
6/75	G	8/15/75	6	Greatest Hits	A&M 4519
11/75	G	1/15/76	13	Numbers	A&M 4555
5/77	G	6/13/77	7	Izitso	A&M 4702
				RAY STEVENS	
3/69	G	6/16/69	8	Gitarzan Ray Stevens/Bill Everette • Fred Foster/ Stevens/Jim Malloy	Monument 1131
3/70	G	6/26/70	1	**Everything Is Beautiful** Stevens • Stevens	Barnaby 2011
4/74	G	8/24/74	1	**The Streak** Stevens • Stevens	Barnaby 600
11/84	G	2/26/87	118	He Thinks He's Ray Stevens	MCA 5517
9/85	G	7/9/89	—	I Have Returned	MCA 5635
				STEVIE B.	
2/89	G	8/16/89	75	In My Eyes	LMR 5531
				AL STEWART	
10/76	G P	1/14/77 3/24/77	5	Year Of The Cat	Janus 7022
9/78	G P	10/25/78 3/16/79	10	Time Passages	Arista 4190
				AMII STEWART	
12/78	G P	3/22/79 8/1/79	1	**Knock On Wood** Eddie Floyd/Steve Cropper • Barry Leng	Ariola 7736

Release Date	Certification	Date of Certification	Chart Peak	ARTIST/Title Songwriter ● Producer (singles only)	Label & Number
2/79	G	2/26/79	19	Knock On Wood	Ariola 50054
				ROD STEWART	
7/71	G	10/1/71	1	**Maggie May** Rod Stewart/Martin Quittenton • Stewart	Mercury 73224
9/76	G	11/30/76	1	**Tonight's The Night** Stewart • Tom Dowd	Warner 8262
10/77	G	2/8/78	4	You're In My Heart Stewart • Dowd	Warner 8475
12/78	G P	1/30/79 2/21/79	1	**Do Ya Think I'm Sexy** Stewart/Carmine Appice • Dowd	Warner 8724
5/71	G	8/2/71	1	**Every Picture Tells A Story**	Mercury 609
7/72	G	7/28/72	2	Never A Dull Moment	Mercury 646
6/73	G	10/12/73	31	Sing It Again Rod	Mercury 680
8/75	G	12/19/75	9	Atlantic Crossing	Warner 2875
5/76	G	5/25/78	90	The Best Of Rod Stewart	Mercury 7507
7/76	G P 2P	10/20/76 11/23/76 10/22/84	2	A Night On The Town	Warner 2938
11/77	G P 3P	11/22/77 12/20/77 10/22/84	2	Foot Loose & Fancy Free	Warner 3092
12/78	G P 3P	12/13/78 12/27/78 10/22/84	1	**Blondes Have More Fun**	Warner 3261
11/79	G P	2/26/80 2/26/80	22	Greatest Hits	Warner 3373
11/80	G P	1/14/81 3/4/81	12	Foolish Behaviour	Warner 3485
11/81	G P	1/7/82 1/28/82	11	Tonight I'm Yours	Warner 3602
6/84	G	8/21/84	18	Camouflage	Warner 25095
5/88	G P	8/9/88 12/6/88	20	Out Of Order	Warner 25684
				STEPHEN STILLS **[see also Mike Bloomfield]**	
11/70	G	11/24/70	3	Stephen Stills	Atlantic 7202
7/71	G	8/26/71	8	Stephen Stills 2	Atlantic 7206
4/72	G	5/30/72	4	Manassas	Atlantic 903

Release Date	Certification	Date of Certification	Chart Peak	ARTIST/Title Songwriter ● Producer (singles only)	Label & Number
				STILLS-YOUNG BAND	
9/76	G	1/12/77	26	Long May You Run	Reprise 2253
				STING	
6/85	G P 2P	8/28/85 8/28/85 2/3/86	2	The Dream Of The Blue Turtles	A&M 3750
10/87	G P	12/15/87 12/15/87	9	…Nothing Like The Sun	A&M 6402
				STOP THE VIOLENCE MOVEMENT	
1/89	G	8/2/89	—	Self-Destruction Various • D-Nice/Lawrence Parker	Jive 1178
				STORIES	
5/73	G	8/22/73	1	**Brother Louie** Errol Brown/Tony Wilson • Kenny Kerner/ Richie Wise	Kama Sutra 577
				GEORGE STRAIT	
9/81	G	4/19/88	—	Strait Country	MCA 5248
6/82	G	2/26/87	—	Strait From The Heart	MCA 5320
10/83	G	11/16/84	163	Right Or Wrong	MCA 5450
10/84	G	4/8/85	139	Does Fort Worth Ever Cross Your Mind	MCA 5518
3/85	G P	11/22/85 2/26/87	157	Greatest Hits	MCA 5567
9/85	G	2/4/86	—	Something Special	MCA 5605
5/86	G	9/18/86	126	#7	MCA 5750
1/87	G P	3/16/87 12/1/87	117	Ocean Front Property	MCA 5913
9/87	G P	11/16/87 6/23/88	68	Greatest Hits Volume Two	MCA 42035
2/88	G	4/22/88	87	If You Ain't Lovin' (You Ain't Livin')	MCA 42114
2/89	G	4/24/89	92	Beyond The Blue Neon	MCA 42266
				STRAWBERRY ALARM CLOCK	
7/67	G	12/19/67	1	**Incense And Peppermints** John Carter/Tim Gilbert • Frank Slay/Bill Holmes	Uni 55018

Release Date	Certification	Date of Certification	Chart Peak	ARTIST/Title Songwriter ● Producer (singles only)	Label & Number
				STRAY CATS	
6/82	G P	11/5/82 12/1/82	2	Built For Speed	EMI America 17070
8/83	G	10/19/83	14	Rant 'n' Rave With The Stray Cats	EMI America 17102
				BARBRA STREISAND	
10/73	G	2/6/74	1	**The Way We Were** Marvin Hamlisch/Alan & Marilyn Bergman • Marty Paich	Columbia 45944
11/76	G	3/31/77	1	**Evergreen (Love Theme From "A Star Is Born")** Barbra Streisand/Paul Williams • Streisand/ Phil Ramone	Columbia 10450
6/79	G	8/30/79	3	The Main Event Paul Jabara/Bruce Roberts/Bob Esty • Esty	Columbia 11008
8/80	G	11/7/80	1	**Woman In Love** Barry & Robin Gibb • Barry Gibb/Albhy Galuten/Karl Richardson	Columbia 11364
2/63	G	10/16/64	8	The Barbra Streisand Album	Columbia 8807
8/63	G	5/12/64	2	The Second Barbra Streisand Album	Columbia 8854
2/64	G	2/11/65	5	The Third Album	Columbia 8954
4/64	G	9/21/64	2	Funny Girl	Capitol 2059
9/64	G	3/23/65	1	**People**	Columbia 9015
5/65	G	12/2/65	2	My Name Is Barbra	Columbia 9136
10/65	G P	1/4/66 11/21/86	2	My Name Is Barbra, Two…	Columbia 9209
3/66	G	4/20/66	3	Color Me Barbra	Columbia 9278
10/67	G P 2P*	1/21/76 11/21/86 11/21/86	108	A Christmas Album	Columbia 9557
8/68	G P	12/23/68 11/21/86	12	Funny Girl [S]	Columbia 3220
2/70	G P 2P	5/4/71 11/21/86 11/21/86	32	Barbra Streisand's Greatest Hits	Columbia 9968
2/71	G P	4/28/71 11/21/86	10	Stoney End	Columbia 30378
9/71	G	12/6/71	11	Barbra Joan Streisand	Columbia 30792
11/72	G P	2/13/73 11/21/86	19	Live Concert At The Forum	Columbia 31760
2/74	G P	2/26/74 11/21/86	1	**The Way We Were**	Columbia 32801

Release Date	Certification	Date of Certification	Chart Peak	ARTIST/Title Songwriter ● Producer (singles only)	Label & Number
11/74	G	1/6/75	13	Butterfly	Columbia 33095
2/75	G	9/8/75	6	Funny Lady [S]	Arista 9004
10/75	G	4/14/76	12	Lazy Afternoon	Columbia 33815
6/77	G P	6/22/77 8/9/77	3	Streisand Superman	Columbia 34830
5/78	G P	5/31/78 8/25/78	12	Songbird	Columbia 35375
11/78	G P 4P	11/16/78 11/16/78 10/26/84	1	**Barbra Streisand's Greatest Hits, Volume 2**	Columbia 35679
6/79	G	9/12/79	20	The Main Event [S]	Columbia 36115
10/79	G P	2/22/80 2/22/80	7	Wet	Columbia 36258
9/80	G P 4P 5P	11/19/80 11/19/80 10/26/84 8/9/89	1	**Guilty**	Columbia 36750
11/81	G P 2P 3P	1/29/82 1/29/82 10/26/84 8/9/89	10	Memories	Columbia 37678
11/83	G P	1/9/84 1/9/84	9	Yentl [S]	Columbia 39152
10/84	G P	12/18/84 12/18/84	19	Emotion	Columbia 39480
11/85	G P 2P 3P	1/13/86 1/13/86 1/13/86 4/14/86	1	**The Broadway Album**	Columbia 40092
4/87	G P	8/11/87 2/8/88	9	One Voice	Columbia 40788
10/88	G P	12/21/88 12/21/88	10	Till I Loved You	Columbia 40880
				BARBRA STREISAND & NEIL DIAMOND	
10/78	G	11/16/78	1	**You Don't Bring Me Flowers** Neil Diamond/Alan & Marilyn Bergman • Bob Gaudio	Columbia 10840
				BARBRA STREISAND & BARRY GIBB	
10/80	G	3/3/81	3	Guilty Barry, Maurice & Robin Gibb • Charles Koppelman	Columbia 11390

Release Date	Certification	Date of Certification	Chart Peak	ARTIST/Title Songwriter ● Producer (singles only)	Label & Number
				BARBRA STREISAND & KRIS KRISTOFFERSON	
11/76	G P 4P	12/23/76 1/21/77 10/26/84	1	A Star Is Born [S]	Columbia 34403
				BARBRA STREISAND & DONNA SUMMER	
10/79	G	2/11/80	1	No More Tears (Enough Is Enough) Paul Jabara/Bruce Roberts • Gary Klein/ Giorgio Moroder	Columbia 11125/ Casablanca 20199
				STRYPER	
5/86	G	4/6/88	149	Soldiers Under Command	Enigma 73217
10/86	G P	2/19/87 1/6/88	32	To Hell With The Devil	Enigma 73237
6/88	G	9/15/88	32	In God We Trust	Enigma 73317
				THE STYLISTICS	
10/71	G	1/3/72	9	You Are Everything Thom Bell/Linda Creed • Bell	Avco 4581
2/72	G	4/17/72	3	Betcha By Golly, Wow Bell/Creed • Bell	Avco 4591
9/72	G	12/13/72	10	I'm Stone In Love With You Bell/Creed/Anthony Bell • Bell	Avco 4603
1/73	G	4/6/73	5	Break Up To Make Up Bell/Creed/Kenny Gamble • Bell	Avco 4611
2/74	G	5/22/74	2	You Make Me Feel Brand New Bell/Creed • Bell	Avco 4634
12/71	G	2/16/73	23	The Stylistics	Avco 33023
10/72	G	6/14/73	32	Round 2	Avco 11006
5/74	G	8/12/74	14	Let's Put It All Together	Avco 69001
				STYX	
9/79	G	1/28/80	1	Babe Dennis DeYoung • Styx	A&M 2188
1/83	G	5/16/83	3	Mr. Roboto DeYoung • Styx	A&M 2525
7/73	G	5/1/75	20	Styx II	Wooden N. 1012

1. "Special Lady" is a second golden moment for Harry Ray, Al Goodman & Billy Brown. They acquired gold in 1970 with "Love On A Two-Way Street" as...the Moments.

2. Eddie Rabbitt was one of the biggest stars of the "urban cowboy" era, with a pair of gold singles, three gold albums, and one platinum LP. Not bad for a good ol' boy from Brooklyn.

3. When you're hot, you're hot. Jerry Reed was in 1970, with the self-composed "Amos Moses," which grabbed a Grammy as well as a gold disc.

4. With 18 gold and 11 platinum albums, Kenny Rogers is the king of country music — always assuming you agree that he sings country.

5. The Rolling Stones have accumulated more gold albums (28) than any other group, but fewer platinum (6) than many — and their multi-platinum peak is only 4 million. Their bank managers are not worried.

1

2

3

4

5

6

7

8

9

6. Epic Records' biggest-selling album of the '80s by a group was REO Speedwagon's *Hi Infidelity.* It was issued in November 1980, and has since sold 7 million.

7. Grammy voters like country music that goes gold: they selected Charlie Rich's million-selling "Behind Closed Doors" as the best country song of 1972.

8. Helen Reddy gave songwriter Alan O'Day his first gold hit in 1974 by recording "Angie Baby." A couple of years later, O'Day sang his own way to a million with "Undercover Angel."

9. Smokey Robinson's gold 45, "Being With You," was the work of producer George Tobin, who was also responsible for Robert John's "Sad Eyes" million-seller and, yes, Tiffany's multi-platinum first album.

Release Date	Certification	Date of Certification	Chart Peak	ARTIST/Title Songwriter ● Producer (singles only)	Label & Number
11/75	G	8/25/77	58	Equinox	A&M 4559
10/76	G	11/10/78	66	Crystal Ball	A&M 4604
7/77	G P 3P	10/19/77 12/22/77 11/14/84	6	The Grand Illusion	A&M 4637
9/78	G P 3P	10/10/78 10/10/78 11/14/84	6	Pieces Of Eight	A&M 4724
10/79	G P 2P	2/5/80 2/5/80 11/14/84	2	Cornerstone	A&M 3711
5/80	G	7/31/84	—	Best Of Styx	RCA 3597
1/81	G P 3P	3/19/81 3/19/81 11/14/84	1	**Paradise Theater**	A&M 3719
2/83	G P	4/29/83 4/29/83	3	Kilroy Was Here	A&M 3734

DONNA SUMMER
[see also Barbra Streisand]

Release Date	Certification	Date of Certification	Chart Peak	ARTIST/Title Songwriter ● Producer (singles only)	Label & Number
11/75	G	2/19/76	2	Love To Love You Baby Donna Summer/Giorgio Moroder/Pete Bellotte ● Bellotte	Oasis 401
7/77	G	11/9/77	6	I Feel Love Summer/Moroder/Bellotte ● Moroder/Bellotte	Casablanca 884
4/78	G	7/19/78	3	Last Dance Paul Jabara ● Moroder	Casablanca 926
9/78	G	10/26/78	1	**MacArthur Park** Jim Webb ● Moroder/Bellotte	Casablanca 939
12/79	G	3/5/79	4	Heaven Knows Summer/Moroder/Bellotte ● Moroder/Bellotte	Casablanca 959
4/79	G P	4/20/79 8/1/79	1	**Hot Stuff** Bellotte/Harold Faltermeyer/Keith Forsey ● Moroder/Bellotte	Casablanca 978
5/79	G P	6/19/79 9/4/79	1	**Bad Girls** Summer/Bruce Sudano/Joe Esposito/Eddie Hokenson ● Moroder/Bellotte	Casablanca 988
8/79	G	12/11/79	2	Dim All The Lights Summer ● Moroder/Bellotte	Casablanca 2201
1/80	G	3/11/80	5	On The Radio Summer/Moroder ● Moroder	Casablanca 2236
9/80	G	12/2/80	3	The Wanderer Summer/Moroder ● Moroder/Bellotte	Geffen 49563

Release Date	Certification	Date of Certification	Chart Peak	ARTIST/Title Songwriter ● Producer (singles only)	Label & Number
4/89	G	7/11/89	7	This Time I Know It's For Real Summer/Mike Stock/Matt Aitken/Pete Waterman • Stock/Aitken/Waterman	Atlantic 88899
9/75	G	1/19/76	11	Love To Love You Baby	Oasis 5003
3/76	G	6/29/76	21	A Love Trilogy	Oasis 5004
10/76	G	11/11/76	29	Four Seasons Of Love	Casablanca 7038
5/77	G	7/13/77	18	I Remember Yesterday	Casablanca 7056
11/77	G	12/9/77	26	Once Upon A Time…	Casablanca 7078
9/78	G P	9/14/78 10/19/78	1	**Live And More**	Casablanca 7119
5/79	G P	5/3/79 5/3/79	1	**Bad Girls**	Casablanca 7150
10/79	G P	2/21/80 2/21/80	1	**On The Radio/Greatest Hits Volumes I & II**	Casablanca 7191
10/80	G	12/12/80	13	The Wanderer	Geffen 2000
7/82	G	9/21/82	20	Donna Summer	Geffen 2005
6/83	G	8/30/83	9	She Works Hard For The Money	Mercury 812 265
				SUN	
2/78	G	10/5/78	69	Sunburn	Capitol 11723
				SUPERTRAMP	
10/74	G	8/2/77	38	Crime Of The Century	A&M 3647
4/77	G	7/13/77	16	Even In The Quietest Moments…	A&M 4634
3/79	G P 4P	4/9/79 5/8/79 11/14/84	1	**Breakfast In America**	A&M 3708
9/80	G	12/10/80	8	Paris	A&M 6702
10/82	G	1/5/83	5	…Famous Last Words…	A&M 3732
				AL B. SURE!	
4/88	G P	6/28/88 8/16/88	20	In Effect Mode	Warner 25662
				SURFACE	
10/88	G	6/13/89	57	Second Wave	Columbia 44284

Release Date	Certification	Date of Certification	Chart Peak	ARTIST/Title Songwriter ● Producer (singles only)	Label & Number
				SURVIVOR	
5/82	G P	7/26/82 8/23/82	1	**Eye Of The Tiger** Jim Peterik/Frankie Sullivan • Peterik/Sullivan	Scotti 02912
5/82	G P	8/9/82 9/21/82	2	Eye Of The Tiger	Scotti 38062
9/84	G P	3/11/85 6/24/85	16	Vital Signs	Scotti 39578
				BILLY SWAN	
9/74	G	12/2/74	1	**I Can Help** Billy Swan • Swan/Chip Young	Monument 8621
				KEITH SWEAT	
10/87	G	6/13/89	5	I Want Her Keith Sweat/Teddy Riley • Sweat	Vintertn. 69431
11/87	G P 2P	3/11/88 5/9/88 11/15/88	15	Make It Last Forever	Vintertn. 60763
				SWEET	
8/72	G	4/25/73	3	Little Willy Nicky Chinn/Mike Chapman • Phil Wainman	Bell 45251
10/75	G	2/23/76	5	Fox On The Run Sweet • Sweet	Capitol 4157
5/75	G	5/25/76	25	Desolation Boulevard	Capitol 11395
				SWING OUT SISTER	
7/87	G	4/22/88	40	It's Better To Travel	Mercury 832 213
				THE SYLVERS	
11/75	G	4/20/76	1	**Boogie Fever** Freddie Perren/Keni St. Lewis • Perren	Capitol 4179
9/76	G	1/3/77	5	Hot Line Perren/St. Lewis • Perren	Capitol 4336
				SYLVESTER	
7/78	G	2/13/79	28	Step II	Fantasy 9556

Release Date	Certification	Date of Certification	Chart Peak	ARTIST/Title Songwriter ● Producer (singles only)	Label & Number
				SYLVIA	
2/73	G	5/21/73	3	Pillow Talk Sylvia Robinson/Michael Burton • Robinson/Burton	Vibration 521
				SYLVIA	
5/82	G	12/21/82	15	Nobody Kye Fleming/Dennis Morgan • Tom Collins	RCA 13223
5/82	G	2/15/83	56	Just Sylvia	RCA 4312
				T	
				TACO	
6/83	G	11/8/83	4	Puttin' On The Ritz Irving Berlin • David Parker	RCA 13574
				TAKE 6	
3/88	G	7/11/89	71	Take 6	Reprise 25670
				TALKING HEADS	
7/78	G	11/16/83	29	More Songs About Buildings And Food	Sire 6058
8/79	G	9/17/85	21	Fear Of Music	Sire 6076
10/80	G	9/17/85	19	Remain In Light	Sire 6095
6/83	G P	9/20/83 12/15/86	15	Speaking In Tongues	Sire 23883
10/84	G P	3/1/85 7/2/86	41	Stop Making Sense [S]	Sire 25121
6/85	G P	8/20/85 11/13/85	20	Little Creatures	Sire 25305
9/86	G	11/18/86	17	True Stories [S]	Sire 25512
3/88	G	5/17/88	19	Naked	Fly/Sire 25654
				A TASTE OF HONEY	

4/78	G
	P
		8/8/78
		10/10/78
			1	**Boogie Oogie Oogie**
				    Janice Marie Johnson/Perry Kibble • Fonce
				    & Larry Mizell
					Capitol 4565

1/81	G	7/17/81	3	Sukiyaki Hachidai Nakamura/Rokusuke Ei • George Duke	Capitol 4953

Release Date	Certification	Date of Certification	Chart Peak	ARTIST/Title Songwriter ● Producer (singles only)	Label & Number
5/78	G P	8/2/78 10/4/78	6	A Taste Of Honey	Capitol 11754
				TAVARES	
5/76	G	9/22/76	15	Heaven Must Be Missing An Angel Freddie Perren/Keni St. Lewis • Perren	Capitol 4270
				JAMES TAYLOR **[see also Carly Simon]**	
5/71	G	9/13/71	1	**You've Got A Friend** Carole King • Peter Asher	Warner 7498
2/70	G P 3P	10/16/70 10/13/86 10/13/86	3	Sweet Baby James	Warner 1843
3/71	G P	4/30/71 10/13/86	2	Mud Slide Slim And The Blue Horizon	Warner 2561
12/72	G	12/18/72	4	One Man Dog	Warner 2660
5/75	G	9/12/75	6	Gorilla	Warner 2866
6/76	G	10/19/76	16	In The Pocket	Warner 2912
10/76	G P 2P 3P	12/22/76 11/21/77 10/22/84 6/1/89	23	Greatest Hits	Warner 2979
6/77	G P 2P	7/5/77 9/1/77 7/6/89	4	JT	Columbia 34811
5/79	G	5/15/79	10	Flag	Columbia 36058
3/81	G	5/5/81	10	Dad Loves His Work	Columbia 37009
10/85	G	12/23/85	34	That's Why I'm Here	Columbia 40052
1/88	G	4/11/88	25	Never Die Young	Columbia 40851
				JOHNNIE TAYLOR	
10/68	G	11/15/68	5	Who's Making Love Homer Banks/Bettye Crutcher/Don Davis/ Raymond Jackson • Davis	Stax 0009
5/73	G	10/23/73	11	I Believe In You Davis • Davis	Stax 0161
1/76	G P	3/11/76 4/22/76	1	**Disco Lady** Davis/Harvey Scales/Al Vance • Davis	Columbia 10281

Release Date	Certification	Date of Certification	Chart Peak	ARTIST/Title Songwriter ● Producer (singles only)	Label & Number
2/76	G	4/5/76	5	Eargasm	Columbia 33951
				TEARS FOR FEARS	
6/85	G	5/9/89	1	**Shout** Roland Orzabal/Ian Stanley • Chris Hughes	Mercury 880 294
3/85	G P 2P 3P 4P	5/16/85 6/25/85 8/29/85 10/24/85 1/27/86	1	**Songs From The Big Chair**	Mercury 824 300
				10cc	
12/76	G	4/18/77	5	The Things We Do For Love Eric Stewart/Graham Gouldman • 10cc	Mercury 73875
				10,000 MANIACS	
7/87	G P	7/7/88 8/10/89	37	In My Tribe	Elektra 60738
5/89	G	7/11/89	13	Blind Man's Zoo	Elektra 60815
				TEN YEARS AFTER	
8/71	G P	12/9/71 11/21/86	17	A Space In Time	Columbia 30801
				TESLA	
11/86	G*	9/15/87	32	Mechanical Resonance	Geffen 24120
2/89	G	4/11/89	18	The Great Radio Controversy	Geffen 24224
				JOE TEX	
10/68	G	1/26/68	10	Skinny Legs And All Joe Tex • Buddy Killen	Dial 4063
12/71	G	3/22/72	2	I Gotcha Tex • Killen	Dial 1010
1/77	G	6/9/77	12	Ain't Gonna Bump No More Buddy McGinty/Killen • Killen	Epic 50313
				THIN LIZZY	
3/76	G	10/22/77	18	Jailbreak	Mercury 1081

Release Date	Certification	Date of Certification	Chart Peak	ARTIST/Title Songwriter ● Producer (singles only)	Label & Number
				.38 SPECIAL	
2/81	G P	6/10/81 2/24/82	18	Wild-Eyed Southern Boys	A&M 4835
5/82	G P	7/2/82 2/4/83	10	Special Forces	A&M 4888
11/83	G P	1/31/84 5/21/84	22	Tour De Force	A&M 4971
4/86	G	7/7/86	17	Strength In Numbers	A&M 5115
7/87	G	4/24/89	35	Flashback	A&M 3910
				B.J. THOMAS	
10/68	G	2/24/69	5	Hooked On A Feeling Mark James • Chips Moman	Scepter 12230
10/69	G	12/23/69	1	**Raindrops Keep Fallin' On My Head** Burt Bacharach/Hal David • Bacharach/David	Scepter 12265

1/75	G	5/23/75	1	**(Hey Won't You Play) Another**
				    Somebody Done Somebody Wrong Song
				    Moman/Larry Butler • Moman
					ABC 12054

12/69	G	7/22/70	12	Raindrops Keep Fallin' On My Head	Scepter 580
				MARLO THOMAS	
12/72	G	10/28/76	68	Free To Be…You And Me	Bell 1110
				THOMPSON TWINS	
2/84	G P	4/24/84 10/2/84	10	Into The Gap	Arista 8200
9/85	G	11/26/85	20	Here's To Future Days	Arista 8276
				GEORGE THOROGOOD & THE DESTROYERS	
10/78	G	7/18/80	33	Move It On Over	Rounder 3024
8/82	G	8/7/85	43	Bad To The Bone	EMI America 17076
1/85	G	8/5/85	32	Maverick	EMI America 17145
9/86	G	12/22/86	33	Live	EMI America 17214
1/88	G	4/8/88	32	Born To Be Bad	EMI Manhattan 46973

Release Date	Certification	Date of Certification	Chart Peak	ARTIST/Title Songwriter ● Producer (singles only)	Label & Number
				THE THREE DEGREES	
9/74	G	12/9/74	2	When Will I See You Again Kenny Gamble/Leon Huff • Gamble/Huff	Phila. Int. 3550
				THREE DOG NIGHT	
4/69	G	7/23/69	5	One Harry Nilsson • Gabriel Mekler	Dunhill 4191
5/70	G	7/14/70	1	**Mama Told Me (Not To Come)** Randy Newman • Richard Polodor	Dunhill 4239
2/71	G	4/9/71	1	**Joy To The World** Hoyt Axton • Polodor	Dunhill 4272
10/71	G	12/29/71	4	An Old Fashioned Love Song Paul Williams • Polodor	Dunhill 4294
7/72	G	10/2/72	1	**Black And White** David Arkin/Earl Robinson • Polodor	Dunhill 4317
5/73	G	7/24/73	3	Shambala Daniel Moore • Polodor	Dunhill 4352
3/74	G	5/14/74	4	The Show Must Go On Leo Sayer/David Courtney • Jimmy Ienner	Dunhill 4382
10/68	G	8/15/69	11	Three Dog Night	Dunhill 50048
6/69	G	12/12/69	16	Suitable For Framing	Dunhill 50058
10/69	G	1/16/70	6	Captured Live At The Forum	Dunhill 50068
3/70	G	7/14/70	8	It Ain't Easy	Dunhill 50078
11/70	G	4/9/71	14	Naturally	Dunhill 50088
2/71	G	4/12/71	5	Golden Bisquits	Dunhill 50098
10/71	G	10/13/71	8	Harmony	Dunhill 50108
7/72	G	7/28/72	6	Seven Separate Fools	Dunhill 50118
2/73	G	3/6/73	18	Around The World With Three Dog Night	Dunhill 50138
10/73	G	10/12/73	26	Cyan	Dunhill 50158
3/74	G	4/17/74	20	Hard Labor	Dunhill 50168
12/74	G	1/14/75	15	Joy To The World/Their Greatest Hits	Dunhill 50178
				TIFFANY	
6/87	G P 2P 3P 4P	11/16/87 12/3/87 12/28/87 2/18/88 4/5/88	1	**Tiffany**	MCA 5793
11/88	G	1/20/89	17	Hold An Old Friend's Hand	MCA 6267

Release Date	Certification	Date of Certification	Chart Peak	ARTIST/Title Songwriter ● Producer (singles only)	Label & Number
	P	1/20/89			
				'TIL TUESDAY	
3/85	G	9/11/85	19	Voices Carry	Epic 39458
				THE TIME	
8/81	G	2/18/82	50	The Time	Warner 3598
9/82	G	11/3/82	26	What Time Is It?	Warner 23701
7/84	G	9/18/84	24	Ice Cream Castle	Warner 25109
	P	1/0/85			
				THE TOKENS	
10/61	G	1/9/62	1	**The Lion Sleeps Tonight** 　　Hugo Peretti/Luigi Creatore/George David Weiss/ 　　Albert Stanton/Paul Campbell/Roy Ilene • 　　Peretti/Creatore	RCA 7954
				TOM TOM CLUB	
10/81	G	5/26/82	23	Tom Tom Club	Sire 3628
				TONE LOC	
10/88	G	1/10/89	2	Wild Thing 　　Marvin Young/Tony Smith/Mike Ross/Matt Dike • 　　Ross/Dike	Delicious 102
	P	2/3/89			
	2P	2/3/89			
2/89	G	5/9/89	3	Funky Cold Medina 　　Young/Ross/Dike • Ross/Dike	Delicious 104
	P	5/9/89			
1/89	G	5/9/89	1	**Loc'ed After Dark**	Delicious 3000
	P	5/9/89			
	2P	5/9/89			
				TOO SHORT	
1/89	G	5/16/89	37	Life Is…Too Short	Jive 1149
				TOTO	
9/78	G	2/15/79	5	Hold The Line 　　David Paich • Toto	Columbia 10830
9/78	G	12/12/78	9	Toto	Columbia 35317
	P*	1/23/79			

Release Date	Certification	Date of Certification	Chart Peak	ARTIST/Title Songwriter ● Producer (singles only)	Label & Number
11/79	G	3/6/80	37	Hydra	Columbia 36229
4/82	G P 2P	6/30/82 12/30/82 10/26/84	4	Toto IV	Columbia 37728
11/84	G	2/28/85	42	Isolation	Columbia 38962
				PETE TOWNSHEND	
4/80	G	8/11/80	5	Empty Glass	Atco 100
11/85	G	1/22/86	26	White City—A Novel	Atco 90473
				THE TOYS	
8/65	G	12/7/65	2	A Lover's Concerto Sandy Linzer/Denny Randell • Linzer/Randell	Dynovoice 209
				TRAFFIC	
6/70	G	12/21/70	5	John Barleycorn Must Die	United Art. 5504
11/71	G	2/7/72	7	The Low Spark Of High Heeled Boys	Island 9306
1/73	G	3/7/73	6	Shoot Out At The Fantasy Factory	Island 9323
9/74	G	11/5/74	9	When The Eagle Flies	Asylum 1020
				THE TRAMMPS	
1/77	G	5/31/78	46	Disco Inferno	Atlantic 18211
				TRAVELING WILBURYS	
10/88	G P 2P	1/4/89 1/4/89 3/1/89	3	Traveling Wilburys Vol.1	Wilbury 25796
				RANDY TRAVIS	
6/86	G P 2P	10/10/86 2/10/87 4/8/88	85	Storms Of Life	Warner 25435
5/87	G P 2P 3P	7/14/87 7/14/87 1/29/88 8/30/88	19	Always & Forever	Warner 25568
7/88	G P	9/13/88 9/13/88	35	Old 8 10	Warner 25738

Release Date	Certification	Date of Certification	Chart Peak	ARTIST/Title Songwriter ● Producer (singles only)	Label & Number
				JOHN TRAVOLTA [see Olivia Newton-John]	
				TRIUMPH	
9/81	G	6/30/82	23	Allied Forces	RCA 3902
1/83	G	9/30/83	26	Never Surrender	RCA 4382
				ROBIN TROWER	
3/74	G	9/10/74	7	Bridge Of Sighs	Chrysalis 1057
2/75	G	10/29/76	5	For Earth Below	Chrysalis 1073
9/76	G	12/13/76	24	Long Misty Days	Chrysalis 1107
9/77	G	11/18/77	25	In City Dreams	Chrysalis 1148
				ANDREA TRUE CONNECTION	
2/76	G	9/28/76	4	More, More, More Gregg Diamond • Diamond	Buddah 515
				TANYA TUCKER	
2/75	G	12/14/78	—	Greatest Hits	Columbia 33355
11/78	G	2/23/79	54	TNT	MCA 3066
				IKE & TINA TURNER	
1/71	G	5/6/71	4	Proud Mary John Fogerty • Ike Turner	Liberty 56216
6/71	G	9/11/72	25	Live At Carnegie Hall/ What You Hear Is What You Get	United Art. 9953
				TINA TURNER	
5/84	G	8/21/84	1	**What's Love Got To Do With It** Terry Britten/Graham Lyle • Britten	Capitol 5354
5/84	G P 3P 4P 5P	7/25/84 8/21/84 2/5/85 6/5/85 9/9/87	3	Private Dancer	Capitol 12330
9/86	G P	11/6/86 11/6/86	4	Break Every Rule	Capitol 12530

Release Date	Certification	Date of Certification	Chart Peak	ARTIST/Title Songwriter ● Producer (singles only)	Label & Number
				THE TURTLES	
1/67	G	5/4/67	1	**Happy Together** Gary Bonner/Alan Gordon • Joe Wissert	White Whale 244
11/67	G	4/12/68	7	Golden Hits	White Whale 7115
				TWISTED SISTER	
6/84	G P 2P	8/28/84 10/3/84 3/19/85	15	Stay Hungry	Atlantic 80156
11/85	G	1/21/86	53	Come Out And Play	Atlantic 81275
				CONWAY TWITTY	
6/70	G	5/15/72	65	Hello Darlin'	Decca 75209
6/72	G	10/29/81	—	Greatest Hits Volume I	Decca 75352
8/73	G	4/29/76	134	You've Never Been This Far Gone Before/Baby's Gone	MCA 359
11/76	G	11/29/88	—	Conway Twitty's Greatest Hits Vol. II	MCA 2235
5/78	G	12/8/83	—	The Very Best Of Conway Twitty	MCA 3043
5/82	G	11/29/88	—	Number Ones	MCA 5318
				CONWAY TWITTY & LORETTA LYNN	
2/71	G	11/29/88	78	We Only Make Believe	Decca 75251
2/72	G	10/29/81	106	Lead Me On	Decca 75326
7/79	G	11/29/88	—	The Very Best Of Conway Twitty & Loretta Lynn	MCA 3164
				2 LIVE CREW	
12/86	G	5/13/88	128	The 2 Live Crew Is What We Are	Luke Skyywalker 100
4/88	G	11/28/88	68	Move Somethin'	Luke Skyywalker 101
				BONNIE TYLER	

3/78	G	6/16/78	3	It's A Heartache
				    Ronnie Scott/Steve Wolfe • Scott/Wolfe/
				    David Mackay
					RCA 11249

6/83	G	10/3/83	1	**Total Eclipse Of The Heart** Jim Steinman • Steinman	Columbia 03906

1

2

3

1. The 2 million buyers of Diana Ross and Lionel Richie's "Endless Love" may have outnumbered those who went to see the Brooke Shields movie from which the song came.

2. Out of the fleeting moment that was Silver Convention, German producer Michael Kunze managed a pair of gold 45s and a gold album. For the record, "Fly, Robin, Fly" was the second-largest single of 1975.

3. Shannon may owe her "Let The Music Play" gold to top-notch vocal tutors Andrew Frierson of the New York Metropolitan Opera and Denni Moorman, brother of Melba Moore. Now there's trivia.

4. Grammy voters and record buyers were united in their appreciation of Sam & Dave's "Soul Man." The Stax wax sold a million copies and won a award for best R&B group vocal performance.

7

6. Santana's first 11 albums all reached gold, and most reached platinum. The best-seller by these pioneers of Latin jazz/fusion was 1970's *Abraxas,* at 4 million.

7. Sade: first three albums, first three platinum. The Nigerian's first song? "Kisses From The Karma Sutra."

7. At triple platinum, Run-DMC's *Raising Hell* album is the best-selling rap album by a black act. The Caucasian crew who matched that number: the Beastie Boys, with *Licensed To Ill.*

8. Dancing on "Soul Train" can lead to gold. Just ask Jody Watley and Jeffrey Daniel, who were recruited from the show to help turn Solar Records' studio creation, Shalamar, into a real group.

9. Linda Ronstadt has eight platinum and 16 gold albums, and just one female singer — Barbra Streisand — can better that tally.

9

Release Date	Certification	Date of Certification	Chart Peak	ARTIST/Title Songwriter ● Producer (singles only)	Label & Number
5/78	G	6/27/78	16	It's A Heartache	RCA 2821
7/83	G P	10/3/83 11/7/83	4	Faster Than The Speed Of Night	Columbia 38710

U

Release Date	Certification	Date of Certification	Chart Peak	ARTIST/Title Songwriter ● Producer (singles only)	Label & Number
				UB40	
8/88	G	1/25/89	1	**Red Red Wine** Neil Diamond • Ray Falconer/UB40	A&M 1244
9/83	G P	7/15/86 9/8/88	14	Labour Of Love	A&M 4980
				URIAH HEEP	
5/72	G	10/27/72	23	Demons And Wizards	Mercury 630
11/72	G	1/22/73	31	The Magician's Birthday	Mercury 652
5/73	G	10/12/73	37	Live	Mercury 7503
9/73	G	3/5/74	33	Sweet Freedom	Warner 2724
				USA FOR AFRICA	
3/85	G P 4P	4/1/85 4/1/85 4/1/85	1	**We Are The World** Michael Jackson/Lionel Richie • Quincy Jones	Columbia 04839
4/85	G P 2P 3P	4/1/85 4/16/85 4/16/85 6/24/85	1	**We Are The World**	Columbia 40043
				U2	
9/88	G	1/10/89	3	Desire U2 • Jimmy Iovine	Island 99250
4/83	G P	7/15/83 2/25/85	12	War	Island 90067
11/83	G P	2/27/84 7/18/85	28	Under A Blood Red Sky	Island 90127
10/84	G	12/3/84	12	The Unforgettable Fire	Island 90231

Release Date	Certification	Date of Certification	Chart Peak	ARTIST/Title Songwriter ● Producer (singles only)	Label & Number
	P	2/7/85			
3/87	G	5/13/87	1	**The Joshua Tree**	Island 90581
	P	5/13/87			
	2P	5/13/87			
	3P	9/30/87			
	4P	12/22/87			
	5P	10/6/88			
10/88	G	12/6/88	1	**Rattle And Hum [S]**	Island 91003
	P	12/6/88			
	2P	12/6/88			
	3P	1/17/89			

Release Date	Certification	Date of Certification	Chart Peak	ARTIST/Title Songwriter ● Producer (singles only)	Label & Number
				FRANKIE VALLI	
4/67	G	9/13/67	2	Can't Take My Eyes Off You Bob Crewe/Bob Gaudio • Crewe	Philips 40446
10/74	G	4/1/75	1	**My Eyes Adored You** Crewe/Kenny Nolan • Crewe	Private S. 45003
5/78	G	7/27/78	1	**Grease** Barry Gibb • Gibb/Albhy Galuten/Karl Richardson	RSO 897
	P	10/17/78			
				VAN HALEN	
1/84	G	4/3/84	1	**Jump** Van Halen • Ted Templeman	Warner 29384
2/78	G	5/24/78	19	Van Halen	Warner 3075
	P	10/10/78			
	5P	10/22/84			
	6P	2/1/89			
4/79	G	4/3/79	6	Van Halen II	Warner 3312
	P	5/8/79			
	3P	10/22/84			
3/80	G	5/29/80	6	Women And Children First	Warner 3415
	P	6/2/80			
	2P	10/22/84			
5/81	G	7/7/81	5	Fair Warning	Warner 3540
	P	11/18/81			
4/82	G	6/30/82	3	Diver Down	Warner 3677
	P	6/30/82			
	2P	10/22/84			
	3P	2/22/89			
1/84	G	3/12/84	2	1984	Warner 23985
	P	3/12/84			

Release Date	Certification	Date of Certification	Chart Peak	ARTIST/Title Songwriter ● Producer (singles only)	Label & Number
	4P 5P 6P	10/22/84 1/23/85 7/1/87			
3/86	G P 2P 3P 4P	5/28/86 5/28/86 5/28/86 10/10/86 1/18/89	1	**5150**	Warner 25394
5/88	G P 2P 3P	7/26/88 7/26/88 7/26/88 1/18/89	1	**OU812**	Warner 25732
				RICKY VAN SHELTON	
2/87	G P	4/11/88 7/24/89	76	Wild-Eyed Dream	Columbia 40602
9/88	G	12/2/88	78	Loving Proof	Columbia 44221
				LUTHER VANDROSS	
8/81	G P	12/8/81 12/8/86	19	Never Too Much	Epic 37451
9/82	G P	11/29/82 3/7/83	20	Forever, For Always, For Love	Epic 38235
12/83	G P	2/6/84 1/2/85	32	Busy Body	Epic 39196
3/85	G P	5/21/85 5/21/85	19	The Night I Fell In Love	Epic 39882
9/86	G P	12/8/86 12/8/86	14	Give Me The Reason	Epic 40415
9/88	G P	12/19/88 12/19/88	9	Any Love	Epic 44308
				VANGELIS	
9/81	G P	3/1/82 4/8/82	1	**Chariots Of Fire [S]**	Polydor 6335
				VANILLA FUDGE	
8/67	G	7/23/68	6	Vanilla Fudge	Atco 224
				VANITY FARE	

2/70	G	7/8/70	5	Hitchin' A Ride
				    Peter Callander/Mitch Murray • Roger
				    Easterby/Des Champ
					Page One 21029

Release Date	Certification	Date of Certification	Chart Peak	ARTIST/Title Songwriter ● Producer (singles only)	Label & Number
				VANITY 6	
8/82	G	8/1/85	45	Vanity 6	Warner 23716
				GINO VANNELLI	
9/78	G P	11/7/78 1/18/79	13	Brother To Brother	A&M 4722
				RANDY VANWARMER	
2/79	G	7/31/79	4	Just When I Needed You Most Randy Vanwarmer • Del Newman	Bearsville 0334
				STEVIE RAY VAUGHAN & DOUBLE TROUBLE	
6/84	G	12/23/85	31	Couldn't Stand The Weather	Epic 39304
9/85	G	8/11/87	34	Soul To Soul	Epic 40036
				BILLY VAUGHN & HIS ORCHESTRA	
8/56	G	10/10/69	—	The Golden Instrumentals	Dot 3016
3/58	G	2/16/62	5	Sail Along Silv'ry Moon	Dot 3100
5/59	G	2/16/62	7	Blue Hawaii	Dot 3165
3/60	G	2/16/62	1	Theme From A Summer Place	Dot 3276
				BOBBY VEE & THE STRANGERS	
4/67	G	10/16/67	3	Come Back When You Grow Up Martha Sharp • Dallas Smith	Liberty 55964
				SUZANNE VEGA	
4/87	G	7/15/87	11	Solitude Standing	A&M 5136
				THE VENTURES	
12/62	G	5/19/70	8	The Ventures Play Telstar, The Lonely Bull & Others	Dolton 8019
8/67	G	5/19/70	50	Golden Greats By The Ventures	Liberty 8053
4/69	G	7/21/71	11	Hawaii Five-O	Liberty 8061

Release Date	Certification	Date of Certification	Chart Peak	ARTIST/Title Songwriter ● Producer (singles only)	Label & Number
				BILLY VERA & THE BEATERS	
9/86	G	2/6/89	1	**At This Moment** Billy Vera • Jeff Baxter	Rhino 74403
8/86	G	3/24/87	15	By Request (The Best Of Billy Vera & The Beaters)	Rhino 70858
				VILLAGE PEOPLE	
4/78	G	10/30/78	25	Macho Man Jacques Morali/Henri Belolo/Victor Willis/ Peter Whitehead • Morali	Casablanca 922
10/78	G P	12/18/78 1/25/79	2	Y.M.C.A. Morali/Belolo/Willis • Morali	Casablanca 945
3/79	G	3/15/79	3	In The Navy Morali/Belolo/Willis • Morali	Casablanca 973
8/77	G	9/18/78	54	Village People	Casablanca 7064
2/78	G P	8/4/78 12/26/78	24	Macho Man	Casablanca 7096
10/78	G P	10/13/78 12/13/78	3	Cruisin'	Casablanca 7118
4/79	G P	4/4/79 4/4/79	8	Go West	Casablanca 7144
9/79	G	1/25/80	32	Live And Sleazy	Casablanca 7183
				BOBBY VINTON	
4/62	G	8/13/62	1	**Roses Are Red** Paul Evans/Al Byron • Bob Morgan	Epic 9505
10/68	G	12/19/68	9	I Love How You Love Me Barry Mann/Larry Kolber • Billy Sherrill	Epic 10397
8/74	G	12/5/74	3	My Melody Of Love Bobby Vinton/Henry Mayer/George Buschor • Morgan	ABC 12022
9/64	G	12/12/66	12	Bobby Vinton's Greatest Hits	Epic 26098
11/74	G	12/5/74	16	Melodies Of Love	ABC 851
				VIOLENT FEMMES	
4/83	G	12/2/87	—	Violent Femmes	Slash 23845

Release Date	Certification	Date of Certification	Chart Peak	ARTIST/Title Songwriter ● Producer (singles only)	Label & Number
				VIXEN	
8/88	G	2/6/89	41	Vixen	EMI 46991
				THE VOGUES	
5/68	G	9/24/68	7	Turn Around, Look At Me Jerry Capehart • Dick Glasser	Reprise 0686
				ANDREAS VOLLENWEIDER	
9/83	G	7/25/89	149	Caverna Magica	CBS 37827
2/85	G	8/11/86	86	White Winds	CBS 39963
7/86	G	2/2/87	60	Down To The Moon	CBS 42255
				HERBERT VON KARAJAN/BERLIN PHILHARMONIC ORCHESTRA	
9/63	G	7/8/77	—	Beethoven: The Nine Symphonies	DGG 101/8
				W	
				JOHN WAITE	
6/84	G	9/4/84	10	No Brakes	EMI America 17124
				RICK WAKEMAN **[see also Anderson/Bruford/Wakeman]**	
2/73	G	10/20/75	30	The Six Wives Of Henry VIII	A&M 4361
6/74	G	9/4/74	3	Journey To The Centre Of The Earth	A&M 3621
				JERRY JEFF WALKER	
11/73	G	12/16/77	160	Viva Terlingua!	MCA 382
				JOE WALSH	
6/73	G	11/2/73	6	The Smoker You Drink, The Player You Get	Dunhill 50140
12/74	G	1/14/75	11	So What	Dunhill 50171
5/78	G P	5/31/78 8/7/78	8	But Seriously, Folks…	Asylum 141

Release Date	Certification	Date of Certification	Chart Peak	ARTIST/Title Songwriter ● Producer (singles only)	Label & Number
				WAR **[*Eric Burdon & War]**	
4/70	G	9/28/70	3	Spill The Wine * War • Jerry Goldstein	MGM 14118
11/71	G	6/26/72	16	Slippin' Into Darkness War • Goldstein	United Art. 50867
10/72	G	3/2/73	7	The World Is A Ghetto War • Goldstein	United Art. 50975
3/73	G	3/6/73	2	The Cisco Kid War • Goldstein/Lonnie Jordan/Howard Scott	United Art. 163
4/75	G	8/19/75	6	Why Can't We Be Friends? War • Goldstein/Jordan/Scott	United Art. 629
6/76	G	9/14/76	7	Summer War • Goldstein	United Art. 834
11/71	G	6/26/72	16	All Day Music	United Art. 5546
11/72	G	12/13/72	1	**The World Is A Ghetto**	United Art. 5652
8/73	G	9/11/73	6	Deliver The Word	United Art. 128
3/74	G	3/13/74	13	War Live!	United Art. 193
6/75	G	7/25/75	8	Why Can't We Be Friends?	United Art. 441
8/76	G P	8/24/76 1/6/77	6	Greatest Hits	United Art. 648
7/77	G	8/10/77	23	Platinum Jazz	Blue Note 690
11/77	G	11/28/77	15	Galaxy	MCA 3030
3/79	G	7/21/79	41	The Music Band	MCA 3085
				JENNIFER WARNES **[see Joe Cocker; Bill Medley]**	
				WARRANT	
1/89	G P	7/6/89 8/25/89	10	Dirty Rotten Filthy Stinking Rich	Columbia 44383
				DIONNE WARWICK **[see also Stevie Wonder]**	
10/67	G	2/15/68	4	I Say A Little Prayer Burt Bacharach/Hal David • Bacharach/David	Scepter 12203
6/79	G	10/19/79	5	I'll Never Love This Way Again Richard Kerr/Will Jennings • Barry Manilow	Arista 0419

Release Date	Certification	Date of Certification	Chart Peak	ARTIST/Title Songwriter ● Producer (singles only)	Label & Number
12/67	G	8/6/70	18	Here Where There Is Love	Scepter 555
2/68	G	8/6/70	6	Valley Of The Dolls	Scepter 568
7/69	G	2/24/69	31	Dionne Warwick's Greatest Motion Picture Hits	Scepter 575
10/71	G	12/23/71	48	The Dionne Warwick Story	Scepter 596
6/79	G P	9/23/79 3/11/80	12	Dionne	Arista 4230
11/85	G	1/21/86	12	Friends	Arista 8398
				DIONNE WARWICK & FRIENDS **[with Elton John/Gladys Knight/Stevie Wonder]**	
10/85	G	1/15/86	1	**That's What Friends Are For** Burt Bacharach/Carole Bayer Sager • Bacharach/Sager	Arista 9422
				DIONNE WARWICK & THE SPINNERS	
7/74	G	10/8/74	1	**Then Came You** Sherman Marshall/Phil Pugh • Thom Bell	Atlantic 3022
				GROVER WASHINGTON JR.	
10/80	G P	3/10/81 5/6/81	5	Winelight	Elektra 305
				JODY WATLEY	
3/89	G	8/23/89	2	Real Love Jody Watley/Andre Cymone • Cymone	MCA 53484
2/87	G P	4/24/87 12/7/87	10	Jody Watley	MCA 5898
3/89	G	5/26/89	16	Larger Than Life	MCA 6276
				JOHNNY "GUITAR" WATSON	
6/76	G	6/2/77	52	Ain't That A Bitch	DJM 3
3/77	G	6/2/77	20	A Real Mother For Ya	DJM 7
				WEATHER REPORT	
3/77	G	6/19/81	30	Heavy Weather	Columbia 34418

Release Date	Certification	Date of Certification	Chart Peak	ARTIST/Title Songwriter ● Producer (singles only)	Label & Number
				TIM WEISSBERG [see Dan Fogelberg]	
				ERIC WEISSBERG	
11/72	G	3/7/73	2	Dueling Banjos Arthur Smith • Eric Weissberg	Warner 7659
1/73	G	3/7/73	1	**Dueling Banjos/Deliverance [S]**	Warner 2683
				BOB WELCH	
9/77	G P	12/9/77 5/1/78	12	French Kiss	Capitol 11663
2/79	G	2/23/79	20	Three Hearts	Capitol 11907
				LAWRENCE WELK & HIS ORCHESTRA	
11/60	G	2/14/61	1	**Calcutta** Heino Gaze/Paul Vance/Lee Pockriss • Welk/ George Cates/Randy Wood	Dot 16161
1/61	G	3/16/61	1	**Calcutta!**	Dot 3359
11/66	G	4/17/67	12	Winchester Cathedral	Dot 25774
				FRED WESLEY & THE JB's	
4/73	G	7/23/73	22	Doin' It To Death James Brown • Brown	People 621
				DOTTIE WEST [see Kenny Rogers]	
				WHAM!	
8/84	G	12/18/84	1	**Wake Me Up Before You Go-Go** George Michael • Michael	Columbia 04552
12/84	G	3/11/85	1	**Careless Whisper** Michael/Andrew Ridgeley • Michael	Columbia 04691
7/83	G	8/9/89	83	Fantastic	Columbia 38911
10/84	G P	12/26/84 12/28/84	1	**Make It Big**	Columbia 39595

Release Date	Certification	Date of Certification	Chart Peak	ARTIST/Title Songwriter ● Producer (singles only)	Label & Number
	3P 4P	7/8/85 12/23/85			
6/86	G P	8/29/86 10/8/86	10	Music From The Edge Of Heaven	Columbia 40285
				THE WHISPERS	
12/79	G	3/18/80	19	And The Beat Goes On Leon Sylvers/Stephen Shockley/William Shelby • Dick Griffey/The Whispers	Solar 11894
12/79	G P	3/18/80 3/18/80	6	The Whispers	Solar 3521
1/81	G	3/12/81	23	Imagination	Solar 3578
1/82	G	11/9/82	35	Love Is Where You Find It	Solar 27
4/87	G P	7/20/87 2/9/88	22	Just Gets Better With Time	Solar 72554
				WHITE LION	
6/87	G P	4/6/88 6/1/88	11	Pride	Atlantic 81768
6/89	G	8/10/89	19	Big Game	Atlantic 81969
				BARRY WHITE	
2/73	G	6/6/73	3	I'm Gonna Love You Just A Little Bit More Baby Barry White • White	20th Century 2018
10/73	G	2/7/74	7	Never, Never Gonna Give Ya Up White • White	20th Century 2058
7/74	G	9/11/74	1	**Can't Get Enough Of Your Love, Babe** White • White	20th Century 2120
10/74	G	12/18/74	2	You're The First, The Last, My Everything White/Tony Sepe/P. Sterling Radcliffe • White	20th Century 2133
8/77	G	10/18/77	4	It's Ecstasy When You Lay Down Next To Me Nelson Pigford/Elcundayo Paris • White	20th Century 2350
2/73	G	11/6/73	16	I've Got So Much To Give	20th Century 407
10/73	G	2/7/74	20	Stone Gon'	20th Century 423
8/74	G	9/19/74	1	**Can't Get Enough**	20th Century 444
3/75	G	4/8/75	17	Just Another Way To Say I Love You	20th Century 466
11/75	G	3/9/76	23	Barry White's Greatest Hits	20th Century 493
9/77	G P	9/20/77 11/15/77	8	Barry White Sings For Someone You Love	20th Century 543

Release Date	Certification	Date of Certification	Chart Peak	ARTIST/Title Songwriter ● Producer (singles only)	Label & Number
9/78	G P	12/22/78 12/22/78	36	The Man	20th Century 571
3/79	G	5/29/79	67	The Message Is Love	Unlimited Gold 35763
				KARYN WHITE	

7/88	G	3/9/89	7	The Way You Love Me
				    Antonio "L.A." Reid/Kenny "Babyface"
				    Edmonds/Darryl Simmons • L.A. & Babyface
					Warner 27773

11/88	G	4/18/89	8	Superwoman L.A. & Babyface/Simmons • L.A. & Babyface	Warner 27783
9/88	G P	1/18/89 4/4/89	19	Karyn White	Warner 25637
				WHITESNAKE	
4/84	G P	4/15/86 11/10/87	40	Slide It In	Geffen 4018
3/87	G P 2P 3P 4P 5P	6/2/87 7/1/87 8/19/87 9/15/87 12/2/87 1/7/88	2	Whitesnake	Geffen 24099
				KEITH WHITLEY	
5/88	G	7/25/89	121	Don't Close Your Eyes	RCA 6494
				ROGER WHITTAKER	
3/75	G	12/29/78	31	The Last Farewell And Other Hits	RCA 0855
3/77	G	7/14/80	—	The Best Of Roger Whittaker	RCA 2255
				THE WHO	
5/69	G	8/18/69	4	Tommy	Decca 7205
5/70	G	8/6/70	4	Live At Leeds	Decca 79175
8/71	G	9/16/71	4	Who's Next	Decca 79182
11/71	G	1/17/72	11	Meaty Beaty Big And Bouncy	Decca 79184
10/73	G	10/29/73	2	Quadrophenia	MCA 100004
10/74	G	12/9/74	15	Odds And Sods	Track 2126
10/75	G	12/10/75	8	The Who By Numbers	MCA 2161

Release Date	Certification	Date of Certification	Chart Peak	ARTIST/Title Songwriter ● Producer (singles only)	Label & Number
8/78	G P	8/24/78 9/20/78	2	Who Are You	MCA 3050
6/79	G P	6/26/79 10/5/79	8	The Kids Are Alright [S]	MCA 11005
3/81	G P	5/20/81 9/18/81	4	Face Dances	Warner 3516
9/82	G	11/3/82	8	It's Hard	Warner 23731
				WHODINI	
10/84	G P	1/24/85 5/22/87	35	Escape	Jive 8251
4/86	G	6/23/86	35	Back In Black	Jive 8407
9/87	G	1/20/88	30	Open Sesame	Jive 8494
				WILD CHERRY	
5/76	G P	8/23/76 10/15/76	1	**Play That Funky Music** Robert Parissi • Parissi	Epic 50225
7/76	G P	9/8/76 12/17/76	5	Wild Cherry	Sweet City 34195
				WILL TO POWER	

8/88	G	1/23/89	1	**Baby I Love Your Way/Freebird Medley**
				    Peter Frampton/Allen Collins/Ronnie Van Zant
				    • Bob Rosenberg
					Epic 08034

				ANDY WILLIAMS	
4/62	G	10/14/63	3	Moon River & Other Great Movie Themes	Columbia 8609
4/63	G	9/19/63	1	**Days Of Wine & Roses**	Columbia 8815
10/63	G P	12/18/64 11/21/86	—	The Andy Williams Christmas Album	Columbia 8887
12/63	G	8/17/64	9	The Wonderful World Of Andy Williams	Columbia 8937
4/64	G	12/18/64	5	Call Me Irresponsible	Columbia 8971
9/64	G	9/17/65	5	The Great Songs From "My Fair Lady" And Other Broadway Hits	Columbia 9005
3/65	G	7/30/65	4	Dear Heart	Columbia 9138
10/65	G*	5/23/68	—	Merry Christmas	Columbia 9220
4/66	G	9/27/66	6	The Shadow Of Your Smile	Columbia 9299
4/67	G	7/6/67	5	Born Free	Columbia 9480
11/67	G	5/14/68	8	Love, Andy	Columbia 9566

1

2

3

4

5

1. Frank Sinatra's sole million-selling single was his duet with daughter Nancy, "Somethin' Stupid." But his gold album count is a distinguished 17, spanning 24 years of recording.

2. Paul Simon and Art Garfunkel have the biggest-selling albums by a duo in recording industry history: *Bridge Over Troubled Water* and *Simon & Garfunkel's Greatest Hits*, both certified at 5 million.

3. Carly Simon joined the career-reviving club at Arista Records (founding members are Aretha, Dionne) and collected her first gold album in nine years.

4. Bruce Springsteen's *Born In The USA*, released in June 1984, is the largest-selling album in the history of Columbia Records. It's been certified at 11 million.

8

5. Mom always wanted you to have a gold album first! Neverthless, both Tom and Dick Smothers earned RIAA certification with three of their comedy albums for Mercury Records.

6. Simple Minds accrued a gold album, *Once Upon A Time,* eight years after the band was born in Glasgow from the, uh, ashes of Johnny & The Self-Abusers.

7. For a band which barely toured, Steely Dan's countdown of five gold and three platinum albums is close enough to ecstacy. Donald Fagen added extra thrills with his own gold *The Nightfly* in 1982.

8. Ringo Starr's solo gold album collection is the smallest of all the ex-Beatles. Just two, to George's nine, John's eight, and Paul's sixteen.

9. Sister Sledge's "We Are Family" was Nile Rodgers' first gold award as a producer outside Chic, which he helped form. Later, he mined precious metal for David Bowie and Diana Ross, among others.

9

Release Date	Certification	Date of Certification	Chart Peak	ARTIST/Title Songwriter ● Producer (singles only)	Label & Number
5/68	G	11/1/68	9	Honey	Columbia 9662
5/69	G	8/20/69	9	Happy Heart	Columbia 9844
10/69	G	2/19/70	27	Get Together With Andy Williams	Columbia 9922
2/70	G	9/13/71	42	Andy Williams' Greatest Hits	Columbia 9979
2/71	G P	3/22/71 11/21/86	3	Love Story	Columbia 30497
3/72	G	8/29/73	29	Love Theme From "The Godfather"	Columbia 31303
				DENIECE WILLIAMS **[see also Johnny Mathis]**	
3/84	G	6/13/84	1	**Let's Hear It For The Boy** Tom Snow/Dean Pitchford • George Duke	Columbia 04417
8/76	G	3/9/77	33	This Is Niecy	Columbia 34242
				DON WILLIAMS	
4/79	G	10/7/80	—	Best Of Don Williams Volume II	MCA 3096
8/80	G	12/2/80	57	I Believe In You	MCA 5133
				HANK WILLIAMS	
4/63	G	6/11/69	—	Greatest Hits	MGM 3918
5/71	G	3/1/77	—	24 Greatest Hits	MGM 4755
				HANK WILLIAMS, JR.	
12/64	G	6/11/69	16	Your Cheatin' Heart [S]	MGM 4260
4/79	G	12/23/83	—	Family Tradition	Elektra/Curb 194
10/79	G	11/2/81	—	Whiskey Bent & Hell Bound	Elektra/Curb 237
1/81	G	5/31/85	82	Rowdy	Elektra/Curb 330
8/81	G P	4/13/82 4/7/86	76	The Pressure Is On	Elektra/Curb 535
4/82	G	4/7/86	123	High Notes	Elektra/Curb 60100
9/82	G P 2P	8/21/84 8/21/84 10/18/88	107	Hank Williams, Jr.'s Greatest Hits	Elektra/Curb 60193
1/83	G	1/22/86	64	Strong Stuff	Elektra/Curb 60223
9/83	G	1/29/85	116	Man Of Steel	Warner/Curb 23924
5/84	G	1/10/85	100	Major Moves	Warner/Curb 25088

Release Date	Certification	Date of Certification	Chart Peak	ARTIST/Title Songwriter ● Producer (singles only)	Label & Number
4/85	G	10/29/85	72	Five-0	Warner/Curb 25267
10/85	G	5/13/86	183	Greatest Hits Volume 2	Warner/Curb 25328
6/86	G	12/22/86	93	Montana Cafe	Warner/Curb 25412
1/87	G	8/11/87	71	Hank "Live"	Warner/Curb 25538
7/87	G P	9/15/87 2/23/88	28	Born To Boogie	Warner/Curb 25593
6/88	G	8/23/88	55	Wild Streak	Warner/Curb 25725
2/89	G*	4/11/89	61	Greatest Hits III	Warner/Curb 25834
				LENNY WILLIAMS	
7/78	G	1/16/79	87	Spark Of Love	ABC 1073
				ROBIN WILLIAMS	
7/79	G	8/1/79	10	Reality…What A Concept	Casablanca 7162
				ROGER WILLIAMS	
2/57	G	1/20/67	6	Songs Of The Fabulous Fifties	Kapp 5000
3/58	G	1/20/67	4	Till	Kapp 1081
5/59	G	1/20/67	11	More Songs Of The Fabulous Fifties	Kapp 1130
1/62	G	1/20/67	44	Greatest Hits	Kapp 3260
2/66	G	7/30/68	24	Somewhere My Love [a/k/a I'll Remember You]	Kapp 3470
9/66	G	4/24/67	7	Born Free	Kapp 3501
				VANESSA WILLIAMS	
6/88	G	3/28/89	38	The Right Stuff	Wing 835 694
				BRUCE WILLIS	
1/87	G	3/24/87	14	The Return Of Bruno	Motown 6222
				AL WILSON	
9/73	G	12/17/73	1	**Show And Tell** Jerry Fuller ● Fuller	Rocky Road 30073
				FLIP WILSON	
2/70	G	7/22/70	17	The Devil Made Me Buy This Dress	Little David 1000

Release Date	Certification	Date of Certification	Chart Peak	ARTIST/Title Songwriter ● Producer (singles only)	Label & Number
				MERI WILSON	
5/77	G	10/26/77	18	Telephone Man Meri Wilson • Boomer Castleman/Jim Rutledge	GRT 127
				WINGER	
7/88	G P	1/27/89 6/13/89	21	Winger	Atlantic 81867
				WINGS **[see Paul McCartney]**	
				GEORGE WINSTON	
11/80	G P	4/2/85 12/17/87	142	Autumn	Windham Hill 1012
7/82	G P	12/10/85 12/17/87	127	Winter Into Spring	Windham Hill 1019
12/82	G P	12/12/84 12/10/85	54	December	Windham Hill 1025
				THE WINSTONS	
5/69	G	7/24/69	7	Color Him Father Richard Spencer • Don Carroll	Metromedia 117
				THE EDGAR WINTER GROUP	
2/73	G	6/19/73	1	**Frankenstein** Edgar Winter • Rick Derringer	Epic 10967
3/72	G	12/18/74	23	Roadwork [EDGAR WINTER'S WHITE TRASH]	Epic 31249
11/72	G P 2P	4/30/73 11/21/86 11/21/86	3	They Only Come Out At Night	Epic 31584
5/74	G	7/18/74	13	Shock Treatment	Epic 32461
				JOHNNY WINTER	
2/71	G	1/28/74	40	Live/Johnny Winter And	Columbia 30475
				STEVE WINWOOD	
1/81	G P	4/7/81 6/26/81	3	Arc Of A Diver	Island 9576

Release Date	Certification	Date of Certification	Chart Peak	ARTIST/Title Songwriter ● Producer (singles only)	Label & Number
6/86	G P 2P 3P	9/8/86 10/10/86 4/21/87 1/12/88	3	Back In The High Life	Island 25448
11/87	G P	1/12/88 5/19/88	26	Chronicles	Island 25660
6/88	G P 2P	8/17/88 8/17/88 11/28/88	1	**Roll With It**	Virgin 90946
				BILL WITHERS	
6/71	G	9/21/71	3	Ain't No Sunshine Bill Withers • Booker T. Jones	Sussex 219
4/72	G	6/20/72	1	**Lean On Me** Withers • Withers	Sussex 235
8/72	G	10/12/72	2	Use Me Withers • Withers	Sussex 241
5/72	G	9/7/72	4	Still Bill	Sussex 7014
10/77	G	5/18/78	39	Menagerie	Columbia 34903
				BOBBY WOMACK	
11/72	G	2/14/73	31	Harry Hippie [with PEACE] Jim Ford • Bobby Womack/Joe Hicks	United Art. 50946
1/74	G	4/8/74	10	Lookin' For A Love J.W. Alexander/Zelda Samuels • Womack	United Art. 375
				STEVIE WONDER **[see also Paul McCartney; Dionne Warwick]**	
8/84	G	11/8/84	1	**I Just Called To Say I Love You** Stevie Wonder • Wonder	Motown 1745
9/80	G P	2/3/81 2/3/81	3	Hotter Than July	Tamla 373
5/82	G	7/9/82	4	Stevie Wonder's Original Musiquarium I	Tamla 6002
8/84	G P	11/8/84 11/8/84	4	The Woman In Red [with DIONNE WARWICK] [S]	Motown 6108
9/85	G P 2P	11/13/85 11/13/85 12/4/85	5	In Square Circle	Tamla 6134
11/87	G P	1/8/88 1/8/88	17	Characters	Motown 6248

Release Date	Certification	Date of Certification	Chart Peak	ARTIST/Title Songwriter ● Producer (singles only)	Label & Number
				BETTY WRIGHT	
10/71	G	12/30/71	6	Clean Up Woman Clarence Reid/Willie Clarke • Reid/Clarke	Alston 4601
				GARY WRIGHT	
11/75	G	4/20/76	2	Dream Weaver Gary Wright • Wright	Warner 8167
7/75	G P	3/8/76 10/13/86	7	The Dream Weaver	Warner 2868
				TAMMY WYNETTE	
7/69	G P	4/16/70 6/9/89	37	Tammy's Greatest Hits	Epic 26486
				Y	
				"WEIRD AL" YANKOVIC	
2/84	G	4/30/84	17	"Weird Al" Yankovic In 3-D	Rock 'n' Roll 39221
6/85	G	1/27/86	50	Dare To Be Stupid	Rock 'n' Roll 40033
3/88	G	7/18/88	27	Even Worse	Rock 'n' Roll 44149
				YARBROUGH & PEOPLES	

10/80	G	4/27/81	19	Don't Stop The Music
				    Alisa Peoples/Lonnie Simmons/Jonah Ellis •
				    Simmons/Ellis
					Mercury 76085

12/80	G	3/11/81	16	The Two Of Us	Mercury 3834
				YAZ	
9/82	G P	10/10/86 2/22/89	92	Upstairs At Eric's	Sire 23737
				YES	
3/71	G	3/17/73	40	The Yes Album	Atlantic 8243
1/72	G	3/10/72	4	Fragile	Atlantic 7211
10/72	G	10/30/72	3	Close To The Edge	Atlantic 7244
3/73	G	3/17/73	12	Yessongs	Atlantic 100

Release Date	Certification	Date of Certification	Chart Peak	ARTIST/Title Songwriter ● Producer (singles only)	Label & Number
1/74	G	2/8/74	6	Tales From Topographic Oceans	Atlantic 908
12/74	G	12/18/74	5	Relayer	Atlantic 18122
7/77	G	8/2/77	8	Going For The One	Atlantic 19106
10/78	G P	10/10/78 11/8/78	10	Tormato	Atlantic 19202
11/83	G P	1/17/84 1/17/84	5	90125	Atlantic 90125
9/87	G P	12/8/87 4/29/88	15	Big Generator	Atlantic 90522
				DWIGHT YOAKAM	
3/86	G P	1/21/87 5/10/89	61	Guitars, Cadillacs, Etc., Etc.	Reprise 25372
4/87	G	10/21/87	55	Hillbilly DeLuxe	Reprise 25567
8/88	G	1/4/89	68	Buenas Noches From A Lonely Room	Reprise 25749
				NEIL YOUNG **[see also Stills-Young Band]**	
1/72	G	4/21/72	1	**Heart Of Gold** 　Neil Young • Elliot Mazer	Reprise 1065
5/69	G P	10/16/70 10/13/86	34	Everybody Knows This Is Nowhere	Reprise 6349
8/70	G P 2P	11/2/70 10/13/86 10/13/86	8	After The Gold Rush	Reprise 6383
2/72	G P 3P	2/18/72 10/13/86 10/13/86	1	**Harvest**	Reprise 2032
10/73	G	12/7/73	22	Times Fades Away	Reprise 2151
7/74	G	9/23/74	16	On The Beach	Reprise 2180
6/77	G	10/11/77	21	American Stars 'n' Bars	Reprise 2261
10/77	G P	8/9/79 12/22/86	43	Decade	Reprise 2257
10/78	G	11/21/78	7	Comes A Time	Reprise 2266
6/79	G P	8/28/79 2/7/80	8	Rust Never Sleeps	Reprise 2295
11/79	G P	3/11/80 2/17/88	15	Live Rust	Reprise 2296

Release Date	Certification	Date of Certification	Chart Peak	ARTIST/Title Songwriter ● Producer (singles only)	Label & Number
				PAUL YOUNG	Columbia 39957
5/85	G	8/13/85	19	The Secret Of Association	
				THE YOUNG RASCALS **[see The Rascals]**	
				THE YOUNGBLOODS	RCA 9752
7/67	G	10/7/69	5	Get Together Chester Powers Jr. • Bob Cullen	
				YOUNG-HOLT UNLIMITED	Brunswick 55391
10/68	G	1/20/69	3	Soulful Strut Eugene Record/Sonny Sanders • Carl Davis/Record	
				# Z	
				ZAGER & EVANS	RCA 0174
5/69	G	7/8/69	1	**In The Year 2525 (Exordium & Terminus)** Rick Evans • Denny Zager/Evans	
				ZAPP	
9/80	G	11/18/80	19	Zapp	Warner 3463
7/82	G	9/21/82	25	Zapp II	Warner 23583
				FRANK ZAPPA **[see also Mothers Of Invention]**	DiscReet 2175
3/74	G	4/7/76	10	Apostrophe (')	
				WARREN ZEVON	Asylum 118
1/78	G	4/17/78	8	Excitable Boy	
				THE ZOMBIES	Date 1628
10/68	G	4/11/69	3	Time Of The Season Rod Argent • Argent/Chris White	

Release Date	Certification	Date of Certification	Chart Peak	ARTIST/Title Songwriter ● Producer (singles only)	Label & Number
				ZZ TOP	
7/73	G	5/23/74	8	Tres Hombres	London 631
4/75	G	6/27/75	10	Fandango!	London 656
1/77	G	1/18/77	17	Tejas	London 680
11/77	G	12/30/77	94	The Best Of ZZ Top	London 706
11/79	G P	3/3/80 5/11/84	24	Deguello	Warner 3361
7/81	G	10/22/81	17	El Loco	Warner 3593
3/83	G P 4P 5P 6P	6/21/83 9/14/83 10/22/84 7/22/85 7/1/87	9	Eliminator	Warner 23774
10/85	G P 2P 3P	1/6/86 1/6/86 1/6/86 6/24/86	4	Afterburner	Warner 25342

ORIGINAL SOUNDTRACKS

This details every gold, platinum, and multi-platinum movie soundtrack. It includes all those albums which appear in the main section of the book under specific artist entries. In this section, the artist's name (where applicable) appears in brackets after the soundtrack title.

Where a soundtrack album title differs from the name of the film—e.g. Prince's music from the film *Under The Cherry Moon* was issued as *Parade*—the movie title is listed before the album title. Releases such as Talking Heads' *True Stories*—based on a movie's music, if not the exact soundtrack—may also be included here.

Release Date	Certification	Date of Certification	Chart Peak	ARTIST/Title Songwriter ● Producer (singles only)	Label & Number
3/84	G	5/2/84	12	Against All Odds	Atlantic 80152
8/84	G	2/27/86	56	Amadeus	Fantasy 1791
2/80	G	4/8/80	7	American Gigolo	Polydor 6259
8/73	G	12/21/73	10	American Graffiti	MCA 8001
5/82	G	7/9/82	35	Annie	Columbia 38000
	P	7/9/82			
7/85	G	9/6/85	12	Back To The Future	MCA 6144
6/89	G	8/29/89	1	**Batman** [PRINCE]	Warner 25936
	P	8/29/89			
	2P	8/29/89			
11/88	G	3/21/89	2	Beaches [BETTE MIDLER]	Atlantic 81933
	P	5/16/89			
5/84	G	7/20/84	14	Beat Street, Volume 1	Atlantic 80154
12/84	G	2/11/85	1	**Beverly Hills Cop**	MCA 5547
	P	4/1/85			
	2P	9/20/85			
5/87	G	8/11/87	8	Beverly Hills Cop II	MCA 6207
	P	8/11/87			
9/83	G	12/12/83	17	The Big Chill	Motown 6062
	P	3/29/84			
	2P	9/27/85			
4/84	G	6/20/85	85	The Big Chill/More Songs From The Original Soundtrack	Motown 6094
10/61	G	12/21/61	1	**Blue Hawaii** [ELVIS PRESLEY]	RCA 2426
6/80	G	9/10/80	13	The Blues Brothers [BLUES BROTHERS]	Atlantic 16017
8/61	G	10/30/62	1	**Breakfast At Tiffany's** [HENRY MANCINI]	RCA 2362
2/85	G	6/11/85	17	The Breakfast Club	A&M 5045
5/84	G	7/27/84	8	Breakin'	Polydor 821 919
	P	7/27/84			

Release Date	Certification	Date of Certification	Chart Peak	ARTIST/Title Songwriter ● Producer (singles only)	Label & Number
9/88	G	1/10/89	54	Buster	Atlantic 81905
10/69	G	5/22/70	16	Butch Cassidy & The Sundance Kid [BURT BACHARACH]	A&M 4227
2/72	G	8/17/73	25	Cabaret	ABC 752
10/67	G P	9/17/68 10/13/86	11	Camelot	Warner 1712
8/76	G	12/21/76	14	Car Wash [ROSE ROYCE]	MCA 6000
1/56	G	1/15/64	2	Carousel	Capitol 694
9/81	G P	3/1/82 4/8/82	1	**Chariots Of Fire [VANGELIS]**	Polydor 6335
9/78	G	10/10/78	14	Children Of Sanchez [CHUCK MANGIONE]	A&M 6700
3/74	G	6/7/74	35	Claudine [GLADYS KNIGHT & THE PIPS]	Buddah 5602
1/78	G	1/9/78	17	Close Encounters Of The Third Kind	Arista 9500
3/80	G	1/11/82	40	Coal Miner's Daughter	MCA 5107
7/88	G P 2P 3P 4P	9/27/88 9/27/88 11/15/88 12/12/88 1/10/89	2	Cocktail	Elektra 60806
4/88	G	7/12/88	31	Colors	Warner 25713
1/73	G	3/7/73	1	**Deliverance/Dueling Banjos [ERIC WEISSBERG]**	Warner 2683
8/87	G P 2P 3P 4P 5P 6P 7P 8P 9P 10P	10/22/87 10/22/87 12/1/87 12/15/87 2/3/88 2/26/88 3/29/88 5/20/88 7/12/88 8/19/88 12/1/88	1	**Dirty Dancing**	RCA 6408
3/88	G P 2P 3P	5/20/88 5/20/88 5/20/88 7/22/88	3	More Dirty Dancing	RCA 6905
8/67	G	3/13/68	55	Doctor Doolittle	20th Century 5101
1/66	G	8/11/66	1	**Doctor Zhivago**	MGM 6
8/69	G	1/19/70	6	Easy Rider	Dunhill 50063
9/83	G P 2P	8/31/84 10/5/84 12/16/86	9	Eddie And The Cruisers [JOHN CAFFERTY & THE BEAVER BROWN BAND],	Scotti Br. 38929
12/79	G	7/3/80	52	The Electric Horseman [WILLIE NELSON]	Columbia 36327
12/70	G	6/28/73	21	Elvis—That's The Way It Is [ELVIS PRESLEY]	RCA 4445

Release Date	Certification	Date of Certification	Chart Peak	ARTIST/Title Songwriter ● Producer (singles only)	Label & Number
4/80	G	6/23/80	4	The Empire Strikes Back	RSO 4201
7/81	G	9/8/81	9	Endless Love	Mercury 2001
6/82	G	10/26/82	37	E.T.—The Extra-Terrestrial	MCA 6109
1/61	G	3/12/63	1	**Exodus**	RCA 1058
5/80	G P	8/19/80 9/15/81	7	Fame	RSO 3080
9/71	G	10/18/71	30	Fiddler On The Roof	United Art. 10900
4/83	G P 5P	6/17/83 6/17/83 10/12/84	1	**Flashdance**	Casablanca 811 492
4/78	G P	4/24/78 5/10/78	5	FM	MCA 12000
2/84	G P 5P 6P	4/2/84 4/2/84 10/19/84 8/9/89	1	**Footloose**	Columbia 39242
6/81	G	1/20/82	—	The Fox And The Hound	Disney 3823
2/71	G	4/6/71	36	Friends [ELTON JOHN]	Paramount 6004
8/68	G P	12/23/68 11/21/86	12	Funny Girl [BARBRA STREISAND]	Columbia 3220
2/75	G	9/8/75	6	Funny Lady [BARBRA STREISAND]	Arista 9004
6/84	G P	8/15/84 8/23/84	6	Ghostbusters	Arista 8246
6/89	G	8/11/89	14	Ghostbusters II	MCA 6306
10/60	G	3/12/63	1	**G.I. Blues** [ELVIS PRESLEY]	RCA 2256
3/58	G	4/17/68	1	**Gigi**	MGM 3641
11/62	G	8/13/63	3	Girls! Girls! Girls! [ELVIS PRESLEY]	RCA 2621
10/84	G	12/26/84	21	Give My Regards To Broad Street [PAUL McCARTNEY]	Columbia 39613
10/78	G	11/6/78	98	Goin' Coconuts [DONNY & MARIE OSMOND]	Polydor 6169
1/88	G P	3/28/88 7/18/88	10	Good Morning Vietnam	A&M 3913
1/68	G	8/14/68	4	The Good, The Bad And The Ugly	United Art. 5172
2/68	G	3/27/68	1	**The Graduate** [SIMON & GARFUNKEL]	Columbia 3180
4/78	G P 8P	5/2/78 5/9/78 11/7/84	1	**Grease**	RSO 4002
3/74	G	7/8/74	85	The Great Gatsby	Paramount 3001
3/79	G	5/16/79	65	Hair	RCA 3274
3/84	G P	7/10/84 7/10/84	16	Hard To Hold [RICK SPRINGFIELD]	RCA 4935

Release Date	Certification	Date of Certification	Chart Peak	ARTIST/Title Songwriter ● Producer (singles only)	Label & Number
7/81	G	9/18/81	12	Heavy Metal	Asylum 90004
8/65	G	8/23/65	1	**Help!** [THE BEATLES]	Capitol 2386
8/80	G P	10/15/80 11/12/80	11	Honeysuckle Rose [WILLIE NELSON]	Columbia 36752
3/63	G	6/11/69	4	How The West Was Won	MGM 5
9/88	G	1/5/89	31	Imagine: John Lennon [JOHN LENNON]	Capitol 90803
11/80	G P	1/14/81 1/14/81	3	The Jazz Singer [NEIL DIAMOND]	Capitol 12120
6/73	G	9/5/73	21	Jesus Christ Superstar	MCA 11000
10/73	G P 2P	10/30/73 11/21/86 11/21/86	2	Jonathan Livingston Seagull [NEIL DIAMOND]	Columbia 32550
8/67	G	12/5/68	19	The Jungle Book	Disneyland 3948
6/79	G P	6/26/79 10/5/79	8	The Kids Are Alright [THE WHO]	MCA 11005
6/56	G	1/15/64	1	**The King And I**	Capitol 740
6/87	G P 2P	9/15/87 9/15/87 12/2/87	1	**La Bamba**	Slash 25605
11/87	G	2/8/88	31	Less Than Zero	Def Jam 44042
5/70	G	5/26/70	1	**Let It Be** [THE BEATLES]	Apple 34001
6/87	G	9/30/87	15	The Lost Boys	Atlantic 81767
12/70	G	2/1/71	2	Love Story	Paramount 6002
7/57	G	4/9/68	1	**Loving You** [ELVIS PRESLEY]	RCA 1515
8/70	G	8/31/70	2	Mad Dogs & Englishmen [JOE COCKER]	A&M 6002
11/67	G	12/15/67	1	**Magical Mystery Tour** [THE BEATLES]	Capitol 2835
6/79	G	9/12/79	20	The Main Event [BARBRA STREISAND]	Columbia 36115
10/66	G	8/22/67	10	A Man And A Woman	United Art. 5147
8/64	G	12/31/64	1	**Mary Poppins**	Buena Vista 4026
5/86	G P	8/19/86 3/24/87	33	Maximum Overdrive/Who Made Who [AC/DC]	Atlantic 81650
6/69	G	5/4/70	19	Midnight Cowboy	United Art. 5198
7/79	G	12/6/79	32	The Muppet Movie [MUPPETS]	Atlantic 16001
7/62	G	3/27/63	2	The Music Man	Warner 1459
10/64	G	12/18/64	4	My Fair Lady	Columbia 2600
8/55	G	7/8/58	1	**Oklahoma!**	Capitol 595
11/68	G	7/25/69	20	Oliver!	Colgems 5501
8/80	G	10/14/80	12	One-Trick Pony [PAUL SIMON]	Warner 3472
9/69	G	10/19/70	28	Paint Your Wagon	Paramount 1001

1

2

3

4

1. Three consecutive platinum double-albums — that's Donna Summer's platinum achievement, matched by none other. Her 12 gold singles aren't exactly chopped liver, either.

2. No doubt that America's best-loved female singer is Barbra Streisand, with 31 gold and 19 platinum albums to her credit over the past 25 years.

3. In ten years with Sire Records, the Talking Heads have earned eight gold albums — more than anyone else on the label. Also gold: the band's 1981 spinoff project, Tom Tom Club.

4. Rod Stewart's 13 gold albums places him behind only Elton John and Paul McCartney as Britain's most-certified male vocalist. And he does have what they don't: a platinum single, for "Do Ya Think I'm Sexy."

5

6

7

8

5. Johnnie Taylor's "Disco Lady" was the RIAA's first platinum single, marking two million sales. The record achieved that on April 22, 1976 — 42 days after going gold.

6. Millionaire Dutchman Stanley August Miesegaes must have been gratified when the band his cash created — Supertramp — turned that investment into five gold and three platinum albums.

7. George Strait leads the pack of country artists breaking through in the '80s, with a remarkable 11 consecutive gold albums.

8. Were Three Dog Night onto something? You'll notice that Dunhill Records released all but two of their 12 gold albums for the label at very precise numerical intervals.

9. After the sweetness of their first million-seller in 1978, A Taste Of Honey signed up for the remake club three years later with "Sukiyaki." It was first a hit for Japan's Kyu Sakamoto in 1963.

9

Release Date	Certification	Date of Certification	Chart Peak	ARTIST/Title Songwriter ● Producer (singles only)	Label & Number
3/64	G	10/5/65	8	The Pink Panther [HENRY MANCINI]	RCA 2795
6/59	G	10/21/63	8	Porgy And Bess	Columbia 2016
1/86	G	4/14/86	5	Pretty In Pink	A&M 3901
6/84	G P 8P 9P 10P	8/29/84 8/29/84 11/13/84 1/16/85 2/22/89	1	**Purple Rain** [PRINCE & THE REVOLUTION]	Warner 25110
10/71	G	12/9/71	15	Rainbow Bridge [JIMI HENDRIX]	Reprise 2040
10/88	G P 2P 3P	12/6/88 12/6/88 12/6/88 1/17/89	1	**Rattle And Hum** [U2]	Island 91003
12/76	G P	4/21/77 6/22/77	4	Rocky	United Art. 693
6/82	G	8/16/82	15	Rocky III	Liberty 51130
10/85	G P	1/13/86 2/21/86	10	Rocky IV	Scotti B. 40203
3/78	G	2/23/81	49	The Rocky Horror Picture Show	Ode 21653
10/68	G	7/3/69	2	Romeo & Juliet	Capitol 2993
12/79	G P	4/10/80 6/11/80	12	The Rose [BETTE MIDLER]	Atlantic 16010
11/64	G	5/20/88	1	**Roustabout** [ELVIS PRESLEY]	RCA 2999
6/86	G P	8/18/86 1/3/78	20	Ruthless People	Epic 40398
11/77	G P 11P	11/22/77 1/3/78 11/7/84	1	**Saturday Night Fever** [THE BEE GEES]	RSO 4100
7/78	G P	7/19/78 7/19/78	5	Sgt. Pepper's Lonely Hearts Club Band	RSO 4100
10/80	G	12/4/87	187	Somewhere In Time	MCA 5154
10/76	G P 2P	11/3/76 11/15/76 10/30/84	2	The Song Remains The Same [LED ZEPPELIN]	Swan Song 201
3/65	G	3/30/65	1	**The Sound Of Music**	RCA 2005
3/58	G	12/18/59	1	**South Pacific**	RCA 1032
6/76	G	7/6/76	18	Sparkle [ARETHA FRANKLIN]	Atlantic 18176
6/85	G	10/23/85	21	St. Elmo's Fire	Atlantic 81261
8/86	G	12/10/86	31	Stand By Me	Atlantic 81677
11/76	G P 4P	12/23/76 1/21/77 10/26/84	1	**A Star Is Born** [BARBRA STREISAND & KRIS KRISTOFFERSON],	Columbia 34403

Release Date	Certification	Date of Certification	Chart Peak	ARTIST/Title Songwriter ● Producer (singles only)	Label & Number
6/77	G P	7/18/77 8/17/77	2	Star Wars	20th Century 541
6/83	G P	8/30/83 8/30/83	6	Staying Alive [THE BEE GEES]	RSO 813 269
1/74	G	4/19/74	1	**The Sting**	MCA 390
10/84	G P	3/1/85 7/2/86	41	Stop Making Sense [TALKING HEADS]	Sire 25121
11/77	G	12/5/77	36	The Story Of Star Wars/ From The Original Soundtrack	20th Century 550
7/72	G	9/7/72	1	**Superfly** [CURTIS MAYFIELD]	Curtom 8014
9/85	G	4/2/87	29	Sweet Dreams [PATSY CLINE]	MCA 6149
9/84	G	11/21/84	34	Teachers	Capitol 12371
4/78	G P	5/16/78 6/8/78	10	Thank God It's Friday	Casablanca 7099
3/75	G P 2P	4/9/75 11/21/86 11/21/86	1	**That's The Way Of The World** [EARTH, WIND & FIRE],	Columbia 33280
3/67	G	4/7/67	16	Thoroughly Modern Millie	Decca 71500
3/75	G	3/18/75	2	Tommy	Polydor 9502
5/86	G P 2P 3P 4P 5P	7/21/86 7/21/86 9/23/86 12/8/86 4/6/87 7/6/89	1	**Top Gun**	Columbia 40323
9/86	G	11/18/86	17	True Stories [TALKING HEADS]	Sire 25512
11/83	G P	1/16/84 1/16/84	26	Two Of A Kind [OLIVIA NEWTON-JOHN/JOHN TRAVOLTA]	MCA 6127
6/68	G	4/24/69	24	2001: A Space Odyssey	MGM 13
3/86	G P	6/3/86 6/3/86	3	Under The Cherry Moon/Parade [PRINCE]	Paisley Park 25395
4/80	G P	7/14/80 7/24/80	3	Urban Cowboy	Asylum 90002
2/85	G P	4/9/85 7/16/85	11	Vision Quest	Geffen 24063
1/73	G	3/7/73	28	Wattstax: The Living Word	Stax 3010
1/74	G	5/17/74	20	The Way We Were	Columbia 32830
8/61	G P 3P	1/7/63 11/21/86 11/21/86	1	**West Side Story**	Columbia 2070
10/85	G	1/22/86	17	White Knights	Atlantic 81273
7/87	G	9/29/87	7	Who's That Girl [MADONNA]	Sire 25611

Release Date	Certification	Date of Certification	Chart Peak	ARTIST/Title Songwriter ● Producer (singles only)	Label & Number
	P	9/29/87			
9/78	G	9/29/78	40	The Wiz	MCA 14000
8/84	G	11/8/84	4	The Woman In Red	Motown 6108
	P	11/8/84		[STEVIE WONDER/DIONNE WARWICK]	
5/70	G	5/22/70	1	**Woodstock**	Cotillion 500
4/71	G	4/1/71	7	Woodstock Two	Cotillion 400
6/80	G	8/19/80	4	Xanadu [OLIVIA NEWTON-JOHN/ELO]	MCA 6100
	P	8/19/80			
	2P	10/12/84			
1/69	G	2/5/69	2	Yellow Submarine [THE BEATLES]	Apple 153
11/83	G	1/9/84	9	Yentl [BARBRA STREISAND]	Columbia 39152
	P	1/9/84			
10/77	G	11/1/77	17	You Light Up My Life	Arista 4159
12/64	G	6/11/69	16	Your Cheatin' Heart [HANK WILLIAMS JR.]	MGM 4260

ORIGINAL CAST ALBUMS

This details every gold, platinum, and multi-platinum original cast album. These are not listed elsewhere in the book, except Barbra Streisand's *Funny Girl*, which does appear under her own artist entry in the main section. Most of these albums feature Broadway casts.

Release Date	Certification	Date of Certification	Chart Peak	ARTIST/Title	Label & Number
5/77	G	6/19/79	81	Annie	Columbia 34712
	P	12/22/80			
1/61	G	2/9/62	1	**Camelot**	Columbia 2031
1/83	G	12/3/85	113	Cats	Geffen 2031
	P	12/5/88			
7/75	G	12/16/77	98	A Chorus Line	Columbia 33581
10/79	G	9/14/81	105	Evita	MCA 11007
	P	10/6/86			
10/64	G	10/28/65	7	Fiddler On The Roof	RCA 1093
1/59	G	2/9/62	1	**Flower Drum Song**	Columbia 2009
4/64	G	9/21/64	2	Funny Girl [BARBRA STREISAND]	Capitol 2059
7/71	G	12/12/72	34	Godspell	Bell 1102
6/68	G	3/25/69	1	**Hair**	RCA 1150
2/64	G	6/2/64	1	**Hello, Dolly!**	RCA 1087
11/70	G	12/21/70	1	**Jesus Christ Superstar**	Decca 7206
6/66	G	5/14/67	23	Mame	Columbia 3000
1/66	G	6/28/67	31	Man Of La Mancha	Kapp 4505

Release Date	Certification	Date of Certification	Chart Peak	ARTIST/Title Songwriter ● Producer (singles only)	Label & Number
5/87	G	3/14/89	117	Les Miserables	Geffen 24151
1/58	G	11/16/59	1	**The Music Man**	Capitol 990
4/56	G P 3P	1/8/64 11/21/86 11/21/86	1	**My Fair Lady**	Columbia 2015
10/62	G	5/4/66	4	Oliver!	RCA 2004
4/87	G P	5/10/88 8/3/89	33	Phantom Of The Opera	Polydor 831 273
11/59	G	12/7/60	1	**The Sound Of Music**	Columbia 2020
5/49	G	5/16/66	1	**South Pacific**	Columbia 2040
10/57	G	1/12/62	5	West Side Story	Columbia 2001

CHILDREN'S RECORDS

The RIAA has certified dozens of children's records gold and platinum over the past 30 years. Most are not by recording artists *per se*, and so are listed here as a separate category. If a specific "artist" (for example, the Muppets) or performer (such as Raffi) *is* associated with a record, that artist's name appears in brackets after the title. It is also entered in the main section of the book.

Since none of the gold/platinum children's singles ever charted in *Billboard*, the Hot 100 peak position column is omitted for this section only. For the 10 children's albums that charted, the peak position is shown in brackets at the right of the album title.

SINGLES

Release Date	Certification	Date of Certification	Chart Peak	ARTIST/Title	Label & Number
4/79	G	4/11/88		Alice In Wonderland	Disneyland 306
8/77	G P	2/23/83 4/11/88		Bambi	Disneyland 309
7/77	G	7/1/83		Brer Rabbit & The Tar Baby	Disneyland 363
8/77	G	2/23/83		Cinderella	Disneyland 308
8/77	G	4/12/83		Dumbo	Disneyland 324
9/80	G	5/26/82		The Empire Strikes Back	Buena Vista 451
12/82	G	6/15/83		E.T.—The Extra-Terrestrial	Disneyland 456
6/81	G	2/23/83		The Fox And The Hound	Disneyland 383
8/77	G	7/22/85		The Hobbit	Buena Vista 368
6/78	G	6/8/83		It's A Small World	Disneyland 323
8/77	G	6/11/84		The Jungle Book	Disneyland 319

Release Date	Certification	Date of Certification	Chart Peak	ARTIST/Title Songwriter ● Producer (singles only)	Label & Number
6/79	G	3/22/83		The Lady And The Tramp	Disneyland 307
8/77	G	4/12/83		Mary Poppins	Disneyland 302
7/82	G	5/11/89		Mickey's Christmas Carol	Disneyland 386
5/79	G	7/22/85		Mother Goose Rhymes	Disneyland 312
3/82	G P	5/11/89 5/11/89		101 Dalmatians	Disneyland 305
6/78	G	7/1/83		Pete's Dragon	Disneyland 369
8/77	G	2/23/83		Peter Pan	Disneyland 304
8/77	G	3/22/83		Pinocchio	Disneyland 311
6/78	G	2/29/84		The Rescuers	Disneyland 367
4/83	G	8/1/83		Return Of The Jedi	Buena Vista 455
8/77	G	5/23/84		Robin Hood	Disneyland 365
8/77	G	6/8/83		Sleeping Beauty	Disneyland 301
7/77	G P	3/22/83 4/11/88		Snow White	Disneyland 310
4/79	G P	5/11/82 11/21/84		Star Wars	Buena Vista 450
6/78	G	6/8/83		The Three Little Pigs	Disneyland 303
6/78	G	7/22/85		Winnie The Pooh And The Blustery Day	Disneyland 327
5/79	G	4/11/88		Winnie The Pooh And The Honeytree	Disneyland 313
8/77	G	7/1/83		Winnie The Pooh And Tigger Too	Disneyland 366
6/78	G	7/22/85		The Wizard Of Oz	Disneyland 347

ALBUMS

Release Date	Certification	Date of Certification	Chart Peak	ARTIST/Title	Label & Number
7/78	G	3/30/84		The Best Of Disney Volume I	Disneyland 2502
7/78	G	7/22/85		The Best Of Disney Volume II	Disneyland 2503
8/75	G	11/8/84		Bullfrogs And Butterflies [CANDLE]	Birdwing 2010
8/84	G	6/21/84		Cabbage Patch Dreams [THE CABBAGE PATCH KIDS]	Parker Bros. 7216
5/79	G P	3/22/83 4/9/86		Children's Favorites Volume I	Disneyland 2505
7/79	G P	10/5/83 10/13/86		Children's Favorites Volume II	Disneyland 2508
6/86	G	12/7/88		Children's Favorites Volume III	Disneyland 2525
8/64	G	12/7/72		The Chilling, Thrilling Sounds Of The Haunted House	Disneyland 1257
8/79	G	4/11/88		The Chilling, Thrilling Sounds Of The Haunted House	Disneyland 2507
10/81	G	1/17/84	[72]	A Chipmunk Christmas [THE CHIPMUNKS]	RCA 4041
6/80	G	10/14/80	[34]	Chipmunk Punk [THE CHIPMUNKS]	Excelsior 6008

Release Date	Certification	Date of Certification	Chart Peak	ARTIST/Title Songwriter ● Producer (singles only)	Label & Number
9/79	G P	12/28/84 4/11/88		Disney's Christmas Favorites	Disneyland 2507
6/81	G	1/20/82		The Fox And The Hound [S]	Disneyland 3823
12/72	G	10/28/76		Free To Be…You And Me [MARLO THOMAS] [68]	Bell 1110
8/67	G	12/5/68		The Jungle Book [S] [19]	Disneyland 3948
8/64	G	12/31/64		**Mary Poppins [S]** [1]	Buena Vista 4026
9/79	G P 2P	4/11/80 5/30/80 10/18/84		Mickey Mouse Disco [35]	Disneyland 2504
2/82	G P	5/13/83 4/11/88		Mousercise	Disneyland 2516
7/79	G	12/6/79		The Muppet Movie [S] [32]	Atlantic 16001
8/75	G	2/26/81		The Music Machine [CANDLE]	Birdwing 2004
7/70	G	10/23/70		The Sesame Street Book And Record [THE MUPPETS] [23]	Columbia 1069
8/78	G	11/21/78		Sesame Street Fever [THE MUPPETS] [75]	Sesame St. 79005
11/84	G	5/23/89		Singable Songs For The Very Young [RAFFI]	Shoreline 0202
5/64	G	1/2/69		The Story And Songs From Walt Disney's Mary Poppins	Disneyland 3922
5/81	G	8/28/81		Urban Chipmunk [THE CHIPMUNKS] [56]	RCA 4027

MISCELLANEOUS ALBUMS

Release Date	Certification	Date of Certification	Chart Peak	ARTIST/Title Songwriter ● Producer (singles only)	Label & Number
10/71	G	12/31/71	8	All In The Family [ORIGINAL TV CAST]	Atlantic 7210
12/73	G	7/26/77	—	Alleluia—Praise Gathering For Believers	Impact 3171
6/73	G	7/20/73	27	Dick Clark/20 Years Of Rock 'N Roll	Buddah 5133
9/85	G P 2P 3P 4P	11/22/85 11/22/85 11/22/85 12/2/85 2/27/86	1	**Music From The TV Series Miami Vice**	MCA 6150
7/79	G	8/21/79	21	A Night At Studio 54	Casablanca 7161
8/88	G	10/26/88	31	1988 Summer Olympics Album/ One Moment In Time	Arista 8551
12/79	G	9/15/80	19	No Nukes/The MUSE Concerts For A Non-Nuclear Future	Asylum 801
10/59	G	2/17/60	2	60 Years Of Music America Loves Best	RCA 6074
10/87	G P	12/15/87 12/15/87	20	A Very Special Christmas	A&M 3911
12/60	G	8/19/64	—	Victory At Sea, Vol. 1 [TV SOUNDTRACK]	RCA 2335
10/85	G	12/17/87	172	A Winter's Solstice	Windham Hill 1045

SONG TITLES

Song Title	Song Title
Artist	Artist

Abracadabra
The Steve Miller Band

Abraham, Martin And John
Dion

Addicted To Love
Robert Palmer

After All
Cher & Peter Cetera

After The Love Has Gone
Earth, Wind & Fire

After The Lovin'
Engelbert Humperdinck

Afternoon Delight
The Starland Vocal Band

Against All Odds (Take A Look At Me Now)
Phil Collins

Ain't Gonna Bump No More
Joe Tex

Ain't No Stoppin' Us Now
McFadden & Whitehead

Ain't No Sunshine
Bill Withers

Ain't No Woman (Like The One I've Got)
The Four Tops

Ain't Understanding Mellow
Jerry Butler & Brenda Lee Eager

Air That I Breathe, The
The Hollies

All By Myself
Eric Carmen

All Night Long (All Night)
Lionel Richie

All Out Of Love
Air Supply

All You Need Is Love
The Beatles

Alone Again (Naturally)
Gilbert O'Sullivan

Always And Forever
Heatwave

American Pie
Don McLean

American Woman
The Guess Who

Americans
Byron MacGregor

Amos Moses
Jerry Reed

And The Beat Goes On
The Whispers

And When I Die
Blood, Sweat & Tears

Angel
Madonna

Angel In Your Arms
Hot

Angel Of The Morning
Juice Newton

Angie
The Rolling Stones

Angie Baby
Helen Reddy

Annie's Song
John Denver

Another Brick In The Wall
Pink Floyd

Another One Bites The Dust
Queen

Aquarius/Let The Sunshine In
The 5th Dimension

Song Title	Song Title
Artist	Artist

Bend Me, Shape Me
American Breed

Bennie And The Jets
Elton John

Best Of My Love
Emotions

Best Thing That Ever Happened To Me
Gladys Knight & The Pips

Betcha By Golly, Wow
Stylistics

Beth
Kiss

Bette Davis Eyes
Kim Carnes

Big Bad John
Jimmy Dean

Billie Jean
Michael Jackson

Billy, Don't Be A Hero
Bo Donaldson & The Heywoods

Black & White
Three Dog Night

Black Water
Doobie Brothers

Blinded By The Light
Manfred Mann's Earth Band

Blue Bayou
Linda Ronstadt

Bohemian Rhapsody
Queen

Boogie Fever
The Sylvers

Boogie Nights
Heatwave

Boogie Oogie Oogie
A Taste Of Honey

Boogie Wonderland
Earth, Wind & Fire with The Emotions

Born To Be Alive
Patrick Hernandez

Born To Be Wild
Steppenwolf

Boy Named Sue, A
Johnny Cash

Brand New Key
Melanie

Brandy (You're A Fine Girl)
Looking Glass

Break Up To Make Up
The Stylistics

Breaks, The
Kurtis Blow

Bridge Over Troubled Water
Simon & Garfunkel
Aretha Franklin

Bring The Boys Home
Freda Payne

Brother Louie
The Stories

Buffalo Stance
Neneh Cherry

Build Me Up Buttercup
The Foundations

Burning Love
Elvis Presley

Bustin' Loose
Chuck Brown & The Soul Searchers

C

Calcutta
Lawrence Welk

1

2

3

1. America was malled by Tiffany Renee Darwish, and the outcome was quadruple platinum at age 17. No other female artist on MCA Records has sold so many copies of one album.

2. Voices don't always carry — and Boston's 'Til Tuesday was another of those groups whose first gold album was a tough act to follow. They couldn't.

3. USA For Africa's all-star recording of "We Are The World" went simultaneously gold, platinum, and quadruple platinum on April 1, 1985. The RIAA waived certification rules to allow this just days after the charity record's release.

4. Four of Conway Twitty's six solo gold albums were compilations of previously-released material, as was one of his three gold duets with Loretta Lynn.

4

5

6

7

8

9. No female singer who's been making hits for as long as Tina Turner — 29 years — has an album that's sold more than *Private Dancer*.

5. UB40 turned "Red, Red Wine" into gold on the second attempt. The single was originally released in 1984, when it barely hit the Top 40.

6. Suzanne Vega's second album, *Solitude Standing*, became her first gold success, largely on the strength of a hit single, "Luka."

7. Van Halen is the only Warner Bros. act with two albums which have sold six million copies: their label debut in 1978, and their sixth album, *1984*.

8. The Time was the first taste of gold for Jimmy Jam and Terry Lewis, who subsequently left the band to become the hottest black producers of the late '80s.

Song Title / Artist	Song Title / Artist
California Dreamin' The Mamas & Papas	**Catch Me (I'm Falling)** Pretty Poison
Call Me Blondie	**Cecilia** Simon & Garfunkel
Call Me (Come Back Home) Al Green	**Celebration** Kool & The Gang
Can I Change My Mind Tyrone Davis	**Centerfold** The J. Geils Band
Can't Buy Me Love The Beatles	**Chain Of Fools** Aretha Franklin
Can't Fight This Feeling REO Speedwagon	**Cherish** The Association David Cassidy
Can't Get Enough Barry White	**Cherish** Kool & The Gang
Can't Help Falling In Love Elvis Presley	**Chevy Van** Sammy Johns
Can't Smile Without You Barry Manilow	**Chewy Chewy** Ohio Express
Can't Take My Eyes Off You Frankie Valli	**Chokin' Kind, The** Joe Simon
Candida Dawn featuring Tony Orlando	**Cisco Kid, The** War
Candy Man, The Sammy Davis Jr.	**Clair** Gilbert O'Sullivan
Car Wash Rose Royce	**Clean Up Woman** Betty Wright
Careless Whisper Wham!	**Close My Eyes Forever** Lita Ford with Ozzy Osbourne
Caribbean Queen Billy Ocean	**Close The Door** Teddy Pendergrass
Casanova Levert	**Closer I Get To You, The** Roberta Flack & Donny Hathaway
Cat's In The Cradle Harry Chapin	**Cold Hearted** Paula Abdul
Catch A Falling Star Perry Como	**Color Him Father** The Winstons

Song Title Artist	Song Title Artist

Come And Get Your Love
Redbone

Come Back When You Grow Up
Bobby Vee & The Strangers

Coming Up (Live at Glasgow)
Paul McCartney

Convoy
C.W. McCall

Cool It Now
New Edition

Copacabana (At The Copa)
Barry Manilow

Could It Be I'm Falling In Love
The Spinners

Cover Of Rolling Stone
Dr. Hook & The Medicine Show

Coward Of The County
Kenny Rogers

Cowboys To Girls
The Intruders

Cracklin' Rosie
Neil Diamond

Crazy For You
Madonna

Crazy Little Thing Called Love
Queen

Crocodile Rock
Elton John

Cry Like A Baby
The Box Tops

Crying In The Chapel
Elvis Presley

Cum On Feel The Noize
Quiet Riot

D

Da Doo Ron Ron
Shaun Cassidy

Daddy Don't You Walk So Fast
Wayne Newton

Dance, Dance, Dance
Chic

Dancing Queen
Abba

Dark Lady
Cher

Day After Day
Badfinger

Day Dreaming
Aretha Franklin

Daydream Believer
The Monkees

December, 1963 (Oh, What A Night)
The 4 Seasons

Delta Dawn
Helen Reddy

Desire
U2

Devil Went Down To Georgia, The
The Charlie Daniels Band

Devil Woman
Cliff Richard

Didn't I (Blow Your Mind This Time)
The Delfonics

Dim All The Nights
Donna Summer

Dirty Laundry
Don Henley

Disco Duck
Rick Dees & His Cast Of Idiots

Song Title	Song Title
Artist	Artist

Disco Lady
Johnnie Taylor

Disco Nights (Rock-Freak)
G.Q.

Dizzy
Tommy Roe

Do It Anyway You Wanna
People's Choice

Do It ('Til You're Satisfied)
B.T. Express

Do That To Me One More Time
The Captain & Tennille

Do They Know It's Christmas?
Band Aid

Do Ya Think I'm Sexy
Rod Stewart

Do You Wanna Make Love
Peter McCann

Doesn't Somebody Want To Be Wanted
The Partridge Family

Doin' It To Death
Fred Wesley & The J.B.s

Don't
Elvis Presley

Don't Be Cruel
Bobby Brown

Don't Bring Me Down
Electric Light Orchestra

Don't Cry Daddy
Elvis Presley

Don't Give Up On Us
David Soul

Don't Go Breaking My Heart
Elton John & Kiki Dee

Don't It Make My Brown Eyes Blue
Crystal Gayle

Don't Knock My Love (Part 1)
Wilson Pickett

Don't Let The Green Grass Fool You
Wilson Pickett

Don't Let The Sun Go Down On Me
Elton John

Don't Play That Song
Aretha Franklin

Don't Pull Your Love
Hamilton, Joe Frank & Reynolds

Don't Stop The Music
Yarbrough & Peoples

Don't Stop 'Til You Get Enough
Michael Jackson

Don't Worry, Be Happy
Bobby McFerrin

Don't You Want Me
The Human League

Double Dutch Bus
Frankie Smith

Double Vision
Foreigner

Down By The Lazy River
The Osmonds

Down On The Corner
Creedence Clearwater Revival

Down Under
Men At Work

Downtown
Petula Clark

Dream Weaver
Gary Wright

Dreams
Fleetwood Mac

Drift Away
Dobie Gray

| Song Title | Song Title |
| Artist | Artist |

Drivin' My Life Away
Eddie Rabbitt

Drowning In The Sea Of Love
Joe Simon

Dueling Banjos
Eric Weissberg

Dust In The Wind
Kansas

E

Easy Come, Easy Go
Bobby Sherman

Easy Lover
Phil Collins with Philip Bailey

Easy Loving
Freddie Hart

Ebony And Ivory
Paul McCartney & Stevie Wonder

Eight Days A Week
The Beatles

Electric Avenue
Eddy Grant

Electric Youth
Debbie Gibson

Elvira
The Oak Ridge Boys

Emotion
Samantha Sang

Endless Love
Diana Ross & Lionel Richie

Enjoy Yourself
The Jacksons

Entertainer, The
Marvin Hamlisch

Escape (The Pina Colada Song)
Rupert Holmes

Eternal Flame
The Bangles

Evergreen (Love Theme From "A Star Is Born")
Barbra Streisand

Everlasting Love, An
Andy Gibb

Every Breath You Take
The Police

Every Little Step
Bobby Brown

Every Rose Has Its Thorn
Poison

Everybody Loves Somebody
Dean Martin

Everybody Plays The Fool
The Main Ingredient

Everyday People
Sly & The Family Stone

Every 1's A Winner
Hot Chocolate

Everything Is Beautiful
Ray Stevens

Express
B.T. Express

Express Yourself
Madonna

Eye Of The Tiger
Survivor

F

Fallin' In Love
Hamilton, Joe Frank & Reynolds

Fame
David Bowie

Family Affair
Sly & The Family Stone

Song Title	Song Title
Artist	Artist

Feel Like Makin' Love Roberta Flack	**For The Love Of Money** The O'Jays
Feelings Morris Albert	**Forever Your Girl** Paula Abdul
Fifth Of Beethoven, A Walter Murphy	**Fox On The Run** The Sweet
50 Ways To Leave Your Lover Paul Simon	**Frankenstein** The Edgar Winter Group
Fight The Power (Part 1) The Isley Brothers	**Freak, Le** Chic
Fire The Crazy World Of Arthur Brown	**Freddie's Dead** Curtis Mayfield
Fire The Ohio Players	**Freeze-Frame** The J. Geils Band
Fire The Pointer Sisters	**Funky Cold Medina** Tone Loc
First Time Ever I Saw Your Face, The Roberta Flack	**Funky Worm** The Ohio Players
Flash Light Parliament	**Funkytown** Lipps, Inc.
Flashdance . . . What A Feeling Irene Cara	**Funny Face** Donna Fargo

G

Float On The Floaters	**Galveston** Glen Campbell
Fly Like An Eagle The Steve Miller Band	**Garden Party** Rick Nelson & The Stone Canyon Band
Fly, Robin, Fly Silver Convention	**Georgy Girl** The Seekers
Fool Such As I, A Elvis Presley	**Get Back** The Beatles with Billy Preston
Fooled Around And Fell In Love Elvin Bishop	**Get Down** Gilbert O'Sullivan
Footloose Kenny Loggins	**Get Down On It** Kool & The Gang
For All We Know The Carpenters	

Song Title	Song Title
Artist	Artist

Get On The Good Foot (Part 1) James Brown	**Good Vibrations** The Beach Boys
Get Together The Youngbloods	**Goodbye Yellow Brick Road** Elton John
Get Up And Boogie Silver Convention	**Goodnight Tonight** Paul McCartney
Getaway Earth, Wind & Fire	**Got My Mind Made Up** Instant Funk
Ghostbusters Ray Parker Jr.	**Got To Be Real** Cheryl Lynn
Girl Is Mine, The Paul McCartney & Michael Jackson	**Got To Get You Into My Life** Earth, Wind & Fire
Girl Watcher The O'Kaysions	**Grazing In The Grass** Hugh Masakela The Friends Of Distinction
Girl You Know It's True Milli Vanilli	**Grease** Frankie Valli
Girls Just Want To Have Fun Cyndi Lauper	**Green Onions** Booker T. & The M.G.s
Gitarzan Ray Stevens	**Green Tambourine** The Lemon Pipers
Give Me Just A Little More Time The Chairmen Of The Board	**Groove Line, The** Heatwave
Give Your Baby A Standing Ovation The Dells	**Groove Me** King Floyd
Gloria Laura Branigan	**Groovin'** The Young Rascals
Go All The Way Raspberries	**Groovy Kind Of Love, A** Phil Collins
Go Away Little Girl Donny Osmond	**Groovy Situation** Gene Chandler
Going In Circles The Friends Of Distinction	**Guilty** Barbra Streisand & Barry Gibb
Gonna Fly Now (Theme From "Rocky") Bill Conti	**Gypsy Woman** Brian Hyland
Good Times Chic	**Gypsys, Tramps & Thieves** Cher

Song Title Artist	Song Title Artist

H

Hair
Cowsills

Half-Breed
Cher

Hangin' Tough
New Kids On The Block

Hanky Panky
Tommy James & The Shondells

Happiest Girl In The Whole U.S.A., The
Donna Fargo

Happy Together
The Turtles

Hard Day's Night, A
The Beatles

Hard Headed Woman
Elvis Presley

Hard To Say I'm Sorry
Chicago

Harper Valley P.T.A.
Jeannie C. Riley

Harry Hippie
Bobby Womack & Peace

Have You Ever Seen The Rain?
Creedence Clearwater Revival

Have You Never Been Mellow
Olivia Newton-John

He Don't Love You (Like I Love You)
Dawn featuring Tony Orlando

He's Got The Whole World In His Hands
Laurie London

He's So Shy
The Pointer Sisters

Heart Of Glass
Blondie

Heart Of Gold
Neil Young

Heartache Tonight
The Eagles

Heartbeat—It's A Lovebeat
DeFranco Family featuring Tony DeFranco

Heaven Knows
Donna Summer

Heaven Must Be Missing An Angel
Tavares

Heaven On The 7th Floor
Paul Nicholas

Hello
Lionel Richie

Hello Goodbye
The Beatles

Hello, I Love You
The Doors

Help!
The Beatles

Help Me Make It Through The Night
Sammi Smith

Here I Am (Come And Take Me)
Al Green

Here You Come Again
Dolly Parton

Hey Deanie
Shaun Cassidy

Hey Girl
Donny Osmond

Hey Jude
The Beatles

Hey! Paula
Paul & Paula

Hey There Lonely Girl
Eddie Holman

Song Title Artist	Song Title Artist
(Hey Won't You Play) Another Somebody Done Somebody Wrong Song B.J. Thomas	**House Of The Rising Sun** Frijid Pink
Higher And Higher Rita Coolidge	**How Can You Mend A Broken Heart** The Bee Gees
Hit Me With Your Best Shot Pat Benatar	**How Deep Is Your Love** The Bee Gees
Hitchin' A Ride Vanity Fare	**How Do You Do?** Mouth & MacNeal
Hold The Line Toto	**Hurting Each Other** The Carpenters
Holly Holy Neil Diamond	**Hurts So Good** John Cougar Mellencamp
Hollywood Swinging Kool & The Gang	**The Hustle** Van McCoy
Honey Bobby Goldsboro	
Honky Tonk Women The Rolling Stones	**I**
Hooked On A Feeling B.J. Thomas Blue Swede	**I.O.U.** Jimmy Dean
Hopelessly Devoted To You Olivia Newton-John	**I Am Woman** Helen Reddy
Horse, The Cliff Nobles & Co.	**I Believe In You** Johnnie Taylor
Horse With No Name, A America	**I Can Help** Billy Swan
Hot Blooded Foreigner	**I Can See Clearly Now** Johnny Nash
Hot Child In The City Nick Gilder	**(I Can't Get No) Satisfaction** The Rolling Stones
Hot Line The Sylvers	**I Can't Go For That (No Can Do)** Daryl Hall & John Oates
Hot Stuff Donna Summer	**I Can't Stop Loving You** Ray Charles
Hotel California The Eagles	**I Don't Know If It's Right** Evelyn "Champagne" King
	I Feel Fine The Beatles

Song Title Artist	Song Title Artist
I Feel For You Chaka Khan	**I Say A Little Prayer** Dionne Warwick Aretha Franklin
I Feel Love Donna Summer	**I Shot The Sheriff** Eric Clapton
I Get Around The Beach Boys	**I Think I Love You** The Partridge Family
I Got Stung Elvis Presley	**I Wanna Be Your Lover** Prince
I Got You Babe Sonny & Cher	**I Wanna Dance With Somebody (Who Loves Me)** Whitney Houston
I Gotcha Joe Tex	**I Wanna Have Some Fun** Samantha Fox
I Honestly Love You Olivia Newton-John	**I Want A New Drug** Huey Lewis & The News
I Just Called To Say I Love You Stevie Wonder	**I Want Her** Keith Sweat
I Just Can't Stop Loving You Michael Jackson with Siedah Garrett	**I Want To Hold Your Hand** The Beatles
I Just Want To Be Your Everything Andy Gibb	**I Want To Know What Love Is** Foreigner
I Like Dreamin' Kenny Nolan	**I Want You To Want Me** Cheap Trick
I Love A Rainy Night Eddie Rabbitt	**I Want Your Love** Chic
I Love How You Love Me Bobby Vinton	**I Was Made For Lovin' You** Kiss
I Love Music The O'Jays	**I Will Survive** Gloria Gaynor
I Love Rock 'n' Roll Joan Jett & The Blackhearts	**I Write The Songs** Barry Manilow
I Love The Nightlife (Disco 'Round) Alicia Bridges	**I'd Like To Teach The World To Sing** The New Seekers
I Never Cry Alice Cooper	**I'd Love You To Want Me** Lobo
I Never Loved A Man (The Way I Love You) Aretha Franklin	**I'd Really Love To See You Tonight** England Dan & John Ford Coley

Song Title	Song Title
Artist	Artist

If I Can't Have You
Yvonne Elliman

If You Don't Know Me By Now
Harold Melvin & The Blue Notes
Simply Red

If You Leave Me Now
Chicago

If You Love Me (Let Me Know)
Olivia Newton-John

If You Want Me To Stay
Sly & The Family Stone

If You're Ready (Come Go With Me)
The Staple Singers

I'll Always Love You
Taylor Dayne

I'll Be Around
The Spinners

I'll Be Good To You
The Brothers Johnson

I'll Be Loving You (Forever)
The New Kids On The Block

I'll Never Fall In Love Again
Tom Jones

I'll Never Love This Way Again
Dionne Warwick

I'm A Believer
The Monkees

I'm Alive
The Electric Light Orchestra

I'm Gonna Love You Just A Little Bit More Baby
Barry White

I'm Henry VIII, I Am
Herman's Hermits

I'm Leaving It Up To You
Donny & Marie Osmond

I'm Sorry
John Denver

I'm Still In Love With You
Al Green

I'm Stone In Love With You
The Stylistics

I'm That Type Of Guy
L.L. Cool J.

In The Ghetto
Elvis Presley

In The Navy
The Village People

In The Summertime
Mungo Jerry

In The Year 2525
Zager & Evans

Incense And Peppermints
The Strawberry Alarm Clock

Indian Giver
The 1910 Fruitgum Company

Indian Reservation
Paul Revere & The Raiders

Instant Karma (We All Shine On)
John Lennon

Instant Replay
Dan Hartman

Into The Groove
Madonna

Island Girl
Elton John

Islands In The Stream
Dolly Parton & Kenny Rogers

It Don't Come Easy
Ringo Starr

It Never Rains In Southern California
Albert Hammond

It Takes Two
Rob Base & DJ E-Z Rock

Song Title Artist	Song Title Artist
It's A Heartache Bonnie Tyler	**Joanna** Kool & The Gang
It's Ecstacy When You Lay Down Next To Me Barry White	**Joker, The** The Steve Miller Band
It's Now Or Never Elvis Presley	**Joy To The World** Three Dog Night
It's Still Rock And Roll To Me Billy Joel	**Judy In Disguise (With Glasses)** John Fred & The Playboy Band
It's Too Late Carole King	**Juicy Fruit** Mtume
It's Your Thing The Isley Brothers	**Julie, Do Ya Love Me** Bobby Sherman
I've Got Love On My Mind Natalie Cole	**Jump** Van Halen
I've Got To Use My Imagination Gladys Knight & The Pips	**Jungle Boogie** Kool & The Gang
(I've Had) The Time Of My Life Bill Medley & Jennifer Warnes	**Jungle Fever** Chakachas
	Just Don't Want To Be Lonely The Main Ingredient

J

Jack And Diane
John Cougar Mellencamp

Jack And Jill
Raydio

Jam Up Jelly Tight
Tommy Roe

Jean
Oliver

Jesse
Carly Simon

Jessie's Girl
Rick Springfield

Jingle Jangle
The Archies

Jive Talkin'
The Bee Gees

(Just Like) Starting Over
John Lennon

Just The Way You Are
Billy Joel

Just When I Needed You Most
Randy Vanwarmer

Just You 'n' Me
Chicago

K

Karma Chameleon
Culture Club

Keep On Loving You
REO Speedwagon

Keep On Movin'
Soul II Soul

Song Title	Song Title
Artist	Artist

Killing Me Softly With His Song
Roberta Flack

King Is Gone, The
Ronnie McDowell

King Of The Road
Roger Miller

King Tut
Steve Martin

Kiss
Prince & The Revolution

Kiss An Angel Good Mornin'
Charley Pride

Kiss And Say Goodbye
The Manhattans

Kiss On My List
Daryl Hall & John Oates

Kiss You All Over
Exile

Knock On Wood
Amii Stewart

Knock Three Times
Dawn featuring Tony Orlando

Kokomo
The Beach Boys

Kung Fu Fighting
Carl Douglas

L

La La La (If I Had You)
Bobby Sherman

Ladies' Night
Kool & The Gang

Lady
Kenny Rogers

Lady Madonna
The Beatles

Lady Marmalade
LaBelle

Lady Willpower
Gary Puckett & The Union Gap

Last Dance
Donna Summer

(Last Night) I Didn't Get To Sleep At All
The 5th Dimension

Last Song
Edward Bear

Last Train To Clarksville
The Monkees

Laughing
Guess Who

Lay Down Sally
Eric Clapton

Lead Me On
Maxine Nightingale

Lean On Me
Bill Withers
Club Nouveau

Leave Me Alone (Ruby Red Dress)
Helen Reddy

Leaving Me
The Independents

Leaving On A Jet Plane
Peter, Paul & Mary

Let 'Em In
Paul McCartney

Let It Be
The Beatles

Let Me Be There
Olivia Newton-John

Let The Music Play
Shannon

Let's Dance
David Bowie

1

2

3

4

1. The Who's rock opera *Tommy* has produced triple gold over the years: the band's own original in 1969, the London Symphony Orchestra extravaganza (with various artists) in 1971, and the movie soundtrack in 1975.

2. Barry White ties with fellow love man Teddy Pendergrass when it comes to gold albums (eight), but the latter has twice the number of platinum awards (four).

3. Andy Williams was Columbia Records' most successful recording artist of the '60s. Fourteen of his albums released that decade were certified gold.

4. Deniece Williams' "Let's Hear It For The Boy" was one of two gold singles from the soundtrack of *Footloose*. The other was Kenny Loggins' title song.

5

6

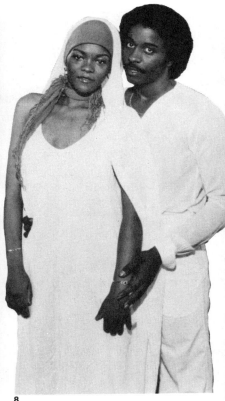

8

7

9

5. Roger Williams is the most-certified pianist of the past 30 years. And somewhere, my love, there's an elevator where you'll hear him and Ray Conniff duking it out over the *Doctor Zhivago* theme.

6. Neil Young's triple-platinum *Harvest* is the biggest-selling solo-artist album on Reprise Records. It also spun off the Canadian's one gold single, "Heart Of Gold."

7. The Wonder years include Stevie's million-selling "Ebony And Ivory" (with Paul McCartney) and "I Just Called To Say I Love You." A long distance from "Fingertips"...

8. There must have been gold dust in the air. Cavin Yarbrough hung out with the Gap Band and toured with Leon Russell before he and Alisa Peoples cut "Don't Stop The Music."

9. Talk about the many facets of Roger Troutman. The Ohio-based musician successfully panned for gold with a group (Zapp), as a solo performer (Roger), and as the producer of Shirley Murdock.

Song Title	Song Title
Artist	Artist

Let's Do It Again
The Staple Singers

Let's Go Crazy
Prince & The Revolution

Let's Groove
Earth, Wind & Fire

Let's Hear It For The Boy
Deniece Williams

Let's Stay Together
Al Green

Letter, The
The Box Tops

Light My Fire
The Doors

Lightnin' Strikes
Lou Christie

Like A Prayer
Madonna

Like A Virgin
Madonna

Lion Sleeps Tonight, The
The Tokens
Robert John

Listen To What The Man Said
Paul McCartney

Little Bit Me, A Little Bit You, A
The Monkees

Little Bit O' Soul
The Music Explosion

Little Green Apples
O.C. Smith

Little Jeannie
Elton John

A Little More Love
Olivia Newton-John

Lil' Red Riding Hood
Sam The Sham & The Pharaohs

Little Willy
The Sweet

Little Woman
Bobby Sherman

Live And Let Die
Paul McCartney

Livin' It Up (Friday Night)
Bell & James

Loco-Motion, The
Grand Funk Railroad

Lonely Days
The Bee Gees

Lonely Night (Angel Face)
The Captain & Tennille

Long Cool Woman (In A Black Dress)
The Hollies

Look, The
Roxette

Look Away
Chicago

Look What You Done For Me
Al Green

Lookin' For A Love
Bobby Womack

Lookin' For Love
Johnny Lee

Lookin' Out My Back Door
Creedence Clearwater Revival

Looks Like We Made It
Barry Manilow

Lord's Prayer, The
Sister Janet Mead

Lost In Your Eyes
Debbie Gibson

Love (Can Make You Happy)
Mercy

Song Title Artist	Song Title Artist
Love Grows (Where My Rosemary Goes) Edison Lighthouse	**Loves Me Like A Rock** Paul Simon
Love Hurts Nazareth	**Lovin' You** Minnie Riperton
Love I Lost, The Harold Melvin & The Blue Notes	**Lowdown** Boz Scaggs
Love Is A Battlefield Pat Benatar	**Lucille** Kenny Rogers
Love Is Blue Paul Mauriat & His Orchestra	**Lucy In The Sky With Diamonds** Elton John

M

(Love Is) Thicker Than Water Andy Gibb	
Love Jones Brighter Side Of Darkness	**MacArthur Park** Donna Summer
Love On A Two-Way Street The Moments	**Macho Man** The Village People
Love Rollercoaster The Ohio Players	**Maggie May** Rod Stewart
Love So Right The Bee Gees	**Magic** Olivia Newton-John
Love Theme From "Romeo & Juliet" Henry Mancini & His Orchestra	**Magic** Pilot
Love To Love You Baby Donna Summer	**Magic Carpet Ride** Steppenwolf
Love Train The O'Jays	**Magnet And Steel** Walter Egan
Love Will Keep Us Together The Captain & Tennille	**Main Event, The** Barbra Streisand
Love Won't Let Me Wait Major Harris	**Make It With You** Bread
Love You Inside Out The Bee Gees	**Makin' It** David Naughton
Love's Theme The Love Unlimited Orchestra	**Making Love Out Of Nothing At All** Air Supply
Lover's Concerto, A The Toys	**Mama Can't Buy You Love** Elton John

Song Title Artist	Song Title Artist
Mama Told Me (Not To Come) Three Dog Night	**Mr. Jaws** Dickie Goodman
Mandy Barry Manilow	**Mr. Roboto** Styx
Maneater Daryl Hall & John Oates	**Mrs. Brown You've Got A Lovely Daughter** Herman's Hermits
Me And Mrs. Jones Billy Paul	**Mrs. Robinson** Simon & Garfunkel
Me, Myself And I De La Soul	**Music Box Dancer** Frank Mills
Mellow Yellow Donovan	**Muskrat Love** The Captain & Tennille
Mickey Toni Basil	**My Ding-A-Ling** Chuck Berry
Midnight Confessions The Grass Roots	**My Eyes Adored You** Frankie Valli
Midnight Train To Georgia Gladys Knight & The Pips	**My Life** Billy Joel
Miss You The Rolling Stones	**My Love** Paul McCartney
Mockingbird Carly Simon & James Taylor	**My Melody Of Love** Bobby Vinton
Monday, Monday The Mamas & Papas	**My Prerogative** Bobby Brown
Monster Mash Bobby "Boris" Pickett & The Crypt Kickers	**My Sharona** The Knack
More, More, More The Andrea True Connection	**My Sweet Lord** George Harrison
More Than I Can Say Leo Sayer	**My Way** Elvis Presley
Morning After, The Maureen McGovern	
Morning Train (Nine To Five) Sheena Easton	

N

Na Na Hey Hey Kiss Him Goodbye
Steam

Most Beautiful Girl, The
Charlie Rich

Nadia's Theme (The Young And The Restless)
Barry DeVorzon & Perry Botkin Jr.

Song Title Artist	**Song Title** Artist

Natural High
Bloodstone

Never Gonna Give You Up
Rick Astley

Never Knew Love Like This Before
Stephanie Mills

Never My Love
The Association

Never, Never Gonna Give Ya Up
Barry White

New Kid In Town
The Eagles

Nice To Be With You
Gallery

Night Chicago Died, The
Paper Lace

Night Fever
The Bee Gees

Night The Lights Went Out In Georgia, The
Vicki Lawrence

Night They Drove Old Dixie Down, The
Joan Baez

Nights In White Satin
The Moody Blues

9 to 5
Dolly Parton

96 Tears
? & The Mysterians

99 Luftballons
Nena

No More Tears (Enough Is Enough)
Barbra Streisand & Donna Summer

Nobody
Sylvia

Nobody Does It Better
Carly Simon

Nothing From Nothing
Billy Preston

Nothing's Gonna Stop Us Now
Starship

Nowhere Man
The Beatles

Ode To Billie Joe
Bobbie Gentry

Off The Wall
Michael Jackson

Oh Happy Day
The Edwin Hawkins Singers

Oh Pretty Woman
Roy Orbison

Old Fashioned Love Song, An
Three Dog Night

On And On
Gladys Knight & The Pips

On My Own
Patti LaBelle & Michael McDonald

On Our Own
Bobby Brown

On The Radio
Donna Summer

Once Bitten Twice Shy
Great White

One
Three Dog Night

One Bad Apple
The Osmonds

One In A Million You
Larry Graham

One Less Bell To Answer
The 5th Dimension

| Song Title | Song Title |
Artist	Artist

One Nation Under A Groove Funkadelic	**Patches** Clarence Carter
One Of A Kind (Love Affair) The Spinners	**Patience** Guns N' Roses
One That You Love, The Air Supply	**Patricia** Perez Prado
1, 2, 3, Red Light The 1910 Fruitgum Company	**Payback (Part 1), The** James Brown
Only In My Dreams Debbie Gibson	**Penny Lane** The Beatles
Only Sixteen Dr. Hook	**People Got To Be Free** The Rascals
Only The Strong Survive Jerry Butler	**Philadelphia Freedom** Elton John
O-o-h Child The Five Stairsteps	**Photograph** Ringo Starr
Our Love Natalie Cole	**Physical** Olivia Newton-John
(Our Love) Don't Throw It All Away Andy Gibb	**Pick Up The Pieces** The Average White Band
Outa-Space Billy Preston	**Pillow Talk** Sylvia
Over You Gary Puckett & The Union Gap	**Planet Rock** Africa Bambaata & The Soulsonic Force

P

Pac-Man Fever Buckner & Garcia	**Play That Funky Music** Wild Cherry
Paper Roses Marie Osmond	**Playground In My Mind** Clint Holmes
Paperback Writer The Beatles	**Pleasant Valley Sunday** The Monkees
Parents Just Don't Understand D.J. Jazzy Jeff & The Fresh Prince	**Please Mr. Please** Olivia Newton-John
Party All The Time Eddie Murphy	**Please Mr. Postman** The Carpenters
	Pop Muzik M

Song Title	
Artist	

Power Of Love
Joe Simon

Power Of Love, The
Huey Lewis & The News

Precious And Few
Climax

Precious, Precious
Jackie Moore

Private Eyes
Daryl Hall & John Oates

Proud Mary
Creedence Clearwater Revival
Ike & Tina Turner

Pump Up The Volume
M/A/R/R/S

Puppy Love
Donny Osmond

Purple Rain
Prince & The Revolution

Push It
Salt-N-Pepa

Put A Little Love In Your Heart
Jackie DeShannon

Put Your Hand In The Hand
Ocean

Puttin' On The Ritz
Taco

Queen Of Hearts
Juice Newton

Song Title	
Artist	

R

Rag Doll
The 4 Seasons

Rain, The Park & Other Things, The
The Cowsills

Raindrops Keep Fallin' On My Head
B. J. Thomas

Rainy Days And Mondays
The Carpenters

Rainy Night In Georgia
Brook Benton

Rapper, The
The Jaggerz

Rapture
Blondie

Real Love
Jody Watley

Red, Red Wine
UB40

Relax
Frankie Goes To Hollywood

Respect
Aretha Franklin

Return To Sender
Elvis Presley

Reunited
Peaches & Herb

Rhinestone Cowboy
Glen Campbell

Rich Girl
Daryl Hall & John Oates

Ride Captain Ride
The Blues Image

Right Back Where We Started From
Maxine Nightingale

Song Title Artist	Song Title Artist
Right Here Waiting Richard Marx	**Saturday In The Park** Chicago
Rise Herb Alpert	**Saturday Night** The Bay City Rollers
Rock Me Gently Andy Kim	**Say, Has Anybody Seen My Sweet Gypsy Rose** Dawn featuring Tony Orlando
Rock On David Essex Michael Damian	**Say, Say, Say** Paul McCartney & Michael Jackson
Rock Steady Aretha Franklin	**Say You, Say Me** Lionel Richie
Rock The Boat The Hues Corporation	**Scorpio** Dennis Coffey & The Detroit Guitar Band
Rock With You Michael Jackson	**Seasons In The Sun** Terry Jacks
Rockin' Pneumonia—Boogie Woogie Flu Johnny Rivers	**Second Time Around, The** Shalamar
Rose, The Bette Midler	**See Saw** Aretha Franklin
Rose Garden Lynn Anderson	**Self-Destruction** Stop The Violence Movement
Roses Are Red Bobby Vinton	**September** Earth, Wind & Fire
Rubberband Man, The The Spinners	**Sexual Healing** Marvin Gaye
Ruby Tuesday The Rolling Stones	**Sexy Eyes** Dr. Hook
Rudolph The Red-Nosed Reindeer Gene Autry	**Sha-La-La (Make Me Happy)** Al Green
	Shadow Dancing Andy Gibb

S

Sad Eyes Robert John	**Shake Your Body (Down To The Ground)** The Jacksons
Sara Smile Daryl Hall & John Oates	**Shake Your Groove Thing** Peaches & Herb
	Shake Your Love Debbie Gibson

Song Title	**Song Title**
Artist	Artist

Song Title	**Song Title**
Artist	Artist
Shambala Three Dog Night	**Show And Tell** Al Wilson
Shame Evelyn "Champagne" King	**Show Must Go On, The** Three Dog Night
Shannon Henry Gross	**Sideshow** Blue Magic
Sharing The Night Together Dr. Hook	**Signs** Five Man Electrical Band
She Believes In Me Kenny Rogers	**Silly Love Songs** Paul McCartney
She Bop Cyndi Lauper	**Simon Says** The 1910 Fruitgum Company
She Drives Me Crazy Fine Young Cannibals	**Sing** The Carpenters
She's A Bad Mama Jama Carl Carlton	**Sing A Song** Earth, Wind & Fire
She's A Lady Tom Jones	**(Sittin' On) The Dock Of The Bay** Otis Redding
She's Not Just Another Woman The 8th Day	**Skin Tight** The Ohio Players
She's Out Of My Life Michael Jackson	**Skinny Legs And All** Joe Tex
Sheila Tommy Roe	**Slip Away** Clarence Carter
Shining Star Earth, Wind & Fire	**Slippin' Into Darkness** War
Shining Star The Manhattans	**Slow Hand** The Pointer Sisters
Shop Around The Captain & Tennille	**Smile A Little Smile For Me** The Flying Machine
Short People Randy Newman	**Smoke On The Water** Deep Purple
Shout Tears For Fears	**Smokin' In The Boys Room** Brownsville Station
Show, The Doug E. Fresh & The Get Fresh Crew	**Snoopy Vs. The Red Baron** The Royal Guardsmen

Song Title	Song Title
Artist	Artist

Snowbird Anne Murray	**Spinning Wheel** Blood, Sweat & Tears
Somebody's Been Sleeping 100 Proof Aged In Soul	**Spirit In The Sky** Norman Greenbaum
Somebody's Watching Me Rockwell	**Stand Tall** Burton Cummings
Someone Saved My Life Tonight Elton John	**Star Wars Theme/Cantina Band** Meco
Somethin' Stupid Nancy & Frank Sinatra	**Stars On 45** Stars On 45
Something The Beatles	**State Of Shock** The Jacksons with Mick Jagger
Sometimes When We Touch Dan Hill	**Stay Awhile** The Bells
Song Sung Blue Neil Diamond	**Stayin' Alive** The Bee Gees
Sorry Seems To Be The Hardest Word Elton John	**Stick Up** The Honey Cone
Soul Man Sam & Dave	**Stoned Soul Picnic** The 5th Dimension
Soulful Strut Young-Holt Unlimited	**Stormy** Classics IV
Sounds Of Silence, The Simon & Garfunkel	**Straight Up** Paula Abdul
Southern Nights Glen Campbell	**Stranger On The Shore** Mr. Acker Bilk
Space Race Billy Preston	**Strawberry Letter 23** The Brothers Johnson
Spanish Harlem Aretha Franklin	**Streak, The** Ray Stevens
Special Lady Ray, Goodman & Brown	**Stumblin' In** Suzi Quatro & Chris Norman
Spiders And Snakes Jim Stafford	**Sugar Shack** Jimmy Gilmer & The Fireballs
Spill The Wine Eric Burdon & War	**Sugar, Sugar** The Archies

Sugar Town
Nancy Sinatra

Sukiyaki
A Taste Of Honey

Summer
War

Summer In The City
The Lovin' Spoonful

Summer Nights
Olivia Newton-John & John Travolta

Sundown
Gordon Lightfoot

Sunny
Bobby Hebb

Sunshine
Jonathan Edwards

Sunshine Of Your Love
Cream

Sunshine On My Shoulders
John Denver

Superbowl Shuffle
The Chicago Bears Shufflin' Crew

Superfly
Curtis Mayfield

Supersonic
J. J. Fad

Superstar
The Carpenters

Superwoman
Karyn White

Suspicious Minds
Elvis Presley

Swayin' To The Music (Slow Dancin')
Johnny Rivers

Sweet And Innocent
Donny Osmond

Sweet Caroline
Neil Diamond

Sweet Child O' Mine
Guns N' Roses

Sweet Dreams (Are Made Of This)
Eurythmics

Sweet Pea
Tommy Roe

Sweet Soul Music
Arthur Conley

(Sweet, Sweet Baby) Since You've Been Gone
Aretha Franklin

Sweet Thing
Rufus featuring Chaka Khan

Swingin'
John Anderson

Sylvia's Mother
Dr. Hook & The Medicine Show

T

TSOP (The Sound Of Philadelphia)
MFSB

Take A Chance On Me
Abba

Take A Letter Maria
R.B. Greaves

Take It On The Run
REO Speedwagon

Take Me Home
Cher

Take Me Home, Country Roads
John Denver with Fat City

Take Your Time (Do It Right)
The S.O.S. Band

Tear The Roof Off The Sucker
Parliament

Song Title	Song Title
Artist	Artist

Teddy Bear Red Sovine	**These Eyes** The Guess Who
Telephone Line The Electric Light Orchestra	**They Just Can't Stop It (The Games People Play)** The Spinners
Telephone Man Meri Wilson	**(They Long To Be) Close To You** The Carpenters
Tell It To My Heart Taylor Dayne	**Thin Line Between Love And Hate** The Persuaders
Tell Me Something Good Rufus	**Things We Do For Love, The** 10cc
Thank God I'm A Country Boy John Denver	**Think** Aretha Franklin
Thank You (Falettinme Be Mice Elf Again) Sly & The Family Stone	**This Diamond Ring** Gary Lewis & The Playboys
That Lady (Part 1) The Isley Brothers	**This Guy's In Love With You** Herb Alpert
That'll Be The Day Buddy Holly & The Crickets	**This Magic Moment** Jay & The Americans
That's Rock 'N' Roll Shaun Cassidy	**This Time I Know It's For Real** Donna Summer
That's What Friends Are For Dionne Warwick & Friends	**Those Were The Days** Mary Hopkin
Theme From "A Summer Place" Percy Faith & His Orchestra	**Tide Is High, The** Blondie
Theme From "S.W.A.T." Rhythm Heritage	**Tie A Yellow Ribbon Round The Ole Oak Tree** Dawn featuring Tony Orlando
Theme From "The Greatest American Hero" Joey Scarbury	**Tighten Up** Archie Bell & The Drells
Theme From "The Dukes Of Hazzard" Waylon Jennings	**Time After Time** Cyndi Lauper
Then Came You Dionne Warwick & The Spinners	**Time In A Bottle** Jim Croce
There's A Kind Of Hush Herman's Hermits	**Time Of The Season** The Zombies
These Boots Are Made For Walkin' Nancy Sinatra	**Tired Of Being Alone** Al Green

Song Title	Song Title
Artist	Artist

To All The Girls I've Loved Before
Julio Iglesias & Willie Nelson

To Sir With Love
Lulu

Tom Dooley
The Kingston Trio

Tonight's The Night
Rod Stewart

Too Hot
Kool & The Gang

Too Late To Turn Back Now
Cornelius Brothers & Sister Rose

Too Much Heaven
The Bee Gees

Too Much, Too Little, Too Late
Johnny Mathis & Deniece Williams

Too Weak To Fight
Clarence Carter

Top Of The World
The Carpenters

Torn Between Two Lovers
Mary MacGregor

Total Eclipse Of The Heart
Bonnie Tyler

Touch Me
The Doors

Toy Soldiers
Martika

Tragedy
The Bee Gees

Trapped By A Thing Called Love
Denise LaSalle

Travelin' Band
Creedence Clearwater Revival

Travelin' Man
Ricky Nelson

Treat Her Like A Lady
Cornelius Brothers & Sister Rose

Troglodyte (Cave Man)
The Jimmy Castor Bunch

Truly
Lionel Richie

Tryin' To Love Two
William Bell

Turn Around, Look At Me
The Vogues

Turn Back The Hands Of Time
Tyrone Davis

Twelfth Of Never, The
Donny Osmond

Two Out Of Three Ain't Bad
Meat Loaf

U

Uncle Albert/Admiral Halsey
Paul & Linda McCartney

Undercover Angel
Alan O'Day

Until You Come Back To Me
Aretha Franklin

Up Around The Bend
Creedence Clearwater Revival

Up Where We Belong
Joe Cocker & Jennifer Warnes

Upside Down
Diana Ross

Uptown Girl
Billy Joel

Use Me
Bill Withers

Use Ta Be My Girl
The O'Jays

Song Title Artist	Song Title Artist

V

Valleri
The Monkees

Venus
Shocking Blue

W

Waiting For A Girl Like You
Foreigner

Wake Me Up Before You Go-Go
Wham!

Walk Like An Egyptian
The Bangles

Walkin' In The Rain With The One I Love
Love Unlimited

The Wanderer
Donna Summer

Want Ads
The Honey Cone

Wasted Days And Wasted Nights
Freddy Fender

Way Down
Elvis Presley

Way I Want To Touch You, The
The Captain & Tennille

Way We Were, The
Barbra Streisand

Way You Love Me, The
Karyn White

We Are Family
Sister Sledge

We Are The Champions
Queen

We Are The World
USA For Africa

We Built This City
Starship

We Can Work It Out
The Beatles

We Got The Beat
The Go-Go's

We're All Alone
Rita Coolidge

We're An American Band
Grand Funk Railroad

We've Only Just Begun
The Carpenters

Wear My Ring Around Your Neck
Elvis Presley

Wedding Bell Blues
The 5th Dimension

Welcome Back
John Sebastian

What A Fool Believes
The Doobie Brothers

What You Don't Know
Expose

What's Love Got To Do With It
Tina Turner

What's On Your Mind (Pure Energy)
Information Society

When A Man Loves A Woman
Percy Sledge

When Doves Cry
Prince & The Revolution

When I Need You
Leo Sayer

When I'm With You
Sheriff

Song Title
Artist

When Will I See You Again
The Three Degrees

When You're In Love With A Beautiful Woman
Dr. Hook

Where Is The Love
Roberta Flack & Donny Hathaway

Which Way You Goin' Billy?
The Poppy Family

Whip It
Devo

Who's Making Love
Johnnie Taylor

Whole Lotta Love
Led Zeppelin

Why Can't We Be Friends?
War

Why Me
Kris Kristofferson

Wichita Lineman
Glen Campbell

Wild Thing
Tone Loc

Wild, Wild West
The Escape Club

Wildfire
Michael Murphey

Will It Go Round In Circles
Billy Preston

Winchester Cathedral
The New Vaudeville Band

Wind Beneath My Wings
Bette Midler

Windy
The Association

Without Love
Tom Jones

Song Title
Artist

Without You
Nilsson

Woman
John Lennon

Woman In Love
Barbra Streisand

Woman, Woman
Gary Puckett & The Union Gap

Wonder Of You, The
Elvis Presley

Wooly Bully
Sam The Sham & The Pharaohs

Working My Back To You
The Spinners

World Is A Ghetto, The
War

Worst That Could Happen, The
The Brooklyn Bridge

Yellow Submarine
The Beatles

Yes, I'm Ready
Teri DeSario With K.C.

Yesterday
The Beatles

Yesterday Once More
The Carpenters

Y.M.C.A.
The Village People

Yo-Yo
The Osmonds

You Ain't Seen Nothing Yet
Bachman-Turner Overdrive

You Are Everything
The Stylistics

Song Title Artist	**Song Title** Artist
You Don't Bring Me Flowers Barbra Streisand & Neil Diamond	**You're The First, The Last, My Everything** Barry White
You Don't Have To Be A Star Marilyn McCoo & Billy Davis Jr.	**You're The One That I Want** Olivia Newton-John & John Travolta
You Gonna Make Me Love Somebody Else The Jones Girls	**You've Got A Friend** James Taylor
You Got It (The Right Stuff) The New Kids On The Block	**You've Made Me So Very Happy** Blood, Sweat & Tears
You Light Up My Life Debby Boone	**Young Girl** Gary Puckett & The Union Gap
You Make Me Feel Brand New The Stylistics	**Your Mama Don't Dance** Loggins & Messina
You Make Me Feel Like Dancing Leo Sayer	**Yummy Yummy Yummy** The Ohio Express
You Needed Me Anne Murray	
You Ought To Be With Me Al Green	
You Sexy Thing Hot Chocolate	
You Should Be Dancing The Bee Gees	
You Take My Breath Away Rex Smith	
You'll Never Find Another Love Like Mine Lou Rawls	
(You're) Having My Baby Paul Anka	
You're In My Heart Rod Stewart	
(You're My) Soul And Inspiration The Righteous Brothers	
You're Sixteen Ringo Starr	
You're So Vain Carly Simon	

THE
BEST
SELLERS

THE 20 BIGGEST-SELLING ALBUMS

(Based on RIAA multi-platinum certifications;
year of release/record label follows title)

Michael Jackson
Thriller (1982/Epic) 20,000,000

Fleetwood Mac
Rumours (1977/Warner Bros.) 13,000,000

Original Soundtrack
Saturday Night Fever (1977/RSO) 11,000,000

Bruce Springsteen
Born In The U.S.A. (1984/Columbia) 11,000,000

Original Soundtrack
Dirty Dancing (1987/RCA) 10,000,000

Prince & The Revolution
Purple Rain (1984/Warner Bros.) 10,000,000

Lionel Richie
Can't Slow Down (1983/Motown) 10,000,000

Boston
Boston (1976/Epic) 9,000,000

Def Leppard
Hysteria (1987/Mercury) 9,000,000

Whitney Houston
Whitney Houston (1985/Arista) 9,000,000

Bon Jovi
Slippery When Wet (1986/Mercury) 8,000,000

Guns N' Roses
Appetite For Destruction (1987/Geffen) 8,000,000

Original Soundtrack
Grease (1978/RSO) 8,000,000

Def Leppard
Pyromania (1983/Mercury) 7,000,000

Journey
Escape (1981/Columbia) 7,000,000

Huey Lewis & The News
Sports (1983/Chrysalis) 7,000,000

Madonna
Like A Virgin (1984/Sire) 7,000,000

George Michael
Faith (1987/Columbia) 7,000,000

Pink Floyd
The Wall (1979/Columbia) 7,000,000

REO Speedwagon
Hi Infidelity (1980/Epic) 7,000,000

MOST PLATINUM ALBUMS BY ARTIST

1. BARBRA STREISAND 19
2. CHICAGO 14
3. NEIL DIAMOND 11
   KENNY ROGERS 11
4. BILLY JOEL 10
   WILLIE NELSON 10
5. ALABAMA 9
   KISS 9

MOST MULTI-PLATINUM ALBUMS BY ARTIST

1. BILLY JOEL 7
   JOURNEY 7
   BARBRA STREISAND 7
   VAN HALEN 7
2. AEROSMITH 6
   CHICAGO 6
   EARTH, WIND & FIRE 6
   WILLIE NELSON 6
3. ALABAMA 5
   FLEETWOOD MAC 5
   FOREIGNER 5
   LYNYRD SKYNYRD 5
   BARRY MANILOW 5
   BRUCE SPRINGSTEEN 5

MOST GOLD ALBUMS BY ARTIST

1. ELVIS PRESLEY 32
2. BARBRA STREISAND 31
3. THE ROLLING STONES 28
4. THE BEATLES 25
5. NEIL DIAMOND 23
   ELTON JOHN 23

MOST GOLD SINGLES BY ARTIST

1. THE BEATLES 20
2. ELVIS PRESLEY 17
3. ARETHA FRANKLIN 14
4. ELTON JOHN 13
5. PAUL MCCARTNEY 12
   DONNA SUMMER 12

MOST GOLD SINGLES BY PRODUCER

(Credited as producer/co-producer;
artists produced under name)

GEORGE MARTIN 23
  Beatles   (20)
  Paul McCartney   (1)
  Paul McCartney/Michael Jackson   (1)
  Paul McCartney/Steve Wonder   (1)

KENNY GAMBLE & LEON HUFF 18
  O'Jays   (5)
  Harold Melvin & Blue Notes   (2)
  Joe Simon   (2)
  Jerry Butler   (1)
  Intruders   (1)
  Jacksons   (1)
  Jones Girls   (1)
  MFSB   (1)
  Billy Paul   (1)
  Teddy Pendergrass   (1)
  Lou Rawls   (1)
  Three Degrees   (1)

BEE GEES (BARRY GIBB)/ALBHY GALUTEN/KARL RICHARDSON 15
  Bee Gees   (8)
  Andy Gibb   (5)
  Kenny Rogers & Dolly Parton   (1)
  Barbra Streisand   (1)

JERRY WEXLER 14
  Aretha Franklin   (14)

THOM BELL 13
  Spinners   (5)
  Stylistics   (5)
  Delfonics   (1)
  Elton John   (1)
  Dionne Warwick/Spinners   (1)

ARIF MARDIN 13
  Aretha Franklin   (6)
  Average White Band   (1)
  Bee Gees   (1)
  Brook Benton   (1)
  Phil Collins   (1)
  Roberta Flack   (1)
  Chaka Khan   (1)
  Bette Midler   (1)

MOST GOLD SINGLES BY LABEL

COLUMBIA 81
ATLANTIC 64
RCA 64
CAPITOL 62
EPIC 45
WARNER BROS 39

MOST GOLD ALBUMS BY LABEL

COLUMBIA 429
WARNER BROS 237
RCA 230
CAPITOL 216
ATLANTIC 150

MOST PLATINUM ALBUMS BY LABEL

COLUMBIA 199
WARNER BROS 106
RCA 61
CAPITOL 51
EPIC 51
ATLANTIC 48

ANNUAL GOLD CERTIFICATION TOTALS

	Gold Singles	Gold Albums
1958	4	1
1959	1	6
1960	0	16
1961	2	15
1962	5	37
1963	2	27
1964	7	28
1965	11	36
1966	23	58
1967	34	61
1968	45	75
1969	64	94
1970	56	114
1971	55	91
1972	66	124
1973	70	116
1974	68	127
1975	48	125
1976	55	149
1977	55	183
1978	61	193
1979	60	112
1980	42	160
1981	32	153
1982	24	130
1983	47	111
1984	26	131
1985	14	138
1986	7	140
1987	3	142
1988	4	158
1989	125	195

ANNUAL PLATINUM CERTIFICATION TOTALS

	Platinum Singles	Platinum Albums	Multi-Platinum Albums
1976	4	37	NA
1977	3	68	NA
1978	10	102	NA
1979	12	42	NA
1980	3	66	NA
1981	2	60	NA
1982	4	55	NA
1983	2	49	NA
1984	2	59	109
1985	1	65	61
1986	0	204	108
1987	0	79	71
1988	2	89	76
1989	30	130	104